An Autobiography

Richard G. Clark

Copyright © 1987 by Richard G. Clark. All rights reserved.

No part of this publication may be reproduced, distributed, or transmitted in any form by any means, nor stored in a database or retrieval system, without the prior written permission of the author's estate.

Second Edition published in 2024.

ISBN: 978-1-7365738-8-4 (Paperback Edition)
ISBN: 978-1-7365738-6-0 (eBook Edition)

Book Cover and Interior Book Design by
Casey L. Jones — http://www.CaseyBelle.com

Contents

Foreword by Thomas R. Clark	v
1918	1
1933 – 1935	25
1935 – 1940	34
November 1942 — September 1945	100
September 1945 — February 1951	162
April 1951 – October 1958	218
1958 – 1964	255
January 1965 – October 1971	276
October 1971 – September 1981	296
Retirement	343
Afterword by Courtney Jo Barr	357
A More Perfect Union	362
Addendum By Evelyn	365
Also by Richard G. Clark	367

Dear Clark Family,

My dad and the author of this book was an extraordinary father, historian, and an incredible mentor in the practice of law. This book TORTS AND DRY MARTINIS is first an autobiography of my father's life, but also it is a history lesson discussing the years between the 1920's-'70's from a different perspective. I hope you enjoy this book as much as I have cherished it.

It's incredibly rare that a son can receive such a gift and is able to pass it on to future generations of the Clark Family.

Go Buckeyes,

Thomas R. Clark

1918

Ruth Clark and Jon Richard Clark

I was told that I was born in a hospital in Columbus, Ohio on August 29, 1918, but I really do not remember much about it. The Armistice occurred shortly thereafter, ending "the war to end all wars." I remember none of that either; nor do I recall much of anything until my third birthday when my mother had a party for me. I was given a coaster wagon with steel wheels on that occasion. The wheels made a helluva racket as I scooted up and down the sidewalk causing complaints from all the old crabs in the neighborhood.

My father was a pharmacist, commonly called a druggist in those days, and was always referred to as "Doc," as were all pharmacists. I never found out why. My mother was a pianist. When she was in high school, she played the piano at the motion picture theater and got to see all the silent movies free and made spending money. I do not think pharmacists made much money in that time, and I know they worked long hours for whatever their compensation. I was an only child. My folks must have decided that one like me was enough.

When I was two, we moved to a really small town: LaRue (pronounced "lay rew" by the natives), Ohio. The village is located on the banks of the Scioto River about fifty miles northwest of Columbus, and fourteen miles west of Marion, the county seat. Purportedly, the town had a population of eight hundred. The count must have been taken on Christmas Day when they were all at home. LaRue was the center of a rich farming area.

Located there were the drug store, which my father ran, a couple of groceries, a meat market, restaurant, dry goods store, two hard wares, a pool room, bank, dairy, movie theater, a printshop which produced the weekly newspaper, two barber shops, two gasoline stations, a bakery, and a combination funeral parlor and furniture store, and there may have been more. In addition, the town had both a Ford and a Willy's Overland garage and dealership. Naturally any community so large had a post office, school building, railroad depot, three or four churches and a combination town hall and jail. A dentist and two doctors—one full-time and the other the county health commissioner—had offices there. There were no lawyers in the entire area—they may have been prohibited. The town was also distinguished by the fact that the famous Airedale Kennels were located there.

Richard at two years old

While I did not then know the difference, the town had a most noteworthy lack of indoor plumbing. I doubt very much whether there were more than three or four bathrooms in the whole territory.

The roads into town were partly paved and partly graveled. The gravel roads were very dusty and, after a hard rain, extremely muddy. Side roads in the country were either gravel or mud. Many farmers came to town by horse and buggy or horse and wagon. Some rode on horseback. Hitching posts were in front of every business building, and the smell of horse manure permeated the air. Many town residents did not own either a horse or an automobile. They were isolated in LaRue, unless they took a train to Marion or depended on others to transport them on rare trips out of town.

Few farm residents had telephones. The telephone system was crude—one cranked for the operator, who then placed the call. Most callers did not ask for telephone numbers. The operator was just told with whom the caller wanted to talk. The operator knew who was at home, who was away, where they were if they were not at home, who was ill, how the weather was, etc.

Radio was in its very early stages and few people owned one because of the cost and the novelty. There was, of course, no television. Victrolas were common, with poor recordings, and had to be wound by a crank on the side of the machine.

Ruth Clark

Automobiles were not a novelty. Quite a few townspeople had them, as did outlying farmers. In LaRue, the vast majority of car owners drove Model T Fords. Most others drove Overland's. Glassed-in autos were relatively new; most autos I saw were "touring cars" or "roadsters." In either case, they had a cloth top which could be raised or lowered manually, with some effort, and came equipped with side curtains which were put on during inclement weather. Heaters, radios and, certainly, air conditioning were not yet in use. Windshield wipers were hand-operated. This ensured that the driver got wet when it rained. Headlights were in vogue by then, but the visibility at night was poor.

To the best of my knowledge, my parents did not own an automobile until 1924, at which time they purchased a Model T Ford coupe. It had a starter for the engine which did not work in cold weather. A crank was attached to the lower front end which, with considerable effort and some risk, would get the car started. The car's color—black! All Fords were painted black.

We did have a telephone. We had neither a radio nor a Victrola so long as we were in LaRue. My mother had a piano, however; at first an upright, and later on, a grand piano, which was the marvel of the community because it was probably the only one in town. It was always necessary to find a place that could accommodate the damned thing.

The house in which we lived had two outdoor pumps—one for rainwater and one for drinking water. My mother boiled water on an oil stove for dishwater and washed the dishes in a dish tub. When the dishes were washed, she threw the dishwater out into the back yard. Baths were taken in water similarly heated, in a gigantic wash tub, which was also used for washing clothes. A three-hole privy was at the back end of the lot. Naturally, each bedroom had a slop jar and pot for use at night, or when it was very cold.

The house itself was fairly large. There were two living rooms (or as they then called them, a parlor and living room), a dining room, a kitchen and two bedrooms on the first floor. We did not use them much, but I think the upstairs contained three bedrooms. There was a basement with a coal furnace providing central heat. Most houses in town had coal stoves instead. We had a large porch in front, and partially on one side. At the rear of the house, in addition to the privy, was a chicken house and what passed for a garage. The lot was large enough that we were able to have a garden. Naturally, since we had the chicken house, we raised chickens.

Richard on his tricycle

In reflecting on LaRue sixty years later, it seems to have been a dull, rather bleak place. It was not that way at all to me as a small boy. It was all I knew, and I was happy with my surroundings and with my parents. I believe that they were happy as well, even though they had lived in a city environment during all of their earlier adult years.

I played with other children, now only dimly remembered. I loved my wagon, a small tricycle, and automobile which I pedaled. I had indoor toys and games, and always books for small children. Very often at night in the winter my parents read to me, and I loved it. We popped corn on Sunday nights in the winter, my mother occasionally made candy, and I did not know what underprivileged meant, even though I now know that we were not in more than extremely moderate circumstances. So was everyone else.

I was allowed to wander all around town. I knew just about everyone, and I do not recall anyone ever treating me badly. Often, I visited "Ma" and "Mart" Clark—no relation. They were probably in their sixties, and their children were already grown. Occasionally, I was permitted to eat chicken pot pie with them on Sunday and, regardless of the day of the week, I was always given a sugar cookie or two. The town marshal made his rounds on horseback and once in a while, to my great delight, he placed me on the front of his saddle and took me for a ride around town.

The Scioto River flooded the town annually, causing great inconvenience to most of the townspeople, but serving as a source of recreation for the kids. We played in the water and mud as the floods receded, and usually were spanked as a result.

From my memory of those years, I am sure that most of the adults enjoyed life too. I know that my mother was a member of two ladies' social clubs. I do not think they had any great purpose, but the ladies gossiped, played auction bridge and Five Hundred, and ate good food. Mother also played the piano for various community operettas, Christmas performances, minstrels, and other musical activities. My father loved to hunt pheasant, rabbit, and squirrel in season. In the spring and summer, he fished in the muddy Scioto. Carp and catfish were the usual catch. I know that he also played on a volleyball team, so, I assume, there was a league. I know that about every other week he played poker and other card games. I am sure the stakes were small.

Father was a member of the Masonic order and became Worshipful Master of the local lodge. Mother, of course, was an Eastern Star. Although my parents were not overly religious, they saw to it that I attended Sunday School on a fairly regular basis.

There were all sorts of community activities ice cream socials, church suppers, a town Halloween costume event, street dancing, band concerts, high school football and basketball games, and many other activities of a similar nature.

My parents entertained other "young marrieds," and were in turn entertained. There were no babysitters, so we children tagged along. I remember that I loved the food and the chance to play, and fight, with the other kids.

Even though Prohibition was the law of the land, I am certain that my parents and their friends drank some alcoholic beverages, perhaps sparingly, and certainly not in public. My grandmother Guy, who lived in the small town of Plain City about sixty miles to the south, visited us occasionally. She was a lifelong member of the Women's Christian Temperance Union and wore the "White Ribbon" on her breast. She was buried with it. On one of her visits, my dad had a batch of home-made dandelion wine fermenting in the basement. She found it and poured hot ashes in it. When dad discovered it, he was madder than hell! One of the few times I remember him that way.

LaRue had a fleeting moment of fame. The owner of the Airedale Kennels conceived the idea of sponsoring a professional football team, at least the nucleus of which was made up of former members of the famous Carlisle Indians. They were called the "Oorang Indians" and if not members of the early National Football League —which they may have been—they at least traveled extensively. I do not remember most of their names, but I do remember that the great Jim Thorpe was one of them. Thorpe and many of the others were in our home frequently. One, whose name for professional reasons was "Chief Long Time Sleep," loved to drink whiskey, and I think of him when I hear the expression "drunken Indian." One night, while under the influence he broke into the bakery. The town marshal discovered him devouring pastry and whatever else he could find. He refused to come out and was subdued by the marshal, other brawny townspeople, and the marshal's blackjack, and was taken to jail after throwing pies and other goodies.

As I said earlier, my mother was a fine piano player. She had many piano students in LaRue. At the age of five, I became one of them. I could read music before I could read words. Before I was six, I appeared in one of her recitals at the local high school auditorium-gymnasium. I hated all of it and, at the age of nine, was finally permitted to quit. Despite my mother's warning that I would regret it,

I never have. I cannot now read one note of music and do not even remember how to play the scales.

Richard at six years old.

I was barely six years old when I entered the first grade. I loved it. I particularly liked the little girls and chased them in order to try to kiss them, until the teacher and my father forcibly persuaded me of the error of my ways. I had been read to a lot by my parents from my earliest recollection and was eager to learn. The result was that I read exceptionally well at the end of my second year in school. I do not know whether the teaching methods employed then were superior to those used now, but I do know that reading skill which I attained in those two years has served me well ever since. In the summer of 1926, the drug store was sold. I guess my folks could not, or would not, raise the money to buy it. As a result, I made the first of two or three traumatic moves.

We pulled up stakes and returned to Columbus, moving into half a double house with indoor plumbing, a gas range, washing machine and other things which I had known nothing about until then. I missed LaRue and, as a small boy of eight had a big adjustment to make.

Columbus, then, did not rival New York or Chicago as a population center. I believe that the city and its suburbs boasted of about two hundred fifty thousand people. To me, it was enormous. Actually, as I got older and acclimated to new friends, new schools and "modern" conveniences, Columbus was a wonderfully pleasant place in which to live. I know now that the city was then an overgrown small town. I do not think that there were serious crime problems. Traffic was not really bad. Most people rode the street cars when they went downtown. Street car fares were cheap. I remember that it cost three cents for children and five cents for adults to ride, and transfers to other lines were free.

There was little heavy industry in Columbus then, and indeed this did not change until the 1940's. Ohio State University, although not the huge knowledge factory it now is, employed a large number of people. The state capitol is there, and the State of Ohio was a leading employer.

There were, and are, home offices of insurance companies and many, many other white-collar employers. Columbus was not a blue-collar town. Indeed, it epitomized white, middle-class, middle-America. There were blacks, poor people, and even some members of the Democratic Party other than my father, who lived there. However, they were all in the minority.

Calvin Coolidge was President of the United States and, even in spite of that fact, prosperity seemed to be everywhere. I know now that my parents really had no money other than my father's rather ordinary weekly salary. I really doubt that most families in any area in which I lived were wealthy, but it seemed to me then, and still does, that there was always enough food, decent clothing, comfortable housing, "movie money," and everything else that I could have thought of. I felt neither inferior nor superior to my peers. We all lived pretty much alike.

During their married life, my parents moved twenty-seven times in twenty-five years. They never owned a house. I am certain that they could not afford one. I don't know whether they paid their rent; my mother just seemed to have a hobby of moving every so often. I remember that she read the rental ads in the classified section of *The Columbus Dispatch* every Sunday. Frequently on Sundays when my father was working, she and I would go look at houses. When we lived in LaRue, she had bought a grand piano with money she made teaching. It took up a lot of space in any living room, and for that reason she always looked for a place with either a long living room or two rooms —one of which could be used for a music room.

From late summer of 1926 until May of 1927, we moved three times, and I attended two different schools in different areas while in the third grade. I do not remember the names of any of my classmates or of the children in the first two neighborhoods, nor do I remember much about the two schools I attended. The first was in Grandview Heights. It was a new building complete with a combination stage-gymnasium and contained a cafeteria. It had a wonderful playground with all sorts of equipment and a grassy area adjacent to the school. The second school was on the near north side in Columbus. It was old and offered nothing except wooden floors, old desks, and dingy walls. I lived several blocks from the school and on the way home at night after school, usually got into a fight. I guess I was the new kid, and all of the others wanted to test me. I didn't lose every fight, but I did decide at the tender age of eight that I would not become a professional boxer.

When we moved to the north end of Columbus, we moved into the upstairs apartment of a duplex. It was old and the entrance had smelled of garbage. The only reason for living there was that it was very close to the drug store which my father started. There were no children in the neighboring apartments, but I did not mind for the reason that both of my parents worked in the drug store, and I spent more time there than I did in the duplex.

I ate restaurant food twice a day, seven days a week, and played in the streets, alleys, and apartment back yards near the store. Needless to say, I learned a lot about city life quickly. The kids who lived around that drug store were street smart and mostly ornery.

One group called themselves the "Alley Rats." They were a little older than me and allowed me in on only the fringes of their activities. I am sure that was fortunate for me. I do not recall much of what I learned in school that year, but I do remember that I read a lot from the last half of the third grade on throughout the rest of my life.

The drug store had a circulating library, which was common then, and I read some of the novels. I became a devotee of western stories. The store also contained a magazine rack, and I read western short stories. It was not great literature, but it helped me develop an interest that later on transferred to reading good literature and a lot of history which, I think, proved to be worthwhile.

In May of 1927, shortly before Lindbergh made his historic flight, we moved into a double house at 397 East 13th Avenue. It was a great move for me. There were, about evenly divided, double and single houses on the block extending from north Fourth Street to the railroad tracks. Children seemed to live in every abode on the block. The street had little traffic, and we all played together—usually in the street. We played touch football and softball, roller skated, rode on sleds down the railroad embankment, regularly got chased out of one old woman's yard when an errant ball got into her flower bed, and generally had fun. On long summer evenings we played hide and seek, tappy on the ice box, Rover Red Rover, and May I. In winter, we visited in each other's homes. We played with toy soldiers complete with cannon which shot everything from toothpicks to small marbles. We played card games such as Old Maid and Rook. We played with toy trains and all of the other toys that were popular during that time. My parents and I lived at that location for more than three years. It was a great place to be!

Present-day environmentalists would perhaps have considered this a slum neighborhood, although for that period it was, in fact, a good middle-class location. The bulk of the dwellings were equipped with furnaces which burned soft coal. The main lines of the Pennsylvania and Big Four railroads were practically in our front yards. All the locomotives were coal-fired. Coal smoke and soot permeated the air to the extent that sometimes at night the smoke partially obscured the streetlights. This was the air we breathed. Neighborhood housewives scrubbed their wooden porches, floors, walls, and ceilings frequently and yet soot continued to be ever present on them. Some days the air was clear enough to hang the family washing outside. At other times, this would have been impossible.

The Ohio State Fairgrounds were due east across the railroad tracks. The State Fair took place the latter part of August, and, as I now remember, it was always steaming hot. The cattle, sheep, hog, and horse barns were adjacent to the railroad tracks. The smell was unbelievable. The animals and their manure brought flies in huge quantities. They remained in the area until fall. In spite of these "minor" problems, all the kids looked forward to the fair. We had no problem in either crossing the tracks and climbing a fence, or, in the alternative, just sneaking in. One year during fair week, one of the neighborhood kids enlisted my help in selling ice cold pop near the Eleventh Avenue entrance to the fairgrounds. We were a success, even though we had no legal right to be there selling anything. We were successful until one Thursday morning when I ran across the street with my hands full of pop bottles, directly into the path of a truck. My left leg was cut to the bone, and I have scars to this day as a reminder of the occasion. I was hospitalized for a time and missed the first six weeks of school.

During the late 1920's and early 1930's, radio was becoming commonplace. At seven o'clock in the evening, Monday through Friday, the streets were deserted, and the evening meal was either consumed or held until later. "Amos and Andy" was on, and adult and child alike listened. For those who missed that marvelous program, two men portrayed the voices of all of the characters. There were such wonderful people such as Amos, Andy, Lightnin', Ruby, Madam Queen, Miss Blue, the Kingfish, Brother Crawford, and Algonquin J. Calhoun; such memorable institutions as the Fresh Air Taxicab Company, the Mystic Knights of the Sea, and the Calhoun Law Offices. Some of the expressions used became a part of our language – "Buzz me, Miz Blue," "I's regusted!," and "Holy Mack'rel!, Andy!" Some of the nicknames still carried came from this program. It brought radio to prominence.

Other radio programs that I remember at this early time included Lowell Thomas and the evening news, which he always ended by saying, "and so long until tomorrow;" Rudy Vallee, the A & P Gypsies, and, of course, broadcasts of football games with Graham MacNamee speaking. As a child growing up, I didn't care much about the popular songs of the day. I do remember "In a Little Spanish Town," "Minnie the Moocher," "Tiptoe Through the Tulips," "Chloe," "Ramona," "Button Up Your Overcoat," and "Mammie." And, although there were many Broadway hit tunes, I didn't hear them and they were not popular with the average person in Columbus, Ohio. Broadway was a long, long way from Columbus then.

Adult recreation was not much different in Columbus in the late 1920's from what it had been in LaRue three or four years earlier. My parents played more bridge, they listened to the radio, attended an occasional movie, and took rides around the city and out into the surrounding countryside.

"The talkies" came to Columbus in 1928, and with them, a real interest in motion pictures on the part of everyone with money enough to go. Movies kept skyrocketing in popularity for years thereafter and became probably the single greatest source of recreation outside the home.

Automobiles improved greatly in a short span of years. Electric windshield wipers were standard, headlights were brighter, and the self-starter improved so much that hand cranks were no longer necessary. Heaters were available and many cars were equipped with this luxury. Chevrolet became a popular car. Ford abandoned the Model T and replaced it with the Model A, complete with gear shift and in various colors other than black. Buick, too, became a popular car, as did Studebaker, Hudson, Essex, Dodge, and Chrysler. Among higher-priced cars were the Pierce Arrow with its unusual headlights, Cadillac, Cord, and the Stutz. The Pontiac was introduced and caught on reasonably well fairly soon. But automobiles come and go. The Marmon disappeared, Hupmobile faded from the scene, and so did some of the others in short order, including the Overland and Willys-Knight.

An innovation of the late 1920's that really made the automobile even more popular with young unmarrieds was the "rumble seat." It was a relatively easy change. All the manufacturer needed to do was change a coupe by eliminating the trunk, reversing the lid, placing a seat in it, and putting two steps on the rear fender for entrance and exit. A lot of love was made in those rumble seats. I doubt that the participants even knew they were uncomfortable.

In September of 1927, I entered the fourth grade at Indianola Elementary School, located at Sixteenth and Indianola Avenues. The school was at that time a combination elementary and junior high. The building was first occupied in 1909. It was the first junior high school in the United States when it opened. It has been only in the last few years that the junior high has been replaced by the middle-school concept. I am probably old-fashioned, but I wonder whether or not real progress in education has been made by the change.

The school building was vastly overcrowded with the result that the fourth, fifth, and part of the sixth grades were in "portable" classrooms. A "portable," so far as I can figure out, was not really portable, but could be done away with as quickly as it was constructed. Each portable contained one complete classroom which could house about forty pupils and, of course, one teacher comfortably. Each building had a cloakroom, a large coal stove which provided all of the heat, windows all along one side of the classroom, and blackboards across two walls. There were electric lights in each building, but no plumbing of any kind. The restrooms we used were located in the basement of the main school building. Room temperature was not regulated by any type of thermostat. During cold days, the windows were closed; during very cold days, we wore long underwear and overcoats. As the weather warmed up, windows were opened. During hot weather, the doors and all windows were open wide and we still sweltered. The playground area surrounding these buildings was almost non-existent and covered with gravel; our shoes wore out quickly and were always scuffed. The knees of our knickers, corduroy and otherwise, developed holes from our falling on the gravel, and our hands and knees were frequently skinned.

Despite the crudeness of the facilities, we received a fine education. The teaching was excellent, and the attitudes, discipline and learning process were exceptional. When I think about it fifty years later—it makes me wonder whether all of the so-called modern school plants are really giving the dollar-for-dollar value that should be demanded by the taxpayer. Bright, willing students and good teachers are really what are required for successful education. With those ingredients present, classes could be held in a barn, a tent, an open field, or under an oak tree.

The Indianola school district was located in The Ohio State University area. A large number of the children in the district were sons and daughters of university professors. Many others came from homes wherein the male parent was either a highly-skilled, well-known professional man, a banker, a scientist, or the owner of a successful business or manufacturing plant. These were, generally, very gifted, highly intelligent people. So were their progeny. The result was that competition was keen in the classroom. Teachers pushed us much harder than could possibly have been the case with less learning ability present on the part of the students. True, there were some dumb kids. I do not now remember them, nor do I remember how they progressed. I believe firmly, however, that the average student learned much more than would have been the case in a less competitive situation. I think a mistake is made in our educational system when teachers do not demand that pupils work and learn to the limits of their ability. Too many children just sit and do little or nothing in the classroom when they could be forced, driven, or cajoled into a reasonably productive pursuit of a decent basic education. In any event, Indianola was a very fast track for me. I learned a great deal, both educationally and socially, during those years. My development as a person is largely traceable to that period in my life.

What did we learn? We learned to read and write well. We had spelling drills every day. We were required to memorize the meaning of the words we spelled. We were taught to use the words in intelligent sentences, and were drilled hard in basic fractions. We were taught geography and were indoctrinated with a very patriotic version of our country's history, and we *knew* that the United States was the greatest, strongest, most prosperous, kindest and most altruistic nation in the history of mankind.

Calvin Coolidge was our President. Prosperity was rampant. Our *The Columbus Dispatch*, an ultra-conservative, Republican newspaper, extolled Coolidge's virtues in each edition. He was known as "Cautious Cal," when he announced, "I do not choose to run," at least the *Dispatch* was practically in mourning.

At the 1928 national conventions, the Democrats nominated Al Smith, "the Happy Warrior," and the Republicans, with Coolidge's blessing, nominated "the Great Engineer," Herbert Hoover. Smith was Catholic in a predominantly Protestant country. He was a Democratic liberal (at least more liberal than Hoover).

When the mood of the country was Republican conservative, Smith was for the repeal of the Prohibition Amendment before the nation was ready to scuttle "the Great Experiment." Hoover ran on the Republican record of prosperity, and promised "two chickens in every pot, and two cars in every garage." Naturally enough, Mr. Hoover won by a landslide. Our teachers led us to expect this result, and cheered it, as did the vast majority of our parents. God was in His heaven and all was right with the world.

Each morning at the beginning of school we said the Lord's Prayer, recited the Pledge of Allegiance, and sang either "America" or "America the Beautiful." Once each week we went to the Protestant church across the street from the school for one hour of religious education during school hours. There was no protest to any of this by the parents, or anyone else for that matter. We were regimented in our thinking and propagandized in the American way of life in a "WASP" environment.

Although my parents and I lived on Thirteenth Avenue for only about three years and lived in four other places from the summer of 1930 until August of 1933. I remained in the Indianola School District for six years. This gave me more continuity than I ever had at any other time during my public-school years. I knew the kids, I knew the teachers, I knew several different neighborhoods in the university area. As a result of so many moves, I learned how to meet people and get along with them was almost like an "Army brat," I really had no roots.

As I indicated earlier, I entered the fourth grade at Indianola Elementary in September of 1927. Even the portables were crowded to the extent that there really were not enough seats for all of those entering the first semester. The result was that another boy and I were arbitrarily promoted to the second semester class after two weeks. We were "4As" and no longer "4Bs." Many of this group of "4As" became my best friends and remained so for years; one until his death more than thirty years later, another still today. One afternoon in the late Spring of 1928, when I walked from school to my father's drug store, I found the front door locked. A sign on the door read "In the Hands of Receiver." I had no idea who or what a "receiver" was, but I was sure that there was something really wrong. I ran home and found a note on the table, together with some money. The note told me to take a taxi to my uncle's home in the east part of town. I was scared and cried. I do not know to this day where my parents were that afternoon. I went to my uncle's home and was comforted by one of my old maid aunts who told me not to worry, that Uncle Louis would take care of everything. However, Uncle Louis did not solve the problem. Dad lost his drug store. I never did find out what happened; I presume that he was not able to pay his creditors. It probably was a simple case of starting a new business without enough working capital. Whatever caused the failure, my father went to work for Walgreen Drug Company and continued with them until August of 1933. As it worked out, my father had a very good job during some very hard times for many people.

In January 1930, my classmates and I entered Indianola Junior High School as seventh graders. The junior high school had moved to a new and wonderful building at north Fourth Street and Nineteenth Avenue on what had been part of the property known as Indianola Park. The Indianola Park swimming pool and dance hall were immediately across Nineteenth Avenue from the school. The school grounds were more than spacious, they were huge and beautifully kept. The building was large and, I feel certain, the ultimate school facility of its time. It was equipped lavishly. Courses offered were in keeping with the entire operation. It was truly a fantastic place in which to be educated.

The school functioned like a high school. We changed classes at forty-five-minute intervals throughout the school day. Each teacher specialized in the subject matter which he or she taught. I know that I was required to take three years of history, mathematics, English, and Latin. I know that I was exposed to one year of art. My only artistic accomplishment occurred the morning I vomited all over the art teacher. I do not think she wanted me back for any more art training. Physical education was required two days a week. We had to wear shorts and shirts and tennis shoes in these classes. We also were required to shower after each session. The gymnasium contained all sorts of mats, parallel bars, and similar equipment in addition to a good-sized basketball floor which, upon occasion, was converted to about three volleyball courts. Each pupil had a locker for gym clothes.

Manual training, metalworking, and printing were offered. I took manual training for a year, as required, but no advanced courses—at the teacher's request. The girls had what was called "domestic science," and quite a few took typing, shorthand, and other secretarial courses. We all were required to have one year of music, and some elected to continue for two more years. There was even an orchestra which played for all of the assemblies. Courses were offered in dramatics, which could be taken as an elective. The dramatics teacher put on two or three rather major productions each year, and every year or two, with the music teacher, an operetta. The auditorium was always sold out for both matinee and evening performances. I had "leads" in a couple of them, and even had the part of the father in "Hansel and Gretel," I sang a duet with a girl who later appeared in musicals on Broadway. She was great! I was lousy. But my mother, being the musician that she was, felt that the part was not suited to my "talents."

The school had a large library with a trained librarian. We were required to learn how to locate books by the use of the Dewey Decimal System. This training was helpful to me throughout my college days. I learned then how to do research. We had a monthly school magazine which was produced by the printing classes. (One year I was sports editor.) There was a fully equipped, very well-run cafeteria. Lunches were good and hot, and cost about twenty cents. This took place long before there were federally subsidized school lunch programs.

There was a large motion picture screen in the auditorium, and movies were shown during lunch periods at a cost of a nickel. We saw Our Gang comedies, Laurel and Hardy, Harold Lloyd, Buster Keaton, Charlie Chaplin and other popular comics of the twenties and thirties.

There were school teams in basketball, baseball, and speedball. There were diverse school clubs which met weekly during a school activity period. We had school sponsored dances and parties. There was a student council and even a student police patrol called "Indianola Traffic Cops," or, as the purple and white armbands read, "TIC." There was even a sight-saving class for those who had visual problems. I had the problems, but neither my parents nor I felt that I needed such a program, Thank God!

Indianola was a truly remarkable school for its time. The faculty was well-trained, the students were generally bright, and discipline never a problem. I owe a great deal to my years in both the elementary and junior high schools.

During the same years, my educational experience included a good amount of religious, social, and moral indoctrination. With my peers, I attended the Sunday School and church services at Indianola Methodist Church. Lessons learned there were progressive for the times. This church was heavily attended by students and faculty from The Ohio State University. Sunday School teachers often were either prominent professional or businessmen. One teacher was a student leader at Ohio State. The minister was Doctor Robert Leonard Tucker, a relatively young Ph.D. from Yale. His sermons and the emphasis of the Sunday School teachers were directed toward the social doctrines of Jesus Christ. We were taught to live the good life, to help others, to love one another, and to love our neighbors. We were not taught "hell fire and damnation," or held to the Victorian standards which still were pervasive in Ohio, the Midwest, and the South.

Religion at this church was far from being fundamentalistic in nature. We had parties at the church and even a little dancing. When we entered the ninth grade, we attended Sunday School at the Student Center located a couple blocks from the church. There were many social activities which became available to us there. Partly because of our age and partly because of the environment, we developed a new and much more appreciative viewpoint toward the opposite sex. I had always liked girls. I got so I liked them better.

Through the church, we attended what was then called "Epworth League," a Methodist youth fellowship organization, on Sunday evenings. Some of the programs were good, but I seem to remember that we all attended regularly so that we could get out of the house on Sunday nights and, after the meeting, go to one of the girl's houses for an hour or so of socializing.

In the eighth and ninth grades, there were school parties, church parties and picnics, and parties given by various parents for all of us. Some of these events were memorable and somewhat unusual for our ages and the time period. I attended a dance, sponsored by The Ohio State University Band director, in a large suite at a downtown hotel. We got there in a chauffeur-driven limousine owned by parents of one of my friends. I was invited to a dinner party at the home of a Jewish rabbi whose genius daughter was in our class. I went to a party at a very nice cottage at Buckeye Lake, about thirty miles east of Columbus. We were treated to speedboat rides in the family's speedboat, a sailboat, swimming and, of course, an unbelievable amount of food. One of the teachers drove a group of us to the party. He was young, unmarried, and, from our point of view, a great chaperone. In "9A" (the last half of the ninth grade), we did begin to have dates for special events such as school dances, a Christmas party at one of the homes, and the like. Occasionally, one of my friends got the family car, but usually we walked. I admit it was not too romantic, but all of us thought we were being very adult.

The period during which I attended Indianola Junior High School —1930 to January 1933—was a traumatic time for America. But neither myself nor my friends and schoolmates were much affected by the Great Depression. Our fathers were fortunate enough to have jobs. My uncle, though, who had been a very wealthy real estate broker and entrepreneur, lost his fortune and never really made a comeback. Our parents may have worried, but we seemed insulated from the problems. I do remember that there were many men on the downtown streets selling apples, pencils and other low-cost items; some with signs saying, "help the unemployed." I saw children walking along the railroad tracks picking up coal that had fallen from the coal cars and putting it in burlap bags. I read in *The Columbus Dispatch* about the millions of unemployed, and the misery that occurred as a consequence. I read about families who were cold and begging; and we all took canned food to school and church for "welfare baskets" for the poor. We were far from rich, but we ate well, wore decent clothing, and even had some money to spend. I knew about the World War I Veterans bonus march on Washington, and of the way they were treated. We all were told about the fortunes that were lost in Wall Street, and we read about numerous bank failures and mortgage foreclosures. This was interesting to me, and I deplored it as did the teachers, the minister, and my parents and their friends, but the difference was that I did not feel it directly at that time.

I have always loved history and reading about great men, wars— particularly the Civil War—what people wore in earlier days, and how they lived. I spent quite a few Sunday afternoons wandering through the Ohio State Museum. I loved the newsreels at the movies. I listened religiously to the six forty-five news on the radio. I announced to everyone that when I grew up, I was going to become a history professor.

Through my interest in history, I developed an interest in current affairs, particularly political affairs.

By the summer of 1932, I became an avid follower of the Republican and Democratic national conventions. I listened to all of it on the radio. Although we had been taught in elementary school about the wonderful things accomplished by "Cautious Cal" Coolidge and the brilliance of "the Great Engineer" Hoover, it was obvious that even the conservative *The Columbus Dispatch* and most of the nation were disenchanted with the anxiety of the Depression, its empty factories, and its genuine hardships. Hoover got the blame—whether deserved or not. After all, he had promised an ever-greater, ever-ongoing prosperity. He had no solution for the Depression. Sadly, he kept repeating the statement that "prosperity is just around the corner"—this, in the face of what amounted to a farm revolt in the mid-west, vacant smokestacks, fear and hunger. The country needed new leadership desperately.

The Republicans really had no choice. They had to nominate Herbert C. Hoover again. His acceptance speech was so typical of everything else he said: "Let no man say it cannot be worse. It can be so much worse that the grass will grow in the streets of every large city in America." I heard it then and I remember it yet. Young as I was, I knew that this attitude would solve nothing. The message was delivered in somber tones, much like those of an old-fashioned funeral director greeting the deceased's family and friends at the door of the funeral parlor.

The Republican convention was dull. The Democrats, as usual, put on a helluva show. They fought over the platform, the seating of delegates and, probably, hotel rooms and nomination. They each had a lengthy, impassioned nominating speech followed by a parade around the convention hall accompanied by their band, organ (or both) playing their campaign song. I remember that the major prospective candidates were the governor of Maryland, whose name now escapes me; Byrd—then, I believe, the governor of Virginia; Al Smith – "the Happy Warrior" who had been the nominee in 1928; John Nance Garner, the majority leader of the House of Representatives; and Franklin D. Roosevelt, the governor of New York who had succeeded Al Smith. The three major contenders turned out to be Smith, Garner, and Roosevelt.

Of course, I knew nothing about the political shenanigans which transpired behind the scenes in the smoke filled rooms, but the debates were bitter on the convention floor. After numerous ballots, Franklin D. Roosevelt was nominated for President and John Nance Garner, Vice President.

Roosevelt immediately captured the imagination and the hearts of the American people. He broke precedent by asking that the convention not adjourn in order that he might fly from New York to Chicago to make his acceptance speech directly to the delegates. It was a heartwarming speech after the gloom which everyone felt. He said, "One third of the American people are inadequately fed, inadequately clothed, and inadequately housed, and I propose to do something about it." At last, there was hope! His aristocratic voice gave confidence where there had been despair. This voice and the wording used by him continued to bring solace to us through much of his time in office. He was elected easily in November. I decided at that time that I was a Roosevelt Democrat. Some eight years later my mind was changed permanently, but to this day I think that F.D.R. saved the nation from revolution.

During my junior high school days, I became a sports fan. I loved to read about, listen to, and watch baseball, basketball, and football games. I was never much of an athlete, but I liked to try. We played softball and hardball on makeshift diamonds on vacant lots, and occasionally on open areas on the Ohio State Campus. "Touch" football was played in the streets, and "tackle" football usually on a vacant field at Ohio State. I suppose that we could have gotten hurt. We had neither uniform, pads, nor any other protective equipment. Basketball was usually played in an alley with a basket nailed to a telephone pole or a garage.

In summer, I swam from morning until night at the Indianola Swimming Pool. We all had season tickets which cost about ten dollars for the summer. We really got our money's worth. We had a professional baseball team which was in the original American Association. Originally, they were known as the "Senators" and it was a lousy team of misfits. Games were played in a ramshackle park. Boys, not girls, could become members of the "Knot Hole Gang," and were admitted free through the week to seats in the right-field bleachers. Neil Park was located adjacent to the Kroger Bakery and along towards the late innings, the smell of hot baked goods wafted into my nostrils. God, I got hungry! The only thing I could afford to buy to quell my appetite was a chocolate peppermint patty for five cents, but the trouble was that after eating one, I got thirsty, and Cokes were a dime. I could not afford both.

The St. Louis Cardinals purchased the Columbus franchise in 1931; consequently, the caliber of play improved almost at once. The ball club was re-christened the "Columbus Red Birds." In the spring of 1932, the new and beautiful Red Bird Stadium was opened, lights were installed, and night baseball began. Columbus was among the first in the country to have night ball on a professional level. Even though we were in the throes of the Depression, the crowds were huge. I do not remember the seating capacity of the stadium (it was probably twelve or thirteen thousand), but several times there was standing room only, and I have seen fans standing in the outfield along the right field fence. Many of the players on those early Red Bird teams went on to the major leagues and stardom. Most of the Cardinal championship teams after 1934 were made up almost entirely of former Columbus Red Birds. Even the 1934 "Gas House Gang" had Paul Dean, Delancey and Jack Hunt from the earlier Red Bird teams.

I read about the major league teams. Naturally, I was a Cardinal fan, but I also had quite an interest in the Philadelphia Athletics in their championship years. Connie Mack still managed, as he continued to do for too many years. Some of his star players included Lefty Grove, George Earnshaw, Jimmy Foxx, and Mickey Cochrane. Every night at about dinner time, I listened to Bob Newhall's sports program. He told some great sports stories and talked faster than anyone else I ever heard on the radio, television, or in person. He advertised Mail Pouch chewing tobacco and wound up every program by saying, "So long from Mail Pouch."

Football was my other favorite spectator sport. Columbus North High School had some great teams, coached by a wonderful guy named Mike Hagley. His teams were unbeaten for several years, and most of them played college football later. Bob Harbride played tackle for The Ohio State University and became an All-American; Lew

Hindsman, Bill Carroll and Buzz Wetzel made up three favorites of a later Ohio State backfield, and there were others who played for State and other schools. I got to see an occasional North game. I watched Ohio State frequently! Once or twice we "snuck" into the stadium. I ushered one year as a Boy Scout, and, because the early season games had small crowds—perhaps only thirty-thousand in that tremendous horseshoe stadium—I was able to sit and watch most of the games. Ohio State's early season football games then were played against small Ohio colleges such as Wittenberg and Ohio Wesleyan. One year Ohio Wesleyan, to everyone's surprise and State's chagrin, almost won. In addition to seeing all of the former North High players who were on the Ohio State team, I watched one of the all-time greats and later coach, Wes Fesler, and his buddy and a later athletic director, Dick Larkins. I did not see very many of the great players from other schools because I could not get into the games.

Knute Rockne coached Notre Dame, the Fighting Irish, who were the darlings of the sports pages and seemed to be on a national radio hook-up every game. I thrilled to Graham MacNamee's descriptions of those games and cheered for Carrideo, Savaldi, Schwartz, Brill, Leahey, and other Notre Dame stars.

Michigan was the great team in the Big Ten, and it was a momentous event in Columbus when Ohio State was able to defeat them. This seldom happened. In fact, Sam Willaman coached the Ohio State team and lost three games in three years—all to Michigan. He was fired.

In either 1927 or 1928, I saw my first talking picture. It was, I think, the first "talkie" made—Al Jolson in "The Jazz Singer." After the first talkie, others came fast. Within a year, every movie theater in Columbus had talking films. Many of the early ones were musicals featuring Broadway Melody series, Jeanette MacDonald and Lawrence Tibbett, and others. Some of the early stars included Janet Gaynor, Gloria Swanson, Norma Shearer, Greta Garbo, Edward G. Robinson, the Marx Brothers, George Arliss, Richard Barthelmess, and others who do not now come to mind.

Popular music, beginning with a couple of early favorites such as "St. Louis Blues" and "My Blue Heaven," included all of the Broadway hits – "Old Man River," "Lullaby of Broadway," "Broadway Melody,"

"Sunny Side of the Street," "Star Dust," "Shuffle Off to Buffalo," "Happy Days Are Here Again," and the Depression song, "Side by Side."

On the radio, in addition to the continuing phenomenon of Amos and Andy, were "The Little Theater Off Broadway," Fannie Brice, George Burns and Gracie Allen, Eddie Cantor, and Jack Benny. There was also an astrologist by the name of Evangeline Adams, who predicted the stock market crash of 1929.

1933–1935

In January of 1933, I completed the ninth grade at Indianola Junior High, and commenced my sophomore year at North High School. This represented a change to me mostly because of the (for that time) hugeness of the school. There were about sixteen hundred students attending North; however, I did not feel lost there because many of the sophomores had attended Indianola with me, and many of the upperclassmen were at least known to me because they, too, had gone to Indianola and lived in the general neighborhood.

Ralph Clark, Richard's father.

Although my dad had gone to "Old North High School" almost twenty-five years earlier, many of the older teachers remembered him and asked—in class and otherwise-whether I was "Ma" Clark's son. I learned that my father was one of the school's greatest football stars and had played on three undefeated teams, captaining the 1909 team.

His picture hung in the hall right beside the door to my history room. One day I was called out of class and summoned to the principal's office. I thought some of my sins had caught up with me and was scared, but it turned out that Mr. Swain, the principal, had been my dad's coach and just wanted to talk to me. I had no problems at North, made a lot of new friends, got excellent grades, and probably would have played football had I remained there. At any rate, the semester passed quickly, and I looked forward to returning that fall. It did not happen.

I do remember the attempted assassination of Franklin Roosevelt. I heard his inaugural address and was thrilled when he said, "The only thing we have to fear is fear itself." I experienced the Bank Holiday, when all of the banks in the country were closed and no one had money. We rode the street cars free. We ate lunch in the school cafeteria on credit. Somehow, we got through it. Roosevelt conducted a series of "Fireside Chats" on Sunday nights and everyone listened and gained confidence as the First Hundred Days of the Roosevelt New Deal with all of its revolutionary programs unfolded. This famous Hundred Days changed the social, economic, and political philosophy —and structure—of the nation far more than anything that had occurred in our entire previous history. Had he done nothing else during his four terms of office, he would have still gone into history as one of the greatest of our Presidents. Had strong action not been taken, and had the people not developed the confidence in "F.D.R." that they did, some sort of revolution would have necessarily taken place. The people had become desperate, despondent, and without hope. Roosevelt gave them that hope, faith and a sense of a new beginning. Some of the experiments worked, some did not. Prosperity did not return by pushing a few buttons. The country was still suffering dire economic straits at the beginning of World War II. But we remained together as the United States; revolution was averted.

The summer of 1933 began as other summers had before hot, sunny, lazy days complete with swimming, girls, baseball and reading. I had, despite the Depression, a sense of security and feeling that all was right with my world. This was the summer of the National Recovery Administration (N.R.A.), the "Blue Eagle" emblem and General Hugh Johnson. The emblem contained the phrase, "We do Our Part." Every business was, voluntarily, supposed to raise the wages of its employees and, whenever possible, hire new personnel. The businesses which did not sign up to participate were virtually ostracized by the weight of public opinion fanned to a hot flame by Johnson. The drug chain for which my father worked subscribed to the Program, raised wages, and fired their higher-salaried pharmacists (who were considered professionals and not subject to the Act). My father lost his job about July of 1933 during the worst of the Depression. It shook my parents up to no end and ruined my sense of ambience. For the first time in my life, I felt insecure.

Within a matter of two or three weeks, dad announced that he had a job in Marion, Ohio, and that we would move there. In August of 1933, seven years after making the transition from LaRue to "the big city," yet another major change was made. Marion was, and is, the county seat of Marion County. Its population was about forty thousand. Its chief claim to fame was that it had been President Warren G. Harding's home. He had conducted much of his Presidential Campaign in 1920 from his front porch on Mt. Vernon Avenue. The town was surrounded by excellent farmland, but farmers were in distress in 1933. Marion was the home of a major manufacturing company, Marion Steam Shovel. This was, of course heavy industry and the company was in trouble almost before the Depression began. Unfortunately, we had moved to a town even more depressed than most of the rest of the nation. There was no money, few jobs, nearly bankrupt small businesses, and much unease among the few who were fortunate enough to be reasonably well off financially. God, what a town to move into!

I found where the high school was located and made my first visit to Marion Harding High School for the purpose of enrolling as a second-semester sophomore. I saw the principal, a very distinguished looking old gent wearing pince-nez glasses, whose name was Marshall. I remember that he appeared to be very well-dressed and spoke in such a cultured tone that I was impressed with his dignity and his complete confidence in his ability to handle any situation which could possibly arise. I doubt that anyone (probably including his wife) ever called him anything other than "mister." He handled my situation decisively: Marion Harding had no semester plan, and I would either have to repeat the first semester or become a first-semester junior. Mr. Marshall decreed that I should become a junior, with the promise that at mid-year I would be required to complete the second half of the plane geometry course. I thought I was smarter than hell! As it turned out, in the short run, I would have been much better off had I repeated some of my previous courses.

Harding High was an old building located in the center of Marion. There were no school grounds at all. The school had no auditorium, no cafeteria, a very small gymnasium, no shop instruction, no art department, and no charm. School assemblies were held in two large study halls located at opposite ends of the building. The building did have classrooms and a library. Academic courses were not only offered, but they were stressed. It turned out to be a good school for any student who planned to attend college. Unfortunately, few students ever saw a college. I don't think many of the students knew the difference or cared. It was not until several years later that vocational training began to emerge in most public high schools.

Athletic facilities at the school were minus zero. Football players dressed at the school (there were no showers), practiced on a field about a mile and a half away, and played their home games in the centerfield of the racetrack at the county fairgrounds. The teams were lousy, and no wonder. The basketball team practiced and played their games at the Marion Steam Shovel gymnasium. For its time, it was an excellent basketball court. Perhaps for this reason, the basketball teams were very successful. There was no track team because there were no track and field facilities in town. There was no baseball team either.

The school itself was not at all like what I had taken for granted in Columbus. But the teachers did a good job of instructing, considering the fact that there was almost a complete lack of teaching aids. High-performance standards were maintained, and good grades were hard to come by. Until then, I had always been an excellent student and was used to receiving high grades without working very hard. I still was able to accomplish this in English, History, and French at Marion Harding. I never understood chemistry. The teacher taught it like a college course—lectures, laboratory, lengthy assignments, frequent tests. I hated it. I never understood anything about it, and most of the year, I was failing.

Miraculously, I passed a very comprehensive final examination at the end of the school year and avoided having to repeat the course.

Had I not passed, I doubt that I would have ever graduated from high school.

The second half of the school year, I resumed my pursuit of plane geometry. I did not expect that this would be difficult. I had gotten good grades when I took the first semester at Columbus North. I don't know what happened, but I failed the course. The teacher was a well-dressed, urban young man with an unusual sense of humor. His sense of humor may have disarmed me, but either he couldn't teach, or I couldn't learn—or both. Had I stayed in Marion, I would probably still be taking plane geometry, old though I may be.

I really believe that I went through a period of adolescence in Marion that darned near did me in. I was a nut. I did not think straight, nor did I act normal. I suppose that some of the problem was adjusting from the security of Columbus to a completely-changed environment in Marion. In addition to not learning as I should, I did everything ornery that I could think of, aided, and abetted by some other boys who were at least as screwy as I was.

We rode around town in a new Rockne convertible operated by a doctor's son who had too much money and shot out streetlights with B.B. guns. We upset the only outside privy in town—with a man in it. How could we know he was in it? We threw tomatoes and other produce at houses, after ringing the front doorbell to make sure someone came out to get hit. We stole things which were useless to us, just for the hell of it. We picked up a kid bodily and sat him on the drinking fountain at the Y.M.C.A. in the dead of winter, then ran him outdoors so that his pants froze. We drove our parents' automobiles at whatever their top speed was and raced one another on curving, hilly roads. When the streets and roads were icy, we deliberately threw the cars into skids. We smoked cheap cigars and cigarettes, and chewed plug tobacco. When we could get it, we drank anything with alcohol in it. God forgive us, but we even did our best to break up an old-fashioned tent revival meeting, but that group of Christians did not turn the other cheek. They chased us for a couple of blocks, and we kept on sinning. Those folks were mad. In a couple of "fundraising activities," I wound up in the principal's office. Once another smart kid and I picked some suckers to join us in matching coins. One of us turned up "heads," the other "tails," and we split our profit. I was also involved in selling tickets for seats in the school library to the incoming sophomores. I was very impressed when I was told that, if I wound up in the office again, I would be suspended. Because my grades were not up to par, I was not allowed to go out at night (even on weekends) for the last two months of my junior year. However, when my parents were not at home, I went out anyway, but managed to get back before they returned.

In spite of everything, I was accepted favorably by my fellow students and most of the faculty. I was in as many activities as I had ever been in Columbus. I had the lead in the class play, was elected to the Student Council about a month after I commenced school, and I became a member of the school chorus and glee club. I joined the Hi-Y Club and the Epworth League at the Methodist Church. I even went to Sunday School, and occasionally to church. Unfortunately, I did not follow the advice I picked up from those Christian organizations. I did not have many dates my junior year in high school. The family car was hard to come by at night - partly because of my grades and partly because I was only fifteen. Naturally, I had very little spending money and girls then, as now, cost money. Most of my female companionship came with "the girl across the street." She was damned good-looking, and we sort of practiced with each other.

One of the many characters with whom I became friends was a tall, skinny, light-haired, slovenly kid whose full name was—and I hope still is—Roger Gomer Bovie Morgan. His father was a doctor. His mother was one of the most prominent and powerful Democratic politicians in Ohio. They lived in a big house on one of the nicer streets in Marion. The house was unkempt—as were they. The paint was peeling, the house cluttered, and they did not seem to worry about anything.

Rog and I combined our "wealth" about May of 1934 and purchased a 1917 Dodge touring car. We paid eleven dollars for it, drove it all summer, and sold it in the fall to the junk yard for thirteen dollars. What a deal! What a car! It was all ours. I recently saw a 1918 Dodge touring car in the Ford Museum at Dearborn, Michigan, which was either a preserved new car, or a completely-restored one. Ours did not look at all like the one in the museum—beautiful. Ours looked like a rusty piece of junk—which it was. Ours had character, though. It had fenders, running boards, frosted head lights, rust, dust, mud, torn leather seats, a cloth top which was so frayed that it flapped in the breeze and, with the top on, the car looked like hell! When we took the top off, it looked only terrible. The radiator leaked, but we slowed that down by throwing flax seed in it. Gasoline was seventeen cents a gallon, kerosene was thirteen cents, so we used a mixture of four gallons of kerosene to one gallon of gas. The engine knocked loudly but kept running. We got used oil free from the corner filling station. We got money to operate our vehicle by collecting pennies, nickels, and, occasionally, dimes from all the idiots who insisted on riding with us. We loved that old car. It was the talk of most of Marion. One night we got dates with two girls from very prominent Marion families. My date was the daughter of the local Congressman; Morgan's date was the daughter of the owners of the town's only mansion. Morgan picked me up. He was dressed in a linen cap, goggles, and a linen duster, and wore gauntlets. He looked like something from about 1912. We put the top on and drove over to pick up my date. Morgan drove the car into their front yard and stopped next to the porch. The entire family was assembled, and they were not amused. After some rather heated debate, my date was permitted to go with us. We then drove over to the mansion, up the long drive, and parked under the portico. We were warmly greeted, and all of those folks enjoyed it, including the servants. Fortunately, nothing bad happened either to the car or the girls.

We had a lot of experiences with the car. We chewed tobacco and spit on new cars. We tried to get arrested for speeding, but the cops just laughed at us. On our speedometer, the Dodge ran thirty-five miles per hour in second and fifty-five in high. We blew a tire and stole two from the junk yard that fit.

My social life picked up that summer. All of us were allowed to drive the family cars, and girls seemed to enjoy going for rides, parking, and doing a little necking. We could count on spending about twenty cents for cokes at the high school hangout. We all went to an Epworth League convention for a week at Lakeside, Ohio. Boys and girls stayed in the same cottage and were chaperoned by an old maid who simply could not keep up with our activities. The Methodist girls at Lakeside did not drink or smoke, but they knew how to have a good time. That fall, we went to a lot of dances. We were always dressed in suits and ties and wore well-shined shoes. We thought we were "smooth."

The music we listened to on the radio and danced to included "Star Dust," "Stormy Weather," "Smoke Gets in Your Eyes," "Winter Wonderland," "The Champagne Waltz," and "Moonglow." It was a romantic period.

In addition to the radio programs that I mentioned earlier, Fred Waring and the Pennsylvanians became popular, as did Ed Wynn, "The Fire Chief," and Fred Allen. I did not have enough money to be able to attend the movies very often, but I do remember Wallace Beery, Lana Turner, John Barrymore, and Will Rodgers as being stars. My parents had little entertainment other than listening to the radio, giving and attending small dinners, and playing bridge with friends. No one that I knew ever took much of a vacation, though a few managed to make it to the Chicago World's Fair, which was considered quite an event. Sally Rand with her fan dance was probably the most publicized attraction at the Fair.

The Depression continued unabated. Everyone in Marion felt its hardship in some manner, even though the young had fun anyway. In the fall of 1934, the drug store which my father operated was forced to go out of business. My folks were very worried, and so was I. My already limited spending money was further curtailed. While we didn't miss any meals, we began to eat quite inexpensive food. I got a lot of bean soup, vegetable soup, wieners, and cheap lunch meat sandwiches. My father quit smoking cigarettes even though they were only fifteen cents a pack. At Christmas, we did not have a tree, and the only present any of us received was a warm jacket which my mother had bought for me with money she made helping a friend clean house. Christmas Day, we drove to my grandmother's house in Plain City. I remember that the meal was not the usual holiday fare, but I do not recall exactly what was served. I also remember that my grandmother gave me a five-dollar bill. I did offer it to my parents on the way home, but they refused it.

During the late fall, my parents took several one-day trips. I thought my father was job hunting until one evening in mid-December when they arrived home to tell me that dad had bought a drug store in Grove City, Ohio, and would take it over January 1, 1935. I was also told that I would finish the mid-year semester in Marion, and that we would then move to Grove City where I would complete my senior year in high school. I had not wanted to leave Columbus North to go to Marion, but now I wanted, desperately, to stay in Marion at least through high school graduation. Two or three of my friends' parents said that I could stay with them until June, but my parents did not agree. I think, now, that this was a wise decision on their part. God knows what I might have gotten involved in had I stayed in Marion without parental supervision.

Despite the Depression, the minimum school facilities, my father's job loss, and all of the things I did that were a little far out, I loved Marion. I think that it may have slowed up my development in some ways but, on the other hand, I really learned what not to do. I liked all the people I met. I know I learned a lot about girls, developed socially, and found out that school was not always easy and that even getting passing grades could be hard to do. I did not have anywhere near the problems in college, graduate school, or law school that I had had with my school days in Marion.

On a cold, gray Sunday, early in January of 1935, my mother and I drove from Marion to Grove City to visit my father to take a look at the town. Grove City is about five miles southwest of Columbus. During the time I lived in Columbus, I had never heard of the place. In 1935, its population was about twelve hundred. It had no charm. Where they got the "Grove" is still beyond me. The town had no tree-lined streets. The word "city" was also a misnomer. It was certainly no city, and on that bleak January day, had no allure for me. The drug storeroom was smaller than any that I remembered. The fixtures were obviously old. There was an old-fashioned soda fountain and chairs and tables that looked as though they had come from an ice cream parlor equipped at the turn of the century. I never knew where my parents got the money with which to purchase this store, and I did not learn what they paid for it, but whatever the amount was, on that day I would have thought the price too high. Later that month, after tearful farewells, we moved from Marion to Grove City into a furnished house. There were no other places for rent in the town. The house, itself, was ancient—the furniture was worse. The bathtub looked as though it had come out of the Civil War, and the bath water was almost black in color, as was the drinking water. I guess the town's water supply came from wells with a very high iron content. Most houses had water softeners, but not that one.

The Monday after our move, I enrolled in what was officially called the Jackson Township High School. It was a small three-story building located on what was then the outskirts of Grove City. This was another "no frills" building. It had been constructed about 1926 on spacious grounds. To the south were corn fields overlooking the football field, directly behind the building. The school was equipped with radiators and steam heat. There was no ventilation other than windows. The day of my arrival it was cold, the windows were closed, and the smell of unwashed clothing and bodies was everywhere. Most of the teachers were older than I had been used to seeing, poorly-dressed, and discouraged-looking. I found out later that, for several months in the fall of the year, these teachers went unpaid. The School Board had run out of money. No wonder they looked discouraged and poorly dressed!

My classmates did not look all that great to me either. Some of the boys wore overalls, and many of the others looked to be fairly poor. Everyone stared at me as though they were sizing me up. All in all, nothing bore any resemblance to anything I had ever been used to. I was discouraged and felt a little lonely. I found out quickly, that about half of the students came from farms and even smaller villages around the area. They were bussed to and from school and most did not participate in the few activities offered either at school or in the town.

The school was poorly-equipped, except for the Agriculture and Home Economics departments which were funded from the state. There was a library room with neither books nor a librarian. There was no cafeteria, no art or vocational programs, and completely outdated textbooks. There was a good music program staffed by an excellent teacher though, and there was also a good business training program and a stenographic course for the girls. The physical education teacher and coach for the entre boys' sports program was a balding, heavy-set man in his late thirties. We took physical education in our school clothes, and most of the boys wore street shoes. Showers after physical education? Forget it!

There were fewer than three hundred students in the entire high school, including the ninth graders. However, they had interscholastic football, basketball, and baseball. I went to some of the basketball games and was amazed at how crowded the small gymnasium became.

School athletics was one of the few winter recreational activities in the community.

Grove City in some ways was a typical small country village. Much of the retail business came from the local farmers. In fact, the biggest business in town was the Farmers Exchange. However, most of the townspeople who were employed worked in Columbus. It was not a wealthy community, and most of those who were employed there had very ordinary jobs, barely making a living. Many were "On relief," or were employed in one of the federal work programs. The difference between Grove City and thousands of other similar small towns across the country was that it was, and is, the location for Beulah Park—a racetrack for thoroughbred racehorses. During the spring and fall of each year, the town would become overrun with race trackers, or in other words, owners, trainers, jockeys, grooms, gamblers, and hangers on. This had a very favorable impact on the town's economy and quite an impact on the town overall, which was not altogether a good thing.

Within a few days after I entered school, I began to get acquainted with my classmates and with some of the other town citizens. Almost everyone was friendly, and I finally began to enjoy myself. One of the first things I noticed was that all of the boys had nicknames. I had not run into this phenomenon previously.

Some of the names I still recall are "Pic," "Rip," "Fenny," "Miser," "Dopey," "Poozle," "Butch," "Hammer Gut," "Dutch," and three brothers called "Tubby," "Quiffy," and "Pickle Nose." Some were aptly named, whereas others I never learned how their names came about. Within a couple of months, I was given the nickname "Joe" because of the mountain music song, "Fare Thee Well, Old Joe Clark." The name stuck, and many longtime residents of the area still call me "Joe."

The hangout for the high school boys was a place called Bernard's, which sold bad ice cream and worse sandwiches. The price was right, and Bernard permitted card games, "profanity," and young guys who either were, or thought they were, drunk. Everybody smoked cigarettes whenever anyone was lucky enough to have enough money to afford a pack. The routine went something like this: The pack owner would light a cigarette, someone would then say, "first butts," someone else "second butts," another "third butts," and finally "short pants." The cigarette passed through several hands, and I'm sure the process was very unsanitary. I was extremely popular with this group because I usually had cigarettes which I stole from the drug store. I never knew what brand I would pick up, since I had to make a blind grab at anything in the cigarette rack.

I do not remember too much about the academic part of the school. The teachers seemed rather dull and plodding, the classrooms dreary, many of the students not overly bright. All in all, I didn't learn much; there was no incentive for learning. I did manage to pass plane geometry, and graduate.

School activities were sort of fun, but not inspiring. I joined the glee club, but most of the voices were below average. The Marion Harding Glee Club had won awards in competition; I had been a member and was proud of it. The Grove City Hi-Y Club had a faculty advisor who was a "jerk" and an embarrassment to be with when we met with other clubs. The class play, a horrible thing called "Tea Toper Taverns," supposedly a comedy, was a disaster. But I got so that I liked the boys in the school with whom I associated, and I sure as hell liked the girls. I was invited to a few parties, attended a couple of school dances, went to the high school basketball games, and had some dates. After having been at school a month or so, I began to take special notice of a girl in the junior class. I checked around and discovered that no one ever attempted to take her out because she was not permitted to have dates. Her father was one of the town doctors and was rumored to be meaner than hell. Naturally, all of this intrigued me, so I asked her for a date. She said that she would like to go but would have to ask her parents and would let me know. We had the date, but with the stringent restriction that she arrives home no later than eleven o'clock.

I dated Ann a lot after that for about a year. She was a fine girl — attractive, intelligent, well-dressed, well-groomed, with a great sense of humor. Gradually, the barriers were let down, and we went out together whenever we wanted to. Her mother was a very lovely woman, and "Doc" was really a good guy, after he decided that he liked me. They took us to the movies and to dinner, and eventually I borrowed his car for a date with his daughter when my folks were using ours. We had moved across the street from their house and his office, so, on a hot summer afternoon while walking home from the drug store, I detoured to their front porch swing with Ann. Doc came out of his office and told me to go home. About a half hour later he came out again, saw me, and said, "I thought I told you to go home." I replied that I would in a few minutes. He looked at me and asked, "Are you scared, Joe?" I said, "No, sir." He then said, "It's hot; how about a beer?"

From that time on, "Doc" and I became friends. He developed a routine to get rid of me when I was staying later than he thought I should. He descended the stairs loudly and appeared in the living room clad in a ragged pair of bedroom slippers, old-fashioned night gown and night cap, carrying a "slop jar," which he sort of swung back and forth while staring at me. It was effective and I always took the hint. A year or so later he died. Ann and I had previously quit dating, sort of by mutual agreement. Later she married a very good-looking, successful man and raised a family in a city in another state. I lost track of her entirely. Not many years ago, I learned that she had committed suicide. I wondered why and was saddened by the news.

Although the Great Depression continued without let up, my father's drug store was moderately prosperous. Both of my parents worked in the store. My father was there as many as fourteen hours a day, seven days a week. I graduated a month early, because the school district had no money to keep the school in operation. The morning after, I went to work in the drug store—my first job other than as a "bag salesman" for *Liberty Magazine* for a couple of years when I was about eleven or twelve. I would have loved to have had a job when I lived in Marion, but there were none—not even paper routes.

I recall that the first thing I did was wash the display windows on the store front. They streaked. I dusted shelves and old packages of patent medicine in order to learn the merchandise. I swept the floor, fired the furnace, burned trash, learned how to wait on customers, operate a cash register, wrap packages, weigh, and sell candy, and do all the other assorted duties of a drug clerk. Most pleasurable of all, I got to work behind a soda fountain. I also learned how to mix improbable and exotic concoctions for my own enjoyment, and sometimes amazement. I believe that rare part of American small-town life was lost with the disappearance of the drug store soda fountain.

We had very little family life in Grove City. Most of my father's waking hours were spent in the drug store. My mother was there a great deal as well, and I worked upon occasion when someone needed time off, or when it was exceptionally busy. Most of our meals were eaten in restaurants. Sometimes the food was lousy, and always repetitious. Dinner—meat, potatoes, salad, bread, and butter and coffee—cost from thirty-five to fifty cents; a T-bone steak about eighty-five cents. A piece of pie or cake was ten cents: a la mode, fifteen cents. Needless to say, my parents had virtually no social life—they were too busy working. We became well-acquainted with most of the townspeople. The drug store was one of the meccas for news, leafing through magazines from the magazine rack, sipping a coke, or just loafing and telling stories.

There were two funeral homes in this small town, and both funeral directors, always properly-dressed in case of a "call," frequented the store. One of them drank an occasional milkshake, which was probably his lunch—and stared out the front door. The other, more successful one bought very little but hovered over the magazine rack, reading the "girlie" magazines. Another, almost permanent resident was called "preacher" because he gave lengthy discourses on virtually anything—usually he did not know what he was talking about. Another regular, named Vernon, was a skinny youth who had no job. He stood around and absorbed heat, fired the coal furnace, took out the ashes, ran errands, and generally adopted the store in exchange for an occasional coke and package of cigarettes or tin of Prince Albert tobacco.

Other townspeople drifted in and out, just to loaf and pass the time of day, drink a coke or a milkshake, glance at the new magazines and, of course, purchase anything they needed that was sold in the store. The school kids hit the soda fountain or the candy case at lunch time and after school. Those who were fortunate enough to have jobs stopped in either on their way home from work, or in the evening after dinner. Usually, they were serious customers; although, from about eight-thirty until closing time, the soda fountain was usually busy.

I remember some of the soda fountain prices. Ice cream cones were a nickel; chocolate "dopes" (ice cream with syrup over it), a dime; sundaes with syrup, whipped cream, nuts, and a cherry, fifteen cents; milkshakes, ten cents; malted milks, fifteen cents; and banana splits (a banana sliced down the center, three dippers of ice cream, syrup, whipped cream, nuts and a cherry), twenty cents. Cigarettes, generally, were fifteen cents a pack. The best cigars we had cost a quarter.

Saturday was the busiest day of the week. The farmers came to town on that day and did practically all of their weekly shopping. Saturday afternoons and nights entire farm families showed up. All of the stores remained open on Saturday night. They were busy and the street was crowded. It was not only necessary that the farmers come to town, but it was also a social event for the women and children. Farm life was dull, hard, and unrewarding in those years. Many farms had no electricity, no plumbing, no telephones, no radios, and little communication or social contact outside the home. Times were hard for farmers too. Most of them drove old dirty, sometimes dilapidated, automobiles. The men usually wore clean overalls to town; their wives wore clean dresses which did not reflect latest fashions; the children were similarly clothed. An ice cream cone or a sack of candy was the weekly treat for all of them if the farmer could afford it.

From early spring until after Memorial Day, and from late August until early October, the town changed remarkably. Race trackers came to Beulah Park for the spring and fall race meetings. Bars, restaurants and two drug stores were constantly busy. About half of the homes in town rented rooms to the race trackers, gamblers, and hangers on. Feed stores were swamped supplying feed for the horses. During the actual race meetings, many residents were employed by the track as parking attendants, ticket sellers and takers, program sellers, mutual clerks, etc. Some of the townspeople were horsemen, and a few were officials at Beulah Park. Money flowed freely even in those Depression years. The trouble was that the vast majority of the natives bet on the horses. About the only non-gamblers were the ministers, most members of the Ladies Aid Societies, and a limited few who either had a lot of brains or were "closer than a photo finish" with a dollar.

The racetrack was a mixed blessing. Some did benefit economically, including my family. Some just enjoyed the action, the people, and the gambling. Others lost their businesses, their homes, and their spouses because they became compulsive gamblers and mortgaged their souls to bet the races. Some young girls, and a few older married ones, left town with jockeys, grooms, owners, and some who were just no damned good. Some girls became pregnant and were left behind; some got venereal disease, and some were lucky enough to just get smarter. Some of the boys, usually of high school age, became enthralled with the romance of the racetrack, quit school, and became race trackers. In some cases, they fared well—others became sadder and wiser.

In any event, Beulah Park changed Grove City from a small, sleepy farming community to a hybrid society. A majority of the younger element, consciously or not, adopted the jargon of the track. Apparently "racetrack-ese" is universal in these United States. The expressions are colorful and descriptive: "he win," instead of "he won," as in "he win by as far as you can throw a rock." A battery is called a "Thomas Edison," or a "joint." (Batteries are used to stimulate a racehorse into running faster, and the practice is, of course, illegal.) This horse is a 'shoo in,' means that the horse should win easily. "It's a lead pipe cinch" means that a horse, or anything else, is certain to win or whatever. (No horse is certain to win.) "It's a boat race" means that the race is allegedly fixed. (I have been privy to some "boat races," and about as often as not the horse that all of the wise guys try to boat home gets beat.) "That horse is so loaded that if the jock hits him with the stick, he'll explode" means that the horse has been administered an illegal drug, generally to stimulate it, but sometimes to cause it not to run. "He threw in the tops" means someone got away with using loaded dice in a crap game. An "Ace" is a dollar, a "deuce" is a two-dollar bill, and a "fin" is five dollars. An "ax handle horse" is a sprinter that can run very fast, but for a very short distance. A horse that can "90 the route" is a horse that can run a long distance. A three-legged horse is a horse that has something wrong with one of its legs. The vocabulary goes on and on. Some of it is description, some profane or worse, and all of it is picturesque.

Most of the horsemen frequented the drug store, and we got to know them well. Some were honest, decent, hardworking, rather moral, people. Some were outright crooks and deadbeats. Some could charitably be called gypsies because they had no real home; some were actually fugitives from justice; some had criminal records ranging from murder to extortion, to obtaining money and property under false pretenses, to petite theft. Some were just bums and vagrants. A few were actually quite wealthy people who bred and raised horses as an avocation. Many were well-dressed and wore obviously expensive jewelry. Most wore serviceable clothing suited for working with horses. The jockeys and some trainers were clothed in fancy shirts, pants, and boots. Not a few owners and trainers wore broad-brimmed Stetson hats. The vagrants and bums looked like vagrants and bums and smelled worse. The horsemen, quite naturally, smelled like horses, and — sometimes — horse manure.

During the times when the horses were at Beulah, the drug store prospered. Trainers bought medicine, drugs, leg braces, liniment, rubbing alcohol, "racing plates" (aluminum horseshoes), "blisters," and all sorts of secret concoctions. The horsemen went into the prescription room with "Doc" and handed dad their "recipes," which covered every possible medication that could ever be used for any ailment, real or imagined, that a racehorse could have. Thoroughbred racehorses seem to be much more prone to diseases and leg problems than do other breeds of horses. At any rate, during racing season, the drug store reeked of an unbelievable combination of aromas — ether, iodine, menthol, other drugs, and cheap cigar smoke. It was different! However, the local residents remained customers in spite of it all. Where else could they have gone?

Anyone who has ever read any of Damon Runyon's short stories would have had no problem understanding and identifying those wonderful characters. The language was the same. They all talked pure "Runyon-ese," and many of the stories they told had a similarity to Runyon's.

The nicknames too had a familiar ring. I knew "Smokeless Powder Schmirtz" who allegedly was a member of the Detroit Purple Gang; "Last-Dollar Dan," who sold *Horse and Jockey* and "touted" horses for a price, usually a piece of the action; "Piggy" Friedman, a pint-sized

Jewish hustler, who was called "Piggy" because, years before, he had gotten drunk and was lying in the gutter when a pig chewed his ear off. "Big Danny" Maloney was a "retired" racketeer out of Cleveland who was a consummate crapshooter. I worked with him in the mutuels, and he constantly practiced pulling loaded dice out of various parts of his clothing faster than the naked eye could follow. "Dirty Shirt Jack" was so-named for obvious reasons. He seldom changed his shirt, nor do I believe that he changed his underwear either. "Dirty Shirt" was a trainer who used nefarious items on his own and other people's—racehorses. "Senator" Simmons was an owner, trainer, card shark, con man and thief. He was called "Senator" because he looked like, talked like, and sometimes acted like an old-fashioned southern senator. "Sampson" was a sometime groom and was called "Sampson" because he never got a haircut. "Squeaky Willie" was another groom who periodically rested in various jails because he had an unfortunate propensity for attacking young girls. Naturally, Squeaky had a high-pitched voice that squeaked occasionally. "Lard Ass" was mammoth and never without a beer. He was an agent for a jockey, a "tout," and an expert at collecting unpaid obligations on a percentage basis. His collection methods were simple—he threatened the debtor with great physical harm, and if the deadbeat failed to take heed, inflicted it. "Pimples" was called "Pimples" because he had more than a few. He was an owner and trainer who was so nearsighted that he could scarcely see beyond his nose and wore very thick glasses. It was quite a spectacle to observe him trying to read the *Daily Racing Form*. His nose was virtually pressed against the pages. "Fats" Smith was fat; so was a guy called "Skinny." "Rain or Shine" was the groom for a horse by the same name. Every racetrack had, and still has, characters like these. However, Beulah Park was, as they said, a "leaky" track. The facilities were poor; the purses were small; the mutuel handle was unprofitable. The result was cheap horses and cheating owners, trainers, and jockeys, who had to connive just to eat. Therefore, although there were some fine people around the track, the bulk of them were, at best, undesirables.

Amazingly, there really was honor among thieves with those folks. When an owner or trainer asked for credit in the drug store, my dad extended it, with rare exception. He always was paid and, with few exceptions, was paid on the day when the debtor stated payment would be made — or sooner. This was true not only with my dad. A deal was a deal, a handshake was enough collateral. Hard as it was, they performed their obligations to each other, with the bookies, the merchants, the landlords and anyone else to whom they gave their word. However, if one of them was sharp enough to figure out a way to "con" anyone out of anything, large or small, they did so without compunction and the stories they told were mostly lies, and the tellers knew that the listeners were aware of this, but the marvelous tales were told in their own vernacular - stories of horses they had owned, and how fast they ran; of races they had won, and races they had lost because the jockey "pulled" the horse, the horse broke a leg in the stretch while leading by ten lengths, the jockey fell off, etc. (Incidentally, while I knew they were lies, I have personally had all of the above happen to horses on which I had wagered.) They talked casually about how they had won or lost five or ten grand on a race, when they knew, and their audience knew, that they did not possess even five- or ten-dollars cash money. Then, too, some were just stories. One that I remember goes something like this: A disgruntled owner gave a horse that couldn't run "half past eight" to a black "swipe" who worked for him. The colored guy ran the horse several times and it always finished last, if at all. The owner shipped his horses to Canada for the fall season and the groom smuggled his horse onto the van. The groom entered the horse one day for the next day's races. Overnight it snowed. The races were run, and his horse won by ten lengths. The elated black guy ran out to the track and led his horse back to the barn. He chortled all the way, saying "Man, I got this horse's whole card now; I run him on a fast track, I run him in the slop, I run him in the mud, he finishes last; I run him in the snow, and he win as far as from here to the Rocky Mountains. He's a snow son-of-a-bitch winner and I'm gonna take him to Alaska."

    I dated a racetrack girl for a couple of summers. She was a real southern belle with a drawl you could cut with a knife. Her grandfather had some really good horses, and there must have been quite a bit of money in the family. She went to boarding school in New Orleans in the winter months. Naturally, she knew when the old man was betting his money which, for those years, was always a large sum.

Naturally, too, Marjorie told me, when that old guy bet his money, his horses almost always won. As a result, I made enough to more than keep me in spending money, date money, and gambling money. Besides, I liked the girl. She was sweet, pretty, "stacked," and not overly bright. She was somewhat like a little child looking into a candy store window. She liked everything and everybody.

At the start of winter quarter one year when I was in college, I received a telegram from Marjy. It said, "Irene's Bob goes today. Love, Marjorie." I bet all of my book money, but Irene's Bob got beaten a nose in a photo finish. Needless to say, I had a very serious talk with my father. He gave me more money and cautioned me not to tell my mother. I never did.

In September of 1935, when I was just seventeen, I got a job working in the mutuel windows at Beulah Park. I had to lie about my age in order to get bonded. I worked as a cashier all through my college years. It paid well. I started out getting four dollars a day, and the last time I worked I got all of eight dollars a day in the spring of 1940. I learned a lot. The people I worked with were not all that honest. The first day's lesson from one of them was "always remember three times five is fourteen." They had many ways of cheating the bettors out of the correct amount due them. I never cheated anyone except when I knew that my money box was short, and I did not balance. When that happened, I got even.

Believe me, those people were mostly thieves. I liked them and they accepted me. I was the "kid goin'" to college. I don't think many of them had ever seen a college unless it was passing by on the way to a racetrack. Between races they taught me how to shoot crap, play poker, blackjack, and other "games of skill." I learned well. I also learned to be damned careful who I gambled with. After all, Smokeless Powder, Big Danny, Piggy, and others of a similar ilk, were my mentors. Piggy, Smokeless, Big Danny, and Last-Dollar Dan, all lived in a flea bag in Columbus called the Bliss Hotel. I forget, after all these years, exactly how it happened but Piggy made a big score on a race and wound up with two or three thousand dollars cash money!!!

The Bliss Hotel was no longer good enough for Piggy and his friends, so they all moved to the Deshler which was, in those years, the finest hotel in Columbus. Naturally, they all got drunk in celebration of their new status. No one, including the Deshler employees, knew exactly how it all transpired, but the fact is that "Piggy" somehow appeared in the Deshler lobby completely naked. The Deshler management threw them all out. They were back in the Bliss Hotel the same night.

Because of my acquaintanceship with people like them and the many other characters I met around the racetrack, I received a liberal education even before I graduated from college. It all helped a lot during the years I practiced law.

I always seemed to know that, after completing high school, I would go to college. My parents, apparently, deliberately, indoctrinated me with the point of view that success in life for me could not occur without higher education. Most of the men among their friends had attended a school of some sort beyond high school. The parents of many friends of mine had gone beyond high school. I didn't really have any intention of attempting to follow a trade or enter employment.

In 1935, there would have been little chance of finding work anyway, other than menial jobs, and there were not many of those. In Grove City, those young men who did not go on to some form of advanced training, and most did not, had nothing to do but sit around the pool room. Farmers' sons worked with their fathers on the family farm. One or two became full-time race trackers and drifted around the country aimlessly following the horses, working as grooms. A few enlisted in the Civilian Conservation Corps (a New Deal program to keep young men housed, fed, and off the streets) doing hard, healthful work in reforestation and other environmental activity for the benefit of the nation. A few got jobs as clerks or laborers because of family connections someplace where there was enough business activity to warrant employing someone new.

I really had no concrete goal in mind. I was barely seventeen years old. In those years public schools did not have any student guidance programs, and I certainly had no exposure to career opportunities. I knew nothing about opportunities in business. I knew that there were engineers, accountants, scientists, doctors, dentists, and lawyers. I had no desire to become a doctor or dentist.

I sort of thought that being a lawyer would be nice; after all, they were all rich and influential, I thought. I also thought about my childhood ambition to become a history professor. So, I announced that I would like to become either a professor or a lawyer. I had talked with some older people who suggested that, just maybe, it might be a good idea to prepare to become a high school teacher in case I was not able to complete all of the training required for law or college teaching. My parents felt that way. My father had always discouraged me from becoming a pharmacist. The hours were long, and the financial rewards were usually not great.

There was no discussion as to where I would attend college. My folks could not afford to send me to any school other than the Ohio State University. It was also financially impossible for me to live on campus and pay room and board. I had to live at home and commute to college daily—not always an easy task.

I entered The Ohio State University in late September 1935. I was enrolled in the College of Arts and Sciences and was to work toward a combined degree in Arts-Education. Tuition was thirty-five dollars a quarter when I started. Whenever possible, I bought used books.

Ohio State seemed huge to me. There were twelve or thirteen thousand students on campus. Thank God, they did have an orientation week for entering freshmen. I at least learned where the buildings were where my classes would be held. The week was devoted to a few lectures and movies, physical examinations, getting fitted for the uniforms we were required to wear when taking Military Science—all freshmen and sophomore men were required to take R.O.T.C.— securing tickets for the football games (they were seven dollars for the season) and generally getting prepared to start classes the following Monday. It was also fraternity "rush week." I went to a couple of parties, but I did not take it seriously. My folks had told me that I could not join a fraternity for economic reasons as well as the fact that they thought I should study. I think, now, that they were right! Had I pledged a fraternity that first year, I might well have flunked out.

As it was, college life my first year consisted only of attending classes, eating lunch at the Ohio Union Cafeteria, and shooting an occasional game of pool. It was a lonesome time. The classes were large, the teaching very impersonal, and I knew no one in my classes the first quarter. I became a speaking acquaintance of some of my classmates—I suppose because misery loves company. Most of the courses I took were not really interesting to me. I remember that I was signed up for English Literature, Zoology, and beginning German. None of them challenged me. I liked English Literature, but the instructor was a cipher. I do not remember him at all, but then I find that there really were very few of the instructors and professors throughout college that I now have a very clear recollection of. Zoology, I suffered through. I did not care much about cutting up frogs, and the building was a long walk from any place where those classes were held. The smell of formaldehyde on a daily basis did not do much for one either. German was fun largely because the professor was interesting. He was a short, fat, fiftyish German-Jewish refugee who spoke English with a heavy German accent. No animosity was in that man. One day in class, when someone asked him about the Nazis, he said, "Ah, it's just youth gone mad." I also took R.O.T.C., which I hated. We wore silly-looking uniforms, leggings, riding breeches, dark blue coat with gold buttons with the American eagle on them, and a visored cap, also dark blue. The tie was black, and naturally we wore white shirts. I was in the "horse marines," more formally known as the field artillery. We were supposed to learn all about the duties of a soldier with the French 75, a World War I cannon.

We also learned how to salute, stand at attention and march. We were also given lectures on military discipline and courtesy. The instructors were right out of the "Great War," and I am damned sure they stayed in the Army because they could not have held a job doing anything else. I learned nothing in two years except that I did not want to become an officer, nor become involved with the Army in any way. I also developed a dislike for horses the second year, which compounded itself my senior year. Physical education was also required. I took tennis in the fall quarter. It was fun, but the physical education facilities were a long way from my other classes, with the result that I was invariably late for either class or lunch, or both. The first quarter ended abruptly in early December, and final examinations were at hand. I was scared. Had I learned anything? Could I remember anything I did learn? I crammed for each examination and did amazingly well. I had a little more than a B average, and usually did that well or a little better throughout college, except for one unfortunate spring quarter when I was otherwise engaged.

We all dressed differently to go to college in those years than college students do now. Most of the men wore three-piece suits, neckties, hats, overcoats in season, and very shiny shoes. We shaved daily, and kept our hair cut short. The women wore dresses, skirts and blouses, or sweaters, and always tried to look their best. College was a big deal, and we thought we were all very adult. Many of us smoked either cigarettes or pipes. I think pipes were in vogue in imitation of many of the professors. I guess we thought it was the intellectual thing to do. It was an age of conformists, and we tried to conform by imitating our peers in appearance, action and thought. Anything much beyond the norm was looked down upon.

Winter quarter was little different as to the routine, the classes, and my sense of not really belonging. The people I knew on campus were people I had known before college. I seldom saw them because the campus seemed so huge. The other students with whom I attended classes had no time to become friendly and were different from class to class, and quarter to quarter. The winter of 1936 was extremely cold. There was much snow and a blizzard or two. I drove my parents' car to school that winter because the fellow I had been riding with managed to flunk out the first quarter. The car had no heater - heaters cost extra. It was a 1933 Ford VB and ran 55 miles an hour in second gear, 85 in high. I drove it that way a lot when it wasn't snowing, and when the roads were clear. When it was icy, the car skidded without much prompting from me. There was, of course, no defroster and often I could hardly see to drive. Sometimes it was necessary to drive with my head out the window. It was cold!

Classes again were dull. I continued the same subjects. I even had the wonderful Dr. Hans Spenser (the professor who had escaped Hitler) for second-quarter German. I loved his accent and his gentleness. My English course was in composition and grammar. Many freshmen failed that course each year. I did well. I remember that we were required to write a long theme in the nature of a term paper. I wrote about the 1936 election—the possible candidates, the issues, and a prognosis as to what the results would be the following November. I said that F.D.R. would be the Democratic nominee, and Alf Landon, governor of Kansas, the Republican, and predicted that Roosevelt would win by a landslide. He did.

I recall, painfully, that I signed up to play handball in Physical Education. I did not know what handball was. I wish I had. That damned game might have killed me. I could not see well, and had a helluva time hitting the ball, with the result that the hard, rock-like, round black object hit me every place except on the soles of my feet. I found another student who felt the same way, so we played together a lot, and survived. I cut a lot of those classes, partly because of the cold weather and partly because I wanted to live. I made up the cuts by playing basketball for two consecutive days, cutting all of my classes in order to get it taken care of.

Winter quarter ended in the same way all quarters seemed to for me – fear that I had learned nothing, cramming for final exams, and relief when it was over and decent grades came through. I wonder, now, whether I did truly learn anything of real or lasting value. Spring quarter commenced. The courses were continuations of those which I had previously taken. Zoology was of more interest to me because it was elementary genetics. I learned that heredity does, in fact, play an important role in the lives of us all. I learned that intelligence—or lack of it—is inherited. My father said it very well: "You can't plant peas and get sweet potatoes." I even discovered that baldness, baby size, hair and eye coloring are hereditary, and that our genes do have something to do with longevity. All of this is now quite elementary, but it was a revelation to me then. English was a course in literature of a more modern period. The instructor was young, dynamic, interesting, and challenging. I loved the course. We read George Bernard Shaw's and Eugene O'Neill's plays, poetry by Ogden Nash and other modern (for then) poets and playwrights. We did not read prose to the best of my recollection. It amazed me so much at the meaning, the themes of some of these authors. I did not understand the symbolism of many of them because I did not sense its existence until the instructor pointed it out to us. I wonder whether all of the rather hidden meanings were really there, or whether they existed only for the instructor and the intellectual few. I always thought plays were written to entertain.

Spring quarter in R.O.T.C. was no joy. In addition to all of the crap we had been exposed to before, we had "parade" at 4:00 p.m. each Wednesday. Our uniforms were supposed to be neat, our shoes shined, and, of course, we wore white belts and gloves. We marched in formation the length of the "Oval" (then the center of the entire campus), military bands playing martial music, erect, doing "eyes right" on command. Christ! The officers, university dignitaries, and others for whom we "passed in review" loved it. So did all of the students who watched it. They were not in it. I prayed for rain every Wednesday, but I do not remember a time when the Lord accommodated me.

As for physical education—I got smarter and elected to play softball. I knew what that was and understood very well how the game was played.

College life my freshman year did not have much meaning for me. I did not suddenly grow up as many were required to do. I commuted between home and school, made no lasting friendships that year, recognized those with whom I attended class, spoke to them when I saw them on campus, but never learned their first names. I was never shy or backward with people, but going to school as I did presented no opportunity to socialize. There were many others like me; I am certain we missed a lot. However, there were thousands of male students who lived in rooming houses in the campus area, who spent their entire college life without progressing much socially. They lived in houses with a few other students, ate in restaurants in the area and did little also. On large campuses, I suspect that this is still true today. There were many campus activities available for those who had the good sense to participate and take advantage of them—lectures on all sorts of topics by famous people, concerts, art displays, political clubs, intramural sports, and many, many more. Most students either did not know about them or, for diverse reasons, never got involved.

Today, freshmen male students are required to live in dormitories operated by the university. I know that there has been much criticism of dormitory life at large schools—drugs, noise, inability to concentrate enough to really study as a result of the racket, social intermingling of roommates arbitrarily, and without the consent of either, upper classmen assigned to room with freshmen, etc. I believe, however, that the student forced to live in a dorm necessarily sees more of campus life and has a better opportunity to participate than did we. Perhaps during my time, it would have been a good idea that we be required to meet each week with an upperclassman who could, and would, serve as an adviser, counselor, and friend.

My freshman year in college was not devoid of social life, however. I just continued doing as I had in Grove City before entering college. I had dates, ran around with the same friends, talked about the same things, hung out in the same places, worked in the drug store upon occasion on weekends, went to numerous movies, learned to play pool, drank beer occasionally, and enjoyed life. It was not broadening.

Perhaps as a symbol of our entrance into young manhood my friends and I started to hang out in the local saloon, pool room, and card room. That was an education, although it did nothing positive for me. We called the place the "Hell Hole." It was probably aptly named. The building was an old two-story frame structure. In the larger room on the first floor the long, old-fashioned wooden bar extended almost the length of the room. There were, of course, many bar stools. There were neither tables nor booths. Located in the center of the room were two pool tables. Along the wall opposite the bar there were long wooden benches for spectators, would-be players, and overflow sitters from the bar. The place was filthy.

Spittoons abounded but no one who chewed tobacco ever seemed to hit them. There were a few ashtrays on the bar, but most people flipped cigarette and cigar ashes onto the oily wooden floor and ground the butts with their shoes. In addition to the beer, whiskey, soft drinks, and conversation available, sandwiches were made and sold. The menu was not extensive. Featured were hamburgers and "dog sandwiches" (large hunks of hot baloney) cooked on a very greasy grill, served with or without a thick slice of cold cheese, cheese on rye bread, and cold baked ham. The drink menu was not extensive either. Had anyone ordered anything as complicated as a martini or Manhattan, the bartender would have thrown him out.

The whole place was unsanitary. I doubt that the grill was ever cleaned. The floor was swept about twice a day. There was absolutely no ventilation in the place and as a result, the place reeked of stale grease, smoke, and dirty bodies. The smell permeated our clothes. The bartenders started out each day wearing clean white aprons. They did not stay clean. Harry Storey was a short, fat ex-drunk, who seemed to work all hours. When the cue ball on one of the pool tables "jumped the table," Harry charged from around the bar, rescued it either from the floor or spittoon, wiped it off carefully with his apron, and placed it back on the table in all of its pristine whiteness. With that same apron, he also wiped the dust from the plates before serving sandwiches and the tops of all beer and pop bottles he opened. The restroom always smelled of urine. Ah, it was wonderful!

Poker was not permitted in the card room. Gambling for cash was prohibited. Card games included about three different kinds—rum, euchre, and pinochle. Each participant paid the house five cents a game, and the winner received the proceeds in metal chips shaped and sized exactly like a nickel. The chips were each worth five cents in merchandise and were also useful in pay telephones and pinball machines.

There were quite a few good card players and excellent pool players who frequented the Hell Hole. I learned a lot. I also picked up more profanity than I had known to that time. Customers included men who came to the place every day. Some were just unemployed and restless. Some were complete losers, outcasts, bar flies who had no other place to go where they could gain any acceptance. They were sad, dreary people. I feel sorry for them now, but I laughed at them and made fun of them then.

Needless to say, women never entered the doors of the place, even in search of their husbands.

The summer of 1936 was not especially noteworthy for me. It passed the same as had the summer preceding it and as did the two summers to follow. It was a lazy, fun time for me. I usually slept late or else read in bed. Frequently, I had an egg malted milkshake at the drug store for breakfast while looking at the morning *Ohio State Journal* sports section and the *Daily Racing Form*. It was not intellectual reading, but I did not claim to be very intellectual in those years. Will Rogers had a short column which appeared daily in the *Journal* until his death. I enjoyed it as did millions of others. I loafed or worked in the store. Hell, that drug store was more home to my parents and me than was the house we occupied. I went to the races if there were any around. I went to the bookies. I swam occasionally in a creek or a quarry, played tennis at the Whites (a couple of older girls who enjoyed young people) rode around the area, batted the breeze with my friends, played pool and cards in the Hell Hole and bridge at friends' houses, had dates and enjoyed being a bum. I did work in the mutuels at the race meetings held at the Lancaster Fairgrounds for about three weeks each summer—work which was constructive and enhanced my spending money.

The summer of 1936 was as hot as the preceding winter had been cold. Temperatures soared to over one hundred degrees several times. Heat records, which have not been broken, were set. A ninety-degree day felt cool. There was no air conditioning then except in a few theaters, so we sweltered. The drug store was so hot that the large fans only circulated hot air. The soda fountain flourished. At home, a minimal amount of clothing was worn and I slept in the nude. Everyone sweat a lot, but, curiously enough, deodorants were not as popular as they later became. So, we bathed with Lifebuoy soap, which was supposed to help prevent "B.O." It may have done so to a limited extent, but it smelled like the flea powder used on dogs.

Popular songs during that time included "Deep Purple," "There is a Small Hotel," "The Music Goes Round and Round," "When I Grow Too Old to Dream," "Who," "Marie," and many now forgotten. Kay Kyser, Jan Garber, Tommy Dorsey, and Guy Lombardo led popular orchestras. The age of the Big Bands was dawning. Eddie Cantor, Jack Benny, George Burns and Gracie Allen, were favorite radio comedians. There were numerous weekly radio plays, and Saturday night brought the Lucky Strike Hit Parade.

The presidential campaign between Roosevelt and Alf Landon wore on. It seemed obvious to everyone that Roosevelt would win easily, and he did. But, despite all of the efforts of Roosevelt and his New Deal programs, despite all of the optimism, the Depression continued only slightly abated. Nevertheless, Roosevelt was as popular as ever. Loved by most, hated, and detested by a few, he gave us hope, inspired us, kept us together as a people. He was the great father figure that was needed. Revolution could have occurred, and many believed then, as I do now, that only the Roosevelt charisma prevented bloodshed. We had faith in him, even though most of the ideas adopted by his administration did not really solve our problems.

In the fall of 1936, at the beginning of my sophomore year at Ohio State, I pledged Sigma Nu Fraternity. My campus social life changed immediately, and, although I did not realize it at the time, this act changed me substantially in other ways in later years. God, how I enjoyed fraternity life. It gave me a sense of belonging that I had not experienced during my freshman year. As pledges, we were required to participate in campus activities. We had to join campus organizations which, if nothing else, led us to become acquainted with a lot of other students.

We were required to attend parties with sorority pledges, so we met college girls. We were required to attend Monday night pledge meetings, learning about the fraternity itself and what it stood for. Paddles were used liberally on our behinds every Monday night for various rules infractions—both real and imaginary. As a result, we had sore and red rear ends every Monday night—agony which extended into Tuesday and sometimes Wednesday. Our pledge class developed a great empathy for one another as a result of the liberal use of the paddle on us, and of the enforced Saturday morning work details in which we rather unwillingly participated.

We were taught table manners, if we had none. We were taught how to get along with the sorority girls, if we didn't know how. We learned how to dress well and, as the expression went, how to be "smooth." None of us were perfect by any means after undergoing such training, but all of us were improved. Most importantly, we became disciplined and learned a code of conduct that has remained with me always.

The Sigma Nu Creed, in part, follows: "To believe in the life of love, to serve in the light of truth, to walk in the way of honor." If I got nothing else from fraternity life, those precepts have served as my code of conduct. I do not regret following them. I wish the world had done as much, or yet would.

Fraternity life was more fun than education, however. We had parties, dances, formal dinner dances, beer busts, card games, crap games, hayrides, song fests (fraternity songs generally are great songs of youth and pride), drinking bouts, bull sessions, and almost everything else known to the young. We damned near did it all to the detriment of our studies, but it surely liberalized our general education.

Classwork my sophomore year was a continuation of a generalized liberal arts program. German was still with me, and two years of a foreign language was required. I took a couple of more rather elementary English courses. Beginning Psychology, Educational Psychology, Survey of Education, elementary Political Science, basic Economics, and American History were among other courses pursued. Unfortunately, a second year of R.O.T.C. was also a requirement. I continued to hate it. Since I had opted for the field Artillery, I was required to ride horses fall and spring quarters. What a disaster! We had to saddle and bridle the beasts. We were told that when we cinched the saddle tightly, we should knee the horse in the stomach because they "sucked wind" and thus kept the cinch loose otherwise. One day I must not have done it properly, because when the sergeant gave the command mount, "I placed my left leg in the stirrup and started to swing my right leg up over the horse's back when the damned saddle slipped. I was underneath the horse. The sergeant was alternately blowing his whistle and swearing at both me and the horse, and all of the other suffering bastards in the class damned near fell off their mounts laughing at me. After that experience, I kicked hell out of the horse's belly while saddling it!

In the spring, we once again had dress parade every Wednesday at four o'clock. We had always been told that if we cut parade, we would fail the course. One lovely day in May, I had a couple of hot horses at Beulah Park Race Track that were a cinch to win. I went to the races, the horses got beat; and the officers had not lied to us about missing parade. I flunked Military Science. My God, I had to take it again the last quarter of my senior year!

In April of that year, during spring quarter, I was initiated into the fraternity, as were about one-third of the pledge class with which I had started in the fall. The other two-thirds either had flunked out of school, were kicked out of the fraternity, had dropped out, or just did not make the grades required for initiation. (It took only slightly above a "C" average—2.3—to be initiated.) Formal initiation was preceded by what was aptly called "Hell Week." Hell Week began early on Monday morning when we appeared at the fraternity house where we were to live for the week. All of us wore what resembled old-fashioned B.V.D.'s made out of burlap sacks. We were not allowed to remove this marvelously uncomfortable garment during the entire week, for any reason. We were not permitted to shave, take a bath, wash, brush our teeth, comb our hair, or smoke. We were not permitted to change our clothes. Thank God, we had been told to wear old clothes. We could not speak to any girls and were all addressed as "Scum." We entered the fraternity house by walking backwards up a fire escape to a window on the fourth floor. We walked up and down all steps, both in the fraternity house and on campus, backwards. We exited from the fraternity house by climbing out of a coal hole onto Sixteenth Avenue. To accomplish this feat, it was necessary to crawl atop the coal pile in the furnace room and push up the circular steel cover, which was flush with the sidewalk. Naturally, we got blacker and blacker each trip out.

On Monday at noon, each of us was given an egg and told to carry it in our pants pocket. We were warned not to break the egg. Of course, many did, but if we had not, the active fraternity members broke them for us. When an egg was broken, the initiate now was required to carry two eggs, then three, etc. On Wednesday, I was advised at noon that my hair was too thick, and another Scum was ordered to give me an egg shampoo. This consisted of breaking an egg on top of my head and rubbing it around, shell and another Scum had the "great egg experiment" performed on him. He was required to stick an egg into his rectum while bent over; an active then took a paddle and walloped his rear. The egg, in theory, was supposed to come out of the Scum's mouth. It did not, of course, but he did have a freshly-egged behind. When the damned eggs had run all over our bodies, I can assure you that a horrible odor was created. This, blended with the B.O., bad breath, and filth, made all of us undesirables. On Thursday of that week, I was told that I smelled terrible and was required to go next door to Smitty's Drug Store for a bottle of ten-cent perfume. Believe it or not, the drug store either stocked such a thing, or else imported it or made it especially for the occasion. I returned to the fraternity dining room with my purchase, and a fellow Scum was required to pour it all over me. It was awful! I guess, though, that I probably smelled worse than anyone else afterwards.

We could not cut class that week, and I had German History immediately after lunch. I sat in the front row directly in front of where the professor ordinarily stood while lecturing. He moved.

We spent the week waiting on the actives. Their every whim was our command. We ran errands, shined shoes, did their laundry, sang songs, lit their cigarettes, served them breakfast in bed, recited poetry, turned handsprings, stood on our heads, told jokes, and did anything else that was dreamed up. Nothing that we did suited them, and we were constantly told to "assume the angle." This meant grabbing our ankles with our hands, tucking in our testicles, and getting our butts beat with paddles. Our asses were literally theirs during the entire week, and many a paddle was broken on us. By Wednesday night, I could not sit down in a chair without pain. My rear end had long since passed the red stage and had become black and blue. On Friday afternoon, we were all required to lie naked on our stomachs in the lounge while the actives inspected our behinds. When they got to me, I could hear the "ah's" and "We'd better lay off of him." Then I heard my friend, "Final Fin Fan Fenton," say, "God damn, he's only just beginning to turn pink." As I said earlier, we learned discipline—I had every urge to get up and try to kill him, but I did not move.

After Thursday night, we had sleep. Friday night and Saturday was devoted to fraternity house maintenance with a couple of interruptions. We were taken to the Theta House, blindfolded, and told to lie down and, one by one, open our mouths. Their Hell Week pledges stood or knelt over us, cleared their throats, and made a spitting noise, at which time something resembling what might have been expectoration during a bad head cold went into our mouths and down our throats. As it occurred, each of us gagged, and I for one had a great desire to vomit. Then our blindfolds were removed, and we discovered that those lovely girls had thrown a spoon of egg white into our mouths. I never liked the Thetas much after that.

We then marched to downtown Columbus and invaded the Ionian Room in the Deshler Hotel. At that time, the Ionian Roan was *the* dining and dancing spot in Columbus. We took over the bandstand, sang, danced, told jokes, and generally made asses of ourselves to the delight of the actives, and the disgust of the patrons. The police arrived in about fifteen minutes and ran us out. It was a good thing; we were about out of things to do. I do not know why we were not put in jail. At the time, I hoped they would.

The remainder of Friday night, all day Saturday, and Saturday night, we scrubbed floors, washed walls, cleaned restrooms and bathrooms, washed windows, and generally labored under the jaundiced eyes of various actives, who took turns in our supervision and the creation of further discomfort for us. Saturday night I was assigned the job of whitewashing a basement room. While thus engaged, I created the darndest mess imaginable. I had whitewash on the floor, whitewash on the ceiling, some on the walls, and a lot all over myself.

About midnight, we were given some food, hot coffee and warm clothing and taken, blindfolded, out into the country. Just as we were leaving, "Final Fin Fan" slipped a bottle of whiskey into my coat pocket. When we got to the designated spot, we were dumped out of the automobiles, advised that Hell Week was over and told to find our way back to the fraternity house. The actives even wished us good luck. This "long walk" was quite an experience. Various members of the group passed out at different intervals, and the rest of us helped those in distress. Finally, daylight came, and we ultimately figured out where we were and straggled back. We were dead tired, aching every place, dirty, hungry, but most of all relieved. It was all over.

After shaving, washing our heads, bathing, scrubbing, and generally removing the filth and odor from ourselves, we put on our best clothes, had a big breakfast, and then went to the chapter room, which we had never before entered, for formal initiation. It was an impressive, ritualistic ceremony, but I was much too tired to appreciate it at the time. I was given my fraternity pin, and "pinned" by one of my friends from grade school days at Indianola Elementary.

I understand that Hell Week is no longer permitted by the national fraternities, and that it is outlawed on almost every college campus in the country. Now, forty-odd years afterward, in thinking about it all, I believe that it was at best silly, and at worst brutal, and dangerous. Students have died on various campuses as a result of some of the hazing to which they were subjected. The purpose of it all was to bring those of us going through it closer together. In my case at least, that purpose was not accomplished. With one exception, I was never close to *that* particular group, and I have lost all track of them. Most of their names are dim in my memory. Another purpose was that all of that week's activity supposedly made the fraternity mean more to us. I do not know that this occurred either. A work week, coupled with instruction in fraternity history and fraternity rituals would have been much more useful. Nevertheless, Hell Week was quite an experience. Now I am glad that I went through all of it, but if I were young again and in college, I doubt that I would be interested in undergoing it all.

I enjoyed fraternity life immensely. I wonder how we all did as well as we did in later life. Certainly, there were few signs of genius displayed by any of us while in college. Quite a few flunked out at least once. The fraternity was, it seemed, always on probation for bad grades, drunken, unchaperoned parties, financial difficulties with the merchants and the university, and God knows what else.

Fraternity finances were in horrible shape. We owed grocery bills, we failed to make payments on the house mortgage. We ran up utility bills until loss of service was threatened. There were at least two reasons for these problems. First, because the brothers either did not have the money or else spent it for something else; second, because the chapter spent too much money on dames and parties and failed to pay our other obligations. Our Social Chairman stuttered, studied hard, chain-smoked cigarettes, dressed sloppily, and was not too social. In fact, he was about as unlikely a guy as you could find for the job. Nevertheless, one Monday night in chapter meeting, when the Eminent Commander called for the Social Chairman's report, our boy stood up, saluted, and said "E-e-e-min-ent C-c-commander, I-I-I've got this d-dance arranged, and I c-c-can g-get th-th-this n-n-name band for t-t-twelve hundred d-dollars, a-and it's the sp-sp-spring f-f-formal, and they're d-d-darned good, but the t-t-t-teacher won't let me have the m-money. N-Now my question (pause) is d-d-do I get (pause) the m-money or do y-you guys g-get a new (pause) social chairman?" It broke us all up. Naturally, he got the money, and another creditor remained unpaid.

One of the brethren set an impressive grade mark spring quarter of his junior year. He failed everything he took except Advanced R.O.T.C., in which he received an A. His grade point average was .18, but he got reinstated the next quarter. I guess his father was a friend of the chairman of the Board of Trustees. Another played in the marching band for eight years. When he finally graduated, he received both his bachelor's and master's degrees on the same day. Yet, a third had three hours of "A," three hours of "E" and fifteen hours of Incomplete. Several were in and out so often, it was hard to keep track of them. Some changed majors in order to continue in school. One who flunked out had an influential father who, indignantly, went to see the dean of the college, only to be told that his son had a strong back and a weak mind and would never do much more than dig ditches. There were no Phi Beta Kappas, and very few members of any men's honorary fraternities among us.

Amazingly all of those louts, playboys, and idiots became successes in later life. I know of no one who were failures. Most are now either retired or dead, but they excelled in many fields. One worked on the atom bomb in New Mexico and became a Navy captain. Another retired as an Air Force lieutenant-general. Several received decorations for bravery in World War II. Some became doctors, dentists, lawyers, and optometrists. One was a congressman; another was president of a very large bank. Another, who started from scratch and never graduated, became super rich. One or two were college professors. Quite a few were professional engineers. Several more were corporate executives, and many highly successful in their own businesses. Our Social Chairman was a tax expert, a CPA and senior partner in the accounting firm that bore his name. The guy who set the record for being reinstated with a .18 became chief engineer for one of the largest shipping lines in the world. When I think about what they were all like then, and what they did with their lives, I am astonished — and proud.

Those of us who remained in the Columbus area after the war managed to gravitate. We all became close friends, much closer than we were while in school. Our wives are all friends. Our children know each other. We play together, party together, have Florida homes near each other, help each other when trouble comes, and have cheered each other's successes. Had it not been for the fraternity experience, we would never have become more than nodding acquaintances on the streets of downtown Columbus.

There was a great deal of resistance to fraternities and sororities across the country's campuses subsequent to the war. Some colleges outlawed them entirely. Others did nothing to encourage them. For a time, it seemed that the fraternity system would disappear. Some said that they were snobbish, undemocratic, and that they blighted the lives of many young people who either could not join or were not invited so to do. Thank God, they are making a comeback! My children were involved. I hope my grandchildren become so. I learned discipline, honor, a moral code, a little religion, and what brotherhood, respect, and love for our fellow man means.

Fraternity life was not all there was to college. We were in school to receive an education, weren't we? I did want to become a professor of history, didn't I? It now seems so long ago. The courses I took now seem a jumble. Most of them I enjoyed. I had many courses in history. Some were dull, some extremely interesting. I know that at the time I knew a lot — facts, dates, the interrelation between historical periods, and the repetitive aspects of history from earliest times. All that I retain now is an appreciation for the broad sweep of history and the predictability of what is occurring today. As Henry Adams wrote quite a few years ago in *The Education of Henry Adams*, "Look at the past, compare it in the present, triangulate and see the future."

The many courses in literature, drama and creative writing were mostly enjoyable. I did receive an appreciation for literature and a cultural veneer that otherwise would have escaped me. Courses in philosophy, advanced political science and the like too were grist for the mill.

I took courses in economics which were difficult but very instructive. Some of them gave me knowledge and insight very applicable today. The business cycle, monetary theory, supply and demand, John Maynard Keynes, and the rest are verities which still exist in this ever-changing, greedy world.

Only a very few professors remain in my memory from those courses. Doctor Edward MacNeil was a slight, wizened, absent-minded, dusty old man who taught courses on the Middle Ages. Hell, I think he lived in them. I loved the old man. He seemed to epitomize the proverbial absent-minded professor. Doctor Harold Washburn taught Modern European History and a course in Diplomatic History. He was the antithesis of Doctor MacNeil heavy-set, robust, fast-talking, humorous and tough as hell on grades. H. Gordon Hayes, also a Doctor of Philosophy, was a very liberal professor of economics. He had served in Washington as a "brain trustee" in the early days of Roosevelt's New Deal. Our ultra conservative newspaper, *The Columbus Dispatch*, castigated him on the editorial page for his "socialistic" views. Humorous, brilliant, sarcastic, yes. A Socialist, perhaps. Whatever he was, he became wealthy from playing the stock market in a depressed economy. He taught me economic truths which, when I remember them, help me to this day. He also taught us, in an unobtrusive manner, that there are social, political, and economic injustices abounding in this country and throughout the world. I did think in his classes and never missed one, even though he never bothered to check attendance.

My senior year I was forced to re-think my future rather quickly because of the death of my father, which I will go into later. It was essential that I graduate and go to work right away. I tossed aside the idea of dawdling for three or four more years earning advanced degrees in history. I opted for a degree in the College of Education in order that I might secure a high school teaching position.

I was force-fed education courses: Teaching Methods in English and Social Sciences, History of Education, Philosophy of Education and on and on. I believe the Methods courses were worthwhile. I did learn something about how to teach the courses. I do not think the courses in Educational Philosophy helped, but they were required. The professor who taught History of Education spent most of the class time trying to teach one of Ohio State's more famous halfbacks how to read and understand a paragraph. He wasted his efforts.

Doctor Howard Francis Seeley taught Methods of Teaching English. He was a balding, middle-aged dapper with a penciled moustache, pompous and egotistical. I actively disliked him. The only things he demanded in class recitations were almost exact quotes of excerpts from the textbook which, of course, he had written. We were required to submit a paper a week on a subject assigned to us. I thought I could write. I thought I understood grammar, sentence structure and punctuation. I was wrong. My papers were returned to me battle-scarred, red-marked with really nasty comments and horrible grades. I endured two quarters of this, hated every class, and learned much. Doctor Seeley caused me to tighten up my writing. He preached the truth when he said over and over and over again that "clarity of thought and clarity of expression go hand in hand." They do. He also stressed a theory that I tried to follow when I taught. He told us we must "demand perfection." It is seldom attainable, but if the best a person has to give is brought out of him, the teacher has been successful.

Spring quarter of my senior year, I repeated Military Science because of those damned horses that failed to win. I had to pass the course in order to graduate, but I almost blew it again. Once a year in the spring an event occurred known as "Federal Inspection." We were required to be in uniform complete with white belt and white gloves. A group of officers from God knows where "inspected" us individually, after which we "passed in review." This proceeding took all day. By this time, my uniform was a shambles. It had never been dry cleaned, and there was a hole in the breeches at the knee as a result of my experiences on horseback. The belt and gloves were dirty. Someone had stolen my cap and left an old one with a moth hole in it. I needed a shave, haircut, and shoeshine. I looked like hell. One of the student officers whom I knew took a look at me while I was standing in line, shook his head and said, "Oh, Jesus, Clark." The sergeant was called. He looked at me, swore, and called the only officer I liked. This

_____ captain checked me thoroughly and with a grin that was almost a laugh, said, "Clark, get out of line and get lost. Get clear to hell away from here!" It was wonderful! I had the day free. It was warm and nice. I changed clothes at the fraternity house, and finally wandered to the Oval and watched all of those poor dumb bastards pass in review. I passed the course.

Graduation came and I received the degree of Bachelor of Science in Education. That night I went to a sorority spring formal with a girl I had known since my days at Indianola Elementary, got in a crap game in the men's restroom and won twenty-five or so dollars, and subsequently got suitably drunk. I celebrated graduation with a bang!

On a lovely summer morning in August of 1938, preceding my June 1939 graduation, the telephone jangled at home. The word came that my father had fallen to the floor at the drug store while talking to some of the early morning visitors and was seriously ill. I ran to the store and my dad said, "Here are the keys, Dick; keep the store open."

Those were the last sensible words he ever said to me. A doctor had been called and he arrived shortly after I did. After examination, he stated that my father had had a stroke. He was not paralyzed and was taken home and put to bed.

I was scared but felt that I had to stay in that damned drug store. It was Homecoming in Grove City, and probably the busiest day of the year. I called in all of the help I could get and worked until midnight without pause, except for a quick trip home to check on my father — and also my mother. My father was out of his head and my mother was worried, but friends and neighbors were with her, which reassured me. It was a hard two or three weeks. My father continued to be out of his head, strong as an ox, and determined to dress and go to work. I guess that people were not hospitalized often in that time. Dad should have been.

He had a massive stroke about ten days after the first and then became completely paralyzed and speechless. Finally, he went into a coma, gasping for breath, and died. My mother and I watched him die. I wish I had not. The doctor was present; so were some of his brothers and sisters. All of us were powerless to help him. I wonder whether he knew any of us were there.

The ritual of accepting condolences at the funeral home was followed. It was well meant. It always is. All it did for me was to cause me to feel more and more grief-stricken as I tried to talk to all of the friends and relatives who came. The funeral itself was a relief when it was over. It was such a large funeral that the funeral home overflowed with people who stood in the yard and street, and heard the service over a loudspeaker. The races at Beulah Park were delayed for an hour in tribute to him, and the horsemen, all of whom were his friends, sent a gigantic floral horseshoe to the funeral home. He would have appreciated that.

My father's death was a shocking, sad time. I loved my dad. He was father, friend, confessor, and hero to me. I wish that he might have lived to see my wife and children. Forty-nine is much too young an age for death. Gradually, my mother and I returned to the reality of living without the aura of security that he gave us. There were, of course, a lot of problems. Our lives were changed. We had to sell the drug store and did so about a year later. Running it with my mother and itinerant pharmacists was difficult. My mother had to get another job. Thank God she was a good Republican! She went to work for the State of Ohio and, until her retirement, always had a pretty good job.

As I said earlier, I completed college and was the proud possessor of a degree from the College of Education. But there were, to my sorrow, no jobs for twenty-one-year-old Social Science-English teachers. I had only two interviews and, apparently, did not suit the jaundiced school superintendents who talked to me—despite good grades and great recommendations from various professors with whom I had come in contact. I was discouraged. After four years of college, I could not do a damned thing with my education! There weren't even any clerk jobs around. Times were still hard, and I was not the only unemployed college graduate.

My mother and I talked over the problems involved with her supporting me, at least partially, and I talked to two or three of the professors in the College of Education about my future. It was decided that I should return to school immediately and work toward a master's degree. There really was not much choice unless I started traveling around the country working at various racetracks in order to survive.

I entered Graduate School at Ohio State in June 1939. In a way, it was an entirely new and different experience from that with which I had become familiar. Most of the students were older. All were serious. Many had received their master's degrees and were intent on securing a Doctorate. They were teachers, administrators, instructors, and bright. Competition was fierce. A grade of "C" was tantamount to failure. Term papers were the norm; outside reading, routine; research had to be undertaken. I became very familiar with Ohio State's main library, as well as the library in the College of Education. Attendance was never taken in graduate level courses. Some of the seminars were so small that we sat in a circle around the instructor, drank cokes, and smoked. The discussions were sometimes far out, and I occasionally felt that I was out of my depth, but I survived.

I took a very advanced course in tests and measurements. There were about ten in the seminar group, all of them except me close to receiving their Ph.Ds. All were considerably older and, I thought, brighter. The professor was a genius, well-known nationally for his work. Term papers were assigned to each of us, and dates set for their presentation to the group. My subject was "objectivity." Among other treatises that I researched was Einstein's *Theory of Relativity*. I did not understand a damned thing. After a Friday afternoon beer-drinking session with two or three other lost souls, I commenced to write my paper. When the paper was completed, I did not understand what I had written. My day for presentation arrived and the paper read. The others really discussed it, the professor stated that it was brilliantly done. I received an "A" for both the paper and the seminar. I have no doubt that the thing is still in the College of Education library. Sometimes we all get lucky. I believe that I was so mixed up in my thinking and writing, that no one else understood it either and thought that it was just too complex for them and, therefore, an outstanding study.

When I did practice teaching during my senior year, my professor and critic was Doctor F.C. Lansitel. He was nearing retirement and was truly a college professor out of the past. I thought that he was a wonderful man, and he genuinely thought a lot of me. He intimated as strongly as he could that if I returned to college for post-graduate work, and taught in high school for a few years, a place on the faculty in the College of Education would be available to me. Accordingly, by mutual consent, he became my faculty advisor in Graduate School.

Under Lansitel's supervision, I wrote my thesis. Many topics were suggested by him and some by others, that needed exploration and research. Finally, it was decided that I should work on a social studies curriculum for senior high school students. I did much library research. I know now that I should have gone much further than that before attempting to prepare anything purporting to be significant, original work. Questionnaires should have been prepared and sent to a wide number of social studies teachers; students should have been interviewed, and, most importantly, I should have taught in high school for a few years before making all of the pompous pronouncements that I did. In any event, I completed a Proposed Program for Social Studies in the Secondary Schools. Lansitel and Allen Griffin, another professor in methods of teaching social studies, read it and gave me an "A" for my work. Then came time for the oral examination, conducted by those two and a professor whose field was methods of teaching mathematics. Ordinarily, I understood, the oral exam was routine. Mine was not. The S.O.B. from the math methods section commenced by telling me that my thesis was lousy. I got mad and told him that he was stupid. Things deteriorated from that point. Finally, Lansitel announced a recess and calmed me down, Griffin got the third professor quiet, and the examination continued. I was approved, thank God! In August of 1940, I received the degree of Master of Arts.

Throughout college and graduate school, in addition to studies, fraternity life, football at Ohio State, campus activities and the like, two things which were not college-sponsored formed an important part of my college life. They were the beer joints in the campus area and the campus hangout.

I did not make the beer-drinking scene every day or two as some did. Friday afternoon, sometimes running into Friday night, was my usual time. The beer seemed good, the fellowship and sense of well-being prevailed. Most importantly were some of the conversations. Everything was discussed. We talked about sports. We talked about girls. We talked increasingly about world politics. Many of us fancied ourselves as authorities on the economic situation. We were liberal as hell in our thinking and conversation. Religion and philosophy generally were discussed. We all thought that we were brilliant and the more beer we drank, the smarter we all became. It was fun. I now think that I probably did learn a lot from all of it, but I cannot be specific.

Hennick's, the campus hangout, was located almost directly across High Street from the main entrance to the campus. It was a large, surprisingly good restaurant with many booths and a soda fountain. Neither beer nor any other alcohol was served or tolerated on the premises. It had a coin-operated nickelodeon which was played constantly, two or three pinball machines, numerous male waiters dressed in white jackets, and both male and female students overflowing the place from breakfast until late evening.

Hennick's was the meeting place—a place to see and be seen; a place to get a date, a place to kill time, a place to talk and laugh and enjoy. To those of us who frequented the establishment, it was more nearly a second home than was the fraternity house. Almost daily, I made the scene for lunch, between classes and sometimes when I should have been in class. I met a lot of people there. It was a great place to take a girl for a coke after class, and a lot of romances began there.

A friend of mine preserved a menu from Hennick's. I have it in front of me now, and I marvel at the prices, because this was actually a first-class establishment. Sundaes were a dime, whipped cream and nuts ten cents extra. Fancy sundaes and banana splits were twenty cents. A large Coca Cola was a dime, small Coca Cola five cents. Sodas and milkshakes were fifteen cents. Sandwiches ranged in price from a hamburger or hot dog at ten cents to the most expensive club for fifty cents. Dinners were amazing in quality and price. A porterhouse or sirloin steak was ninety-five cents; two lamb chops, sixty-five cents; ham steak or two pork chops, sixty cents; boneless pickerel, sixty cents; and fried chicken, country style, eighty-five cents. All of these meals included potatoes, vegetable, rolls, drink, and dessert.

It is true that those were depressed times, but living costs were low. The prices quoted above were those of an above-average restaurant. Many other places served food much cheaper. A new Ford automobile could be purchased for around five hundred dollars, and a decent suit cost twenty-two dollars and fifty cents. Prices rose somewhat after the war, but real inflation did not hit us until the late 1960s.

On a hot July afternoon in 1939, I was playing a pinball machine in Hennick's with three or four others when I looked up and saw a tall, blue-eyed, ash-blonde come up the steps into the restaurant. Lighting must have struck me. I did not know who she was, but I knew I had to find out. I immediately got out of the pinball game and grabbed one of the waiters who was a friend of mine and told him to find out who that girl was. I guess I just stared at her. In a day or so, the waiter told me that her name was Evelyn Stark, that she went to Ohio Wesleyan, and was attending Ohio State for the summer school only. I arranged to get acquainted and managed to get a date with her a couple of weeks later. I thought she was wonderful then, and I still do.

Unfortunately, so did several other guys, and while I chased the hell out of her from then on and dated her whenever she would go out with me, I made little progress for a long time. If I got nothing else out of college, I met Evelyn. She was then, and has always been since, the most important person in my life. I do not know what my life might have been like had I not met her, but I do know it has been great with her, and I would not have been as happy. I know that there is not supposed to be such a thing as love at first sight, but I was the exception to the rule. Fortunately, or unfortunately, the same thing did not happen to her. For a long time, she was not very receptive to me. One of the many times when she was trying to get rid of me, she wrote a letter to me and said, "Honey, I love the life you lead, but I couldn't stand it all the time." I guess she still has problems, but she has learned to sort of roll with the punches over the years.

During my college years, radio was family entertainment. Bob Hope became a star, so did Bing Crosby; Eddie Cantor and Jack Benny were going strong. Fibber McGee and Molly and Lum and Abner were hit shows.

The big bands were at their peak. My first date with Evelyn was at Valley Dale to dance and listen to Artie Shaw. I do not know how I got the money, probably gambling, but I heard most of the name bands of the times—Tommy Dorsey with Frank Sinatra as vocalist, Kay Kyser and his Kollege of Musical Knowledge, Woody Herman, Wayne King,

Glenn Miller, Benny Goodman, Duke Ellington, and others, prominent then, mostly forgotten now.

As I said, it was the era of the Big Band sound. "Swing" was as popular as "rock and roll" became later. Some of the tunes I remember are: "Oh Johnny," "Begin the Beguine," "And the Angels Sing," "Annapolis," "Woodchoppers Ball," "String of Pearls," "Chattanooga Choo Choo," "Pennsylvania 6500," "Song of India," and "Red Sails in the Sunset." Most of these were swing tunes—dance tunes. There no doubt were some other good songs too, but they now escape my memory. Star vocalists included Sinatra, Crosby, and Nat King Cole among the male group, and Helen O'Connell, Martha Tilton, and the Andrew Sisters among the girls. The juke boxes were constantly playing, radio shows featured hours of band music. Yes, swing was king.

Musicals were still big at the movies. We wanted to be entertained, and most of our movies were light. We all had enough heavy stuff in our daily lives. Fred Astaire and Ginger Rogers and Dick Powell were stars. Of course, so were Clark Gable, Jean Harlow, Katharine Hepburn, Bette Davis, Rita Hayworth, Gary Cooper, Spencer Tracy, and Hope and Crosby. Lionel Barrymore, William Powell, David Niven, Myrna Loy, Carole Lombard, and Greta Garbo—when they could find her—were popular stars, and Elizabeth Taylor was then young and beautiful. I do not remember the titles of very many movies during this period, except "Mr. Deeds Goes to Town" and "Mr. Smith Goes to Washington" with Gary Cooper, "The Thin Man" series, Hope and Crosby's "Road To" series, and "Knute Rockne," with Pat O'Brien and a second-rate actor named Ronald Reagan.

Ohio State football flourished. Francis Schmidt was the coach. He had some great teams, known as "The Scarlet Scourge." He was called "Shut the Gates of Mercy" because of the high scores his teams ran up. They were called "The Team of a Thousand Plays," and I believe it. Three or four players handed the ball; they used lateral passes, forward laterals, fake punts, end arounds, and even had plays where a big tackle threw the football about 60 yards down the field. I know that Woody Hayes was a great character, but Schmidt was even more colorful. When it came to sheer foul language, Woody was nowhere near as profane as Schmidt—nor as imaginative.

Automobiles came with steel tops, divided windshields, gear shifts on the steering column, fewer and fewer running boards, and almost every car had a heater, and many had radios. VB engines were commonplace, and the four-cylinder engine was almost extinct. Among the autos which were popular then, but forgotten now, were the Packard, LaSalle, DeSoto, and Nash. A foreign-made car was seldom seen, and the Japanese car industry was unheard of. Best sellers were Chevrolet, Ford, and Plymouth; Cadillac, Chrysler, and Lincoln—the luxury cars—are still around.

We were all very aware of the Depression with all of its misery. It was still with us throughout my college days. We also knew about Hitler and his persecution of the Jews, his invasions of surrounding countries and territories in Europe, but we were not too concerned about our own safety. France had the greatest Army in the world, we thought. Britain was strong and we ignored the Japanese, even though we were given lectures in Military Science classes about the Japanese threat to the Philippines. We laughed at Mussolini and at the trouble he had defeating the Ethiopians, who seemed to be armed only with spears.

In late summer 1939, Germany invaded Poland. A widespread war seemed imminent for a time and, although Poland was soon occupied by both Germany and Russia, it was not really subdued. France and England declared war against Germany, but not much action took place. Over the winter of 1939-1940, the war became known as "the Phony War." The French sat behind the Maginot Line and dared the Germans to attack it. The French and British were only prepared, then, to fight World War I.

In early May of 1940, Germany moved quickly through Holland, Luxembourg, and Belgium with a new method of warfare—the Blitzkrieg. Their planes, trucks, tanks, and other vehicles moved swiftly and ruthlessly. The Maginot Line was bypassed; the French really never got any defense mounted. Belgium, Holland, and Luxembourg were helpless to defend themselves. The British retreated to Dunkirk and miraculously got much of their Army home by using a great armada of pleasure boats, cargo vessels, motorboats—everything but row boats—to get across the English Channel. They lost most of their equipment but salvaged their men. The French surrendered quickly. The British, back on their island, were defiant. Winston Churchill finally took over as Prime Minister, and we knew that the war would continue. I think that after Dunkirk, we all knew that sooner or later the United States would be in the fight in spite of Roosevelt's statements to the contrary. Although isolationism ran high, we realized we had to fight sooner or later. I felt in my heart that if war came, I would be in the service whether I wanted to be or not.

The summer of 1940 brought the presidential conventions. Roosevelt announced for a third term and, although there was some grumbling among Democrats about this unprecedented step, he was nominated by acclamation. The Republicans put on a helluva convention that summer—a real show. There were several pros who wanted the chance to take on F.D.R. over the third-term issue, but "a barefoot boy from Wall Street," Wendell Wilkie, got the nomination by packing the convention spectators' section with people who would not stop chanting, "we want Wilkie."

It is still a mystery to me how they got admitted. I know it was a mystery to the Republican hierarchy at the time. In any event, the gallery stampeded the convention in order to nail down Wilkie's nomination. By that time, out of necessity, I had become a Republican—my mother had a state job. If the Democrats had gotten into the State House, she would have been fired. Civil Service was supposedly in effect, but no one paid serious attention to it. Anyway, I had become disenchanted with Roosevelt and the New Deal. The Depression was still with us despite all of the programs the New Deal brought forth. By the summer of 1940, I felt that our entry into the war was almost inevitable, and I believed Roosevelt to be partly responsible. Besides all of this, I was concerned that, should Roosevelt win a third term, it would at the least set a bad precedent and might lead to a dictatorship by whatever name it might be called.

I was twenty-one. This was to be my first presidential vote. Tom White, a friend of mine from grade school on through the fraternity years, had gone to the Republican convention with his father, who was still an important Ohio politician. When the convention was over, Tom propositioned me over a few beers to help organize "The Wilkie First-

Voters Club of the State of Ohio." His father said that he could get us money to finance the operation. Over the beers, it sounded like a great idea, so we went to work on it. Neither of us had anything much else to do. Neither of us had any idea how to proceed but, somehow, we got an organization going. We made a lot of noise, held a lot of meetings, and used someone's idea to sell a campaign key. Naturally, it was called "The Will Key." We did unload a lot of keys, and I think most of the proceeds went to the campaign. When it was over, and Wilkie was defeated, we threw a helluva party for our loyal workers from some left-over funds. A night or two later, Tom said he wanted to talk to me alone. He said that he still had a couple hundred dollars in cash left over and did not know what to do with it. I solved the problem – we split the money. Thus began my political career.

I learned from the history teacher at Grove City High School in the spring of 1939 that he intended to retire at the end of the next school year. I felt that, if all else failed, I could get that job after his retirement. I had not yet obtained a job by the summer of 1940, and by then was damned interested in the Grove City job. It was not so easy to come by as I believed. The president of the Board of Education was a friend of mine, and our doctor. I knew all of the Board members, one extremely well, the other three casually. I talked to them all individually prior to the night the Board was to meet. On that night, there were five candidates interviewed, including me. After a long time, a girl and I were asked to stay, and the others were dismissed. We were each questioned at length by the County Superintendent of Schools and, to a lesser extent, by Barton Griffith - the newly-hired local Superintendent. We waited another hour or so, and I was then told that I was hired. I found out later that the County Superintendent knew the girl and wanted her hired. The doctor and my other "friend" were going along with him. The new Superintendent and the other three Board members were for me. I learned again that one should never take anything for granted. By January of 1940, my mother and I had sold the drugstore and she had a job in Columbus working in the State Welfare Department as a caseworker in the Division of Aid for the Aged. Since I was still attending Ohio State, it seemed logical that we move to Columbus. Therefore, we rented a two-bedroom apartment in

Olentangy Village—a new, very nice apartment complex. Many of the ideas incorporated there are still considered to be top-notch amenities for present-day apartment complexes. The buildings were well-separated by wide streets and much green space. Many apartment units, including ours, had an unobstructed view of the Olentangy River. There were beautiful trees, well-landscaped grounds complete with flower gardens and picnic and playground area. There was a swimming pool for the complex, and everything was faultlessly maintained. At the entrance to the apartment area was a small shopping center and a bowling alley. It was convenience personified. The only drawback was the central heating system for all of the units. Steam heat was provided, and it was always hot. Nothing was thermostatically controlled, with the result that even in winter we kept windows open, and I went around the apartment a lot of times in my underwear. Of course, it was not air conditioned and therefore was hot in the summer as well. This was my introduction to apartment living and I enjoyed it immensely. In the summer of 1940, I spent a lot of great afternoons at the swimming pool.

On the Tuesday after Labor Day in 1940, I commenced teaching school at Grove City High. I was just twenty-two years old and eager to get started, finally, on my career. I received a munificent salary compared to some of my peers lucky enough to find jobs. I got the staggering sum of thirteen hundred dollars for nine months' work. I would have received only twelve hundred but, after all, I had a master's degree!

I was dedicated to really teaching the students all that I possibly could. I wanted to prepare them for life. I found out quickly enough that I was not prepared for them. The College of Education had not taken into account the fact that most of them were not eager to learn and that all too many of them were dumber than hell, at least insofar as formal education was concerned. More than a few should not have been in high school. They could not read a sentence. They could not write a paragraph. They could not spell anything much beyond three- or four-letter words. They had no vocabularies. The teachers were discouraged and passed the kids on year after year in order to get rid of them. Anyway, the school needed the seats.

On the other hand, some were very bright and could absorb more than I was able to teach them. The majority were average or a little below-average students. They were all—bright, dull, and average—basically good kids who went on to become good citizens. There were no serious disciplinary problems. They were not defiant or malicious. Some were ornery; a few were almost too good. I was very young and idealistic. I expected too much. I took myself too seriously.

Educational facilities were almost non-existent. Most of my classes were held in what was supposed to be the school library. There were no books in the library—only library tables. Necessarily, some of the students were forced to sit with their backs to my teacher's desk. The room was crammed with students for each class. Forty students a period was about average. The room contained one small blackboard on a wall to one side. There were no maps, no illustrative material, no projector, no teaching aids of any kind. The American history textbook was dry, dull reading—many of the words unfamiliar to even the average student. The book contained a few pictures. It had not been revised and was not current at all. The text used for the course, called "Problems of Democracy," was really a new elementary civics book. The course was targeted to high school seniors, and unfortunately neither presented nor solved the problems of our democracy. It, too, needed to be brought up to date. I do not know what great educator selected those textbooks, but I do know that they were totally unsuitable for those classes. Unfortunately, the school system did not have money enough to replace them, and they could not have been replaced anyway. They had been adopted for use countywide.

I was disillusioned quickly, and for a time became discouraged. Ohio State's College of Education had not prepared me for teaching. More time should have been given to the practicality of teaching in a poor high school in Ohio and less time to educational philosophy and the progressive education movement then in vogue. I am certain that the vast majority of public high schools in Ohio were no better off than was Grove City both as to the caliber of the students and the equipment and educational facilities available.

I had an additional problem. Many of the kids knew me either personally or by reputation. Most of them called me by the nickname

"Joe," which I had managed to pick up during the semester I attended high school in town. I was only about four years older than some of my students. None of this was conducive to a great deal of respect for me by those students. I had to earn that over a period of time, and I did. They tried me, but a combination of humor and occasional hard discipline solved that problem. Strangely, some of those who knew me best were most cooperative.

I gradually relaxed and began to really enjoy both teaching and the students. There really was not much sense in my taking myself very seriously. No one else did. The whole situation became a challenge. Problems to solve are the best part of working, and there were problems.

I persuaded the school to spend enough money for some good world maps, as well as for two or three weekly magazines. I insisted that my seniors read the daily newspaper, especially the editorial page. They were assigned articles from magazines to read and report on in class. We took up a collection and bought a radio so that we could keep up with the news. I worked with the public librarian, and we came up with a list of historical novels for the American History classes to read and either report on orally in class or in written form. All of my students were assigned research topics which required that they become familiar with the public library. The students hated it at first, but later on became quite interested, and very proud of themselves. I used the textbooks as guides and as material for tests, but I, necessarily, had to lecture more than I would have liked to supplement the material.

I gave paragraph-meaning quizzes frequently and was astounded at the diversity of opinion as to what a simple paragraph had to say. I gave essay-type examinations. My idea was to try to get as many students as possible to read and write intelligently, and to think. Quite a few actually improved. Most of those who did not were simply not mentally able to succeed at anything academically. I passed them, anyway, as did all of the other teachers. The only students I ever gave a failing grade to had just refused to try to do anything even though they had the intelligence and learning skills to succeed. When I did fail a student, I usually heard about it from their parents, but generally after one failure for six weeks, they got the message and produced.

From my lectures and reading assignments, I got all kinds of flak from parents, ministers, and the school administration. I was called an atheist, a communist, a socialist and a son of a bitch. In fact, I was a Republican Methodist who sometimes wishes that I had just stuck to the textbooks, bad as they were.

The other teachers had no better equipment or facilities with which to work than did I. The English teachers had no library either, and complained about outmoded, uninteresting textbooks. The math teacher had textbooks and blackboards. I do not know enough about mathematics to know what else was needed other than apples and oranges. In the sciences there was a laboratory almost devoid of any equipment at all. Textbooks used were, of course, ancient. The only two languages offered were Latin and two years of French. Students who took the courses did learn Latin for whatever good it may have done them. I doubt that the second-year French students could have deciphered a menu in a French restaurant.

Significantly, during that time, none of the academic programs received any money at all from either state or federal government. The Jackson Township (Grove City) local school district was poor with a very small tax base. It did not help any that much of the district was composed of small farms and poor farmers, many of whom had only eighth-grade educations, and most of whom, while proud that their children were getting a better education than they had, did not understand how academic courses could be of much help. Teachers were lucky to get paid and equipment and textbooks were out of the question.

The State of Ohio provided adequate money for vocational training in agriculture and home economics, however. Teachers were hired for eleven months and were well-paid. Those departments were well-equipped, and the programs offered were excellent. The State also supplied some additional funding in vocational education where metal working, cabinet making, and welding were taught, as well as for business and secretarial educational courses. The results were good.

Despite the poor facilities for providing a good academic education, the graduates of this poor school system did surprisingly well in life. Many of the boys, of course, became successful small farmers. Many of the girls became housewives within a year or two after leaving school. Others became factory workers, telephone company employees, grocers and butchers, clerks, and secretaries. They were and are good citizens and fine people. Some went to college and became teachers, engineers, dentists, preachers, doctors, and lawyers. Some of these people were very successful, and all of them were a credit to the school system and to themselves. There was one murderer, another felon or two, one or two prostitutes, several racketeers, and one tout. Generally, those kids became a cross-section of American society. Some rose much above their environmental background. Some even overachieved, based upon their intellectual capacity. However, the vast majority of the brighter students did much better than did those with less innate ability.

We have, as a nation, been stressing education in the last twenty years, and have spent untold sums to upgrade the quality of schooling our students receive. Much of this has been proven wasteful. We are now told that there is mediocrity in the education of our young people. Money will not solve the problem by itself any more than busing will improve the situation for the blacks. This is not a treatise on American education, but I learned enough from the years I taught to know a few things that we seem to overlook.

First of all, education begins at the birth of the child and continues at home until the child goes to school. If the home situation is not capable of providing it, then the Head Start program is a necessity. Second, every student capable of learning at all must be taught to read and write intelligently, and to acquire enough skill to perform the daily, necessary arithmetic problems with which we are all faced. Third, those capable of absorbing knowledge must undergo a stiff academic program at least until high school. Those who want to become trained for employment after high school should receive such training to ensure their success if they are capable of absorbing it. Poor students bring down the level of instruction below what the better students can accomplish. Vast amounts of equipment and instructional aids, while helpful, will not ensure a good education. A skilled teacher with a full and ready knowledge of subject matter is a large part of the answer. However, if the student does not have the capacity to learn, no one can teach him.

After I quit taking myself seriously and began to relax, I commenced to thoroughly enjoy teaching. The kids were fun. If you liked them, they responded. I began to get affection and respect from them and, when this happened, discipline was no longer much of a problem. When we began to enjoy each other in the classroom, learning improved.

I got well-acquainted with the other members of the faculty and liked most of them. The male teachers congregated in the teachers' restroom before school each morning. The stories were great, and some of them were even true. Most of these people, male and female, were dedicated to their work, even though resigned to a life of genteel poverty. I do not know how some of those who were married and had children were able even to exist. I do know that they would have been better teachers had they eaten regularly.

I became a close friend of the coach of all sports, the physical education teacher. He asked that I help him out a little with his football team. I was delighted. I cannot say that my assistance made them a championship team. Nothing could have done that. I did help keep them busy during practice and even did some scouting, which proved helpful.

This red-headed coach was profane, colorful, enthusiastic, and well-liked. His basketball teams were almost always excellent; and, in fact, he had a winning record in all four of the sports he coached—football, basketball, baseball, and track. The girls played basketball, and softball. Tennis, swimming, soccer, and the like were unheard of as a part of a high school program. I enjoyed the athletic teams as much as I did my own classes, and lived and died with Red Trego, the coach, with the rise and fall of each team's fortunes. I really do not know how that one man managed to coach everything, even including reserve basketball. He was at school every night until six o'clock and had a full teaching schedule during school hours.

Athletic facilities and equipment were no better than we were used to in teaching our own subjects. New uniforms were purchased about every five or six years, and the protective pads were not really safe for football. Neither were the crude helmets available able to stave off concussion or worse. Fortunately, there were never any major injuries, and it was rare that a player was unable to participate on game day.

The offense used in football was a very simplified version of the single wing, with an occasional pass or trick play thrown in for variety. The offense had to be simple because the only outstanding athlete on the team was a big black man (he was almost average) who was so dumb that he could not memorize the signals. In the huddle, the quarterback called the play for the rest of the team and then said, "Fred, you get the ball from center and just follow me." It worked well. Fred could have butted and driven his way through a bank vault, and he could run like a deer over almost anyone.

The basketball team my first year was terrible. There simply was no material of varsity caliber in the junior and senior classes, and the freshmen and sophomores were not yet physically mature enough to play on the varsity. The result was that the varsity lost much more often than they won, and the reserves were undefeated. The gymnasium was packed early for every game in order that the fans could watch the reserves play and dream about the good teams ahead. I took tickets at the basketball games and then kept score. I was paid three dollars a night for my labors. It was a bonanza which kept me in beer and cigarette money during the season.

Almost all of the students were basically fine kids. Most of the girls were developed well, to say the least, and some of them were not above attempting to be provocative with a young male teacher. That was a no! No! I would not have dared get involved or my job and reputation would have been gone. I think those girls were aware of this and therefore bolder than they might otherwise have been. Some of the boys were ornery, but none were either defiant or destructive.

In a class I had immediately after lunch, there were some really ingenious junior boys. They did not repeat much, but they went through shooting paper wads from rubber band sling shots, squirt guns, and pea shooters. One of the boys took a nap fairly often, so I told the class one day to save their ammunition until such time as the sleepy one took his next nap, and when they caught him asleep to let him have it. Things quieted down and the boy stayed awake for three or four weeks to the point that I had forgotten about what I had said. One day, however, all hell broke loose, and the poor kid was hit with a barrage of paper, peas, and paperclips. He stayed awake the rest of the year, and the firing ceased.

I was cursed by having about forty students a class sitting at library tables. I do not know how I kept them in line as well as I did. It was not like having fifteen or twenty students sitting in neat rows. Sometime during the winter my after-lunch group would leave to be followed by a class made up mostly of girls. The girls would drop their books on one particular table, and it collapsed almost daily. Obviously, one of my ornery groups was unscrewing the table legs prior to departure. There were six boys at the table when the crime had to have been committed. Any one of five of them, in my opinion, might have done it. Finally, I got the old janitor in the act, and he labored mightily one evening before announcing that the table was so tight that no one could take it apart. No one did—for a week or two—and then it collapsed again. The janitor said that it was impossible, but it happened. The next day when the boys got in, I said, "Okay, there won't be any reprisals, but I want to know which one of you guys took the table apart yesterday." There was silence for a couple of minutes and the big, tall, skinny kid that I had not suspected held up his hand and said, "I did." I asked him how he got it apart. He got a big grin on his face, reached in his pocket, and pulled out a wrench. He could not talk plainly because he did not hear well, so he said, "I used this wench." Same table later on I got complaints about tobacco juice being in the center drawer. I watched for about a week afterwards without having said anything, and then caught the culprit. He was one of our more imaginative ornery ones, so I said, "Come on, Jack. We're going to go talk to Percey (Percey was the principal!) loved, respected, and feared by all. I told Percey that Jack was chewing tobacco, and spitting into the table drawer. Percey nodded, looked at Jack and asked, "Have you still got her, Jack?" Jack nodded affirmatively whereupon the principal said, "Okay, then, swallow her, Jack." We had a sick kid, but the tobacco chewing ceased.

Morally, the students were almost universally way above what the present-day youth seem to have become. Some of the boys smoked; periodically one would be caught smoking in the boys' restroom. If the girls smoked at all, they did not do so at school. Occasionally, we heard rumors of drinking escapades, but these were not the rule. Marijuana and drugs were unheard of during that age of innocence. Unfortunately, every year one or two girls became pregnant during the school year, and had to quit school. This may have been immoral, but it has been going on without interruption since the days of Adam and Eve.

Teachers and other school personnel were expected to be examples for the students. Consequently, our moral standards were supposed to be about as high as those of Methodist ministers. Almost all of the faculty really adhered to these standards either out of fear or else because they did not make enough money to be able to afford any vices. The coaches used fluent profanity with some frequency, and with a lot of good reason, but this was frowned upon by the Board of Education. Two or three of the male teachers smoked pipes away from school, and one chewed tobacco in class, but never spit. He let the tobacco juice trickle down his throat. No teacher ever drank any alcoholic beverage—at least never in Grove City.

I, of course, violated all of the rules, but not publicly. I did smoke cigarettes in school during my free period, but I had to climb down a circular ladder to get to the furnace room in order to do this. The janitor was a friend of mine, and not only encouraged my visits, but provided me with the <u>Daily Racing Form</u> so that I could handicap the horses while I puffed on cigarettes. One of my students, who also played the horses, took my bets to the local bookie at noon when he made his own. When Beulah Park was in operation, the superintendent, the coach, and I almost beat the kids out of school in the afternoon in order to get to the track and get our money in action.

In the fall of 1940, my classes followed the presidential campaign. They heard F.D.R. tell the mothers of America (again, and again, and again) that he would "never, never" send their sons to war. Those kids were smarter than the voters. They did not believe him. We were aware during that year that the Germans completely dominated Europe along with the Russians in the East. When the Draft Act was passed by Congress, it seemed obvious that we were gearing up for war. The British were taking a horrible aerial beating. Prime Minister Churchill was defiant. Almost single-handedly he kept up the British will to fight on when peace with honor was attainable and deservedly so. My students did not really need too much urging to follow those events; neither did I. The draft age was eighteen, and many of the boys were approaching the time for registration. Most of them ultimately did, in fact, enter military service shortly after their graduation from high school. One or two were heroes, three or four or more were wounded, one or two were killed. They knew and I knew what the possibilities were, but we did not worry about it on a daily basis. Life went on about as normally as it always had for all of us.

In the early spring of 1941, I was summoned to appear at the Westerville Armory for a draft physical. I do not remember my draft registration number, but I do know that it was low. I was definitely "draft bait." None of my friends had yet received notices, but were curious and drove to Westerville to see what went on. I do not know how many men were there that evening for their examinations, but the Armory was full of naked men. We lined up single file and progressed from doctor to doctor. After the doctor in charge of eye exams had checked me, he asked in a low tone of voice whether I wanted to be in the Army. I whispered back a quick "no." When I got to the doctor who was checking for hernia, he pointed his index finger at the appropriate spot and started to check me. For some reason I flinched, giggled, and pulled up my knee defensively. He tried two or three more times with about the same results; I got to laughing and so did the doctor. We attracted so much attention that eventually everyone in the Armory was laughing. I must have put on a great performance. The doctor never really did get me checked. Everyone there was hysterical before we got through with the show. The Army should have quit while they were ahead.

I dated Evelyn whenever I could during that school year but did not get to see her as often as I would have liked. She had a job teaching physical education at Crestline, a town in North Central Ohio about sixty miles north of Columbus. Her salary was about eleven hundred dollars a year. Marriage was impossible. Besides, she was not at all sure that she wanted to marry me even if we could have afforded to do so. We did get together most weekends and our romance flourished — slowly.

My first teaching year ended in May of 1941. I had one paycheck coming, which, as often happened, was late. I was broke and needed a summer job. I was bemoaning my fate to Herb Hennick, the owner of the campus hangout, and he surprised me by saying, "You've got a job working the soda fountain and waiting tables. You get fifty cents an hour. Show up Monday morning at seven-thirty." My God, what a job that was! I worked at least twelve hours a day, seven days a week. I was on my feet constantly, and I earned my money. I also knew a large number of the customers, and they took much delight in picking on me. After a few days my feet were killing me, I was exhausted, and about half mad at the world. I hated the damned job, hated Herb, and hated some of my so-called friends for needling me. The truth is, I never really worked hard in my life before this experience.

One of my friends was dating the step-daughter of the chief engineer for the Ohio State Highway Department, Division Six. He got a job with one of the bridge crews. So did another friend of mine because his father had some political influence. They did not kill themselves on the job, worked eight hours a day, six days a week, and felt like running around at night. The chief engineer and his wife ate dinner in Hennick's quite often, knew me pretty well and enjoyed my sore feet. One night the chief said, "For Christ's sake, report Monday morning to the bridge crew George and Tom are on, and get the hell out of here!" I did.

The crew "was assigned" to paint a rather large steel bridge which crossed the Olentangy River in Delaware, Ohio, about twenty miles north of Columbus. "Working hours were supposed to be from seven-thirty in the morning until four-thirty in the afternoon, with half an hour for lunch. The crew was made up entirely of young high school students or immediate graduates and college students or immediate graduates. Almost all of them got their summer jobs on the basis of their parents' political influence. There were no Democrats in that group. Absolutely none of these young men had any desire to work; in fact, they very seldom did. The W.P.A. (a federal government agency noted for inefficient, slow work) estimated completion of the painting job to be six weeks. This would have meant by mid-July. I quit toward the end of August, and I heard that the job finally ended about Labor Day.

The foreman was an older man, a permanent employee of the State Highway Department, afraid of his own shadow, intimidated by those kids, and obviously not overly brilliant. The result was that no one paid any attention to his orders. We worked when we felt like it, stole his Highway Department truck to take rides and check out the girls, dumped paint on some of the bothersome little kids in the neighborhood, threw paint on each other and generally did everything but get arrested. The Delaware Police did pay us a couple of visits when the paint was poured on the kids.

Any of us could have been killed or seriously injured. We had to paint the steel beams supporting the bridge underneath part of the bridge by steel chairs hooked to the girders. One of the young kids was agile enough to attach these chains.

He got to them by means of a long series of ladder arrangements and then, upon occasion, swung from chain to chain high above the river. Once, we removed the ladder and left him hanging about thirty feet above the Olentangy River. He proceeded to climb up the chain hand over hand and pulled himself up to the surface of the bridge – fortunately. Almost daily, we would get the scaffolds swinging back and forth, which was dangerous. We jumped from scaffold to scaffold, which was bad, and we often took naps on the narrow boards, which was even worse. Had anyone accidentally stepped too far or rolled over, he would have either dropped thirty feet into the water or onto sharp, hard rocks.

One day the Highway Engineer sent us all over to division headquarters to unload a carload of cement. I was standing on the tailgate of our truck handing down a fifty-pound bag, when an imbecile foreman, for reasons unknown to anyone, pulled away from the loading dock. I juggled the cement bag and, fortunately, fell backwards rather than to the asphalt below. It scared me, and I called him a dumb son of a bitch. George got mad, went to the Engineer's private office swearing and generally raising hell with his future father-in-law for hiring such a dumb bastard, and got fired on the spot.

All in all, it was a fine job and a wonderful way to spend the summer at state expense. Three of the high school kids on that bridge crew were killed during World War II in the Battle of the Bulge.

The school year 1941-1942 began the day after Labor Day, as usual. My salary for that school year was increased by the large sum of one hundred dollars, so that I received a total of fourteen hundred dollars for nine months' teaching. Naturally, retirement deductions were taken out each month, but I did not pay income tax. None of the teachers were paid much, regardless of experience, teaching ability, or whatever. There was a salary schedule. I do not remember what the maximum salary was, but I am certain it did not exceed two thousand dollars. The school district simply had no money for salaries, equipment, books, teaching aids or anything else. Frequently our checks were late, pending payment of taxes. There was little, if any, State Aid to public schools, and Federal Aid to Education was only a dream in the minds of educational associations.

I did not expect as much of either myself or the students as I had at the beginning of my first year. I was much more at ease with them and much more assured. I had not had a large number of disciplinary problems my first year, and even less the second. The subject matter was easier to teach. I had been through it all once and had learned what worked and what did not. I think that I was a better teacher.

School life and school activities were unchanged. I did help more with the football team than I had the previous year and, as it turned out later, it was a good thing I did. All teachers were required to attend the monthly P.T.A. meetings. I hated them as did all of the teachers, but the parents enjoyed them. The school basketball team was good that winter, and the kids, teachers and indeed the entire community, cheered them on.

We were aware of world events. Class discussions were held for a few minutes each day as to the news and its meaning. The senior boys became very interested and very aware. Most of them faced the probability of being drafted into military service shortly after graduation. Many of my friends had already either been drafted, were placed in Federal Service or a National Guard unit, or had volunteered in order to beat the draft and choose the branch of service they wanted. Several had taken advanced R.O.T.C. in college and entered service as commissioned officers. My own draft status was uncertain. I was placed in a limited-service category with the possibility that I might be taken at some time in the future. The Friday before Pearl Harbor Sunday, I delivered a lecture to my students in American History class and those taking Problems of Democracy to the effect that we would not have war with Japan. I should have remembered the R.O.T.C. lectures I received in college in 1935 and 1936, wherein we were told to expect a Japanese war within a matter of a few years. Later, none of the students thought that the attack on Pearl Harbor was funny, but they all managed to remind me as to what I said. That must have been one day everyone paid attention.

Sunday, December 7, 1941, was a quiet day for me. My mother was not at home, and after a leisurely reading of the Sunday paper, I wrote some letters, graded papers, took a nap, read and was generally lazy and I did not turn on the radio. In the early evening, I became hungry and drove to Hennick's for my Sunday dinner and a little conversation with whomever I knew in the restaurant. As soon as I walked in, I wondered why the place was so quiet. There were no loud voices and there was no laughter. I sat down with some people I knew and asked why the place was so subdued. They looked at me as though I were crazy and asked me where I had been all day. They then informed me that the Japanese had attacked Pearl Harbor. I was shocked, scared, and generally upset immediately. I do not have any idea what I had for dinner that night—I am not certain as to whether or not I ate. I do know that I went home soon and listened to the reports on the radio the rest of the evening. When I went to bed, I slept poorly and awakened in the morning with a truly blinding headache. I called school and told them that I would not be in that day because of illness. I took several assessment in a short period of time, fixed an ice bag, and went back to bed. When I got up in the early afternoon, the headache had disappeared, but I was exhausted. It was nerves, fright, emotional fatigue. I knew that my relatively sheltered life would soon change, and I also feared for my friends who either already were or soon would be in military service. I decided to try to get my mind going in a different direction and went to one of the neighborhood theaters to see *Philadelphia Story*. It was a great movie. Every time it is mentioned today, I think of that afternoon. For me, the film had great therapeutic value. When I came out of the theater, my attack of nerves was over permanently.

The next morning, I went to school prepared to teach and try to answer at least some of the inevitable questions. I packed everyone possible into my classroom and the adjacent study hall for the purpose of hearing President Roosevelt's address to the Congress in which he asked for a declaration of war against Japan, Germany, and Italy. It was, of course, a tremendously emotional speech, delivered by a master in a moment in history when feeling was at its peak. The United States of America was truly united from then on until the war finally ended. We all returned to leading more or less normal lives. Everyone was affected by the war in some way, but everyone had been affected by the Depression. Americans, then, were able to adjust and accept adversity when it came. School continued as usual, but many of the students were well aware of the daily status of the war. Newspapers were filled with stories of the battles in the Pacific, the battles of Bataan and Corregidor, the continuous bombing of London by the Germans, the German invasion of Russia, the German victories against the British in the Desert, the Japanese takeover of the Philippines and all of the British possessions in the Far East. The news was all bad. There was a news program at seven o'clock every evening with Gabriel Heater as the commentator. Every night his opening remark was, "Oh, there's good news tonight." I could have throttled him, cheerfully. The news was all bad. We were losing the war everywhere.

The school year ended, finally, in May of 1942. I think I did as good a teaching job as possible under the circumstances. History was particularly difficult to teach. Hell, it was being made every hour of every day. Current events were not a problem. We discussed the status of the war. Thank God, I did have some maps. We could find the places we were reading about, although at times with difficulty. I was not sorry when school was out for the summer.

During the entire school year, I saw Evelyn as much as possible, but it was becoming increasingly difficult for us to get together. She was still teaching in Crestline, about eighty miles away, though her home was on a farm north of Sunbury, about thirty-five miles away. Gasoline rationing was coming into effect. We did see each other on weekends, and wrote each other almost daily. Perhaps absence really does make the heart grow fonder, because our romance was progressing rapidly. She even started admitting that she loved me. We talked about marriage, but that seemed to be a long way off. My draft status was becoming more and more unclear, and somewhat tenuous. I did not make enough money to support myself very well, and certainly could not have supported both of us. There did not seem to be any jobs available for girls' physical education teachers within easy driving distance of Columbus, so we just talked and dreamed.

By the summer of 1942, almost all of my friends were in the military service, scattered throughout the United States and various parts of the world. I had letters from several of them. Almost to a man, they hated whatever they were doing and certainly disliked wherever they were located. It did not sound to me as though it would be much fun to be in service, and I was not looking forward to it.

Of those friends who did not enter service as officers, almost all went to Officer Candidate Schools and became officers after completing their basic military training. One of the guys who had been a real character in college wrote that he was going to take Air Cadet training in order to get out of the mud at Camp Aberdeen. He assured me that he would never graduate. I did not believe that he could possibly ever fly an airplane. I really did not think anyone in authority would do any more than let him ride in one once or twice. He could not drive an automobile with safety at thirty-five miles an hour. But he graduated and became a pursuit pilot of the hottest airplane we had. A couple of years later I found out that he had become commander of a pursuit squadron in the Pacific. He flew out one morning with his squadron and was never heard from again.

I was not in any hurry to look for a summer job as soon as school was over. I had received my last salary check for the school year soon after the term had ended. I had also been luckier than usual betting on the horses at Beulah Park. I probably had two hundred dollars or more. Who needed to work? Besides, I had started going to my favorite bookie establishment almost daily, and my luck, or skill, in picking winners continued. In those years, one could bet any amount from fifty cents on up on a horse and could even play fifty-cent show parleys. There were a lot of racetracks running, and I kept active every afternoon. I made anywhere from four to eight or ten dollars almost every afternoon. It sure beat working.

Fortunately, or in my opinion, unfortunately, after two weeks, my mother could stand my activities no longer. After all, she had to get up and go to work every morning. She suggested, in no uncertain terms, that I get busy and get a job. My God, did I get a job! When my father had had the drug store, we sold Telling's Ice Cream at the soda fountain. We sold a lot of ice cream, and I was well acquainted with the manager of the ice cream factory. Telling's, by then, had been absorbed by Sealtest. I made an appointment to see Mr. Hughes, the manager. When I got to his office, I told him that I was looking for summer employment and wondered whether or not he had any jobs available. He got a big grin on his face and a gleam in his eye and told me that I could have all the work I wanted. He really meant it. I had all of the work I wanted, and then some! I was paid fifty cents an hour, which seemed to be the going rate for unskilled labor. There was no such thing as time-and-a-half for overtime nor did they believe in paying double time on Sundays. Had they paid on that basis, even at fifty cents an hour, I would have become well-to-do in a few weeks.

I was assigned as a helper and man-of-all-work to assist the plant foreman. He was a nice fellow and a hard worker used to long, hard hours. Although he had graduated from college with a major in dairy technology, I doubt that he made a dollar an hour. I was never certain whether the foreman felt sorry for me and thought that I needed to work all the hours I could get in, or whether he just could not find anyone else dumb enough to put in that much time. In any event, I punched in on the time clock at six-thirty every morning, and usually checked out about seven in the evening, six days a week. We did not work every Sunday, but during the hot weather, some of us did work about eight hours. On those Sundays, the company paid for our lunch. One of my duties included going to the Southern Hotel and purchasing enough sandwiches, coffee, and pie for the crew. Every morning, I was the first employee to report for work. The bulk of the people came in at seven-thirty. My main job during that hour was to connect all of the pipes through which the ice cream mix flowed into the tremendous vat that constituted the mixer. The pipes were disconnected each night and steam cleaned. One morning, I either forgot to put the washers in at the connecting joints, or else did not put them in correctly. Whatever, when the machinery was started, ice cream mix leaked all over the place. It was a real mess and rather chaotic for a while. I thought the foreman was going to have a stroke and his language to me was neither tender nor complimentary. I wish he had fired me.

Most days I assisted the foreman at the vat. I lifted fifty-gallon cans of mix, put in whatever was needed to make the particular flavor being run, hauled mix in the cans on a huge dolly, and ran the machine required for Dixie cups and quarts and pints of "fast-frozen ice cream." At other times, I helped unload supplies shipped in from Cleveland. Several times I had to work in the "cold room" where the ice cream was fast frozen. The temperatures in this ice box were about zero. I wore heavy clothing, a heavy coat, a lined hat which covered my ears, and heavy fur-lined gloves. Every fifteen minutes, we were required to get out into the warmth in order to keep from freezing. I drove a big ice cream truck and made deliveries during emergencies. I ran the equipment to make popsicles and helped make ice cream bars. Some of these jobs may sound easy. None were. I went home exhausted every night. I saved a little money because I was too tired to go any place to spend it.

One day I was making ice cream bars, using faulty molds which cut my fingers a little with each batch. It was necessary to then put my hands into the brine tank, and each time that happened, my fingers stung more and became sorer. When the work was completed, I went upstairs to the office, saw the manager, thanked him for hiring me, and quit. That was undoubtedly the hardest, worst job I ever had. Nothing in the Army that I ever was required to do compared with it. Strange as it may seem, however, I am still very fond of ice cream.

I drove out to Grove City a day or two after my departure from Telling's, and ran into my boss, the Superintendent of Schools. He said that he had a summer job working at the Columbus General Depot, an Army supply facility. He told me that there was a crew of school teachers and administrators working together, that it was a good job and that he thought I could get hired if I wanted to work. I got a job immediately. What a contrast! I worked forty hours a week and got paid a dollar an hour, which was a real bonanza. The job was easy, the crew was fun to work with, and I got neither tired nor dirty. After the ice cream plant, it was a vacation. The reason for our employment resulted from what I later discovered to be a typical Army screw-up! There were three warehouses full of parts, nuts, bolts, and other items. The trouble was that no one knew where anything was or how much of any item was there. We had to count and categorize all of this, then fill out inventory cards. The work was not finished when we went back to our duties as educators. I wonder whether it was ever done. This was my introduction to government waste and inefficiency. I saw many more examples later on.

Sunbury House

Socially, the summer of 1942 did not amount to much as far as I was concerned. Almost all of my friends were in the service, and the few who were still around had gotten married and could not have caroused around even had they wanted to. Besides, when I worked in the ice cream plant, I was too tired to go out. Although Evelyn was not too many miles away, I could not see her until the weekend because she too had a summer job and worked very peculiar hours. She worked at the Nestle's plant in Sunbury. One of her jobs was to wipe the cans of "Nescafé" as they came off the assembly lines. We did see each other on Saturday evenings, and Sundays when I did not work. It was unusual—Evelyn had the aroma of coffee in her hair all summer, no matter how often she washed it. In spite of all of the obstacles, we were very much in love. She finally took my fraternity pin that summer, which, in those years, meant that we were engaged. Hardly anyone could afford an engagement ring. We spent a lot of evenings that summer in the porch swing on the front porch of her family's beautiful, large farm home (3167 North State Route 61). We continued to talk and dream about getting married, but the draft loomed ever closer, and we both knew it. There had been opportunities for advantageous job changes for me which would have made marriage possible, but I did not get favorable consideration because of my draft status. One of those positions very probably would have led to my return to Ohio State as an instructor in the College of Education, and, ultimately, to my then goal of being a professor of education. I have often wondered what might have been. It was a strange time. Everyone's lives, ambitions and dreams were in a state of flux. Today, the expression would be that our lives were "on hold" until the war was ended.

About the end of July that summer, our coach was drafted. We had become close friends, and I hated to see him leave. There was no one around to replace him. All of the young coaches and recent graduates in physical education were in the service. Our Board of Education and Superintendent of Schools were desperate. Football practice was scheduled to commence August twentieth. One of the English teachers had coached football once—about fifteen years previously. He was, arbitrarily, made head football coach. The vocational education teacher, a huge physical specimen who had played tackle on his high school team, was informed that he was the line coach. I had been assisting the coach for two years, knew his system and coaching methods, and was told that I was the backfield coach. I was also informed that I would not have a full schedule of history classes but would be the boy's physical education teacher. That I had no qualifications to teach physical education did not matter; the war caused standards to be completely relaxed.

August twentieth arrived and we got the football equipment issued, put the kids through the usual calisthenics, ran them around the track until they were exhausted from the running and the August heat, then sent them home. The poor English teacher did not want to coach and had lost track of what was then "modern" football. The three of us talked and I tried to tell them what to do, based upon what I had learned from observation and practice. The first couple of weeks were chaotic. We were using an old-fashioned offense and defense without our new "head coach" remembering exactly how they were supposed to work. I persuaded him to let me change the defense to what our drafted coach had been doing, which the boys were used to. We had a practice scrimmage with Columbus North, and Mike Hagely, the long-time, highly successful North High coach told us that he had used our short punt offense in the 1920s and went to his office and gave us his old play book. At least what he gave us made sense and we did have some offense for our first game. After that game, which we lost seven to zero, I took over the team by popular consent. Naturally, we went back to everything with which the team was familiar. We ran a single wing offense with an unbalanced line and used a five and six-man defensive line with either two or three linebackers. Once in a while, we used a spread formation which was effective for passing. We had a long pass out of a deep punt formation, which worked two or three times during the season. I had been reading about how the coach of the Chicago Bears had reincarnated the T formation with a man in motion, and we even tried that. I now knew that I did not know much about it. It seemed to mess us up more than it helped.

It was a strange season. I really do not remember exactly what our won and lost record was. I do know that we lost more games than we won. No one beat us badly. We had too many big, strong players for that. We usually outplayed our opponents but could not take the ball in for a touchdown from inside the ten-yard line. Several times when we were ready to score, our backs fumbled the snap from center. I did not know why this happened and blamed the backs for having "butter fingers" until they told me that our center was passing them curves. I checked him and found that, under stress, he did. We moved the center to guard and brought in someone else to center the ball, and the fumbling stopped.

In the first game of the season, our team was convinced that they could win if they held the opponent and the first series of plays and forced them to punt. We put in our most dependable boy to receive the ball. He was a fine basketball player and ball handler. He always caught the ball in practice. We told him to play deep, signal for a "fair catch" and hold on to the ball. He played deep, signaled for a fair catch, and dropped the damned ball. They recovered on our five-yard line, scored, and defeated us, as I said, seven to zero. In another game, we kicked off and the other team's kickoff return man ran it back about ninety yards for a touchdown. In still another game, our fullback, linebacker, passer, kicker, and best ballplayer got mad at a big kid on the other team, slugged him, and got kicked out of the ball game. We lost that one by a point. The last game of the season, with the other team leading six to zero, I called for the long pass out of punt formation. Our big end caught the ball and had an absolutely open field for a touchdown. He tripped over his own feet and fell down on the ten-yard line.

I had always been a football fan and frustrated coach as are all fans. I thought I knew a lot about the game. I did. I found out that knowledge of the game is far from the entire answer. After that experience, I lost all desire to coach. I could not have gone through my productive years with the certain knowledge that my livelihood depended on what a bunch of kids did or did not do under game conditions.

I was not a good teacher that fall. I was interested in football and my draft status. I hardly remember what did or did not take place in the classroom. I have no clear memory as to the progress of the war. I do remember vividly that I got my notice to report for induction into the Armed Forces on the Tuesday after completion of the football season.

The Friday which marked the last football game of the year was also my last day of teaching. The school held a pep rally and farewell to me at an assembly that afternoon. I sat in the back of the auditorium and was asked to come up front to the stage. I stood up and moved down the aisle to the stage amid loud cheers and the high school band playing. I felt so good, pleased, and emotional that I put my hands on the stage and vaulted up, rather than walking up the steps as I should have done. In the process of vaulting, I ripped the entire seat out of my last decent pair of pants in front of all of the faculty and the entire student body. The roar of laughter replaced the cheering. It was a fitting end to my early career.

The period from 1940 to 1942 was one of the most traumatic in our history. We knew, although we tried to kick the thought under the rug, that after Hitler's Blitzkrieg and complete domination of Western Europe, we would in all probability be drawn into the conflict. Dunkirk and the evacuation of the remnants of the British Army was a courageous action that captured our imagination and sympathy. Roosevelt was completely pro-British. He, with little favorable public opinion in the beginning, took us step by step toward open, all-out aid to England. The "leasing" or our "overage" destroyers, the "arsenal for democracy" speech, the rapid changeover to military production in this country, the implementation of the draft, were all clear indications of our ultimate involvement. There was considerable isolationist sentiment too. Many members of Congress, both Democratic and Republican, were against any involvement in Europe. Charles Lindbergh, a bona fide American hero, was one of the leaders of the isolationists and very much pro-German. Roosevelt's tremendous appeal to the American people discredited Lindbergh and cast a shadow over the patriotism of the other leaders, even though we were not at war.

Whether or not F.D.R. and his staff had advance knowledge that the Japanese would bomb Pearl Harbor, that attack completely changed all of our lives, not only for the war's duration, but to this day. Like it or not, we truly became a superpower on December 7, 1941. We have been the defenders of the Free World ever since. Our thinking, our economy, and our lifestyle changed quickly. We suddenly were out of the Great Depression. Unemployment dropped rapidly. Young men were in military service, women and older men went to work in our hastily created defense industries. It truly did take a war to put the people of America back to work.

After Pearl Harbor, no dissident voices were heard in the land. I am certain that there was still some pro-German sentiment, but it was not brought out openly. Most men of draft age really had no burning desire to enter military service. Most were "handcuffed volunteers," but there was little attempt at draft evasion. We all accepted our fate without questioning our orders. I suppose it was for that reason that I was totally amazed later at the attitude of young Americans at the time of the Vietnam War. I still wonder what has happened to America's attitude toward serving our country during the intervening years. Patriotism seems now to be a dirty word. Either people today are much brighter and better educated than we were, or else the media have exercised tremendous influence over our thinking. Whether this is good for the country, I am not so sure.

Men's clothing was differently tailored from what it is today. Suits had wide coat lapels, many had belted backs, pants were pleated in the front. Neckties were wider. Colored shirts were almost unheard of for dress wear with coats and vests. Women wore skirts much longer than they are now. Hats were worn to church and for dining out and other dress-up occasions. High-heeled shoes seemed to come or go with each new year.

The home radio was probably the single most popular entertainment vehicle. Music, still including the big bands and the Lucky Strike Hit Parade, were still popular. So were Bob Hope, George Burns and Gracie Allen, Jack Benny, Edgar Bergen, and Charlie McCarthy, W.C. Fields, and other comedians. Lum and Abner was a popular fifteen-minute, five-nights-a-week program. Fibber McGee and Molly was a fixture on Sunday evening. Bing Crosby had a program. The Lux Radio Theater was popular. Of course, most of us listened to at least one news program each day from the time of the air battles from Britain until the end of the war.

Motion pictures were extremely popular. One would think that we went to the movies to escape. Many of us did, but there were several war movies. The one I recall best is *Mrs. Minerva. Tobacco Road* was an extremely popular play. To me, however, and, apparently, to everyone else, the most outstanding production of that or any other period was the movie *Gone with the Wind*.

Popular songs included "We're Off to See the Wizard," "White Cliffs of Dover," "Don't Sit Under the Apple Tree," "The Last Time I Saw Paris," "Somewhere Over the Rainbow," and the nonsensical "Hut-Sut Rawlson on the Rillerah," and "Three Little Fiddies."

Finally, in sports, I witnessed the last game that Francis Schmidt coached at Ohio State—a humiliating forty to zero loss to the University of Michigan. Michigan was a truly great football team in 1940. Its star halfback was Tom Hannon, one of the finest I ever saw play the game. Despite much earlier success, Schmidt was on his way out as the Ohio State coach anyway. He had become a little more mentally unbalanced than he had always been, and his team was disorganized. Michigan, the school's greatest rival, was never supposed to beat State, and forty to zero was intolerable.

Ohio State hired a very outstanding young Ohio high school coach to succeed Schmidt. Paul Brown came in and restored discipline, cohesion, and organization out of chaos. He, of course, went on to become one of the most successful coaches in football history, for Ohio State, Great Lakes, the Cleveland Browns, and the Cincinnati Bengals. I watched his 1941 and 1942 teams at Ohio State. His 1941 team was good—amazingly good considering the situation he had taken over. His 1942 team won the National Championship. It was perfection itself. Sitting in the stands, I decided that Mr. Brown was a much better football coach than I was.

In baseball during that time there were many truly fine players, but Ted Williams of the Boston Red Sox and Joe DiMaggio of the New York Yankees were already legends. Williams had a .400 batting average, and DiMaggio set a consecutive game hitting streak in 1941 that has never been broken. As it did with every other part of our lives, the war played havoc with all the great athletes and great teams, both college and professional.

November 1942 — September 1945

A new recruit.

Although vision in my left eye was near 20/20, from birth I had no sight in my right eye. Consequently, shortly after the draft became effective, several of us paid a visit on then Mayor Montgomery, who was the mobilization officer for the Vth Corps Area, and the father of my fraternity brother and closest friend in college. We all wanted to know how the draft would work, and what our chances would be of being drafted. We sat in his living room, drank his Scotch, and had our spirits lifted by what we heard. He questioned us on our individual physical conditions, and told each of us, after listening to our ailments, that we did not meet the minimum standards for induction into military service and would not be drafted. The major was wrong. Everyone in that living room wound up in the service. I was the last to go, earmarked for "Limited Service Only." I guess by late 1942, the draft boards were running short of bodies and decided that my turn had finally arrived.

In any event, on Armistice Day, Tuesday, November 11, 1942, I reported to the Worthington Draft Board, as did quite a few other poor souls. After some confusion, we were transported to downtown

Columbus and dropped off at the American Legion Post. Victims from other draft boards were also present. After some delay, an Army officer showed up and swore us all in to "bear true faith and allegiance to the United States." We were in the Goddamned Army!

After more delays, we were fed and then walked up High Street to Union Station. When we got there, our names were called again to make sure that none of us had strayed or gotten lost, and then were told that we were being shipped to Fort Benjamin Harrison, Indiana.

About an hour later, we boarded a passenger train for Indianapolis. I smoked a lot of cigarettes, stared out the window at the countryside, read a *Time* magazine which I had bought at the train station, and dozed. There was a long article about Dwight D. Eisenhower, who had just been placed in command of air forces in Africa. I think that his picture was on the magazine cover. I had never heard of Ike before that day. Naturally, I thought of Evelyn, my mother, school, and all of the rest. I know that I was a little nervous and apprehensive that entire day, and very sad about the entire matter.

When we arrived in Indianapolis, we were met by an Army Sergeant and led to a bus which took us to "Fort Ben." I never really knew which direction it was from the train station, and I do not remember whether it is in Indianapolis proper, or where it is. I do know that it took up a lot of space. We were taken to a barracks and told to leave our bags there. Then things began to get confusing. I believe that we were first taken to Army supply. That was funny and a little tragic. As we went down the line, the soldiers behind the counters looked at us and threw clothing to us, based on their estimates as to size. We were asked our shoe size, thank God. We stored all of this clothing into our new barracks bags and returned to the barracks to dress in our new uniforms. Some of the clothing fit, some did not. We were able to change around with each other, and I came close to having clothing that almost fit. I felt strange in G.I. clothing, and the G.I. shoes were heavy. We had also received our Army identification tags, ever after known as "dog tags," which we wore around our necks as long as we were in the service. I still remember my Army serial number. I had to memorize it in basic training in order to get a pass to go out. I also had to recite it every payday.

The rest of that day is hazy in my memory. So was the rest of the week. We had a cursory physical examination, the high point of which was my first "short arm" inspection. A very disinterested PFC kept repeating as the lines passed by, "Take it out, roll it over, skin it back, milk it down, next." Occasionally, some unfortunate individual was told to step out of line. I never heard what happened to them. I have always wondered what that soldier dreamed about at night. We had a few shots; I never found out what they were for. We took various classification tests, attended some lectures, and mostly just stood around. It was sad when we had to mail our civilian clothing and suitcases home.

I have no clear recollection of my first meal in an Army mess hall. I know we got a compartmentalized metal tray, and moved through the chow line where a bunch of sadistic kitchen personnel threw food at the various compartments. Frequently ice cream hit in the mashed potatoes, but, hell, we scraped it off. My first breakfast does still stand out in my mind. The main course was creamed wieners. When I ate them and drank my first G.I. coffee at six o'clock in the morning, I was certain that I would vomit. I didn't.

Shipping orders began about Friday of that week, and we were told to stay in our barracks, or in the area until called. There were rumors about where each shipment was going, but no one really knew. Things were so confused I am not certain anyone in the Army knew where anyone was, much less where they were going. There was a branch of the Post Exchange (PX) in our vicinity and I made frequent trips there. Fortunately, I had sold my 1936 Plymouth for seventy-five dollars, so I had money. I bought cigarettes, candy bars, Coca Cola, hot dogs, stationery, beer, and anything else that came to mind. Sitting around sweating out shipping orders was a little nerve-wracking. I called Evelyn and my mother on Sunday, and felt better. They both told me that they loved me and missed me. I did not talk to either of them again for a very long time, but a lot of letters were written. On Tuesday, I was told that I was leaving that day. I packed my barracks bags and carried all of my belongings to the designated area, and waited. Eventually, there were hundreds of us from all over the post. Finally, our names were called and we stepped into waiting buses to be taken to the train station where we were loaded onto a troop train. No one knew where we were going, but wherever it was, a lot of us were headed there. That was a big trainload of newly-created soldiers, destination unknown. The coaches were dirty, the seats uncomfortable; these were old railroad coaches. The locomotive was coal-fired, and when the windows were opened, which was not easy to accomplish, coal smoke and cinders permeated everything. We were filthy within a few hours. When the windows were closed, the coal smoke stayed with us along with stale cigarette smoke and the odor of many dirty human bodies. The windows were so dusty on the outside that it was difficult to look out and get anything but a distorted view of the countryside. The Army did not furnish its soldiers with first-class transportation.

We rode, and we rode, and rode some more. The coaches rattled and swayed. We walked up and down the aisle but were not permitted to walk into the other cars. Finally, it was our turn to be fed, and we moved through several cars into what looked like a box car with slats on the door—the mess car. It was a mess all right. The movement of the train caused some of the food to slop over onto the floor. We used our mess kits for the first time, and carrying Army stew in a tin mess kit and coffee in a tin container on a swaying train caused a few problems. I do not recall what we ate at any meal served on that train, but I am certain that it was at least partially indigestible and, by the time we got back to our coach, cold. We assumed that we were heading south, because we saw signs on an occasional train station containing the name of towns that some recognized as being in Kentucky. Night came. Eventually the coach lights were turned off and we slept sitting up two to a narrow, uncomfortable seat, facing two other miserable G.I.s who had no more leg room or seat room than we did on our side. We were all cramped and tired. When the train stopped or jerked during the night, we were awakened. The train stopped on a siding, and we sat; then we switched engines and lost some of our coaches forever. I assume that those soldiers went to another installation other than where we were going. Before daybreak, we went up a mountain —we knew because the locomotive moved forward slowly and with apparent difficulty. We came to a large city. We could tell it was large from the number of streetlights we passed. We stopped and discovered that we were in Chattanooga, Tennessee.

We awoke to the discovery that there was no water in the cramped men's room on our coach. Something in the water line had broken. We could not wash and the little toilet itself had become clogged and smelled horrible. Its odor added to the general smell of the coach. That day is now completely blanked from my memory. We knew that we were traveling somewhere in Georgia and assumed that we were headed either for Fort Benning and the Infantry or one of the Air Corps training centers in Florida. I saw red clay roads, red clay fields, and pine trees. I saw a little colored boy standing beside the tracks, absolutely naked, waving at the train. We stopped for a while and opened the windows to find out where we were. We were told Valdosta, but none of us knew where that was. As a matter of fact, I did not know where anything was. The only times that I was ever out of Ohio previously had been on two or three trips to Indiana when I was in grade school.

The next night was a repetition of the previous one. We slept, uncomfortably, and awakened frequently to the noise of the train wheels and the rails and the swaying, jerking, stopping, and starting of the train. The third day, when daylight came, we could see palm trees and sandy soil. We knew that we were in Florida, somewhere. We passed through town after town – West Palm Beach, Lake Worth, Fort Lauderdale, and, finally, Miami. As the train stopped, we all cheered. We were certain that we were going to the basic training center for the Army Air Corps on Miami Beach.

God, we were glad to get off that damned troop train! Naturally, we had to sit on our barracks bags and wait. The sun was hot. Our wool uniforms itched; we stank and so did the uniforms. My face itched where my beard had grown, and my stomach was upset from the food and confinement. I had a bad taste in my mouth from not brushing my teeth. All in all, I am certain that I was a pretty unattractive specimen. So were we all, but everyone was happy to be off that train and at Miami. I had heard that this was probably the most desirable basic training center the Army had to offer.

Open Army trucks finally arrived, and we threw ourselves and our barracks bags on them to be transported across the Fifth Street Causeway and up Collins Avenue to 41st Street, where the trucks stopped. I gaped all the way at the streets, Biscayne Bay, hotel after hotel, the droves of soldiers in khaki uniforms, and the great beauty that seemed to be everywhere.

As our names were called, we climbed out of the trucks and went with a sergeant who led us to the hotel to which we were assigned. I was in the Craydon Arms, a relatively small hotel at the corner of 41st and Collins. We were led into the courtyard where we sat on the grass amidst the flowers and under the palm trees. After about fifteen minutes of orientation, we were assigned to our respective rooms, and told to shave, shower, unpack, put on khaki uniforms, and then reassemble in the courtyard where we would receive further instructions. I was assigned to the hotel's penthouse, as were perhaps a dozen or more other men. It sounded damned impressive to be located in a penthouse. It was not quite so good as it sounded. We walked up eight floors to get there, and being exhausted from the train trip, and having to carry two heavy barracks bags over our shoulders was a real test of physical conditioning. Of course, the hotel had an elevator, but we were not allowed to use it.

After cleaning up, unpacking, making up our beds and the like, I began to feel more like a human being and less like a zombie. Youth does have great powers of recuperation. God, though, we were hungry! When we returned to the courtyard, we were greeted by our squadron commander, two or three lieutenants and the non-coms assigned to the squadron. One of these non-commissioned officers was assigned as our drill instructor, Corporal Patrick Joseph Henley, a Boston Irishman in his late thirties, who was Regular Army. We found out a lot more about him as time went on. In due course, we were told to get our mess kits and reassemble in the street in front of the hotel to be marched to chow. The mess hall was just across the street, but we marched over anyway and then lined up. I do not remember what I ate. I do know that, in a mess kit, everything was thrown together anyhow, so I was never positive as to just exactly what I did eat. Almost inevitably when there were mashed potatoes and gravy, ice cream was the dessert, and the ice cream always wound up on top of the mashed potatoes in the middle of the gravy. That combination added a new dimension to the flavor of the ice cream.

Basic training commenced the next day at five-thirty in the morning with reveille. No bugle blew, but the whistle of the S.O.B. who was in charge of waking us up was louder and certainly more shrill than any bugle. We dressed hastily and stumbled downstairs eight floors to the street. It was darker than hell because Miami Beach and Miami were under a blackout. After roll call, we ran back up the stairs, eight floors, to wash, shave, dress and reassemble in half an hour, equipped with those damned mess kits, to be herded across to the mess hall for breakfast.

Mess halls generally all looked alike. What the food tasted like, how it was served and the cleanliness of them varied with the mess sergeant in charge. Supposedly, the Army bought the best food and meat available. It did not always taste so great. Breakfast was the same most mornings—a scoop of scrambled eggs, a couple slices of bacon or small link sausages, toast, marmalade, cereal and coffee or milk. Occasionally, we had "S.O.S." (creamed dried beef on toast). Once in a great while there were pancakes. The coffee was always strong and scalding hot. When canned milk was served for use in the coffee, and sugar added, the combination bubbled and looked as though it might explode. It tasted terrible. I learned to drink black coffee then. Lunch and dinner varied from day to day. We ate a lot of stew, sometimes tough roast beef, occasionally pork, even fried pork chops. Almost always we had mashed potatoes and gravy. Vegetables were always canned and included tomatoes, string beans, mixed vegetables, and corn. There was never either fresh fruit or fresh vegetables. Salads were unheard of. The Army cornered the market on canned peaches and apricots. Ice cream was served frequently as was fruit pie. Fresh bread was in abundance. On Sunday nights, we always seemed to have cold cuts—mostly bologna and peanut butter sandwiches, and damned little else.

The mess kits were dipped in filthy, greasy, steaming hot barrels of water, then carried back to the hotel for further washing and scrubbing with a Brillo pad. As far as I know, miraculously, no one got food poisoning or dysentery.

After breakfast, we made our beds any style, mopped the floors, made sure our uniforms were in order and ran downstairs again for formation, where Corporal Henley took over.

What a colorful character Henley was! He had a Boston Irish accent that was marvelous to hear. He also had a string of profanity which must have taken him years to perfect. I had heard all of the words before, but not in the combinations he used. "Son of a bitch" and "bastard" were normal. The favorite Army word, however, was "fuck," also used as in "fucker" and "fucking," "fuck up" and "fuck off." From generals to privates, some combination thereof formed a part of every soldier's daily vocabulary. Another non-profane expression was "G.I.," for Government Issue. All soldiers were "G. I.s." All equipment was G.I. When we were ordered to scrub the floor, we were told to G.I. the floor. If a G.I. had loose bowels, he was said to have had the G.I.s, etc. In any event, Corporal Henley, Regular Army, had held every noncommissioned rank from private to first sergeant. He was bright, effective, communicative, and an excellent soldier, but Henley had feet of clay. He drank. He drank something every day, and always ran out of money about two days after payday. I understand that, upon ascension, he got falling-down drunk and, when this occurred, he sometimes failed to appear for a few days. He went A.W.O.L., wound up stripped of his rank, and usually spent a few days in the Post Stockade. We had Henley for our "D.I." (drill instructor) while he was on his best behavior. I realize, now, that we were never more than overgrown Boy Scouts dressed in Army uniforms, but he had us looking and acting like soldiers within a week. He taught us how to salute, how to walk, how to march, how to stand at attention, how to wear our uniforms, how to recognize Army rank, how to keep our clothing, our mess kits and personal belongings clean, and—most importantly—how to stay out of trouble, other than that which was self-imposed. God knows, he taught us close-order drill. After about the first week, we won the flag as the best drill unit on the beach and kept it as long as I was with the squadron.

Other than Corporal Henley and his instruction, basic training, Air Force Miami Beach basic training, did little to make fighting combat soldiers out of any of us. We carried no weapons. We went to the rifle range two or three times for instruction. No shots were fired at us, or over our heads, not even blanks. None of us ever saw a helmet. We pitched no tents, nor carried a pack on a hike. There were no night problems, nor was there field training of any kind. Guard duty was a farce. We were armed with Billy clubs and wore arm bands which said "Guard," and patrolled around the hotel. There was a reasonably good physical training program, with lots of running around a golf course, but there was no obstacle course. It was true that most of us were supposedly in limited service, which should have eliminated combat, but many of the men I am certain were shipped overseas, and no doubt were exposed to bombing attacks if nothing more.

The Army Air Force was great for classification tests. I wonder what use they put them to. One of my compatriots had been a Kentucky State Highway Patrolman and wanted to become an "M.P." (Military Policeman) which seemed logical. Unfortunately, he was shipped to Cooks and Bakers School. No wonder the food was bad. Another "handcuffed volunteer" had been an auto mechanic, and wanted to either do the same thing in the Army or else become an airplane mechanic. He went to Radar School. Our two hillbillies from Hazard, Kentucky, could barely read and write, and if in fact they were classified for limited service, it would have had to have been because of no brains at all. They became Military Policemen. If those two morons had been given guns, they might well have killed somebody.

The Army was also great on shots and physicals. The first Saturday we were at Miami Beach, we went through a "shot line," where a series of doctors and other medical personnel hit us with the needles as we walked through. A couple of guys passed out. My arms and rear-end were sore. I was not alone. When we staggered back to the hotel, we were told that we were going to have a "G.I. Party." That meant that we were issued scrub buckets, brushes, and Army scouring soap and were ordered to scrub all of the bare floors in the hotel, on our hands and knees. The object was to exercise our arms, or so we were told. We exercised our arms, and most of the rest of our anatomy.

I do not remember the names or faces of any of the men who were in my training squadron. We were all buddy-buddy then, probably because misery loves company. However, a lot of those men received very little basic training and were shipped out early to various Air Corps training schools. Some were discharged as being unfit for military service. Others just drifted along until someone could determine what to do with them. Most of the squadron were from Kentucky or Southern Indiana. Most of them had very limited educations. Several were really too old to have been drafted, and two or three were so obviously physically unfit that they could not participate in marching or any other physical activity. I blame the draft boards for insisting that these poor fellows be required to enter the service. The Army had to accept what the draft boards sent, but they did cull out the worst.

My own basic training was negligible. I do not remember how many days or weeks I actually participated, but I was pulled out fairly soon and sent to a two-week training course on chemical warfare. Upon its completion, I was qualified to be a gas warfare N.C.O. in an Air Corps squadron. The Army fully expected the Germans to use gas and other chemicals against us. We were also advised that the United States was fully prepared to use these weapons against the enemy. I presume, and hope, that we are prepared for this eventuality today. I returned to the training squadron upon completion of the course and was there at least through Thanksgiving.

Thanksgiving was no holiday. We did march to the golf course and drill as usual. But everyone knew that every soldier in the United States Armed Forces was going to have a traditional Thanksgiving dinner that day. The menu was in the newspapers throughout the country and was posted on the door to the mess hall. We were all homesick that day, but were kept in reasonably good spirits with the thought of turkey, dressing, giblet gravy, candied sweet potatoes, cranberry salad, pumpkin pie, etc. Mess hall lines were long and slow, and our squadron was near the end of the line. As the G.I.s came out, they had satisfied smiles on their faces. We finally entered, eagerly holding out our mess kits. We got a Thanksgiving dinner with all the trimmings, except for the main course. The bastards had run out of turkey, so we were served three generous slices of bologna. Bologna does not go well with the remainder of that menu. I think about it every year at Thanksgiving.

A few days after Thanksgiving when our squadron marched back to the hotel for dismissal for the rest of day, I was told by one of the sergeants to step out of line and report to the squadron commander in his office, immediately. I went in, saluted, and said, "Private Clark reporting as ordered, sir," while standing at attention. He looked at me a moment and then said in almost a hushed tone, "Private Clark, you are to shave, shower, dress in a clean khaki uniform, and report to Captain Logsden at the Shoreham Hotel at 1400 hours. Here is a special pass for you; a guard will escort you to the captain." I was nervous as hell. I knew the Shoreham was a very secret, well-guarded establishment further south on the beach. I wondered what anyone there wanted with me. So did the squadron commander, I think.

I walked to the Shoreham and was stopped by guards at the entrance gate at the front of the grounds. I presented my pass and, after a couple of telephone calls, was taken by an official-looking messenger-guard to Captain Logsden's office. Ultimately, I was ushered into a spacious, almost plush, office and came face to face with Captain Logsden. After the salutes, etc., I was told to sit down. The captain eyed me for what seemed like an hour, looked at the file he had on his desk, and started questioning me about my life. He closed the file and said, "We have had your background checked, and wish to place you for service in our Army Intelligence forces." He asked whether I would be willing to serve. I asked him what I would be doing, and where I would be sent. He stated that he could tell me very little except that I would remain in Miami Beach, at least for a time. I was impressed and more than a little afraid, but I told him that I would be willing to serve. He then read to me from something he had on his desk as to the general nature of intelligence work and asked me to take the oath of secrecy. I did and was both more impressed and no less frightened. He then told me to return to my squadron and not to discuss our meeting with anyone. All the way back to my hotel I looked over my shoulder, sure that "the enemy" was following me. Delusions!

A few days later, I received orders to move to the Lord Tarleton Hotel and to report for duty to Lieutenant Hill in the Cadillac Hotel. The Cadillac was headquarters for North Beach. The Lord Tarleton was squadron headquarters where all of the enlisted men assigned to the Cadillac were quartered. The two hotels were adjacent to each other.

Basic training was over for me. I could not have had more than a month of it, and learned nothing very useful, except how to make a G.I. bed, how to hang my clothes and place my other clothing in a footlocker, how to salute and look a little more like a soldier than a Boy Scout. I know what "real soldiers" went through but, fortunately, I lucked out. Some of our experiences were fun and funny. The two hillbillies never took a bath, so at the suggestion of Corporal Henley, the men who bunked near them grabbed them, put them in the showers, scrubbed them with scrub brushes and G. I. soap and then shaved their heads. The hillbillies swore that they would kill all of the participants, but clean and with their heads shaved they did not appear to be much of a menace. Our particular platoon sang in cadence as we marched to and from our training grounds on the golf course. One day we were singing, "Around her neck she wore a yellow ribbon, she wore it for the soldier who was far, far away." We had just come to the words, "Around the block she pushed a baby carriage," and there was this girl pushing a baby carriage. She looked as though some G.I. had gotten her pregnant again. I went on sick call one morning because I had blisters on both feet, and some sadistic medic taped pieces of sponge on the bottoms of my feet and told me to walk about twenty blocks back to the hotel. There was the time when we were marching back from drill when, at my instigation, the platoon chanted in cadence, "Fin, zwei, drei, vier, who's gonna buy the beer? Henley! Henley! Henley! He marched us directly to a beer joint and probably spent his paycheck or his poker winnings buying beer for all of us. It was almost all fun, but, thank God, it was not very much like the United States Army was supposed to be during a major war.

On the appointed evening, I packed all of my clothes in my two barracks bags, tied them together, threw them over one shoulder, and walked the three blocks to the Lord Tarleton. I was assigned to share the "Al Jolson Suite" with five others, three of whom, I discovered the next day, worked in the same office to which I was assigned. The rooms were on the eighth floor facing the Atlantic Ocean and were directly on the beach. The two rooms were spacious and carpeted, with three bathrooms adjacent. We had three beds in each room and two or three armchairs which, no doubt, belonged to the hotel. For buck privates in the Army, we had damned plush accommodations.

The squadron regulations were virtually non-existent or never enforced. Lights were out at eleven o'clock, but there was no such thing as a bed check. Reveille was at five-thirty in the morning six days a week, and roll call at a quarter of six. Not everyone showed up every morning at roll call. We alternated attending and answering for the others. I actually made roll call once or twice a week. The sergeant who handled calling the roll never looked up --well, almost never—and the result was that only about a fourth of the squadron appeared on any given morning. The roll call sergeant had been an associate professor of history at the University of Chicago. One morning he _did_ look up and appeared to go into a complete state of shock. He looked out over his glasses at the small assembly present and in motley disarray and said in very cultured tones, "Nevah, neither heah nor abroad have I evah witnessed such a fucked-up organization as this!" I broke up.

Our schedules for eating in the mess hall were simple. We could eat whenever the mess hall was open. As a practical matter, most mornings I stayed in bed until seven, showered, dressed, and walked to a drug store in the area for coffee and doughnuts. I ate lunch in the mess hall, and dinner either in a nice restaurant or in the mess hall, depending on my current financial condition. Miami Beach was really not much like the rest of the Army. I reported to the Intelligence Unit as ordered. Originally, it was a fair-sized suite overlooking Collins Avenue on the eighth floor of the Cadillac Hotel. The entrance door contained the designation "S-2" (Intelligence Unit). There was a secretary, two other privates, a tech sergeant and two lieutenants. The entire atmosphere was very informal and friendly. I liked everyone there almost at once. That original group was unusual. The first lieutenant had been a Houston banker. He had a Texas drawl, carried himself like a soldier, and looked like the officer one always saw in the movies. The second lieutenant had been a first-rate Georgia lawyer and politician. He was short, smoked cigars, slouched around, had a Georgia drawl, and a way of speaking similar to that of a real Georgia Cracker. The tech sergeant was a dark, slightly-built, sharp-looking, and extremely reticent former detective. The privates were both about my age. One wore glasses, looked like a scholar, had a New York Irish accent and had been a cub reporter on a New York newspaper. The other was a tall, dark, handsome easterner who had attended one of the good small Eastern colleges, and had a master's degree in history from Harvard. He had worked for the State Department in Washington, was surprised that he was drafted, and was not too thrilled about it; but then neither were the rest of us.

Our cub reporter did not stay in the unit very long. He kept saying that he wanted to become a thirty-year man in the Army and wear those stripes "three up and three down" (a master sergeant). He applied for Cryptography School and was accepted. We were told that there might be a house of prostitution in the area, and the former detective and I were ordered to check it out. I wanted to go to the front door, knock and ask, but he wanted to sneak around and peer through windows. He was climbing over a concrete fence when a "hillbilly" voice cried, "Halt!" He kept climbing. I heard a thump, and the voice said "Goddammit, when ah say 'halt,' you bettah halt." It was a basic trainee on guard duty. I'm glad he had a Billy club rather than a gun. As it was, the medics took several stitches, and our intrepid sleuth had his head bandaged for about a week. The next night, I found out the place in question was not a whore house. I damned near got hurt myself when I went to the door and asked.

Howard the Historian and I became good friends and ate together in some of Miami's better restaurants when we were in funds. In the office, we played the horses and the dogs, and bet on the jai alai games. We did not always win on the horses and dogs, but the jai alai was great. Our tech sergeant spoke Spanish like a native and got acquainted with some of the players. I think those games were really fixed. In any event, we usually avoided the mess hall in the evening, and had plenty of spending money.

One night my friend said he had to talk to me. He told me that his O.C.S. application had not been accepted, and that he could not understand why. He asked me to see what I could find out. I checked the next day and discovered to my amazement that he had failed an intelligence clearance. We were all supposed to have been cleared before becoming members of the unit, so I asked for a complete report. It turned out that the Office of Naval Intelligence had checked him when he had earlier applied for a Navy commission and had him listed as "possibly subversive." This was based on reports that he had been quoted as saying that he liked the German people when he lived there, and thought that they were the cleanest, most industrious people in Europe. The O.N.I. report also stated that he was in Germany in the summer of 1939 when war broke out, living well, without apparent income. It was suspected that he was one of the young Americans recruited by the Nazis. When I got this information, I should have reported it to the officers, but I had dinner with him again, and asked for an explanation. He was shocked. He told me that he did like the German people very much, and no doubt had said so, but that he was neither a Nazi nor a sympathizer. He told me that he had traveled in Europe in the summer of 1939 on his mother's illicit boyfriend's money, which had been given to him as a sort of graduation present. The boyfriend was a very prominent, very rich American. I talked with the Georgia lieutenant early the next morning. After chewing me out for not reporting what I had learned earlier, he set the wheels in motion for a complete investigation and report. Thank God, my boy came out clean! The investigators, among other things, interviewed the boyfriend, who confirmed everything and even produced checks which he had written to finance the 1939 summer trip. Our files were cleared, and my friend went to the next Air Corps O.C.S. class in Miami Beach. While there, his commission as a lieutenant, junior grade in the Navy came through and he became a Navy officer.

The Georgia lieutenant was one of the most remarkable, unforgettable people I ever met. When he talked, he sounded like a real redneck, but, in fact, he was very well educated. We kidded him one day about his conversation style and he said, "Aw hell, fellas. Ah kin talk better'n this, but if ah did I wouldn't nevah have got no wheah in politics in Georgia." We brought up the fact that he was close to the top in a notoriously corrupt state administration. He said, "Why sho' we stole, but we nevah took nothin' from the poor."

He was sympathetic to the fact that we were sometimes broke and slipped me an occasional five or ten dollars. He smoked very expensive cigars, kept a box of them in his desk drawer and invited me to smoke them, which, upon occasion, I did even though I did not really like cigars. He did not treat us as some officers treated privates. He was our friend.

One of the duties he and I shared was the supervision of the emptying and burning of all the trash and other contents from any wastebasket in headquarters. At four o'clock each afternoon, we met two colored G.I.s and followed them room after room as they emptied wastebasket after wastebasket into large trash containers. We then followed them to an area away from the building and watched this debris go up in smoke. When the operation was completed, we each had to sign a certification chart in the office of the base commander to the effect that all papers, etc., had been properly destroyed. Christ, what a waste of time! If the Germans and Japanese had been given copies of everything in headquarters, it would not have made any difference in the outcome of the war.

I do not know whether I am still bound by the Oath of Secrecy which I took, but I will not detail what I did while in S-2. I will say that had the Germans and Japanese had access to all of our activities, it would have availed them little. If I had not known who our enemy was, I would have thought we were fighting the Russians. Now, more than forty years later, it seems to me that we were somewhat ridiculous in our activities.

There were a couple of incidents that were a little unusual. We received a telephone call from a squadron commander of a basic training squadron asking that we try to figure out what was wrong with a new trainee who just sat around and cried and jabbered in some strange language. We said to send him down, but he did not show. Finally, he was escorted to our office by a couple of sergeants. He had gotten lost and was found wandering around the Miami Beach streets. The guy was hysterical and obviously scared almost to death. Our tech sergeant said that he was talking in a language similar to Spanish and suggested that it might be Portuguese. We called Army classification and put them in search of someone who spoke Portuguese. In a few days, they sent over a young man from one of the South American countries whose English was a little vague, but whose native language was Portuguese. We then summoned our problem and sat him down for an interview. The South American looked at Lieutenant Hill and said, "What do you want me to ask him?" The lieutenant thought a minute and said, "Well, ask him what the hell?" I laughed. Finally, our problem poured out his story. He was a Portuguese sailor. His ship had been blown up by a German sub off New Orleans, and he was rescued and hospitalized. When he had recovered, he was immediately drafted into the United States Armed Forces. How this occurred, I never found out. He just wanted to go back to Portugal to his wife and children. It turned out that his story was true. He was discharged and sent home.

As though that were not enough, after we had finished interviewing this poor fellow, our South American told us that he should not be in our Army either. He was the son of an extremely high-ranking South American official—a dictator. He had been sent to the States for flight training. How he got in our Army he did not know, but it turned out that our State Department was trying to find him at the urgent, rather truculent request of his father. We got him discharged from our Army quickly and sent him to Randolph Field.

Later on, the office expanded. We got several adjoining rooms on the eighth floor of the Cadillac overlooking the beach and Atlantic Ocean. I looked out my office window one afternoon and saw General George C. Marshall and other high-ranking officers getting sun and relaxing on the beach below. I was certain, at that moment, that I was in the safest place in the world. Three more G.I.s joined our group. One was fat, had flat feet, and was, of course, a cop in civilian life. Another was a young pink-cheeked Jewish kid we made into a file clerk. The third was an older, sandy-haired corporal who had his Doctorate from Yale, and who supposedly was a leading authority on homosexuality. They had sent him in to ferret out a part of a nest of homosexuals in Miami, he said.

He gave us a series of lectures on how to spot them. He said that to the homos, our young pink-cheeked kid would be a beautiful boy. Some months after I left, I heard that our authority and the kid were arrested for homosexual activity.

From the time I got to Miami until almost Christmas, I was homesick. From November to Christmas, every radio and every music box in every bar kept playing "I'm Dreaming of a White Christmas" with Bing Crosby as the vocalist, I wanted to cry every time I heard it. I went to the movies one afternoon when I was supposed to be working, and "investigated" Humphrey Bogart in <u>Casa Blanca</u> with the song "As Time Goes By." That made me sadder. I missed Evelyn, my mother, school, my friends—everything! Miami Beach was beautiful, and I had a good time, mostly, but it was not home. Then I got some great news that lifted my spirits to no end. Evelyn wrote that she was coming down for a week and would arrive on Christmas morning. Unfortunately, she was to be chaperoned by her aunt.

I was up early Christmas morning, shoes shined, uniform crisp, belt buckle shined and properly centered. I <u>looked</u> like a soldier that day. I took a cab to Miami and was early for the train's scheduled time of arrival. It was a beautiful sunny Florida morning, and I stood outside along the tracks. I was nervous and anxious for Evelyn's arrival. I finally went into what I thought was the train station and sat down. It was small, dirty, and dark, with uncomfortable seats. I thought it was sure a lousy station for Miami. Finally, a colored gentleman came over and said, "Pardon me, sir, but I believe you would rather sit in the white station." I was in the station to which blacks were assigned. There were separate train stations in Miami, Florida in 1942. Evelyn's train was very late; I got more nervous and agitated. Finally, it arrived and off she came. It was worth all of the earlier trauma of the morning just to see her! I was not so glad to see her aunt, but hell, without her Evelyn would never have made it.

Her aunt had friends in Coral Gables, so they stayed there. I did not worry too much that entire week about my military duties. I was covered in the squadron, so I could be gone without any problem. My office knew that my girl was in town and did not ask much of me. It was a wonderful time! I do not remember what we did or where we went but the week went all too fast, and I was awfully lonesome and in love all over again.

January and February of 1943 were not dull. In fact, aside from the sign on the elevator doors in the Cadillac Hotel lobby which said

"Ladies, Officers, then you," it would have been almost like having a civilian job in a great winter vacation spot. True, we did work. Sometimes we were required to perform some duty at night. No one was following us around keeping track of our every move. Results were the criteria. Sometimes it was possible to accomplish a lot in a short time; at other times, it took a long time to produce nothing. I had a pass which permitted me, if questioned by the military police, to be any place in the Miami area day or night. Amazingly, I was stopped only once and, after examining my identification, the M.P. saluted me. I returned the salute very snappily. Most privates were not saluted by M.P.s. I applied for Officer Candidate School, met with the examining board, and was approved. I was all set to go to the next O.C.S. class for the Air Corps at Miami Beach. Unfortunately, I could not pass the eye examination. I was discouraged. I could be in the Army, but I could not become an officer. I talked to my two lieutenants. They told me not to worry about it. They would think of something. Between them, I believe they knew everyone having any authority in Miami Beach. One day I was told to report to a colonel in the Medical Corps, who very likely was the Flight Surgeon. He took me into a room with an eye chart. Shut the door and said, "Son, you see that chart, don't you?" "Yes, sir," I said. "Now you know God-damned well that it says (he read the chart), don't you." "Yes, sir!" "Then I do not see any problem with your physical examination. You are approved for O.C.S." "Thank you, sir!" I replied, saluting, and got out of there quickly before he changed his mind. I could see the chart, of course, and could read most of it with my left eye, but none of it with my right eye.

I was eligible to attend any one of three officer candidate schools—Air Corps, Army Administration, and Medical Administration. The Air Corps class had started; I had missed it because of my eye problem. So had Army Administration. I found out that Medical Administration would have a class starting in two weeks. I was so eager to become an officer that I said I would attend it. After all, administration is administration, and my officers assured me that it would not be any problem for me to come back after graduation. I should not have been so eager. Three months was not a long time, and I did not have it very hard where I was. I wanted to get married, though, and thought I could on a lieutenant's pay. At any rate, I was sent to the Army Medical Administrative Corps O.C.S. at Camp Barkley in Abilene, Texas. Christ! Little did I know!

Once again, I packed all of my belongings into my two barracks bags, said goodbye to everyone I knew on Miami Beach, regretfully, and boarded a train Texas-bound. There was a lot of difference in this train trip from my trip from Indianapolis to Miami. I rode in decent trains, unsupervised. I ate my meals in a dining car and had a lower berth the two nights I slept on a train. I enjoyed the trip and checked the scenery as it passed by. For a person who had never been any place until grabbed by the Army, I was becoming well-traveled. As the train pulled further and further into Texas, I began to hum, "The stars at night are big and bright, deep in the heart of Texas." I thought about all of the western stories I had read as a boy and was thrilled that I was finally right in the middle of the Old West.

Abilene, Texas was no Miami. It was a medium-smallish city. Some of it even looked nice. I changed my mind about it the first time I got a pass to get out of Camp Barkley. Just as Abilene was no Miami, Camp Barkley was certainly no Miami Beach. It was a military base in the strictest sense of the word. Primarily, it was an infantry base, and the Army did not believe in pampering the infantry. They were getting those troops prepared to fight overseas and must have wanted them all damned good and mad. The contrast between an Army-occupied hotel on Miami Beach and the barracks at Camp Barkley was overwhelming. This was the real Army life and not another Al Jolson suite. These barracks were typical of those all over the United States. There were two rows of double decker bunks separated by an aisle which ran the full length of the barracks. There was a large latrine with rows of johns, urinals, sinks, and showers. Even so, one had to wait in line in the mornings to use any of these items.

I might have gotten used to the barracks in a few days; after all, most of our armed forces in the United States survived very well on barracks living. Unfortunately, I did not have long enough to acclimate myself to barracks living. All of the members of my O.C.S. class arrived at various times from Thursday to Sunday. We were not required to do anything during that period. However, on Monday morning, things changed rapidly.

We were all assembled, our names were read alphabetically, and we were, arbitrarily, assigned to platoons. Each platoon was assigned to a second lieutenant known as a Tactical Officer (tac officer for short). These people must have all been born tall, handsome, possessing military bearing, and able to wear any uniform attractively. In my opinion, they were the leftovers from the bright people who came out of Officer Candidate School. They would all have been Nazi Storm Troopers had they lived in Germany, and so far as I could determine, were all complete sons of bitches with absolutely no redeeming virtues. The one to whom I was assigned stood out over the rest of his peers. I hated the bastard from the beginning. In any event, we were ordered to vacate the barracks, draw bedding at supply, and move to what were referred to as "hutments." I think a hutment was simply a large hut.

When we had finally carried our barracks bags, bedding, and footlockers the considerable distance from the barracks to the hutment area, we met our tac officer again. He assigned about ten men to each building, told us to make our beds, then tore them all up. We did not know how to make up a G.I. bed, according to him. After we finally suited him on bedmaking, he explained how, and in what order, our uniforms were to be buttoned and hung up. He explained exactly how our footlockers were to be maintained, where our socks, underwear, and every other permissible item was to be located in the footlocker. He also showed us how to tie and arrange our shoes from the front corner of our bed, told us what brand of shoe polish to use, and how to polish our belt buckles. He also explained how the hutment should be swept, mopped, and scrubbed. Finally, he told us about the operation, use, care, and cleaning of the one coal stove we had for warmth. He explained what uniforms we were expected to wear on all given occasions. He did not tell us how or when to brush our teeth, but he did march us to the latrine for our entire platoon, about fifty yards away, and explained to us how to use the showers, how to clean and maintain all of the other equipment and read the daily latrine duty list.

After lunch, our platoon was marched to one of the post's so-called barber shops, where we were lined up and given G. I. haircuts. I think the haircuts were free—at least they should have been. The barbers were probably meat cutters or sheep shearers in civilian life. They were not equipped with the usual barber tools—just clippers and razors. Four snips with the clippers and a couple of cuts on the neck with the razor, and we were through. All of us looked worse than any movie convict or cartoon character I had ever seen.

Abilene and Camp Barkley are located in West Texas, surrounded by miles and miles of nothing. There are few hills, few trees, sparse grass, some brush, and scrub. It is almost always windy. The State of Oklahoma blows into this area one day and blows back the next. The climate is not temperate. When it rains, it pours, and standing in formation, I sank to the tops of my leggings in the mud while the dust and sand from Oklahoma devastated faces and ruined eyesight. There were days when we had to wear gas masks to protect our eyes and faces from the sandstorms. I know that some influential Texas congressmen picked out the location. Either the politicians or one of his important constituents had to own all of this land. Since that time, I have traveled quite a lot, and I am still convinced that this is the place God forgot.

The hutments were small, crude, one-story buildings. The wind came through the walls and windows. The dirt and sand blew in. The stove heated a few of us too adequately, some froze every night. When it was hot, the sun beat down on this treeless, God-forsaken area. There were no fans, and air conditioning was non-existent. The wind blew only hot air. When it was cold, it was freezing; when it was hot, heat prostration was near; when the weather was normal, it was miserable.

Naturally, we all hoped for passes to get away from Camp Barkley and into Abilene on Saturday night or Sunday. Compared to the camp, the town was an oasis. However, it was too small to handle the volume of soldiers who poured into it on weekends. There were long lines to eat in every one of the several lousy restaurants in the town. There were longer lines to get into the town's two small movie houses. There was nothing else to do in the damned place. I went to a steakhouse with visions of a wonderful honest-to-God Texas steak. I got it. It was tougher than shoe leather, stringy, tasteless, and fried to death. I went to a movie, which was a second-rate film. Before the show began, everyone stood for the playing of the "Star Spangled Banner" and remained standing for "The Eyes of Texas Are Upon You." Had I not stood through the latter, I know that I would have created a real mob scene with myself as the victim.

Abilene was dry in every sense of the word. There were no bars, saloons, carry outs, wine shops, or any other legal public or private establishment for the sale or consumption of any alcoholic beverages. Doctor Pepper was the town's idea of strong drink. There were no dance halls, U.S.O. canteens or known whorehouses. There was more action on the post than in Abilene. According to a <u>Sports Illustrated</u> article I read several years ago, Abe Leman, a famous college basketball coach in the Southwest, took a team to Abilene to play a game against Abilene Christian. He told his players that if they did not play a good game, he would lock them out of their motel until one o'clock a.m. Apparently, the town had not changed much over the years.

The classes taken in O.C.S. were easy. We learned map reading, how to use a compass, military correspondence, orderly room procedure and the like. We had lectures and movies on medical field hospitals, stretcher bearers and other phases of being a platoon leader with a medical battalion. We had close-order drill every day and went on a few hikes carrying field packs; crawled underneath barbed-wire entanglements for a couple hundred years and, generally, received instruction which probably would have been useful for an officer in the Medical Administrative Corps on duty in the field.

Every Saturday morning, we were required to stand inspection beside our beds in the hutment. Our clothes had to be hung in precise order with all buttons buttoned. Our shoes were shined and placed in precise order at the end of the bed; we took a ruler to make certain that they were properly aligned. The stove had to be perfectly clean inside and out on Friday night, and then we put black shoe polish on the exterior. Of course, we could not have any heat on Friday night or Saturday until after inspection. We scrubbed the floor on Friday night and then mopped it on Saturday morning. One cold Saturday a little ice formed on one portion of the floor. We had to pass inspection or else we were all restricted to quarters for a week. Individually, we received demerits for either real or imagined personal lapses. Saturday afternoon, weather permitting, we paraded with much pomp and circumstance, and a very good military band. The entire operation, from the tac officer on, was really, to use a well-known Army phrase, "chicken shit." I hated Texas, Camp Barkley, Abilene, the Medical Administrative Corps, and the tac officer. Within a week I wished that I had waited for the next O.C.S. Miami Beach class. I had made a helluva mistake. I did not know what to do to get out of it gracefully. I wanted to be an officer, but not in that kind of setup. I did not want to wash out and was in no danger of so doing as far as I knew. I heard that during the ninth week of the twelve-week course we would be required to take another physical examination. I knew that, if this were true, I could not pass it. I did not want to go through all of that time and then be dismissed, so I requested an appointment to talk to my tac officer. He condescended to see me one evening a few days later. I saw him in what passed for an office near the classroom area. Much time has passed since that night, and much of the meeting, either conveniently or otherwise, is obliterated from my memory. I know that I saluted and then stood at attention in front of his desk for some time before I was instructed to be seated. Before he asked what I wanted, he told me that he thought I had had a totally insufficient amount of basic training and that I was not measuring up in his opinion. I told him that I thought it a little unusual since my grades were good and I had not been chewed on for anything. "Are you arguing with me?" he asked. "No, sir," I replied. It was obvious that I was madder than hell. He asked me what I had done in the Air Force, and I told him that I was in an Army Intelligence Unit. He asked what I did. I replied that I could not tell him. This made him mad if he wasn't already. Finally, he asked me to state my business with him. I asked whether or not we would be given a physical examination prior to graduation. "Yes, in the ninth week, if you last that long," he said. He then asked, "What's the problem? Can't you pass the physical?" All in all, it was not a happy conference. I thought about it for a couple of days and then resigned.

For a couple of weeks afterward, I was in limbo. I had no duties of any kind and was just awaiting orders to be transferred out. Finally, some twenty-eight of us were assembled and told that we were being shipped to the Air Corps Replacement Training Center at Jefferson Barracks, Missouri. One of our groups, First Sergeant Buckley, was placed in charge of us. Most of these men were staff, tech, or master sergeants. All of us were mad, but relieved to get away from Camp Barkley.

We boarded a train at Abilene and traveled to Fort Worth. On the way, we discussed drinking, eating, and having a night on the town in Fort Worth. All of us agreed to get off the train together. We did! I have absolutely no idea where I was or what I did. I know that whatever else happened, I got falling-down, passing out drunk. The next morning, I woke up in a hotel room somewhere in Fort Worth, sick, hung over and willing to die. Our little group saw to it that I showered, shaved, and ate. We then went to the train station, got on a train, and went to Dallas, where we all disembarked again for the day. Naturally, we ate and drank some more, but stayed, relatively, in good shape because Sergeant Buckley had found out that there was a through train to St. Louis in the late afternoon.

We all climbed on the train, the sergeant leading the way, with orders for the previous day's train in hand. Buckley was a huge man with an authoritative first sergeant's voice. The train conductor was short, skinny, and nasty. He wanted to put us off the train until Buckley told him that he would personally throw the conductor off the rear of the observation car. We got most of the space in a sleeping car, and some complaining civilians were moved out and into coach seats throughout the train. We all thought we would be arrested and taken from the train in Little Rock. Nothing happened when we arrived there. We were certain that we would be arrested in St. Louis, and probably put in the stockade at Jefferson Barracks for being A.W.O.L. We were not arrested any place. No one at Jefferson Barracks was aware that we were supposed to arrive, and no one ever checked our orders as to our departure.

Jefferson Barracks is located on the edge of St. Louis. It existed in Civil War days, and perhaps longer. According to everything I had heard, it was really a hell hole, but after Texas, it seemed like heaven to me. The grass was green, there were flowers, trees, shrubs, sidewalks, paved streets, and permanent buildings. The food in the mess halls was good. The weather was ideal. It was early May and lovely. Passes to St. Louis were given to us about as often as we wanted to go.

There was very little for any of our group to do insofar as Army duties were concerned. A sadistic, loud voiced PFC awakened us every morning at five-thirty blowing a whistle loudly and frequently and yelling the same little rhyme every morning: "Drop your cocks and grab your socks." He kept repeating the whistle blowing and the yelling as he walked through the barracks. We all wanted to strangle him. I doubt whether he had any other job assignment all day. We stood reveille at six, had roll call and then were dismissed to wander over to the mess hall for breakfast. After breakfast we scoured the barracks, made our beds, and stood in formation at eight for announcements, orders, work details, etc. I followed the lead of some of my brethren from Camp Barkley who had been high-ranking sergeants in service for a long time and avoided all work by the simple process of hiding. We would go to the dental building and sit on the chairs as though waiting for our names to be called and read magazines. Other days, we did the same thing in the medical building. In the afternoon, we frequently went to a matinee movie on the post which was shown for those unfortunates who were required to work at night. We all volunteered to dig a "deep pit latrine." I wondered why we boys got into that one voluntarily, but I found out. After we dug the damned thing, we hid in it for a week.

Not everything at Jefferson Barracks was so easy. We all had to take shots again. Among the shots given were those for yellow fever. We all got sick, but after all we were in an Overseas Replacement Training Center, and many of the fellows were sure to need every one of those shots later. We were taken to the firing range. I was not familiar with any weapon. I managed to get by with the rifle. Since I had no vision in my right eye, I had to shoot left-handed. The Army .45 pistol was something else. I put the gun in my left hand, sighted at the target and pulled the trigger. The damned gun kicked on me and jerked my arm back in the air so that I accidentally discharged it again. The range officer and range personnel were all ducking and swearing at me. I then fired the Thompson submachine gun. I really riddled a silhouette target, but no one had told me the damned gun rose as shots were fired. My finger froze and I shot more bullets than a mob assassin. Everyone scattered and hit the ground. Finally, I got stopped and the range officer charged me, grabbed the gun, and screamed, "For Christ's sake. Don't ever come near this range again!" I was glad to follow his orders, and I have been afraid of guns ever since.

One night, though, shortly after my range experience, I was made Corporal of the Guard, and was required to wear an Army .45, complete with belt and holster. Usually, the job did not amount to much but, naturally, the Saturday night I drew the assignment there was a helluva racket in one of the barracks and a call – "Corporal of the Guard, post number seven!" I went—scared to death—to a barracks which housed a bunch of Mexicans and Indians from a western reservation. None of them was very bright, and all of them were dirty. All of them were screaming. It appeared that one of the Indians had procured and drank a bottle of whiskey, pulled out a long knife and was going on the warpath. I assembled about five guards, and we all rushed him and subdued him, then turned him over to the M. P.s, who arrived about the time all the trouble was over.

We received some new clothing and new G.I. shoes, but the one thing that did the most to ruin my morale was when I was issued an Army helmet. We had to wear the damned things from supply all the way back to our barracks, about a mile away. The helmet was so heavy, I could hardly hold my head up. It was then that I thought, "My God. I really am going overseas!"

St. Louis was a great town for soldiers. Streetcars were free, movies were full, beer was free at the Anheuser Busch Brewery, baseball games were free, and I was lucky enough to get to see the St. Louis Cardinals several times. There were U.S.O. canteens, good restaurants, and a generally happy atmosphere. I enjoyed the town a lot and went downtown frequently, either alone or with some of my Texas friends.

One morning, several names were called at the eight o'clock formation, including mine. We were told to report to the orderly room. When we arrived, we were advised that we were "on orders" to be shipped out, and to pack our barracks bags (the "A bag" and the "B bag"). I don't remember what we put in which bag. We were then told that we would receive an overseas furlough, to enable us to go home for five days, plus travel time.

I do not remember how long I had to get word to Evelyn and my mother that I was coming home, but I alerted them somehow. God was I glad to see Columbus and my mother, and—most importantly—Evelyn! I arrived on a Friday afternoon at Union Station carrying a small bag containing a change of uniform, socks, underwear, and toilet articles. I traveled light. I knew that my mother was still at work, and that Evelyn had to drive down from Crestline after completing her teaching for the week, so I walked, bag in hand to the Clock—a restaurant that had been in the same location for years. I had a couple of drinks to celebrate my arrival, ate a sandwich to placate my hunger, and just killed a little time. Finally, I boarded a streetcar to Olentangy Village and my mother's apartment. I looked out the windows all the way up North High Street and loved all of the familiar sights. Nothing had changed in six months, and I loved it all. Columbus was home.

Everything, now, is jumbled in my mind from the time of my arrival on Friday until the following Tuesday. The Army had given me five full days at home, plus a day's travel time each way. The time whizzed by. I do know that somehow Evelyn and I were alone in the apartment late on Friday night. I do not know whether my mother had gone to bed or out in order to give us an opportunity to be together. We were together; that was what mattered. We talked, and loved each other, and discussed getting married. Evelyn says that she had to talk me into it, but I think it was a mutual decision and dumber than hell under the existing circumstances. I had every reason to believe that, upon my return to Jefferson Barracks, I would be shipped overseas someplace for the duration of the war. I was a corporal. My gross pay was sixty-six dollars a month. I had about thirty dollars in my possession, and absolutely no other assets. I guess Evelyn must have loved me, because none of this mattered to her. We figured that we could get married on Tuesday. My, how short a time to plan a wedding. Somehow, Evelyn did it. My mother was not overjoyed when we told her the news. She gave us all of the reasons why we should not even think about it.

We drove to Evelyn's parents at Sunbury and told them the next morning. I think that for the only time in her life, Evelyn's mother was speechless for a while. Her father did not seem too unhappy. When her mother started to talk, I got the impression that she was not elated with the news. However, she did start planning the wedding right away. It was to be at their home, only relatives and close friends were to be invited, and it would be on Tuesday night. Evelyn had to tell her aunt and uncle. There was no joy expressed there either. No one wanted us to get married but us.

In any event, we saw the minister, and he consented to marry us. We got the marriage license on Monday at the Delaware County Court House. All waiting periods, etc., were waived for servicemen. We listened to Evelyn's mother and aunt fight over which one of them had promoted our romance and we listened to my mother raise hell, because Evelyn's aunt had said that my mother and I were fortune hunters. We discovered that none of my friends were around and that I really had no one available to serve as my best man. Still the wedding was on. We were determined to get married. Two of Evelyn's friends, Carey and Adele Pace, agreed to stand up with us. Carey had been a friend of Evelyn's from her earliest childhood. I hardly knew either of them, but we have all been very close friends ever since.

Tuesday night finally came. My mother and her boyfriend were my only allies. A few of Evelyn's friends were there, and some of her relatives. Her aunt came reluctantly. We had purchased a wedding ring, and I really am sorry to say that Evelyn had to pay for it. She also bought a new dress and hat for the occasion. I had on a clean set of khakis. There were flowers and one of her friends played suitable music on the piano. The minister pronounced us husband and wife. There was a small reception complete with a cake. Never did two people get married under less-promising circumstances. The only saving grace was that we really did love one another, and still do.

We received the usual good wishes, said our goodbyes, and departed in Evelyn's car for our honeymoon—one night at the Fort Hayes Hotel in Columbus. I do not know today which of us paid for the room. We had breakfast the next morning with my uncle, who wished us well and gave us twenty-five dollars, which was most welcome. He probably did not have much more money than that.

Believe it or not, we went to Beulah Park to the races that afternoon! I doubt that we either made or lost very much, because I have no clear recollection as to how we came out. That night we stayed in my mother's one-bedroom apartment and slept in her bed. This was a highly unsatisfactory arrangement, but we had no place else to go and no money to spend for accommodations.

The next morning, I had to leave my new bride and return to St. Louis. I hated to go. I was sad about everything, and damned sorry to leave her. As honeymoons go, ours was much too short and unsatisfactory. As I rode on the train toward St.Louis, the numbness of the whole thing gradually wore off and I realized that I was a married man with a wife to worry about. I was alternately happy and scared to death. God, I thought, how crazy we were to have gotten married on the spur of the moment, with me broke and—so far as I knew—not just leaving my bride of less than forty-eight hours to return to Jefferson Barracks, but rather to ship overseas. Evelyn really must have loved me very much, and trusted in God greatly, in order to have agreed to go through what she had and what she probably still would go through. When I thought of this, I was very proud and very sad. With my emotions and my thoughts, the train ride to St. Louis was short. All too quickly, I was at Jefferson Barracks again.

There was a note pinned to my bunk in the barracks which said that I was to report to the personnel office the next morning. I thought that I would receive shipping orders then. I spent an uncomfortable night worrying about Evelyn and wondering where I would be sent. The next morning, I reported as ordered, and was told that I had been taken off overseas assignment entirely because of my eyes! The officer had no idea what to do with me. He sent me to see the Post Intelligence Officer who advised me that he could not use me at Jefferson Barracks. The intelligence officer suggested that I apply for C.I.C. School at Fort Custer, Michigan, for training in Military Police Civilian Intelligence. I filled out the application. Days went by and all of my buddies were shipped out. I had nothing to do except wander around the base and go to St. Louis to baseball games and movies. I was lonesome, blue over being away from Evelyn, apprehensive as to what the fates held in store for me, and damned uncomfortable. The barracks had become infested with bed bugs. I remember that they got underneath my skin, and that my legs and body ached and itched. All in all, I was miserable.

One bright morning in early June, I was summoned once more before the personnel officer. "Corporal, you are shipping to Wright Field, Dayton, Ohio." I know my grin must have nearly cracked my face as I said a very unmilitary thing to him – "Oh shit, Sir." Wright Field was only about two hours from home. I could hardly wait to get there. When I arrived, I was amazed at what I saw. It was a virtual city of office buildings, laboratories, airplane hangars, runways, airplanes flying constantly, high-ranking officers visible everyplace. Civilians sat chatting the night away. What sort of place had I come across? When I finally got "up the hill," things looked more familiar. There were soldiers, barracks, a mess hall, and a squadron headquarters. I reported to the first sergeant and was assigned to a barracks and told that I should report the next morning to the personnel office for assignment.

I went to personnel as scheduled and talked with a very knowledgeable corporal by the name of Booth. He looked at my personnel records, said that he did not know anyone had requested an intelligence specialist and then called the Base Intelligence Officer. When he hung up, he was still puzzled but said that the intelligence officer would see me and told me where to find him. He was a major, older, and also puzzled. He told me that intelligence at Wright Field was handled almost entirely by C.I.C. personnel (Counter Intelligence) and that he did not see how I could be used. I went back to Corporal Booth and told him what I had learned. He replied that I could either be sent someplace else as an intelligence specialist or else be reclassified and remain at Wright Field. "Christ," I said. "Reclassify me. I'm only seventy-five miles from home." He chuckled, looked at me and said that he knew Special Services was looking for someone to do some writing and that, with my background in history, he felt that I might be their answer. I said, "Fine, but what the hell is Special Services?" He laughed and said he'd be damned if he knew for sure, that they seemed to do a little of everything. He again called and then told me where the office was and said I was to see Lieutenant Magee.

Magee was a young, boyish-looking first lieutenant with a crew haircut, a nice grin, and a great Texas drawl. He immediately introduced me to a young, muscular, crew-cut lieutenant named Ray Kruse, who was from Colorado, and had been a lineman for Colorado State. We talked for a long time, and I became a friend of theirs that day. I was introduced to the office secretary and to two privates who were all a part of what seemed like one happy family. Magee finally said that they were starting an Army Orientation program wherein the soldiers at the field were to be indoctrinated as to why we were fighting a war. Magee said that they had no idea what to do and no information as to how to do it. He then called Booth and told him to complete assigning me to Special Services.

They gave me a desk, writing material, a telephone, and a lot of conversation about sports. I found out in a day or two that Special Services was to provide athletics and recreation for the enlisted men. For several days I really did not do much of anything except shoot the breeze with the two young officers and ride around the field and Dayton with two privates, Stanfield, and Fox. Everyone was nice to me; everyone was informative and talkative. I discovered that Special Services at Wright Field had become a catchall for almost everything that the Commanding Officer of Wright Field did not know where else to handle whatever it was. (The sentence does not make sense; neither did many of the duties of Special Services.)

There was a specially-equipped gymnasium located in our office building, manned by a corporal who had graduated in physical education from Springfield College in Massachusetts. This gym was for colonels and above who were required to work out two or three hours a week. It had a steam room, massage table, weights, parallel bars, and everything else known to the trade. The corporal gave the high-ranking officers massage treatments and provided them with physical fitness suggestions. This operation was under Special Services. A large gymnasium was being completed on the hill under the supervision of Lieutenant Belew, a tall, thin, erect, serious officer of about thirty, who had a marvelous Tennessee drawl. He and his enlisted men were in charge of the physical training program for the enlisted men. This, too, was under Special Services. Thirty-five-day rooms were under construction for the various squadrons, and barracks were being built to handle the influx of enlisted men expected. Special services were to somehow furnish and equip the day rooms. A theater was under construction. Special Services was to operate the theater, arrange for U.S.O. shows, etc. The 752nd Army Air Corps Band, under the direction of a master sergeant, with a second lieutenant normally in charge, was a part of Special Services. The officer's club was run by a lieutenant who was under Special Services. Later on, we built, equipped, and operated a service club, with donations from Dayton industry; equipped and staffed a library and hobby shop; had a football team, basketball team and baseball team; sports leagues; and a newspaper all under Special Services. Lieutenant Kruse operated Army Emergency Relief out of the Special Services Office. A major was designated as the Special Services Officer, but he was usually someplace else. There was a captain who was a lawyer assigned to the office for a time, who did not know how he got there, and was eventually assigned to procurement as a Contracts Officer. Poor Magee did most of the work, caught most of the hell, and was usually confused. He should have been. So was I. Wright Field was the headquarters of Air Material Command. As I said, it contained huge office buildings, laboratories, hangars, experimental aircraft of all kinds, thousands of civilian employees, hundreds of high-ranking officers – so many officers that we saluted only colonels, generals, Navy captains, and admirals. There were highly skilled lawyers, accountants, and engineers. Technicians abounded. There were excellent airplane mechanics and flying officers, including several really hot shot test pilots who would—and could—fly anything upside down, sideways, straight up, and sometimes straight down. Conservatively, there was a crash a week at Wright Field. We were the experimental and procurement headquarters for the Air Corps.

 The first Saturday after my arrival, and after work, I hitchhiked to the Columbus outskirts where Evelyn arranged to meet me. We drove to her home that evening. She had packed quite a few of her clothes and announced that she was going back to Dayton with me. We visited my mother the next afternoon and drove that night to Dayton where I got Evelyn a room in the Biltmore Hotel. I had to be in the barracks by midnight, so she drove me to the field, made arrangements to meet me the next evening and said that she would look for a room and job the next day. After she left, I got scared about the whole thing. She knew nothing about Dayton and had little to offer the Dayton job market. After all, she was a teacher, not an office worker, a clerk, a waitress, a cook, nor an engineering technician. Where would she look for a room? Where would she find a job?

When I got to the barracks, I found a job for the next day. I had been assigned to K.P. duty. At five o'clock in the morning, I was awakened and worked like the devil all day until eight o'clock that night. I worried about Evelyn all day. I could not call her. I did not know where she was. When I got to the orderly room, I had a message to call my wife. The telephone number was there. I called, and a woman with a heavy German accent answered. I asked for Evelyn, who was soon on the phone. She had found a room and had been interviewed for a job. I arranged to meet her after work the next evening. She had secured a job at Air Service Command, making what seemed to be a fortune compared to her teaching salary. It was all a miracle.

I was permitted to live off-post, since my wife was with me, but I was required to be present every morning at six o'clock for roll call. Evelyn got up, took me to the field, and went back to the room to get ready for work, stopped to eat breakfast and drove back to her job across the road from Wright Field, where she reported for work at eight. It was hard for her, and not easy for me, but we loved it. We were young and in love and never tired then. I ate breakfast and lunch in the mess hall. Evelyn picked me up every evening and we usually ate in one of the many Dayton restaurants before going to our room. We thought life was wonderful, and for us, it was.

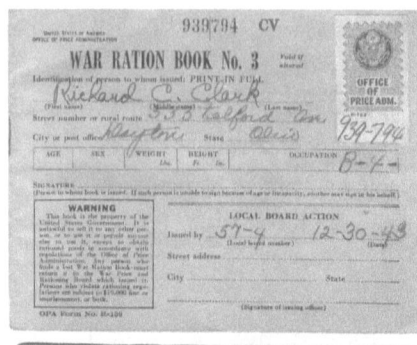

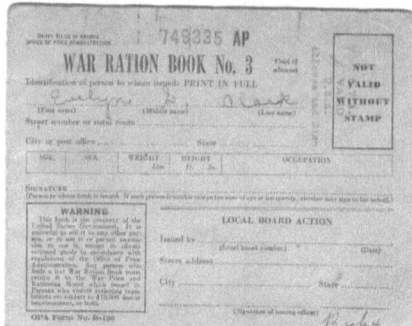

War Ration Book

We could not go home very often on Saturday evenings and Sundays. There was gasoline rationing. But occasionally, we got some extra ration stamps through my mother who was friendly with the guy who ran the Office of Price Administration in Ohio. He was, among other things, in charge of all rationing. In addition to gasoline rationing, there was meat and butter rationing, sugar rationing, tire rationing, and even liquor rationing. In a restaurant, we knew how many ration stamps were required, as well as the price of the meal. Butcher shops posted the number of stamps needed right with the cost of the meat. We managed to do well enough, thanks to my mother's connections. Sometimes the meat selection was pretty limited. Fish cost no stamps. The liquor selection was terrible. I do not know where the good liquor went, but it was not in Dayton, Ohio. I do remember that we could almost always purchase Three Feathers whiskey, which was awful. Naturally, we drank it anyway. It took almost a special dispensation from God to get a certificate to purchase a tire, and when the certificate appeared, all that we could get were recaps made with synthetic rubber.

After I had been at Wright Field for two or three weeks and had become acquainted and learned where everything was located at Wright and in Dayton, Magee gave me information available to him relevant to Army orientation. I commenced work on a rather haphazard basis to put together something for use at Wright Field in the conduct of an orientation program. It was haphazard only because Magee and Kruse both started assigning me some of their work, so I managed to be very busy between research, writing and supervising parts of our Special Services operation. It all worked out well. They made me a buck sergeant after a month or so. By fall, I had completed a book entitled *Orientation at Wright Field*. It was not very good, in my opinion, but my bosses liked it. So did the commanding officer of Wright Field. It was used in the squadrons for a while. After all, it was all that was available, and each squadron commander was required to conduct an orientation course. Basically, all it amounted to was why we were in the war. I was not really too damned sure why we were fighting, but I managed to give the proper historical perspective, and the usual propaganda. In the fall of the year, Evelyn found out about a new apartment development that was being completed. It contained street after street of four-family, one-bedroom apartments with garages underneath. They were all rented, but someone she knew had put up a deposit and for some reason did not want the apartment. We went to the rental office and were able to substitute our deposit, and rented the apartment as soon as it was completed. We, of course, had no furniture, but a trip to her parents', her aunt's, and my mother's homes remedied the furniture problem. Evelyn's uncle, a laborer on his farm, and I took over a load of very used furniture in a farm truck. After Evelyn had purchased slip covers, drapes, and curtains, it looked like heaven on earth to us.

We moved in and settled into the routine of living together in our first home. True, I still had to make early morning roll call, but we were used to that. Shortly after we moved in, orders were issued to the effect that all enlisted men below the first two grades, married or not, were required to live in the barracks on the base. God, what a mess!

As soon as I told my bosses about the problem, they became as mad as I was. "First three grades," included the top three ranks of sergeants, staff sergeants, technical sergeants, and, finally, the highest enlisted rank of master sergeant.

I never knew exactly how Magee arranged it, but I became a staff sergeant practically overnight. I not only got to live off the base, but I received quarters allowance every month, and no longer was required to make early morning roll call. When this occurred, we really had it made as far as Army life was concerned. We lived in our own apartment; our combined salaries gave us a really comfortable income; we drove to work together each morning, and home each evening. It was *almost* like being a civilian.

Socially, we went to the movies, ate dinner out, attended dances sponsored by Special Services, and, when we had enough gasoline stamps, took an occasional ride in the country. We entertained my officers and their wives a couple of times and were entertained by them, even though officers and enlisted men were not supposed to associate. We became very friendly, socially, with Lieutenant Belew and his wife and saw them often. Over a period of time, we became friendly with other G.I.s and their wives. We always had plenty of recreation, entertainment, and social life. We played some bridge, and I played a lot of gin rummy and poker. Some of the poker games were really for far too much money, and it was easy enough to lose ten or fifteen dollars in a gin game.

In December of 1943, the Commanding Officer, Wright Field, decided that Special Services should be located up the hill with the troops. We were arbitrarily moved from our comfortable office into a newly-completed one-story building that resembled a barracks in its architecture. It had few windows, a concrete floor, bad lighting, and worse heat. The winter of 1943-1944 was cold. Our office was colder. It had a concrete slab floor, little or no insulation, a gas blower furnace arrangement and pneumonia potential. I wore long underwear all winter. When it warmed up enough to rain, we were stranded in a sea of mud. When it dried out, the wind blew dust through the walls and windows. It reminded me a lot of Camp Barkley at Abilene.

When a load of gravel was delivered, I told Corporal Fox and

Corporal Stanfield, our two drivers and general handymen, to spread it around in order to get us out of the mud. Stanfield came in about the second day and said, "Sergeant, court martial me if you want to, but my hand don't fit that God-damned shovel." I had no intention of court martialing him, but I had to do something since he was defying my authority. "Stanfield," I said "Where do you want to be shipped?" "Get me a job on the flight line. I'm an airplane mechanic," he responded. I did. About a month later, Stanfield came running into the office so scared he was shaking. It appeared that General Hap Arnold, Commanding General, Army Air Corps, had flown into Wright Field in his converted Barber. Stanfield had entered the plane and through ignorance pulled on a lever which was to open the bomb bay doors so that bombs could be discharged. But, because they had all been wired shut, he caused a lot of damage to the plane. He asked whether I could help him. I called Sergeant Booth, who had become a real wheel in Air Material Command Personnel and was a frequent companion of mine at lunch. He got Stanfield shipped to California the same night. I doubt whether anyone ever knew for sure that Stanfield had caused the damage.

Very early in 1944, Lieutenant Magee attended a staff meeting in the Commanding Officer's office. When he returned, he was glum and very downcast and discouraged. He called me into the small cubbyhole which passed for his private office and told me that a new Special Services Officer would arrive soon, and that he would then revert back from being acting Special Services officer to assistant. He said that all he knew was that the new officer was a captain and that he had completed Special Services School. I felt truly sorry for Magee. He had worked so hard and had accomplished a lot. He wanted the job very badly. He had been wonderful to me and had treated everyone well. A few days later, a captain came into the office and closeted himself with Magee immediately. In a short time, they came out and Magee introduced me to Captain Oliver Joel Hunt. Hunt was erect, about five feet nine inches tall, of medium build, and a handsome thirty-eight years old. He had presence and impressed me immediately. There was no question that a rare one had arrived, and no doubt that our new Special Services officer was a determined, take-charge guy.

I began to find out a lot about him almost at once. He had been Texas A&M's first All-American football player. He was the hero of the 1925 East-West Shrine game. He had played professional baseball for the St. Louis Cardinals and played with the famous Gas House Gang that had won a World Series or two. When he came into service, he had been the head backfield coach at L.S.U. and had previously been the head coach at both Georgia and Wyoming. He was divorced, and the women flocked around him. Men admired him. Joel was truly a man's man, but he was a helluva a ladies' man too.

I found out as time went on that Joel Hunt, despite his fame and glamour, was really a very lonely man. His divorce affected him tremendously. He had a daughter whom he never saw. He told me, in a rare moment of confidence, that his wife could not stand his lack of success at Georgia and Wyoming and the attendant criticism and unfavorable publicity. In many ways, he was a very cold man. In dealing with people, he could be very abrupt, and was personable only when it suited his purposes. I do not believe that he made many friends among the officers. I know that he drank a lot at the Officers Club, but I think that most of the time he drank alone. He trusted few people. He had a good, quick mind, sometimes a quick wit, but he maintained a distance from almost everyone. Whether it was true or not, I believe that he felt that he had been taken advantage of during his years at the top of the baseball profession.

Apparently, he decided to trust me. A week or two after his arrival he said, "Sergeant Clark, I want you to drive over to Columbus with me." Ostensibly we were going to try to pry some athletic equipment out of Capital University and Ohio State. We did talk with the athletic director at Capital University, and the assistant athletic director at Ohio State without much success, but I felt that the captain had anticipated this. During the day, he talked to me about all of our personnel, both officers and enlisted men. I defended Belew, Kruse, and Magee and went over with him the strengths and weaknesses of our enlisted men. He did not say so directly, but I knew that he would replace Magee. We had two other officers who were virtually valueless that he never questioned. Apparently, he felt that they were not a threat to him.

We ate lunch at Hennick's, my old campus hangout, and he seemed amused that some of the old-time waiters greeted me like a long-lost brother. He said that he wondered whether I would have gotten the same kind of greeting from my former professors. Over lunch, he looked across the table at me, his eyes penetrating mine, and said, "Clark, you are to run Special Services on a day-to-day basis. Issue orders, okay supplies, handle the daily correspondence, and, if you get in trouble, I'll back you up!" From then on, under his regime, I did handle the daily operations of the section of Special Services of recreational and athletic facilities and activities. The one or two times I got in trouble, Hunt was as good as his word and backed me to the point of embarrassment. He was afraid of no one.

On matters of policy, Hunt made all decisions. It was up to me to see that his policies were carried out. He did change a lot of things. The Army band became completely independent of our office. Any emergency relief also was taken off and moved in with the American Red Cross office. The Officer's Club was removed from our jurisdiction, as was the officer's gymnasium. He also told Lieutenant Belew to run the physical training program, and not to bother us with it. Belew should have taken the hint and simply asked me to get him such supplies and equipment as he needed but he was too conscientious for his own good. Hunt finally brought in another P.T. officer and Belew wound up as the commanding officer of an all-black maintenance squadron. I felt sorry for Belew, but I also felt sorry for the men in his squadron. It had to be rough on them.

Even after getting rid of all of the above activities, Special Services still was a conglomerate. We operated a newspaper which was published weekly. We provided every squadron with athletic equipment of all kinds, got our motion picture theater in operation, staffed the Service Club with a hostess and W.A.C. assistants, hired a civilian librarian and really had a nice library for those who wanted to read. We set up a hobby shop supervised by an insane G.I. artist who helped with painting, sculpture, and wood carving. We got on the vast U.S.O. circuit and provided great entertainment frequently. We sponsored dances in the gymnasium with Dayton girls for dance partners. The Commanding General, Air Material Command, decided that we should have a "representative" basketball team. We really accommodated him by bringing in college and professional stars from all over the country. We had to provide recreational activities for Vandalia Army Air Base and for a glider base at Wilmington, Ohio. We were busy, but it was fun and a lot of new responsibility for me. After Hunt's arrival, the year 1944 all sort of ran together, things happened so quickly. A headquarters building for Wright Field was completed and all of the administrative staff was moved into it. We had a huge office on the second floor very near the office of the Commanding Officer, Wright Field. Near us were the Red Cross, Public Relations, Administrative Inspector and Station Claims offices. In the building, among others, were the Personnel, Intelligence, Supply, and Maintenance offices for the field. It made it easy to contact the people we needed to see, and everyone became friendly and cooperative. It was the Army, but it was a very gentle version of it.

The Commanding officer was a West Pointer, a pilot, and a full colonel. His name was Rudolph Fink. That name should have made him mean, but he was a very fine individual, and most considerate, so long as everyone did what they were supposed to. He did not have to be a harsh disciplinarian, and his attitude and manner were reflected by his staff officers. It was a relaxed, busy, happy headquarters.

Captain Hunt promoted me to technical sergeant in the spring, which helped Evelyn and me financially and seemed to give me much more prestige and clout at work. There were not too many tech and master sergeants in the Army. Everything went well except one weekend when we had company from Columbus on Saturday night and Sunday. Hunt told me to take Monday off, too, in order to properly see to our guests. When I came in on Tuesday, I was informed that Magee had been shipped out. I never saw him again, and Hunt said that the reason he let me off was because he did not want to argue with me. He quickly replaced Magee with an orientation officer who did get a lot of information out to the G.I.s as to what they were doing in the service, and at Wright Field.

I met a lot of interesting people, some of whom were assigned to Special Services and some of whom were U.S.O. entertainers. Among the entertainers that I actually talked to were Max Baer, the former heavyweight champion, and his brother Buddy. They put on what passed for a boxing exhibition, but they were really clowns. They were as funny to talk to as they were when putting on an act. I supplied Gypsy Rose Lee with Cokes backstage, which she mixed with whiskey. I liked her. She was a good-hearted, down-to-basics old gal to talk to, and when she put on her striptease act, the troops loved it. Shirley Temple came as a young girl of barely eighteen. She was nice, but very nervous, not really very sure of herself. After her performance, we had a dance, and my respect for Hunt increased. A private was dancing with Shirley Temple and obviously enjoying himself. When a West Point major pulled his rank and cut in, the captain saw it, walked out to the dance floor, tapped the major on the shoulder and said, "Sir, you're out of line. Leave this gymnasium. This dance is for the enlisted men." The major started to protest, but Hunt grabbed him, whirled him around and took him to the door, saying as he went past me, "Don't flash that West Point ring at me. I'm from Texas A&M and we've got more officers fighting in this Army than you have." Hunt reported this to Colonel Fink the next morning; the major was shipped out. I had a couple of drinks with Bill Stern, the sports announcer most prominent at that time, but did not like him much. He and Hunt got into a drinking contest later that night and the captain said that I had misjudged Stern. That the more he drank, the less pompous he became.

Special Services attracted characters partly because of the nature of our organization, and partly because personnel sent us several people who were so screwed up that they did not know where else to put them. We picked up our mad artist that way. We were sent a corporal who had been an M.P. but did not fit in because he had a habit of getting drunk and disappearing. He was a sort of handyman, a jack of all trades, so we kept him. He got put in the base stockade for going A.W.O.L. and was busted to private. They sent a W.A.C., blonde, old, with fake teeth, big bust, a lot of makeup, etc., who had been a night club performer who danced in nothing but silver paint. Word came to us from a replacement center that Private Lou Cooper, a concert pianist of great note, could be sent to us on request. None of us had ever heard of him, but we thought that he could be useful in entertaining ladies' groups in Dayton and environs. Lou arrived. He was pale, emaciated, filthy, vague, a total misfit in the Army. Hunt took a look at him, smelled him, and then told me to get him cleaned up. We got him scrubbed, deodorized, and fumigated, had the moss scraped from his teeth, got him new uniforms, and made him shave and shine his shoes. The squadron first sergeant and I explained to him that he was required to perform the acts of shaving, bathing, shoe shining, etc., and the sergeant inspected him every morning thereafter. Cooper looked balefully at me and said, "Someone always took care of these details for me." He could really play the piano and the Dayton ladies were enthralled.

One day a corporal came wandering into our office and announced that his name was Marion Forsman, but "Just call me Bucko." He stated that he had been transferred to us from Procurement and handed me his orders. None of us admitted requesting him, and I still do not know how we got so lucky. Buck was a real operator, and became damned useful to us. He was a promoter who always thought in large terms. Whether he learned it in procurement is doubtful, but he could "procure" anything. He had worked in aircraft procurement as a civilian, had been a bootlegger in Oklahoma, and helped his wife run the biggest dance studio in Tulsa. He took over running our dances, and brought girls out from Dayton by the busload. He promoted himself into conducting dancing classes at the Officers Club, and made a good living from it by working about two nights a week. He knew everything that was going on at Wright Field before anyone else did. Buck drove the newest Chrysler convertible available. (No automobiles were manufactured after early 1942.) He drove around Wright Field with his top down, drinking rum and Coca Cola as he put up posters advertising our activities all over the base. He was also one step away from being in really serious trouble, but always talked his way out of it. After everything had been worked out to his satisfaction, I found out that he had gotten one of our lieutenant's wife pregnant, and—through medication—aborted. He was not allowed to live off the base, but he did. I never knew how he got away with it. He always had plenty of gasoline in spite of rationing. I do not know how that happened either. One afternoon I was screwing off and went to the

Central Tower at Wright Field for a game or two of gin rummy with Sergeant Tiger, who was in charge of the tower. No one knew where I was, I thought. A telephone rang—the call was for me. It was Forsman. He told me he had two phones going and just to listen. His conversation was with his insurance company. He reported that his car had been stolen, and said that it contained,—in addition to his record player—fishing tackle, golf clubs, and God only knows what else—none of which he owned. When he hung up, he said to me, "Christ, isn't that great!" I found out later that he had reported the theft to the insurance company before he called the M.P.s. I always wondered who he talked into stealing the car. Naturally, the car was quickly located, and he received a substantial amount of cash from the insurance company for his "losses."

I got a call one sad day from the personnel office to tell me that Billy Conn the fighter who had been the light heavyweight champion of the world, had washed out of Air Cadets and was available, and that if we could use him, they would requisition him. I talked to Hunt and Magee, and we were all enthusiastic. We thought that he could put on some exhibitions around Dayton, give a real boost to our physical training program, and perhaps—just perhaps—we could work out a rematch with Joe Louis for the heavyweight championship for the benefit of Army Emergency Relief. Conn had damned near defeated Louis in their first fight. He was the "white hope," and a certified hero to sporting America. We got him. He was handsome, had a nice smile, wore tailormade uniforms, drove an expensive car, rented a large home in Dayton, and was absolutely useless to us. He hated the Army, was disrespectful of almost everyone and had too much influence in Washington for any of us to even attempt to discipline. Everybody was either a bum or a "shit bum." The only man I ever heard him say anything nice about was Joe Louis. When he talked about Louis, there was a little fear in his voice and about all he said was "Yeah, he hits hard." I knew that if he ever fought Louis again, he would lose. He did. We set up a three-round exhibition between Billy and an M.P. who had been a third-rate fighter. The poor guy was delighted to get in the same ring with Conn. Billy cut him to ribbons on purpose. We set up no more exhibitions. We tried to arrange a fight with Joe Louis, who was willing, but after being approved through all military channels, such a fight was disapproved by Henry L. Stinson, Secretary of War. I wish I had had brains enough to keep all of that military correspondence. It would be interesting reading today. We tried to interest Conn in setting up a boxing program as part of physical training. He about drove poor Belew crazy, but no program was produced. The only really good that we got out of Billy Conn was access to an unlimited supply of gasoline ration stamps. I don't know how he got them, but he seemed to have more stamps than the government had ever printed. One lucky day, a notice came across my desk that the Chemical Warfare Service was going to make a movie and needed experienced actors. I knew Conn had been in a couple of second-rate movies, so I asked him whether he would like to go to Camp Aberdeen, Maryland, and star in the film. Thank God he liked the idea. We got rid of him. I do not know what happened to the movie; Billy might have disrupted the entire project.

We had a short, fat, curly-haired Jewish kid who had the greatest smile—almost angelic—and the nicest personality around. His name was Leonard Axebrand, and he was a walking ambassador of goodwill. When the G.I.s saw him, they automatically felt better. We sent him to Vandalia Air Base, and there were a lot of happy soldiers there as a result. He came over about once a week, took everything we gave him, and stole whatever else he needed.

At Wilmington, we had an equally fat guy by the name of Stelwein, who had been a professional magician in civilian life. He, too, was a great asset and equally as entertaining as Axebrand, without the happy appearance. Stelwein was not happy. Like most of us, he did not volunteer for service, and waited for the day when he could get out. He published a mimeographed newspaper for the benefit of the G.I.s and officers at Wilmington that was great. I read it every week, looked at his cartoons, laughed at his own personal column entitled "Tough Stuff by Stelwein." It was the greatest job of bitching every week I ever saw. He should have been a national columnist. I know people would have read his work and felt better, because he felt worse than they possibly could have.

Captain Hunt was also a personality. Our office was on the

colonel's intercom system, and the box sat next to my desk. One morning, about an hour or so after we were supposed to be at work, the colonel's voice came over the intercom saying, "Captain Hunt." Hunt had not surfaced yet, so I assumed he had had a hard night someplace. I answered and said, "He is not here right now, Colonel." The colonel told me to have Hunt call when he returned. About a half an hour later, the colonel's voice came on again asking for Captain Hunt. I replied that he had not returned. The colonel said, "Where is he, Sergeant Clark?" I replied that I was not sure, but that he might have gone to Vandalia or Wilmington. There was a pause, and then the colonel said, in a rather exasperated tone, "Find him, sergeant, and get him in here at once." I was scared, afraid the captain was in trouble. I went to the Bachelor's Officer's Quarters (B.O.Q.), got Hunt out of bed, showered, and shaved and into the office sustained by one cup of coffee. Hunt got on the intercom saying, "You wanted me, colonel?" "Captain, where the hell have you been?" demanded the colonel. "Sir, I was God-damned drunk last night, and I've been sleeping it off." There was a pause and the colonel said, "Report to me immediately." When Hunt got back, I asked him what happened. He said, "Nothing new, sergeant. I just got my ass chewed out." All of the young secretaries were enamored with him and dropped by almost daily to say hello. He usually said, "Back up here, honey, and let me give you a little pat. They did and loved it. So did he. He always had a bottle of rum in his desk drawer, and every afternoon whoever was around played "King Bee" to see who bought the cokes to go with the rum. Colonel Fink even participated occasionally. Hunt knew all sorts of star athletes and an unlimited number of football coaches. Mickey Cochrane, one of baseball's Hall of Fame members, was managing the Great Lakes Naval Training Center's baseball team. Hunt called him and chatted on a friendly basis a couple of times. He talked with Ben Hogan on an equally friendly basis. Others called him from all over the country just to chat. The captain, Major Bill Wood, the station claims officer, and I played the football pools on college games every week in the fall. We did well. Hunt knew about the teams in the South and Southwest, Major Wood picked them in the East, and I took care of the Big Ten. One week, we had a game on the west coast that none of us knew much about, so Hunt picked up the telephone and called the head coach at U.C.L.A. to get the required information. It turned out that this coach and Hunt had been assistant coaches at L.S.U. at the same time. It was a wonderful experience for anyone as interested in sports as I was to be associated with a man like Joel.

Major Wood was quite a personality himself. He was much older. He had been a Washington attorney prior to the war. His wife had died, so he pulled strings to get into the service. He had been a star tackle at Princeton in his teens. He flew as a member of the Lafayette Escadrille in World War I and wore his old-fashioned wings on his uniform. He had flown with General Hap Arnold and, whenever Arnold came to Wright Field, he and the major got together for a drink and a chat. The major had a Virginia drawl that was wonderful to hear. He was bald and fat with a cherubic red face. When he became either angry or excited, he could be heard throughout headquarters building. Because of his obvious influence, no officer on the field, regardless of rank, was ever anything but friendly and respectful toward him. He came to our office almost daily for a little conversation and relaxation. Occasionally, he just came in, sat down, and took a nap. He liked Hunt and me, and the feeling was mutual. Later on, I was thankful for his friendship.

In the summer of 1944, Captain Hunt, returning from a staff meeting with the C.O., told me that the colonel wanted to see both of us the following afternoon. Hunt did not know why, and I sure as hell didn't. I was a little nervous. I had never had a meeting in Colonel Fink's office before, or, for that matter, in any other colonel's office. When we arrived, I was immediately relieved. I think the colonel must have sensed my uneasiness. He asked us to be seated, grinned at me, and said, "Sergeant, have a cigarette. I really want to talk to you, but I want Captain Hunt to hear what I want you to do, so that there will be no misunderstanding between the two of you." He then said that he was going to turn over an abandoned mess hall to us for conversion into a club for non-commissioned officers. He said that it would have to be for staff tech, and master sergeants only, since there were so many corporals and buck sergeants. He said that he wanted me to call a meeting of all first three grades to determine how much interest there would be in such a club, and then he said, "I want it to be nicer than the Officers Club, with a damned sight better food." He also said for us to let him know what we needed, and he would see that we got it.

A meeting was held and there really was a lot of enthusiasm among the first three grades for an N.C.O. Club. One staff sergeant came to me after the meeting and told me that he had been a club manager in civilian life and would love to run our club and help organize it. I got him transferred to us immediately and put him to work. God, he was good! He worked out everything needed for a complete club facility.

Hunt and I decided that we needed money for decorating, furniture, and equipment. He told me to see how much I could raise in Dayton without his help and said that it would look better if no officer was involved. I knew how money had been raised earlier, so I called the General Motors vice president in charge of the Dayton G.M. plants, one Charles Wilson—not "Engine Charlie" of Eisenhower fame. He gave me an appointment for the next morning. His office surprised me. It was small, old-fashioned, and very unpretentious. He listened to me politely and said, "I think that a total of fifty thousand dollars should do it; sit still and let me see what l can do." He turned to an old-fashioned upright telephone and called the Chairman of the Board of the National Cash Register Company, one S.C. Allyn. "Chick," he said. "I've got Sergeant Clark in my office. He needs fifty thousand dollars for an N.C.O. club at Wright Field. I'm going to give twenty thousand. I think you should talk to him and do the same thing. I'll call Dayton Power. They ought to give ten thousand. When can you see the sergeant?" He hung up and called the president of Dayton Power and Light and told him about the same thing. Appointments were made with both Allyn and Dayton Power. The Dayton Power president was not overly happy to see me, but did agree to give the ten thousand. Allyn was quite cordial, talked to me for a long time and told me to come back on Friday afternoon at two o'clock for a check. When I went back, his secretary took me to where the N.C.R. Board of Directors was meeting, and ushered me in. Allyn had his feet up on the long, impressive table, obviously waiting for me. He said, "Gentlemen, this is Sergeant Clark. We're giving him twenty thousand dollars today for an N.C.O. club at Wright Field; I just wanted all of you to see where the money is going." With that, he gave me the check. In a matter of a few days, I had raised fifty thousand dollars.

Needless to say, with that money we furnished and equipped the club in a first-class manner. But how could we afford to operate it? Hunt kept telling me not to worry about it, he would take care of operating money when the time came. One day when we were getting close to being ready to open, Hunt called a Cajun he knew in New Orleans and told him that he needed a planeload of slot machines. The Cajun, a New Orleans gambling king and racketeer, agreed to donate them. Hunt took a cargo plane to New Orleans and returned with about ten or twelve slot machines, nickel, dime, and quarter play. We put them in the bar on his advice, and our money worries were over. The club opened, and it really was nice. Our club sergeant had hired a chef from one of Dayton's best hotels, we had G.I.s as waiters and kitchen help in their off-duty time. The food was excellent, decor nice, the service good.

Our bartender mixed great drinks, and, thanks to the slot machines, it was all dirt cheap. It sure beat the mess halls and the civilian cafeterias. The place was crowded every day for lunch; the sergeants dropped in after work for drinks and snacks. Dinner was served on Friday and Saturday nights by reservation only. Dances and parties were held frequently, card games went on constantly. The place was a success, the food so good that the colonel had to issue an order preventing officers from eating there. He was happy, and so was I.

Wright Field Dayton, OH

Wednesday night was poker night, or whatever kind of card games the members wanted to play. I played in the poker game every week. It was a stiff game for any of us. You could bet a dollar anytime, and there was no limit on raises. I took twenty-five dollars with me every week, and one time was back home, broke, before Evelyn even knew that I had left. I won a lot more times than I lost, though. Some of the players were either not very good or overly optimistic. One night I won enough for Evelyn and me to take a furlough and spend a first-class week in Washington. Unfortunately, I got most of it from our first sergeant, who was being honored by us with a farewell dinner because he was being shipped overseas. When the game was over, he still owed me quite a bit of money, which I never expected to see. He sent me a money order for all of it from California his next pay. I never have forgotten this. There are a lot of good, honest, honorable people around.

There has always been an expression to the effect that the sergeants run the Army. With the inception of the N.C.O. club, and our getting well-acquainted with each other, we sergeants had a lot to do with running Wright Field, insofar as our own self-interest was concerned. We helped each other. If someone had a hard time with an officer, the officer very often was suddenly transferred. Our first sergeants and sergeant majors took care of us in the squadrons so that we had very little of the "chicken shit" part of Army life. The supply sergeants kept us in whatever we needed, usually to operate our offices without too much red tape. The administrative inspector's sergeant kept us advised as to when to expect to be checked on. The sergeant major of the medics saw to it that we got proper medical attention without going through the pain in the neck known as sick call. For those who were technical people, everyone cooperated. We were better organized than the West Pointers.

Generally, the spring, summer and fall of 1944 were good to me. Considering the fact that I was in the Army, I lived well, had little or no military discipline to put up with, made a lot of friends both among the officers and the sergeants. Actually, I enjoyed myself, although I knew, as did we all, that there was only one rank above a five-star general, and that was a civilian.

About December of 1944, I got a grim reminder that I was really in the Army. On Saturday afternoon, I found out that Wright Field was "frozen." No enlisted man was permitted to leave the base. But Evelyn and I had friends coming from Columbus to spend Saturday night with us and I wanted out. No one seemed to know what it was all about.

My squadron commander told me he could not let me off base when I called him. I asked him who could get me out, and his reply was, "No one but Colonel Fink, sergeant." Taking my life in my hands, I walked down the hall to the colonel's office, and asked if it would be possible for me to see him for a minute. Thank God I knew all of the people in his office. In about five minutes, the colonel, himself, came out and told me to come in. I was scared, but I told him the problem. He looked at me, grinned and said, "Sergeant, if I let you out, will you be at your squadron headquarters at five-thirty tomorrow morning?" I promised I would, and he wrote out a pass which got me out the gates. We had quite a time that Saturday night, but I was at squadron headquarters on time, sick, hung over and apprehensive. It was a cold, windy, dark morning, but the entire squadron was soon assembled. We stood at attention until the squadron commander put us at ease. He then said, "Those whose names are called, fall out and line up on the left next to the orderly room door." About fifty names were read, but mine was not among them, fortunately. Those men were shipped out that day to an infantry replacement center. We had lost so many men in the Battle of the Bulge that fresh basics were needed. Those poor bastards had never had infantry training, nor combat training, but they were equipped and shipped to Europe two or three weeks later. Several were killed, including the sergeant in charge of our post theater. The Germans almost broke through them, but, surely, the men they took from us that morning could never have helped solve the problem. Sending them into combat was murder.

The year 1944 ended with a wonderful party at the N.C.O. club. Much drinking and dancing, a beautiful refreshment table with figures sculptured in ice, large bowls of fresh shrimp and other delicacies. It was a great way to end what, for me, had been a very good year in the service.

The first few months of 1945 were not so good for me personally, although the year itself turned out to be great.

Our commanding officer, Colonel Fink, received an overseas assignment which suited him perfectly. Since he was a West Point career officer, I hope he made general because he was a fine gentleman, a credit to West Point, and an excellent commanding officer. However, the colonel who succeeded him was different. He wanted to pretend Wright Field was a real, honest-to-God military base, and did his best to convert what had been a very efficient, happy engineering and experimental air base into a modified prison camp. One by one he shipped out the officers who had served as headquarters staff and replaced them with a bunch of military jerks from his previous command at Lincoln, Nebraska.

Everything became very formal, and very "G.I. real chicken shit." For example, in the headquarters building there was one large men's room on each floor, used by officers and enlisted men alike without any dire results. He ordered them to be partitioned, with two doors, one reading "officers," the other "men." We laughed about that one. As changes were made and his version of discipline installed, the men became sullen and disenchanted. Efficiency dropped. Instead of complete cooperation to do the best job possible, there was a silent rebellion. When the engineering and experimental specialists complained to their officers and civilian bosses, and when some of the so-called "military obligations" prevented these men from performing their real jobs, word came to the colonel and his officers from on high to cut out the crap, and many of his orders and regulations were rescinded, but a lot of them were not. The result was that our "sergeants protective association" went to work in order to assure our own survival, and to louse up the new regime as much as possible.

As a part of the new order, Captain Hunt was shipped out. He got further Special Services training and then was to be sent overseas. It suited him just fine, but I really hated to see him depart. He was a good friend, a good officer, and wonderful to work for and be around. Special Services had really progressed while he was in charge, and everyone had enjoyed their duties and worked hard to make a success of the whole program.

The captain was replaced by one of the commanding officer's cronies, Major Norman Perry—a real, first-class, revolting son of a bitch. Perry was of medium height and build, with a moustache just a little larger than Adolph Hitler's. I actively disliked the man at first sight. He had been a lawyer in civilian life and, I'll bet, not well-liked by other members of his local bar association. He had no background in athletics and recreation, but immediately commenced changing things. I tried to tell him a couple of times, as did some of the remaining officers, that he had inherited a truly fine program and that it would be wise to leave things alone. We were, in effect, told that when he wanted our opinion, he would ask for it. Naturally, we shut up and let him go ahead and screw things up. The office was run in military fashion. He even lined up the desks in rows, not for efficiency, but because they looked better. He was God, and all communications came to him through proper channels. Those methods might have been all right in an infantry battalion at the front, but I doubt it. At Wright Field in athletics and recreation, they did not work. It was not possible to plan for a dance, a U.S.O. troop, an intramural league or distribution of new library books in the kind of routine that dumb bastard set up.

There had always been a miraculous method of stretching a three-day pass into five legitimate days off, if one were a "first three-grader" and a friend of the squadron sergeant major. One got assigned for squadron duty as Charge of Quarters (C.Q.) on Tuesday night from six o'clock until seven o'clock Wednesday morning; a day off followed such duty, so the three-day pass was for Thursday, Friday, and Saturday, and Sunday was a day off. I wanted to see the district basketball tournament at home because Grove City had a good team, so early in March I availed myself of the "three-day pass." My friend Forsman had taken one look at Major Perry and got himself transferred to squadron headquarters to replace the departed sergeant major. Evelyn and I were staying with my mother and Forsman knew it. On that Friday the telephone rang in the apartment, and it was Forsman. He was horrified. "Dick, my God, that damned Perry just sent word up here that you are available for reassignment," he said. "Buck, you mean I'm getting fired?" I asked. "I guess so," he replied. Thought I ought to tell you. Maybe you should come back and do something." "No, screw him," I said. "Buck, I'll be in on Monday, and we'll think of something."

I was shocked. I did not tell Evelyn much about it, but I knew that there was a good chance that I would be shipped out, perhaps overseas. I thought, the hell with it, enjoyed the tournament, and had a good five days.

On Monday morning following my "three-day pass," I went to work, early as usual, determined to act as though everything was as it usually was after I had been away for a few days. As the others came in, I tried to act normally, but I felt an air of tension—perhaps imagined. By the time Major Perry arrived, I was at least pretending to be busy at my desk. He nodded and went to his own desk. Eventually, I have no real idea now how much later, the major said in a loud voice," "Sergeant Clark, report to my desk at once." I stood, walked back to his desk, now two rows removed from mine, squared my shoulders, saluted, and stood at attention. He said in a nasty tone loud enough for all to hear, "Sergeant, you disappoint me. You're taking off duty for five days on a three-day pass is irresponsible on your part. You were being considered to become the colonel's sergeant major. Now I have made you available for shipment. I'm going to give you twenty-four hours to find some other spot for yourself on the Field, and if you don't, I'll see that you are shipped out immediately. I don't think there is much room at Wright Field for tech sergeants trying to transfer. What do you think of that?" He should not have asked. His tone, his sarcasm, his god-like attitude had me so angry that I lost all reason, and blurted out, "I think you're a no-good son of a bitch, sir." "Sergeant," he sputtered, "for that I will probably have you court martialed. You are dismissed." I saluted, did a proper about-face, and left the office amidst complete silence.

I went to the men's room, remembering to enter the door marked "men." I rinsed my face in cold water, smoked two or three cigarettes, and tried to calm down. What to do? I had no good idea immediately. I thought about seeing Sergeant Bothe in personnel but decided I had better try to keep myself from getting court martialed first. Major Wood was one of the few of the old guard left. The new colonel did not dare bother him. Major Wood was also chairman of "Carts and Boards" at Wright Field. I did not know whether these duties covered my situation or not, but I went to his office. He greeted me warmly and asked me to sit down. As I did so, he said, "Sergeant, you are clear pale. What's wrong?" I told him the entire story. His big face got red, and he yelled in his normally mad tone of voice, "You're right, sergeant. He is a no-good son of a bitch." He then added to my relief. "Don't worry about getting court martialed, sergeant. I'll take care of it. The bastard ain't gonna do nothin'."

He then asked me to go with him for a cup of coffee and, after a while, he asked, "Sergeant, what are you going to do?" I told him I didn't know. He asked me whether or not I was friendly with Captain Cribbs in the administrative inspector's office. When I told him that I was and that we rode to or from work together occasionally since he lived on the same street I did, the Major said, "Let's go see him. He has a special assignment. Major Applegate screwed up, and Cribbs is supposed to straighten out Base Maintenance Supply records. It looks like there is a big shortage."

When we went into Captain Cribbs' office, the major said, "Sergeant Clark just got fired. He needs a job quick. Can you use a good man?" "Clark, what the hell happened?" Cribbs asked. I told him. He laughed and said, "Okay. You are no longer unemployed. I'll take care of your assignment right now. Come in here after lunch. I'll have your new assignment orders ready." He shook his head and laughed again as he said, "You're the first guy I ever heard of who was looking for a job in the Army." I thanked him, and thanked Major Wood, and walked out relieved.

That afternoon I reported to my new boss. He already had my orders for reassignment to his special duty unit. He grinned as he handed a copy to me and said, "Sergeant, take a copy of these orders to Major Perry, and tell him that they are for his records." This was actually not necessary, and Captain Cribbs knew it. He also knew that I would enjoy delivering those orders.

I went down the hall to my old office and very formally asked to see the major. When he condescended to me, I stood in front of his desk, saluted, stood at attention, and said, "Sir, Captain Cribb told me to deliver this to you." He took the envelope, read the orders, looked up at me and said with a little astonishment in his voice, "Sergeant, you did pretty well at that, didn't you?" I smiled, said "Yes, sir," saluted, and got the hell out of there. The major and I were almost through, but not quite. Early that summer I got the bastard!

I returned to Captain Cribbs' office. He then explained that the base maintenance officer, Major Applegate, was supposed to be transferred out to an overseas assignment and had been relieved of his duties but could not leave because the necessary audit of his records failed to locate several hundred thousand of dollars' worth of equipment, supplies, and inventory for which he was responsible. No one knew whether there was wrongdoing or sloppy record-keeping, but it was our duty to investigate, locate what we could and try to find out what did happen. It was quite an assignment, but Cribbs was brighter than hell and well-trained in accounting and auditing. I knew nothing about either, but I loved to try to solve mysteries, had two good feet and permission to use a jeep when necessary.

The next day we moved out of Headquarters Building to the maintenance supply office. Cribbs went to work on the record-keeping, and I went snooping all over Wright Field, Vandalia, and Wilmington. I was scouting for large items which were "missing," such things as large electric motors, huge ceiling fans, tremendously large blowers, furnaces, two tractors with sundry equipment; and even a coal unloader and conveyor. There were many, many similar items that I do not now remember.

When I first looked over these lists, it seemed obvious that none of these items had been carried away in someone's pocket, nor in the trunk of a car. The damned things were around someplace. But where?

I spent all of the spring of 1945 looking and locating. Each item found was a triumph. I got well-acquainted with every part of Wright Field from building basement boiler rooms to ceilings to roofs. I was in unauthorized, top-secret areas that I knew nothing about. I was in all of the airplane hangars. I was everyplace. Gradually my list dwindled as I located item after item. I was convinced, and so was Captain Cribbs, that Major Applegate was guilty of no wrongdoing, but only of stupidity and sloppy record keeping. Finally, we had a tragedy at the Field. A bomber crashed into a hangar and blew up the hangar and killed quite a few people. Cribbs and I decided that the remaining items on my list were in that hangar—some probably were. So, we surveyed them, and Major Applegate was released from any further accountability and shipped out. Our job was complete.

We expected that Captain Cribbs would return to the administrative inspector's office, and that I would probably go with him. Instead, Cribbs and I both went to base maintenance supply where the captain was ordered to set up a proper record-keeping system and I was to serve as his administrative N.C.O.

During the spring of 1945, two major historical events occurred to affect us all, and, indeed, to affect the world. In April, President Franklin D. Roosevelt died of a stroke at the Little White House in Warm Springs, Georgia. In newsreel pictures of him during the 1944 presidential campaign and, later at the Yalta Conference, he looked to be terribly ill, old, pale, and exhausted. He probably should not have run for reelection to a fourth term. Nevertheless, the world was shocked, and the American people felt sorrow and were apprehensive. He had been President for more than twelve years. We trusted him and relied on him. He had given us a father image. He had led us from the deepest Depression, into war, and almost to victory. His death truly marked the end of an era.

Harry S. Truman was sworn in as President of the United States. Truman was not well-known to us. He had been chairman of a Senate committee which investigated inefficiency and graft in the armed services and got some headlines as a result. We heard that he had been a part of a very corrupt political organization in Missouri. We were afraid. Harry did not look or sound like a President of the United States.

In May, the war in Europe ended with the collapse of Germany and the end of what was left of Italy. V.E. Day was a happy event for the entire nation, but it was really a great thing for everyone in service. We knew that with victory in Europe, the end of the war was not too far away. The sobering fact was that, while we appeared to be winning in the Pacific, the Japanese were still fighting hard. We knew that many more of our troops would die before victory was finally achieved. Nevertheless, Hitler and Mussolini were both dead, and the reign of Nazism and Fascism was over.

It was in May of 1945, shortly after V.E. Day that Evelyn and I went to Washington on my poker winnings from the first sergeant. We had our honeymoon then, two years late. We stayed at the Willard

Hotel at Major Wood's suggestion. It was still a fine hotel, full of history. It has been torn down long since. We saw all the historical sights, and I was absolutely thrilled. We ate in fine restaurants. Thank God that I had drawn that fourth ace.

While we were in Washington, we called one of my fraternity brothers who was stationed as a Navy officer at the Navy Department. Bill was a genius. He was the guy who took eight years to get through college and then got both his bachelor's and master's degrees at the same time in chemical engineering He later stayed in the Navy and retired as a Navy captain. In any event, Bill came to see us and have some drinks with us at the Willard. I asked him what he had been doing in the Navy. In his loud voice, he replied, "I've been in civilian clothes as an associate professor at the University of New Mexico. Here's my faculty card." He then went on to tell us that he had been working with a group of scientists, whom he named, on a "secret project." "I can't tell you about it now," he said, "but you'll hear about it before long." Had there been spies in the Willard corridor, they would have known about the atomic bomb.

The early summer of 1945 was rather dull for me. I was surely no authority on recordkeeping, but it was my job to supervise about thirty civilian employees who spent their days posting entries on Cribbs' new ledger cards. The captain did not have much more to do than I, and we sort of took turns thinking of excuses to get out of the office. We were marking time, waiting for the war to end. I went to the N.C.O. club for lunch every day, and our group of sergeants still connived on ways to preserve ourselves from putting up with the commanding officer's efforts to make Wright Field a proper Army facility.

At a stag party at the club one night, as the sergeant major of the medics and I were drinking and playing gin rummy, he said, "Your old friend Major Perry is up for promotion to lieutenant colonel, and he is taking a physical." "Where are his records?" I asked. "On my desk in my office. I suppose you would like to see them. We got into his car, drove to the medical building and he said, as we stopped, "Take my key. I'm not going in and I don't want to know anything about it." I found the file and buried it some place in the voluminous annals of medical records. I don't know whether they ever surfaced again. The next day, however, I talked to my buddy in Air Material Personnel, and he managed to get the good major shipped out for an assignment overseas. I do not know whether his records ever caught up with him or not, and I have often wondered whether or not he ever got promoted. The sergeants, in many ways, really did run the Army.

One hot August afternoon I was swiveling in my office chair about half awake, with the radio turned on low, when the musical program I was listening to was interrupted with a news bulletin. The first atomic bomb had been dropped on Japan! When the devastation was described and I heard that the research on the bomb had taken place in New Mexico, I knew what my Navy friend had been telling me in the Willard Hotel Washington. I also knew that the war would probably end soon. None of us thought of the consequences. We knew nothing about the frightening possibilities of the Atomic Age which would ensue. With the dropping of the second bomb, we knew that the war would be over very soon. I think that we felt relief and joy rather than anything about the horror of what had happened.

Peace came very quickly. The personnel sergeant and I had lunch at his request, and he said, "Get your classification changed quickly if you can. All administrative N.C.O.s will soon be shipped to discharge centers to supervise the discharging of the entire Army." He suggested that I have an eye examination.

I called my friend, Staff Sergeant Miller, who was an optometrist. His home was in Dayton and, even though he was severely disabled, he had been drafted and assigned to Wright Field. At that time, optometrists could not be directly commissioned as officers. I told Miller I wanted an appointment to have an eye examination as soon as possible. He asked me if it was an emergency, and I told him it was, that I would explain only when I saw him. We arranged to have lunch the next day and then go to his office for an exam.

At lunch, I explained to him that I needed to get my classification changed quickly to avoid discharging everyone else. He asked whether I did a lot of paperwork or not and I lied and told him that I did.

He examined my eyes and asked me several questions. He was extremely formal and professional in his office. He said, when he had completed the examination, that he might be able to help me, but that he was not sure. He told me that he would get in touch with me as soon as he could. I was not encouraged.

After the examination, I went to the office and tried to work. About a half an hour after my return, I received a telephone call. It was Miller. He said, very formally, "Sergeant Clark, this is Sergeant Miller. The Flight Surgeon wants you to report to him immediately." I was scared. I thought that I might have gotten Miller and myself both in trouble.

I hurried to the Flight Surgeon's office and was met by Sergeant Miller, who ushered me into the presence of the most military-looking "chicken colonel" I ever saw. I stopped upon entering, saluted, and stood at attention. The colonel smiled and said, "Sergeant, for Christ's sake, sit down." I collapsed. The colonel looked at my records briefly, and said, "Clark, how in the hell did you ever get in the Army?" "Sir, how the hell do I know?" I replied. He chuckled and asked, "Would you like to get out?" I did not hesitate as I replied, "Yes, sir." He told me that he was sending me to the hospital at Patterson Field for examination by an ophthalmologist stationed there, and said, "If his findings agree with Sergeant Miller's, you will be discharged immediately." I do not remember what I said, but I went back to my office in a daze. I told Captain Cribbs, and he was pleased for my sake. I called Evelyn at the office and got her excited. I did no more work in the Army.

The next morning, I picked up my medical records and was admitted to the hospital at Patterson Field. Like all hospitals, I had to go through the complete routine, complete with a bed and the works. In a day or so, I saw the ophthalmologist and he told me that I would be discharged. In a matter of two or three days I was a civilian. My God, all I set out to do was to see whether I could get reclassified from what was probably the most desirable classification an enlisted man could have to something less. Instead, I got the ultimate classification Civilian!

The period from 1942 to the end of the war changed us all. Most of the young men of America were in military service. Many were in combat; many died. Their parents, wives and sweethearts were affected too, because someone important was absent.

Many women who had never thought of working outside the home took jobs manning our industrial plants. It marked the beginning of woman's changing role from that of mother, wife, and homemaker to that of a competitor in the job market. The family traditions which had governed America commenced to break up as a result of the war effort.

The Great Depression ended. It is true that it took a war to employ the resources of the country. There was full employment for the first time in a decade and a half. We were once again a prosperous nation, but the cost was staggering.

We were the dominant nation in the world, both economically and militarily. Our allies were in terrible shape. England, particularly London, had been devastated by bombing. France had been occupied by German troops and was deeply divided politically. Russia had lost millions of men. All three were virtually bankrupt. Germany was in shambles. It was occupied militarily. Its cities had been bombed to ruins; its young men dead or crippled as a reminder of Hitler's Third Reich. Italy was poverty-stricken and revolutionary. The Japanese fared better. They had lost much but, except for the complete ruin of two of their cities by our atomic bombs, otherwise unscathed. General McArthur ruled the country as an absolute monarch. We lost many men in dead and wounded, but our homes, our farms and our factories had not been touched by war. Indeed, our factories—and our technical and mechanical skills—were at a peak never previously attained.

During the war, the hardships at home were negligible compared to those of the rest of the world. Yes, we had rationing. We could not buy all the meat, sugar, and butter that we wanted. New automobiles were not available, nor were new tires. Somehow, the old automobiles continued to run. We recapped our old tires with synthetic rubber. We did not drive our cars very much for pleasure. Liquor rationing was in effect too, but it always seemed that it was possible to buy some kind of booze with a high alcoholic content. It didn't always satisfy the palate, but we drank it anyway. Cigarettes were in short supply for the civilian population, and even those of us who were in service had trouble finding the brands we wanted. But a cigarette was still a cigarette, and all of us who smoked got enough nicotine.

We saw a lot of movies, most of them forgettable. Many male film stars, including James Stewart, Clark Gable, and David Niven, were in the military. *Casa Blanca* with Humphrey Bogart was probably the best film made during those years. Bing Crosby and Bob Hope carried on as usual. I remember that Lauren Bacall emerged as a young star. Betty Grable was the G.I.s pin-up girl. Jane Russell was a young starlet and quite a pin-up girl too. A great musical starred James Cagney as George M. Cohan in *Yankee Doodle Dandy*.

Some of the hit songs that I recall included "Paper Moon," "Deep in the Heart of Texas," and "Paper Doll." Two of the really good songs were Bing Crosby's "White Christmas" and "As Time Goes By." The big dance bands still played regularly, and swing music was very much in vogue.

Life went on during the war, somewhat differently, but no one at home suffered very much. Although most of the great athletes were in military service, the competition was still good, and sporting events of all kinds continued to be popular.

I think that the moral standards of the country suffered and changed. There were a lot of unfaithful wives and girlfriends at home. There were a lot of unfaithful guys in service and away from home too. Divorces became much more common than they had been. Adultery and promiscuity were rampant everywhere. The general attitude seemed to be that tomorrow might never come.

Yes, the war changed us all for better or for worse, and there has never since been a turning back of the clock to those rather naive years of suffering through hardships without complaint, of fearing God, and trusting one another very much. We had suddenly become an older, more sophisticated nation.

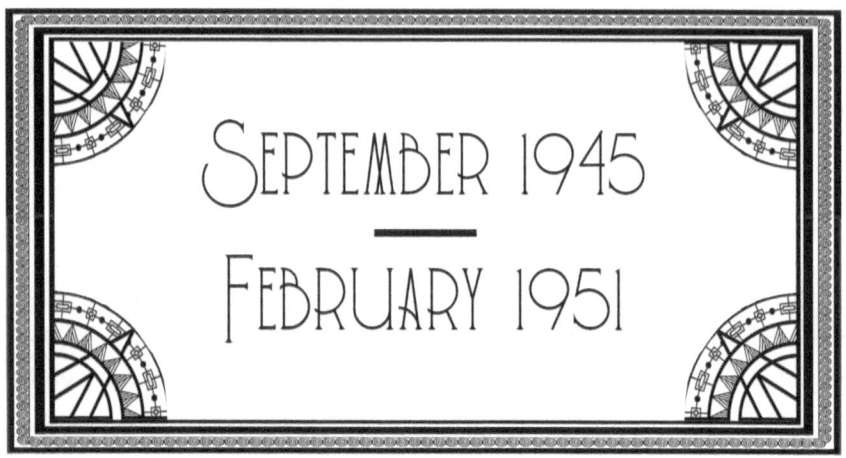

September 1945 — February 1951

Things moved rapidly for Evelyn and me from the moment that I knew that I would be discharged. I contacted the superintendent of schools at Grove City to confirm that I could return to teaching at my old job. Perhaps I should have talked with some of the business leaders in Dayton who had been friendly to me when I was in Special Services, but I wanted to go home and find my roots. I bought civilian clothes, including two expensive (for that time) suits. We went to Grove City and found a house. We said goodbye to Dayton and to our friends there and moved from our apartment. When we got in the car to leave, Evelyn burst into tears. That apartment was our first home, and we were happy there.

The Army experience that I had was generally a happy one. I met a lot of interesting people. I learned discipline. I had much valuable experience. I had quite a lot of responsibility. I learned how to handle men and situations. The only thing that I did not enjoy was that, somehow, I always felt as though I were in prison, because I could not come and go, and do, as I pleased. Being in Dayton was a wonderful thing for Evelyn and me and our marriage. We were really on our own. Neither my mother nor her family could, or did, tell us what to do or how to do it. We became self-sufficient, responsible adults. We depended on each other and, because we were away from home, grew very close.

3618 Connor Street

The little house we rented in Grove City was near the edge of town, almost directly across the road from the cemetery. It was a small, four-room cottage (3618 Connor Street.) Naturally, it was painted white. It had a full basement and a coal furnace, which I had to hand fire. There was no thermostat. One attempted to control the heat by opening and closing a draft. One also shoveled ashes and carried buckets of them outside to a pile at the rear of the lot. We used the furniture that we had accumulated from our families when we set up housekeeping in Dayton and supplemented it with other odds and ends that we either bought cheaply or appropriated from our relatives. One of the great purchases was a very much-used gas stove, which had an oven door that would not stay closed until Evelyn tied its handle to a brick. It may not have looked like much, but she baked some good things in that oven. Evelyn got curtains for the windows and when we were all straightened up and ready for family inspections, we thought it was a palace. Our rent was thirty-five dollars a month.

Grove City had not changed much from what it had been when I first saw it. The population had remained about the same. All of the local businesses were still in operation and mostly owned by the same people with whom I was familiar. The racetrack was still in operation. The farmers still came to town on Saturday night. The local library was still upstairs above the ten-cent store. The beer joints were still in their old locations. I was once again at home.

Going back to my old teaching job was a thrilling experience. Almost all of the teachers with whom I had taught were still there. The redheaded coach and I both got back from service at the same time. Although he had been overseas, he had not changed. The man who had been superintendent of schools when I taught had taken a better job elsewhere, and one of the teachers had taken over as acting superintendent.

The building and classrooms had not changed, and there was no more equipment or supplies available than there had been the first day I taught there. The textbooks were the same dull, inadequate books that I had used earlier. But somehow, the teachers appeared to be more prosperous, more confident, and happier than I remembered. The students seemed well-dressed and, to me, brighter scholars than I remembered. The end of the war was a happy time for everyone. It was a particularly happy time for me.

I was a much better teacher than I had been previously. I did not take myself as seriously as I had earlier. I was older. I was used to giving orders in such a way that they were carried out without question or argument. Discipline was no longer a problem. I did not expect as much from the students and, hence, got more out of them than I expected. Teaching was fun.

Everything in life was fun then, except for payday. My salary for the school year 1945-1946 was fixed at nineteen hundred and seven dollars. Evelyn and I had made more than twice that in Dayton with our combined incomes. My salary first paid for the essentials, and we were forced to live frugally. At Christmastime, we both took jobs as extra help in Columbus' largest department store. Evelyn continued to do this type of work during the winter and did some substitute teaching in order for us to keep afloat. Nevertheless, we enjoyed ourselves. Gradually my friends were being discharged from service and returning home. There were quite a few get-togethers. The food was usually potluck, and whoever came brought whatever they wanted to drink. We saw all of the high school athletic events, and usually got together after each game. We played cards with our friends and served them coffee and an inexpensive dessert. We did not go out for dinner, saw few movies, and generally found extremely inexpensive entertainment. We could not afford to do more.

The war had changed many of my friends. Of course, they were older and more mature, but most were much more serious. Some became very introverted. Some could not adjust to civilian life. One or two were in a strange world of their own.

From having known these men before they went into the service, when they were still overgrown kids, I was astonished at what they had done during the war. One was a battalion commander of an armored division which fought its way through Europe under General George Patton. Another liaison officer with one of the Chinese armies. Yet another received the Air Medal with two oak-leaf clusters for flying over Germany on bombing raids as a volunteer ordinance officer observer and for defusing an unexploded bomb which dropped on the air base where he was stationed. One had been in the Navy, though never on a ship. Each one had war stories to tell, but few really wanted to talk about anything that had happened from the time of their entrance into military service until their discharge. None of them seemed very interested in how I fought the battle of Wright Field.

As I said, the students seemed so much brighter, so much more cooperative, so much more willing to work and to learn that it was a joy to teach them. There were some very good athletes in school that year as well. The redhead took over his coaching duties as soon as he got back. The other English teacher had coached the football team for two years without any help after I left and had started fall practice. The boys were in pretty good physical condition, but they really did not know much football. I helped out quite a lot, and we soon had a team together that, after it once got started, went on to win a championship. The coach ranted and raved and yelled and swore very much as he always had, and the football team accepted it.

I was the idiot who got in trouble, not the coach. I had scouted one of the teams we played. They had a good passer, and two ends who could really catch the ball. We handled them very well during the first half of the game by blocking their ends, and then laying on them. Their passer had no one to throw the football to. The second half, a redhaired referee, doubtless alerted by the opposing coach, called a penalty on us for defensive holding. Of course, he was right, but I felt myself almost propelled out onto the field as the referee was stepping off the fifteen-yard penalty, yelling, "Why don't you mark off fifteen more, you redheaded son of a bitch?" Naturally, the referee just kept walking - fifteen more yards. I was no hero.

The basketball team had been coached for three years by the geometry teacher—a little short, fat, bald, nice, quiet fellow. He had been a coach, successfully, years before and had formerly coached the girls' basketball team at Grove City. He did very well and had one team get to the regional finals in the state tournament. His coaching style and the redheads were different. The basketball team had become used to his gentle, softspoken, low-key approach. Now they got a loud, profane chewing-out on a daily basis. There was a rebellion. On several occasions, the boys came to me to complain, and I interceded for them. Finally, the coach and team got used to one another and went to the district finals. Grove City was proud of its athletic teams that year. They should have been.

Early in January of 1946, Evelyn decided to drive to Florida with her parents who were to spend the winter there. She planned to take three days on the way down, a couple of days in Florida, and then return home on a Greyhound bus. I was a big boy and could certainly survive those few days. Or could I? There were floods in Kentucky, and they were stranded for several days. I do not remember how long she was gone – perhaps two weeks, maybe three. I got very lonesome. When Evelyn climbed out of that bus, I was really happy to see her. Needless to say, she was a basket case from riding on a bus for that long. She had B.O., her ankles were swollen, her back hurt. She was a wreck. She has not been on a bus since that time. It was amazing how close we had become after less than three years of marriage.

Evelyn's 1940 Ford coupe still was our only transportation. Automobiles had not been built since 1942, and by the end of 1945, only a few token models had reached the showrooms. The rear springs collapsed on the Ford; we could not get new ones. Replacement parts were not in production. An alley mechanic and a blacksmith combined their talents and created what passed for a rear spring. I do not know how it was constructed, but the entire back end of the car was raised to the point where the occupants were riding on a downward slant. It was unusual looking to say the least and produced the roughest ride I ever had in any motor vehicle except an Army truck.

As I have said, repeatedly, Evelyn and I were truly happy with our lives. We loved our little cottage, we had a lot of friends, I enjoyed teaching, and Evelyn enjoyed playing housewife. We had some money in the bank, which we had saved while we were in Dayton. Hamburger and chicken were cheap then. We had a wide variety of hamburger and chicken dishes. We wore nice clothes; the car still ran. Life was good to us. I intended to try to get a different teaching job for the next year and hoped that I could go to work for the Columbus school system. We did not want to move, but my salary was totally unacceptable.

One morning in early March 1946, after I got my mail out of the school mailbox, I glanced through it on my way to my registration room. Included in the school mail was a written teaching contract for the next year. I put it in my pocket until I had some free time in which to read it, but I did think it a little unusual because it was the first written contract I had ever been offered. When I had a free period, I read the contract, and discovered that my salary for the next school year was cut to eighteen hundred dollars! I thought that the office had made a mistake, so I went to the school secretary and learned that all of us were being required to take a cut in pay because the Board of Education did not have enough money to pay any more. I told the secretary to tell the superintendent that I definitely would not return the next year and I added that, if I could find a job, I would not even finish that school year.

I talked with the school administration in Columbus about a teaching job but did not receive much encouragement. I then heard that the United States Veterans Administration was hiring people for employment in all sorts of positions. The V.A. had set up a large office in Columbus.

I went in and filled out a job application. An interviewer in the personnel office referred me to the head of Education and Training. I had a job immediately as a Veterans Administration training officer, at a starting salary of thirty-six hundred dollars a year. I thought that I was rich. Needless to say, I quit teaching within two weeks. I never taught again.

I thought then, and I think now, that teachers' salaries were, and are, totally inadequate for the amount of education, training and dedication required of anyone in the teaching profession who really prepares himself properly to do a decent job of educating young people. When I started, many people went into the educational field only because there were few jobs available in anything else. Some became teachers because they were truly dedicated and, in the alternative, others because they felt totally inadequate to handle any other employment. Today, I am very concerned that only the less fit is finding their way into teaching. The result of all of this is that the young student is not receiving a first-class education. Standards for teacher certification must be raised, and teaching salaries must be substantially increased, regardless of where the money comes from.

The United States Congress, in anticipation of assisting the returning veterans of World War II to complete their education and training interrupted by the war, passed two pieces of legislation. Public Law 346 applied to any honorably-discharged veteran. Public Law 16 was for the benefit of those who had developed some degree of disability, either physical or mental, as a result of their military service.

Local Teachers Leave To Accept New Positions

RICHARD CLARK

Richard G. Clark, teacher of history and P. O. D. in the Jackson Township High School, resigned his position here and left Thursday for Columbus. He will enter the branch office of the Veterans' Administration there as a training fa-

Public Law 346 paid for books and tuition for any veteran attending any school, whether college or trade school. It also paid a subsistence allowance for those enrolled in a full-time educational program. In addition, any veteran engaged in training on the job was entitled to receive a subsistence allowance as well as any tools or other equipment required. It was a great thing for most of the many thousands of veterans who took advantage of it. A lot of men received a free college education who otherwise would never have been financially able even to step on a college campus. Many others received adequate training in trade schools or apprentice programs to provide them with skills necessary to secure well-paying jobs that never would have come their way without such training.

Article about Richard.

Public Law 16 provided all of the same benefits as did Public Law 346 and, in addition, gave the disabled veteran a higher subsistence allowance, guidance, counseling, placement training in facilities suitable for them depending upon their type and degree of disability. It also provided for such personnel as might be required for their supervision, encouragement, and assistance of all kinds. But, because both Public Law 346 (always referred to as the G. I. Bill) and Public Law 6 (the Educational and Vocational Rehabilitation Act) were often abused, training officers were hired to make certain that the veteran got the education and training for which the government was paying.

I was sent to Dayton for two weeks of orientation and training for the work which I was to perform, as were perhaps seventy-five other newly-hired training officers from all parts of the southern half of Ohio. I was puzzled as to the qualifications and criteria for the job. Many of us were college graduates. Quite a few had never attended college. I do not think that any of us knew anything about vocational training. During our two weeks' stay, we learned surprisingly little. I do remember that, typical of governmental agencies, the emphasis was on the proper compilation of various forms.

I was really sweating out where I would be assigned. It could have been in any county in the southern half of Ohio. On our last day of training, assignments were given and, fortunately, I was sent to the Columbus office as were many others in the group. Some of them who came to Columbus, however, lived far away from the central Ohio area.

I reported to the Columbus local office eager to get to work, as did the others. The offices occupied an entire floor of an old building at 209 South High Street. Several training officers there had been hired earlier. Most of them were older, veterans of World War I. It seemed to me that their main qualifications were that they had some political influence and were members of the long-standing American Legion. There was a secretary's pool, a file room, and numerous offices for us with three or four desks in each office. One of the older Legionnaires, who was definitely a politician, was in charge. He had a small private office overlooking High Street, with a reception area and a secretary. His assistant was a young redhead who had the adjacent office, with a reception area and a secretary. As nearly as I could ever determine, the boss did damn little, other than serve as a gladhander. The redhead did the work and held the office together.

The boss greeted us with a speech full of patriotism and compassion for "G.I. Joe and G. I. Jill" and then turned us over to the redhead, who promptly told us that no files had been received from the regional office in Cincinnati, and that he had no idea when we would actually go to work, or who would be doing what. He suggested that we make ourselves at home, get acquainted with one another and with the secretaries, and stay out of sight as much as possible. We had all gotten used to this sort of thing when we were in the service. None of us had any trouble entertaining ourselves, and we did get acquainted.

Stories about how each of us won the war flowed freely. Most of the group had been officers during service. Their ranks ran from colonel to second lieutenant. Only three of us had been enlisted men but, after a few days of close association doing nothing, service rank, heroism, medals, and other tales of similar ilk made no difference to anyone.

We, of course, discussed what we had done in civilian life before the war. Several of us had taught school. One had been a coach, another had taught agriculture, another had been a high school principal; there were mathematics teachers, science teachers, etc. The only teacher qualified to supervise vocational training was the ag teacher, and when we were finally assigned, he did supervise agricultural training in several counties. In addition to our teachers, there were two pharmacists, a hardware store worker, a sheet metal man, a couple of youngsters who had not really held any kind of full-time job, an accounting major, and a former employment office employee. None of us was equipped for what we knew we would be required to do if assigned to the supervision of active job training. Those of us who had taught school could have done well handling the problems of those taking college and business school courses. We had no trouble staying out of sight. We took extended lunch hours. We went for rides. We went to the movies about once a week. Several of us took in a couple of matinees at the burlesque house located about a block away.

The entire operation was a complete boondoggle for a while. We all got tired of loafing, and had almost exhausted places to go, movies to see, and places to eat. Finally, everything in the way of files came in at once. The redhead worked night and day preparing the caseloads for assignment to us. He did not do a superior assignment job as far as I was concerned. My cases were all on-the-job trainees scattered all over the Columbus area, engaged in learning widely divergent trades. I had trainees in carpentry, cabinet-making, sheet metal layout, plate glass installation, auto parts location and inventory, appliance repair, sign painting, tool and die making, electric motor repair, and on and on. I did not know a damned thing about any of these trades. I would never know whether they were being trained properly or not for the skill they wished to acquire. All of the other training officers were in the same situation.

I visited all of my trainees and their employers solely for the purpose of introducing myself. The trainees were all on disability. From their test scores as shown in the files, quite a few of them were not overly bright and—to my considerable amazement—several were drawing disability pensions and were in training under Public Law 16 because of varying degrees of psychoneurosis. Others had sustained genuine war injuries, ranging from having only one arm to having no legs. Only a few had been placed in really genuine apprentice programs. Those few who were lucky enough to have become union apprentices needed little supervision from me. Many of the employers were hostile, either because they did not want to be bothered with government red tape, or because they were not really providing training. Many, particularly those who had agreed to train men on the G. I. Bill, were simply using these men as a source of cheap labor. Any training they received was pure coincidence.

I was not aware of a lot of these things as a result of one visit, but as I saw them month after month, I realized that, as most of the on-the-job training was concerned, the government was wasting a lot of money without accomplishing the purposes of the programs. Employment was provided for some who might not otherwise have been able to secure jobs. I talked this over with the other training officers, and they all had similar feelings. I talked with the supervisors and, in effect, was told not to worry about it, but just to make sure that I got the monthly reports required from both the trainee and the employer. This was probably the right solution. Had we insisted on bona fide training as we should have, in theory there would have been a lot of veterans, many with young families, without employment of any kind.

The spring of 1946 brought the news that Evelyn was pregnant. We were both ecstatic at this news. Most young marrieds are with the news of the first pregnancy but, frequently, as pregnancies continued, the news becomes less and less thrilling. We were young. I had a good job, we lived in a little white cottage and life was good. I do not remember any of the rainy days—only the sunshine.

That summer brought another great change to my life. One of my best friends was then, and is now, Tom White. We had been friends from our days at Indianola Elementary. We were fraternity brothers in college. Before the war grabbed him, he had been attending law school at The Ohio State University. His father had been an extremely prominent lawyer and politician in Columbus and was well-known throughout the state. I drove Tom home late one afternoon from a golf game, and as he left, his father rushed out to the car and said that he wanted to talk to me. He told me that he was afraid that Tom would not return to law school in the fall. Tom was just back from the service, had purchased an automobile with his poker winnings, and was spending his time catching up on raising hell. He had an opportunity to get a job in the Veterans Administration, and Mr. White was very afraid that he would take it. He then asked me to consider attending night law school at Franklin University, and told me that if I became a lawyer, I could practice law in his office. He said that he felt sure that, if I would start law school, Tom would return.

I had always thought about becoming a lawyer. In my choice of careers, it was second to that of becoming a college professor. I thought that, if I could practice in Mr. White's law office, I would certainly make a lot of money. After all, Mr. White was successful — I thought. I talked to Evelyn about it that same night. She was enthusiastic, and so was I. We both knew that my Veterans Administration job would not last forever, and I did not want to return to high school teaching at a starvation salary. Shortly after I went to work for the V.A. The Ohio State University had called me and offered me a job as an instructor in the history department at a salary of eight hundred dollars a quarter with the opportunity to work toward a Ph.D. I turned it down, and I now felt that, by doing so, I had ruined any chance I might have had to get into college teaching. There probably might still have been good opportunities for me in Dayton through the contacts I had made when I was in Special Services, but I should have explored them at the time of my discharge. It seemed logical to become a lawyer.

In any event, I checked with Franklin University College of Law and found that I could be admitted. I also learned that classes were held on Monday, Wednesday, and Friday evenings from six until nine o'clock. I finished working at five each evening. Getting from my place of employment to the Y.M.C.A. where classes were held, together with the fact that I had to eat, was going to be difficult. I would have to do a considerable amount of studying on the nights when I was not in school and on weekends. I talked this all over with Evelyn and she encouraged me to go ahead.

Had I really known all of the difficulties involved with being on such a schedule, day after day and week after week, I probably would never have started. The courses were not easy and required much study and concentration, but they were the least of my problems. It was an endurance contest. I ate hamburgers at a little sandwich shop near the Y.M.C.A. three nights a week. Occasionally, I varied this with a waffle and sausage. I got tired both physically and mentally. Evelyn was alone most of the time, and she became tired of the routine too. Many students dropped out of school, not because of the difficulty of the courses, but because of the confining routine. Many, many times I thought about quitting school, and probably would have had it not been for my pride. I did not want anyone to be able to say that I couldn't make it through school.

Franklin Law School was strictly a night school. When I enrolled, it was not even accredited by the American Bar Association for the reason that it did not have a full-time faculty, and its library was not satisfactory. I do not really know the history of the school. It had been in existence for a long time before the war. Interesting to me at the time was the fact that more than a few very successful Franklin County lawyers and many judges had received their legal education from Franklin.

The teaching staff consisted of Columbus lawyers actively engaged in the practice, state officials, and judges. The instruction I received was, by and large, first rate. The "case book method" was used in every course of instruction, which simply meant that we were required to read actual cases (legal opinions) covering the particular subject which we were studying. In each class, when called upon, we were required to recite the facts, the decision, and the rule of law. A very serious, very dignified judge taught the course on contracts where we were required to stand up during our recitation. There was never any fooling around in the judge's class; woe be unto him who was not properly prepared.

By the time I completed school some four years later, Franklin was hiring full-time instructors in an effort to comply with American Bar Association requirements. The result was that the quality of instruction was diminished. But we had had the claims manager of an automobile insurance company for a course called "Torts." A tort is simply a wrong done by one person to another; but of course, he covered the law of negligence and personal injury. A former county prosecutor from a small Ohio county taught criminal law. A lawyer with a large probate practice taught a course in wills and probate procedure. One trial lawyer taught evidence, another taught pleadings and trial practice. And so it went throughout the four years. With one or two exceptions, we received first-class training. No wonder Franklin had had only one failure on the state bar examination in about twenty years. Of course, enrollment in the school was not large until after the war, when the veterans hit the classrooms. In the 1960s, Franklin Law School was absorbed by Capital University, and ultimately became the Capital University College of Law with both day and night classes.

I enrolled in the school for a six-weeks course in the summer of 1946. Naturally, I took advantage of the G.I. Bill, and the Veterans Administration paid for my tuition and books. I was not entitled to a subsistence allowance because I was not a full-time student. There were no full-time students at Franklin Law School. Everyone that I had any contact with worked, and almost everyone worked full time.

Competition in the classroom was excellent. Most of the students were veterans. Those who were not were serious enough to pay their own tuition and purchase their own books, which were not inexpensive. Everyone in school was intent on graduating or they would never have started. No one would undergo that routine who was not serious. After the first year, and into the second year, the mortality rate was extremely high. Most of those who departed did so because of the extreme hardships attached to the routine. There were, of course, quite a few who could not do the work even though they had successfully completed at least three years of study in a college or university. There was no deliberate effort made on the part of the faculty to establish a high attrition rate. It just happened. We all fought for survival.

Evelyn with Marcia Jo

Richard with Marcia Jo

In December of 1946, Evelyn and I had our first child, Marcia Jo. I took Evelyn to the hospital in the middle of the night, and was completely scared to death that she would go into labor on the way to the hospital. We were still driving Evelyn's 1940 Ford with the homemade rear spring, because we could not find any automobile dealer who would sell us a new car. Even on the smooth road to the hospital, in the Ford the ride was rough and bouncy. With every bounce she groaned a little, and I became more nervous. Naturally, I went to the wrong door at the hospital before I finally got her admitted. It was several hours after her admission before she delivered.

Having our first child, as with almost everyone, changed our lives. If we had not been in love with each other before, we were now. We thought that our daughter was the most special child ever born, and that the entire event was a very close second to the birth of Jesus. When I was at home, which was not very often, I carried the little girl around on my shoulder so carefully that one who did not know better, might have thought she would disintegrate into small pieces. Evelyn was no longer lonely. The child occupied her time and my thoughts. If I had not known it earlier, it was brought home to me that marriage was very serious business—supporting a wife and child.

We needed a new automobile at the end of the war. There were none even being manufactured for display until the end of 1945. I doubt that there were any new cars actually sold and delivered to eager customers until sometime early in 1946. Every automobile dealer had a long list of prospective buyers, many of whom put up deposits of one hundred dollars or more in order to have the dealer do them the "favor" of placing them on the list. There were many stories of under-the-table payments to dealers for automobiles as they came in. I had my name on every list in the area that did not require a deposit. I bothered them with frequent calls and personal visits which produced no results. Of course, I was on lists for only the more inexpensive cars. Cadillacs, Lincolns, Packards, Buicks and the like were not within my price range.

As time went on, our situation got worse. Our homemade rear spring not only gave us an extremely uncomfortable ride, it made the car dangerous. Our brakes were bad, our tires were suspect, some of the underneath portions of the car, including the muffler, were held together with wire. The only good thing about it was that the engine ran perfectly. The Ford engine used in those cars was a marvel. I got nastier with the dealers, and they were not overly friendly toward me either. I would not pay a bonus for an automobile. For one thing, I could not afford to. Grove City had a local Dodge dealer who had sold Fords for years before the war. I knew him very well and had played cards with him in the Hell Hole when I was a kid. Naturally, I was on his list. Naturally, he kept lying to me and stalling me. One nice spring Saturday morning, I dropped in to see him and, as usual, was greeted warmly. I sat down at his desk and asked him when I could expect to get a car and got the usual answers. Then I blew up. I told him that he was a liar and that if he did not get me a car within thirty days, I would run a full-page advertisement in our local weekly newspaper telling the community just what kind of son of a bitch he really was. At that point, he got serious and told me he understood I really needed a car, and that he would get me one as soon as he could, but no later than six weeks from then.

In about five weeks he called me and said that he had a new Dodge coming in that week that I could have. Evelyn and I had saved money in Dayton; we did not need to borrow to pay for it. So it was that one bright day in early June 1947, I bought a new Dodge four-door sedan.

We had no choice as to model, color, or equipment. The one we got was black with white steel rims around the wheels, which made the tires appear to be white sidewalls. The car had a radio, a heater, and red-checkered, straw-like seat covers. It also had what was referred to as "fluid drive," which let you drive without shifting gears. It did not work too well, but was one of the forerunners of the present-day automatic shift.

The price of this marvelous car was eighteen hundred dollars. The dealer allowed us four hundred dollars for the Ford. I felt sorry for whoever was unlucky enough to buy it. The dealer even filled the new car full of gasoline. I guess I really did have him convinced that I would have run the ad. When I finally got the car, I was treated fairly.

Life seemed truly wonderful. I had a good job for that time. I had received a raise to forty-eight hundred dollars a year. Evelyn and I lived happily in our little white cottage. We had, in our opinion, the most wonderful baby daughter ever born. I had my first new car. What more could any man ask of life?

My job with the Veterans Administration had settled into a rather boring routine. I saw my trainees each month and listened to their problems, most of which did not seem to have anything to do with their training, and few of which I could solve. Occasionally, one of them would get fired for anything from absenteeism to laziness, to being completely incompetent. When this happened, I was required to make a recommendation as to whether to discontinue the training completely, or locate another training facility, or send him back through an extensive testing and interviewing program with the V.A.'s Advisement and Guidance Section. Many veterans were really not suited for any training because of a complete lack of mental ability beyond elementary manual labor. Those who were both physically handicapped and dumb were really unemployable. Some of them are, no doubt, still alive and existing on some sort of federal or state welfare program. Nothing else could happen, and they should be provided for. Some others were not employable only because they absolutely refused to make any effort to comply with basic job requirements, such as following orders, showing up for work, staying sober on the job, and making an honest effort to work. No doubt some of them are also on some form of welfare and, to me, this is totally wrong.

There were really too many training officers attached to our local office. Even with a so-called full caseload, we all had plenty of free time. None of us was overburdened with our labors. There were still bull sessions in the office. We still took extensive coffee breaks at a restaurant located next to our office building. We still had lengthy lunch hours occasionally. Once in a while we went home when we should have been out visiting our trainees. During the Christmas holidays one year, we started an impromptu party in the office. Someone brought in a bottle. The idea spread and we all got bottles, ice, mix, snacks—and drunk. We were so noisy that we disturbed all of the tenants in the building. Finally, the word got to the manager of the Columbus V.A. office and, after he got through with us, the party ended quickly and permanently. The only thing that saved us was that had we all been fired, the training of veterans in the Columbus area would have ended all supervision.

Sometime in 1947, I was assigned the task of making periodic visits to check on the progress of some fifty veterans enrolled in a school known as the Capitol College of Oratory and Music under the G.I. Bill. This school is not to be confused with Capital University which was, and is, a reputable small college located in Bexley, just outside the Columbus city limits. The Capitol College of Oratory and Music was located in a big old home on Neil Avenue not very far south of The Ohio State University. On my initial visit, I was met at the front door by the president of the college, who introduced himself as Doctor _____ . (He must remain anonymous because of current libel laws). The doctor took me on a tour of the building. I was most impressed with its quietness. There appeared to be neither faculty, nor students. When we returned to the doctor's office, I asked where everyone was, and he told me that the school was on vacation that particular week. I asked him for the reports which we were supposed to receive for the previous semester and was told that, although he had requested the proper forms on numerous occasions, the V.A. had failed to supply them. He then pontificated for at least one hour on various subjects.

God, he was an orator. I finally escaped and, as I left, I told him that I would make sure that he got the necessary reporting forms.

A week or so later, I went back to the school without an appointment to deliver the requisite forms. The place was still quiet. I did hear someone playing a piano. I also heard a male voice singing. I did not stay, and I did not ask any questions. I did not have the time or the desire to listen to the doctor expound that day. I was convinced, however, that there was no full-time instruction taking place, and I was not too sure that *any* training went on. Was a fraud being committed? I was convinced that there was, but I did not know really enough about the place even to report my suspicions to my superiors.

The G.I. Bill provided that a subsistence allowance would be paid to veterans pursuing a full-time course in an accredited college or university, among other learning facilities. A full-time course was in the case of a college or university, to consist of at least fifteen clock hours of classroom instruction a week. In addition to the veterans' subsistence allowance, the Veterans Administration paid the schools an hourly rate for classroom instruction given to each veteran student. Obviously, if billings were made and subsistence paid for full-time instruction, the student should be getting full-time instruction.

In a short period of time, I received all of the reports for the veterans enrolled at, as I started to call it, "The Capitol College of Musical Knowledge." Everything appeared to be in proper order. Not one veteran was absent during the entire semester. All of them, with one or two exceptions, were taking courses in piano, musicology, and voice. All appeared to be "A" students. I sent these progress reports on to our Cincinnati regional office without comment.

Every time I was near Neil Avenue, I made it a habit to drop in at the college for a chat with the president. He always appeared glad to see me. He invariably made a speech on whatever his topic for discussion was for the day. He gave me clippings from the Columbus newspapers containing letters to the editor which he had written. There was never much activity around the school. In the course of our conversations, I asked him where he had received his doctorate, and whether he held the degree of Doctor of Philosophy. He told me that his degree was "DS," which was Doctor of Psychology. I also asked him where all of the students were, and he told me that they started arriving about four o'clock each afternoon.

I made two- or three-night visits and discovered that there were, in fact, students. I also ascertained that these students were there for a music lesson. These lessons were generally for half an hour and, when finished, the student left the building.

I reported all of this to my superiors and was put in touch with one of the contract officers from the Cincinnati office. I also contacted the Ohio State Department of Education and asked that they conduct an investigation as to whether or not the school and its instructors were accredited by the State of Ohio.

The contract officer and I made an appointment to see the president and asked that he have all of his records available as to the exact number of hours each student spent on the premises. It took all afternoon to get through his speech-making, but finally we were told that each student received individual instruction, that there was no classroom instruction as such, and that there were no records as to exactly how much time each student spent at the school.

We left while the good "doctor" was still talking and headed for a bar partly to recover our sanity and partly to compare notes and determine how to proceed. Obviously, a fraud was being perpetrated, whether knowingly or not, against the Veterans Administration and, therefore, the United States Government. We decided that the next move had to come from the Cincinnati regional office based upon the contract officer's report.

I heard nothing further from Cincinnati for a considerable period of time. I did get reports from the Ohio State Department of Education. The Capitol College of Oratory and Music was a "chartered college" which had been founded forty or fifty years earlier. It had been a very legitimate, small music school where good instruction had been provided in voice, piano, and string instruments. Some of the original teachers apparently were still around. With the advent of the G.I. Bill, the "doctor" showed up and moved in on the old man who had run the school for years. The old man was confused and willing to go along with all of the suggestions made by my friend, the president. I also learned that when the president supposedly was in college, he was, in fact, a juggler in a circus; and that during the time that he was ostensibly obtaining a master's degree, he was a lecturer on a Chautauqua circuit. Obviously, he had awarded himself three degrees. However, the college's charter could not be revoked. It was in some sort of grandfather clause and was not under the jurisdiction of the Department of Education. Whatever was to be done had to come from the Veterans Administration.

The next thing I heard was in the form of a telephone call from the very irate president who told me that he had received notice from the Veterans Administration that tuition checks were being withheld for all students on the G.I. Bill at the school. I then began to receive calls from the G.I.'s that they had received notice that they would not receive checks for their subsistence allowance. Calls came in from all sorts of politicians including our local congressman. The V.A. in Cincinnati received a telegram from Senator Robert A. Taft demanding an explanation. I wished I had never heard of the damned school.

Finally, word filtered down to me that the Veterans Administration in Washington had withdrawn approval of this school for veterans' education and training. I was told to set up a meeting of all of the G.I.s who were enrolled and explain to them what the problem was.

By this time, my original boss had been replaced by a man who had been a colonel throughout much of World War II, and who had actually commanded troops. He told me to call a meeting at the school and said that he would go with me and do the talking. I called the president, who agreed to meet on the night suggested, but said, in what I thought was a threatening manner, "You had better make a good explanation. These men are mad." The night of the meeting we had two police cruisers sitting outside and my boss prominently displayed an Army .45 pistol in a shoulder holster. There was no trouble. He got up and said, with all the authority a colonel's voice could contain, "Effective now, this school is no longer approved for veterans training." He walked out and I was happy to join him.

Within a week or two after the meeting, I received a letter of commendation from the Chief of Education and Training in the V.A. regional office, thanking me for the excellent job I had done in eliminating the fraud which had been engaged in. Everyone congratulated me on the fine job I had done. About a month later, along with several of my cohorts, I received a notice that, because of budget restrictions, a reduction in force was necessary ("R.I.F." in governmentese) and that, because of my lack of seniority, I would be temporarily terminated; and perhaps at a later date would be reassigned to another area.

I found out that seniority included any government service, regardless of its level, including time spent in military service. Merit and efficiency reports made no difference. I do not know, but I surmise that federal employment still operates the same way. If an individual is hired into a government position, and survives long enough, it is virtually impossible for that person to be replaced, regardless of his job performance or ability. It was a good lesson for me because I learned that I did not want to attempt to make a career in government service, regardless of how well such a job might pay.

I needed a job quickly – a job in the Columbus area in order that I might continue law school. A teaching position was out of the question at that time of year. One of the training officers who remained had enough seniority to stay forever. He had been a soldier in World War I and, through political connections and American Legion activities, had held state and federal jobs most of his adult life. He told me that he thought it might be possible for me to get his old job in the Ohio State Department of Public Welfare. He introduced me to his old boss and vouched for my status as a good Republican.

I was interviewed by the chief of the Division of Aid for the Aged, State of Ohio, Department of Public Welfare. He had a large, very plush office with a huge desk, a high-backed leather chair, and deep, upholstered leather furniture. He was not a big man physically, but he smoked one huge cigar after another. We liked each other immediately. He told me that he would hire me, and that my title would be Administrative Assistant to the Chief, Division of the Aid for the Aged. He also told me that the title was more impressive than the salary, which would be three thousand dollars annually. He added that the job was strictly political, that I could receive only a temporary appointment because of civil service requirements, and that I would need to obtain the endorsement of the Franklin County Republican Committee chairman.

The salary was very unimpressive, but I needed employment right away in order that we might continue to eat. I had no idea what my duties would consist of, but a job was a job. I saw the county chairman and was endorsed; he knew my mother. I took the endorsement form to the "The Chief," who took steps to put me on the state payroll. He sat and puffed on his cigar while thinking, and then said, "I'll take you down to your office. You will occupy space with our comptroller." It turned out that the comptroller and I had known each other in junior high school, and we immediately became buddies. It also turned out that my duties consisted of doing whatever the Chief, the state welfare director, or the comptroller wanted me to do.

The Division of the Aid for the Aged was established in the early days of the Great Depression to provide the administration of an aid program for the elderly who were virtually indigent, who had no means of supporting themselves, and whose children were not financially able to provide support. There were some minor medical benefits, a small burial allowance, and meager monthly support payments. This program began before the Social Security Act was even thought of. It was strictly a welfare program and was based entirely on need. Those recipients of aid who owned real estate were required to assign their property to the state. The benefits were never great, and, for those who received Social Security, were reduced accordingly.

County offices were operated throughout the state. A caseworker was assigned to each recipient. These caseworkers were supposed to see to the well-being of their clients, counsel with them, and generally assist them in any way possible. There were enough caseworkers to ensure that each client was visited once a month and sometimes more often. The trouble was that the entire program was based on "need," and caseworkers were really investigators to the point that they were required to serve almost as policemen to ensure that no one received a nickel more than they should have, based upon the budget very carefully worked out for them. There were, of course, case work supervisors and an office manager in each office. In the central office, to which I was assigned, there were district case work supervisors, attorneys, a print shop to handle the printing of the voluminous literature and forms, countless secretaries and clerical workers, and others whose duties were never known to me. It was a typical bureaucracy. After I learned about the entire operation, I felt that it would probably have been simpler, and probably cheaper, just to mail each person over sixty-five a check for the maximum amount permitted by law.

I did not work for every governmental agency, state or federal, but I was in the Army, and I worked for the Veterans Administration and finally the State of Ohio Division of Aid for the Aged. I know why we run deficits in this country. It is because of the systems we set up, and people like me who fit into the systems.

I had no other job in my life that was as enjoyable as my employment with the Division of Aid for the Aged. Much of what I did had no relationship to aid for the aged or welfare. It was political. I did a little investigative work where complaints were filed against various county offices and their personnel. I had to check out a few nursing homes that allegedly were not being operated properly. I was involved in two or three fraud investigations. I negotiated leases of office space in some of the counties. All of this, of course, was relevant to the work of the Division. Many other assignments were not, but often developed into trips which I was required to make in the normal course of business.

I did not realize at the time that I was hired that I would be required to travel. However, there are eighty-eight counties in the State of Ohio, and I do not believe I missed visiting very many of them in the few months that I worked for the Division. Traveling around the state was fun. I received a generous mileage allowance for my car; all meals were paid for when I was on the road, and when I required to be out overnight, I was reimbursed for my lodging. There was not an interstate highway system then. There were no freeways, and not many four-lane highways. As a consequence, trips that today could be made easily in a day required a stay overnight. In many of the small counties, accommodations were not very good, and the food in the restaurants was sometimes just awful. Of course, there were also some small cities, and all of the larger cities, with excellent food and hotels. Motels as we know them today were non-existent. There were tourist cabins along the roads, but they had no appeal to me. Thank God there were no fast-food restaurants then.

In order to make the law classes on Monday, Wednesday and Friday nights, I traveled Tuesdays, Wednesdays and Thursdays and, when necessary, stayed overnight on Tuesdays and Thursdays. Studying in hotel rooms was not much fun, but in most of the county seats there was nothing to do anyway. Television was such a novelty that it was shown only in a few bars and hotel lobbies in Cleveland and two or three neighboring counties. I was thrilled in the summer of 1948 when I first saw television in a hotel lobby in Painesville, Ohio. The program was a Cleveland Indians baseball game, and I stood entranced, as did almost all of the other hotel guests, as the black and white picture flashed across the small television screen.

When I went to Cleveland or the northeastern Ohio counties, it was a real struggle to make my law classes on time. Sometimes I did miss my pre-class hamburger, but I really did not feel that that was much of a loss. Evelyn and our daughter were alone a great deal. It was a hard situation for her, but she did not complain. She had no transportation except for her two feet and a baby carriage. Fortunately, the grocery and other stores in which she shopped were only a couple blocks from our house.

Some of my assignments were entertaining. The Chief called me in one day and told me that I had to go to Ironton to fire the subdivision manager, who was both inefficient—and worse--a Democrat. I was to find new quarters for the office as well. Also, before I did anything else, I was to see the president of the bank, the political boss, to get his approval for the firing and his recommendation as to just where I should look for office space.

I drove to Ironton, naturally stopping for lunch on the way. Ironton is the county seat of Lawrence County, located across the Ohio River from Ashland, Kentucky. There were, and still are, a lot of hillbillies from Kentucky, southern Ohio and West Virginia who either live in the town or use it as their source of sustenance and recreation. In that time, the town was known as tough and wide open; gambling houses and houses of prostitution flourished. So did "moonshine" whiskey. Fights, shootouts, and an occasional murder were a normal part of living, particularly in the area along the river.

I checked into the hotel in the middle of the afternoon and was rather impressed with it. It was two or three cuts above the average found in most of the smaller county seat towns I visited. I parked my

Dodge, not a state car, no special license number, and went to my room. As I entered, the telephone was ringing. When I answered, a male voice with a real hillbilly accent said, "Mr. Clark, a'hm, jus' wahnin' yu. Watch what yu do, yu're bein' watched." The telephone then went dead. I had planned to walk around the downtown area and find a restaurant away from the hotel in which to eat dinner. Instead, I made certain that the room was locked, and had dinner in the hotel dining room. I was scared. I never found out who the call was from, or how anyone in Ironton other than the desk clerk knew that I existed.

The next morning after a leisurely breakfast in the hotel coffee shop, and with some fear in my heart, I found the bank. It was a rather imposing building for Ironton. The interior had the usual high ceiling found in most banks at that time. There were numerous teller's windows, and the bank had an air of bigness about it. I was impressed. I walked to the desk at the rear of the bank, assuming that the bank president was in one of the private offices located in that area. The secretary told me that I would find the president at the very front of the bank. I had walked past him on the way in with no more than a glance. I saw a rather plain little man sitting at an old-fashioned desk behind a low iron railing and wearing a green eye shade, elastic arm bands and suspenders holding up a pair of baggy striped pants. This was the most powerful man in Lawrence County. When I identified myself, he rose and shook hands with me and invited me to occupy a rather uncomfortable wooden chair across from him. I told him my reasons for being in Ironton. He rocked in his chair for a few moments, and then told me that it would be all right to fire the subdivision manager, but suggested that it might be better if he were allowed to resign. When I asked him about office space, he told me that a Mr. Roberts handled all of that. He did not say for whom, but I had no doubt that Mr. Roberts was the banker's agent. He said that I could find Mr. Roberts at the train depot that afternoon. We talked for a time about state and national politics. He was sure that our Republican governor would get beat in November, and was equally sure that Tom Dewey, or whoever the Republican Party might run for President, would defeat Harry Truman.

When I left the bank, I went to the county office of the Division of

Aid. I introduced myself to the two or three people in the office, who seemed frightened at my appearance. They soon got over the feeling, and soon were complaining about some of the stupid regulations issued from our central office in Columbus. I agreed with them. The professional social workers who promulgated the regulations were the usual idealistic do-gooders who still are the scourge of every welfare program in every welfare agency in the country. Later that year, I got in trouble in Cleveland for saying in a talk I made representing the chief that if I had a choice between hiring a graduate of The Ohio State University's College of Social Administration and a person with ordinary common sense, I would hire the person with common sense every time.

I then went into the subdivisions manager's office and was greeted warmly. He was a huge, fat slob with a triple chin and a drawl that was pure hillbilly. I sat down, prepared to tell him that he had a choice – either to resign or be fired – but he beat me to it. "Mistuh Clark, ah know why ya ah heah," he said, "and yu-all don't need to worry none. Heah's mah resignation. Ah been waiten on yu to show up." With that he opened his desk drawer and pulled out a typed resignation, dated it, signed it, and handed it to me. He then said, "It's just about time to go to lunch. Wil yu join me?" I told him that I would take him to lunch. God, did he eat! He told me that he lived "out in the country" and that he had eleven children and fourteen coon dogs. He said that he knew he and his wife should not have any more children, but, as he put it, "ever' once in a while I jus' git a hankerin' to have another one of them little felluhs runnin' around." I do not know how the man lived and supported a family that large plus his fourteen coon dogs.

I then got my automobile and drove to the train depot in search of Mr. Roberts. The only person around was a tall, thin, older man wearing a straw hat and coveralls. When I asked where Mr. Roberts was, he said, "That's me. I'm the station master, ticket agent, and janitor. Right now I'm the janitor and I'm cleaning privies. You can't perfume shit, you got to clean it." He then asked what he could do for me. I told him that the banker had sent me to him to talk about leasing space. He told me to wait a few minutes, and he disappeared. When he returned, he had removed the coveralls, but still had on his straw hat.

He climbed into my car and directed me to two or three different locations. None of the space looked good to me, but I knew it was good Republican space. I told him I would get in touch with him soon and took him back to the railroad station. I do not believe that very many trains passed through Ironton because Mr. Roberts' arrival at or departure from his job did not seem to make any difference. I enjoyed Mr. Roberts. He yelled and waved at people all over Ironton during our tour. He too was a very important man in Lawrence County.

I enjoyed the trip but was glad to get out of Ironton without loss of either life or limb.

Of course, the largest county office in Ohio was in Cleveland. It had countless employees, countless problems, and a weak subdivision manager who passed on to the central office all problems possible. We all made more trips to Cleveland than we wanted to for that reason. The office occupied the entire second floor of the Public Square Building in the heart of downtown Cleveland. The building was owned by one H.E. McMullen, who lived in the penthouse on top of the building. The comptroller and I got well acquainted with him. He told us that he had gone broke in Chicago, got drunk when he found out he was broke, and really did not quite know how he got to Cleveland. We were never able to understand how he became the owner of the Public Square Building. He signed all papers with pens holding only green ink, he said, because he had seen too much red ink previously. He wined and dined us lavishly both in the penthouse and in expensive restaurants. Naturally, being good state employees, we enjoyed ourselves.

I received a telephone call from the chief late one afternoon summoning me to his office immediately. He said that he had just received a call from the governor's office to the effect that McMullen had turned off the heat in our Cleveland offices and that the elevators were not running. It seems that the State Auditor had not mailed the rent check as he should have. I was told that I was to be at the airport at eight o'clock the next morning, where the governor's plane was kept; that someone from the State Auditor's Office would meet me and hand me the requisite check; and that the governor's pilot would fly me to Cleveland.

I had never flown, not once in the entire time I was in the Air Corps. I had a close call the time I was supposed to fly around the country to visit various air bases with the Commanding Officer, Wright Field, but he shipped out before the trip was scheduled. Frankly, I spent a nervous night. I had a definite fear of flying.

I was at the proper airport on time; so was the official with the check for McMullen, and so was Bob Werthlin, whom I knew. He too worked for the State Welfare Department and was an Ohio National Guard pilot with the rank of major. It was his duty to fly the governor's plane when necessary. The plane itself was a beautiful thing. It carried four passengers comfortably. It just looked safe to me and I figured that if Bob Werthlin was good enough to fly the governor around, he was probably safe enough for me. We had a beautiful flight to Cleveland on a clear, sunshiny morning. We were flying low enough that I could see the fields, the roads, and the towns easily. I lost all fear and got quite comfortable. The plane landed at Lake Front Airport, downtown just a few blocks from the Public Square Building. I walked there, then climbed the stairs to get to our office. The employees were sitting around with their overcoats on. The office really was cold with the heat off. I went into the manager's office and called McMullen. A husky, sexy female voice answered the phone. I told the woman who I was and what I wanted. After a pause, McMullen came on the line and instructed me to go to his private elevator, which he would send down to me, and to get up to the penthouse quickly.

When I got off the elevator at the penthouse, I buzzed the apartment and, after identifying myself again, the electric lock was opened, and I was able to open the door. I was greeted by a rather dark-complexioned young woman with long black hair. She was completely naked except for a pair of high-heeled shoes. She went ahead of me, hips in constant motion, down the corridor to the large, well-furnished living area where McMullen was seated. He looked up, then stood to greet me. I handed him the check. He glanced at it, then told the young woman to get something on and bring some Bloody Marys. As we sat down, I reminded him to start the elevators and turn on the heat in our offices. He went to his desk and called his maintenance superintendent with instructions to put us back in business. I asked him why there was so much security about getting up to the penthouse. He told me that the young lady was a Cleveland mobster's girlfriend, and that he was afraid of being killed. He told me that he would gladly get rid of the girl, that he was tired of her anyway. I found out who the mobster was, and his telephone number, and with McMullen's blessing called him and made arrangements to deliver her at the side door of the building in half an hour in exchange for the gangster's promise not to harm McMullen. The guy said that the girl had gone with other men too, and that all he wanted was to get her back. We got her dressed, complete with the new fur coat McMullen had bought her. I took her to the side entrance where she was picked up. Everyone was happy and relieved – including me. McMullen was so happy that he signed a new three-year lease, enabling us to keep our office where it was at a very nominal increase in rent. He had been stalling the comptroller and me about executing the lease for at least two months. After a drink or two and a nice lunch catered by a nearby restaurant, I left and went back to the airport. It had been a very successful day for me, and I felt great about flying back to Columbus.

When we took off from the Lake Front Airport in Cleveland, the weather was crisp and clear. About thirty miles south, the weather began to change. It became cloudy, the wind buffeted the small plane around in the air. It rained, it sleeted, the plane dropped suddenly, two or three hundred feet because it could not fly at a high enough altitude to get us above the storm. Naturally, I was nervous and scared. The pilot was calm, intense, and attentive to his instruments and the plane radio. I think I prayed a little. As we got nearer to Columbus, we passed through the worst of the storm and learned from the radio and visual observation that we were in heavy fog.

The pilot could find our airport by instrument only. He was in constant radio communication – there was no radar then, at least not at that airport and not on the airplane we were in. Finally, the airport talked us down and we landed safely. When I got to the ground outside the plane, I was weak. I did insist that we find a bar, when Evelyn picked me up. I did not fly again for almost sixteen years.

The State Welfare Department had, arbitrarily, attached a nursing home inspection unit to our office. The few employees were all nurses.

The unit supervisor was a career employee who had been an Army nurse overseas in World War 1. She was a little tough, swore beautifully, and was efficient as hell. When she wanted to close a nursing home based upon the reports of her inspector nurses, litigation often resulted. Occasionally, prior to the issuance of the order to close, I had to verify the information presented. God, some of those places were really horrible! They were fire traps, the stench was beyond description, the patients were filthy, and the food was slop. Complaints about physical abuse of the patients were always true. Those places were as bad as any poor house or orphanage described in the nineteenth century literature. No one, including myself, looks forward to spending their last few months or years in a nursing home today; but present-day nursing facilities are palaces compared to those I saw then.

Because I was a political appointee, a known Republican, and trusted by both the chief and the director of welfare, I was asked to talk with the Republican County chairman almost every time I took a trip to any county in the state. I would discuss the governor's campaign for reelection and transmit the suggestions and complaints back to state Republican headquarters. The various county chairmen were cordial to me, but almost all of them were mad at the governor, his staff, or his campaign aides. They were not happy with the amounts of money they were receiving from state headquarters. They thought the governor was stupid and resented the complete lack of cooperation they were receiving from everyone. By late August I knew that the governor would lose in November. I talked with Hamilton County chairman—Cincinnati and its environs, who had just received a call from the campaign chairman for Thomas E. Dewey, the Republican presidential candidate who, ostensibly, could not lose to Harry Truman. The Hamilton County chairman told Dewey's man that the Ohio governor would not be reelected and added that Dewey would not carry Ohio and would probably get beat in November. He was right!

In late October, I was in Kenton, Ohio, on a cold, blustery morning. Frank Lausche, the Democratic candidate for governor, was to make a speech on the steps of the Hardin County Court House at eleven o'clock. I decided to go hear him. He had wavy curly hair that came over his forehead, and he always wore a bow tie. He had on only a suit coat, unbuttoned and flying in the breeze. He had to be cold. Lausche was very colorful and a great speech maker. While I was listening, I thoroughly enjoyed myself, until he suddenly pointed his forefinger at me and said, "This man is here at State expense, spying on me, and is in this party only for political purposes. When I am elected, one of my first official acts will be to dismiss him." He meant it.

We all thought the governor would lose his bid for reelection in November of 1948. However, almost everyone, Democrat and Republican alike, was sure that Thomas E. Dewey, former governor of New York, would defeat Harry Truman in the presidential election. We were told that, when this occurred, we would be hired by the new administration in better-paying jobs than those we held.

Dewey ran a statesman-like campaign. He sounded presidential – actually a little pompous. Television did not enter into the 1948 campaign. Candidates were seen in personal appearances throughout the country and in the newsreels at the movie houses. They were heard on the radio in some of their speeches. The various polls showed Dewey leading by a landslide. The Republicans had won control of Congress and many of the state Houses in 1946. The country's newspapers and news magazines were anti-Truman. He was thought to be a lightweight and an unworthy successor to Roosevelt. But Harry Truman was a fighter. He took off across the United States on a train in what came to be known as "the whistle-stop campaign." He made personal appearances from the rear of the observation car from early in the morning until late at night. He talked about the "do nothing" Republican Congress and said that all of the country's problems resulted from Congressional obstructionism. His theme was "Elect me and a Democratic Congress, and our problems will all be solved." Truman was the epitome of the abused little guy, the common man. People identified with him. Shouts of "Give 'em hell, Harry" became heard at each stop. Truman obliged.

Election day 1948 finally arrived. Dewey was heavily favored nationally. It was even thought that Dewey's landslide victory might pull in Tom Herbert—our governor—on his coattails. I was optimistic. Evelyn and I had some of our friends in for an election party. The returns did not start to come in until after nine o'clock; so, we played cards and talked. We were prepared to celebrate the first republican presidential victor in twenty years. A well-known, highly-respected magazine in the 1920's, 1930's and 1940's was the *Literary Digest* which predicted a Dewey landslide. Its presidential poll was always right. The first *New York Times* Wednesday morning edition carried a huge headline indicating a Dewey victory. The first returns were all Dewey. We did some drinking. Then other returns began to come in. Truman was running stronger than expected. Our guests went home. It was late, but I stayed up listening to the radio. Dewey's victory went out the window. Tom Herbert was defeated. I knew that I would be out of a job. The *Literary Digest* went out of business, its credibility lost.

Wednesday morning after election was a gloomy, rainy day. It matched my feelings perfectly. I went to the office tired, discouraged and somewhat hung over. The chief called me into his office. Of course, we discussed the election returns. He knew that he would soon be replaced, and he was almost too old to find other employment. Such is the life of many politicians. More often than not, professional politicians end up on dead-end streets.

He then told me that he wanted me to drive to Zanesville that morning and fire the subdivision manager. Who, was an active Democrat and who "should have been fired a long time ago." I could not believe what I was hearing. I tried to talk the old man out of this folly, but he was adamant and vengeful. I went to Zanesville, went into the manager's office and sat down. He grinned at me, opened his center desk drawer, and handed me his resignation without a word. I read the letter and told him how sorry I was. He told me not to worry about it, that he had been expecting to be fired for almost two years, but that he would be back in a few months now that the Democrats had won again. The whole thing seemed ridiculous to me at that point, but I did as I was told.

Dr. Jim Henry and Dick Clark

Shortly after I moved to Grove City in 1935, I met Jim Henry. He was two years behind me in school and as a sophomore was taking the sophomore course in plane geometry that I was still taking as a senior. He was a small, dark-haired boy, very neat in appearance, and damned bright in class. Jim played baseball and basketball and, despite his lack of stature, was a good young ballplayer. That summer we became good friends and remained so. Jim became a doctor and, after spending time in the Army and a short time in another small town near Columbus, returned to Grove City to take up the practice of medicine. He and his wife (Virginia) and Evelyn and I saw each other as frequently as our busy schedules permitted.

Dr. Jim Henry, Ginnie Henry, and Dick Clark

Evelyn and I had dreams of owning a house someday. So too did the Henrys. We took rides on Sunday afternoons and looked at houses, and poured over the house plans in *Better Homes and Gardens* every month. We still had some money in savings even after buying our new Dodge—enough perhaps for a lot, perhaps enough for a down payment on a house if the house were inexpensive enough. We even talked about buying the little cottage in which we lived.

Our home we built.

Jim Henry never stood on ceremony. One Saturday night in January, as I was taking a bath, I could hear Jim asking where I was. He came into the bathroom, sat on the edge of the tub, and told me that he had just talked to Hal Goldsmith, a builder who lived next door. Goldsmith owned some lots on East Park Street that we coveted, but he had refused to sell them to anyone. He had just told Jim that he and I could buy them provided that we agreed that Goldsmith and Son would build our future houses. Jim and Evelyn and I decided that we could get along as next-door neighbors, and that we would buy the lots together. We paid fifteen hundred dollars for our lot—expensive for Grove City in 1948. (236 East Park Street)

Now that we had bought our lot, we really wanted a home of our own. After all of the various places where I had lived, I thought that it would be nice to take root some place. Evelyn had always lived in her parents' house until she married me and was used to the security of having permanence.

We found we could borrow money from Evelyn's aunt and uncle for the purpose of building. They were able to get only two and half percent interest on the money they had in the banks and in bonds and were glad to loan us money and charge us four and one-half percent. I wish that I could borrow money at that rate today. We saw a floor plan in *Better Homes and Gardens* that we really liked, and then had our plans drawn from it.

Even in 1948, there were shortages of some building materials. Goldsmith told us that it was impossible to get good siding and told us that we should shingle the house. Much of the other lumber that was delivered to the site was sent back to the lumberyard because it was not properly seasoned. The Goldsmiths were particular about everything. We wanted gas heat, but the gas freeze was on. Oil was expensive and electric heat was in its infancy. We did not want a coal furnace because of its inconvenience and, besides, our plans did not call for a basement. But we got a full basement, a coal stoker furnace, a coal chute, and a coal storage room. (The Room was too large to be called a coal bin.) The stoker was the most efficient, but laborious, way to fire a coal furnace, but the ashes still had to be taken out and disposed of, and periodically something would go wrong with the mechanism, which I could not fix. Fortunately, in two or three years, the freeze was lifted, and we were able to convert to gas heat.

The basement was dug on Memorial Day, and we moved into the house on December first. I doubt that I missed very many days of going to the site to see what progress was being made. We were excited the entire time. On moving day, Evelyn cried again, as she had done when we left our Dayton apartment. We were proud of our new home. We thought, and probably said, that we had the finest house in Grove City. It has been remodeled since; but, after thirty-six years, we still love it, and to us it still is the finest house in Grove City.

Evelyn was pregnant again in 1948, but nothing went well. Jim Henry was the doctor, of course, and he ordered her to stay in bed. We were supposed to have taken a vacation and meet friends in Boston, but I wired them explaining in a few words that we could not join them. I spent the vacation time taking care of Marcia and Evelyn. I even cooked. I knew absolutely nothing about cooking beyond frying bacon and eggs, making coffee, opening, and heating a can of soup, and putting lunchmeat between two slices of bread. Under directions given me from the bedroom, I even made meat loaf. Despite all precautions, Evelyn had a miscarriage. Jim was there and I served as best I could as his assistant. I have never forgotten the experience. It was a helluva time for both of us.

After the 1948 election results were in, it was obvious that I had to find yet another job as quickly as I possibly could. Whether Frank Lausche, the victor in the gubernatorial race, would have really made it a point to fire me on inauguration day was doubtful. However, there was no question that my days were numbered after January. I was a political appointee. The Democrats were in, and most certainly I would be among the early dismissals. This was the way the game was played, and I understood it. The spoils system was still in effect in 1948 and, from what I understand, is very much alive today. Many government jobs are truly so protected by civil service that it is virtually impossible to dismiss even the most inefficient employee. Political jobs are still political and shift with the winds of political change.

I needed to work. I was tired of job changes and really, in my heart, wanted job security with an opportunity for advancement if I did well. On the other hand, I wanted to complete law school. To do this, I could not look for a position with long-term possibilities. I talked with some of my friends who still remained with the Veterans Administration and found out that one of the trade school owners wanted someone who knew about V.A. regulations and procedure for the purpose of ultimately managing a small business college that he was about to purchase and later move into one of the trade schools. I was not enthusiastic about talking to him because I did not think much of the training provided by most of these schools, including his. I thought that the trade school operators were out to make a fast dollar at the expense of the veteran and the Veterans Administration. Most of them were. Nevertheless, I did not let my ideals interfere with the necessity to feed myself and my family. I arranged to talk to the "Old Man."

He was a small, very well-dressed, neat individual. His shoes were always perfectly shined, and his manicured fingers showed his diamond rings to their best advantage. His upper lip had a pencil moustache, and he invariably wore a hat wherever he was. One would have thought him bald, but he had a rather heavy head of neatly-parted black hair. It was never easy to see him. Much of the time it was impossible to locate him. He was never available in the morning or early afternoon. It was only late afternoon and early evening through the dinner hour that he made an appearance. Very seldom did he enter one of the offices. He usually went to a bar nearby and called to announce his arrival. He was always accompanied by Chester, his colored chauffeur, confidant, advisor, and – I think financial backer.

The two occupied bar stools and drank together. I never knew what they discussed, but they were always deep in conversation.

I was told to go to the auto mechanics school, which was located at that time in the heart of the black area in Columbus, for my initial conference. I was to show up around five o'clock in the evening. It was dark and I felt somewhat apprehensive about being in the area, but I later discovered that I need not have worried. The Old Man was a friend of everyone in the area, and no one interfered with anyone or anything around that school. I went to the office and met the Old Man's son, who was about my age. Theoretically, he was second in command to his father, but he was never given any real authority. He knew who I was and why I was there. We got along fine. He told me that he had no idea when his father would show up, but about two hours later, the Old Man called and wanted to see me at the Pine Tree bar across the street from the school. I went over. He was easy to spot because he was the only white man in the place. He motioned for me to take an adjoining bar stool, and he introduced me to Chester. We had a couple of drinks while we talked. He did not really interview me. Finally, he looked at me and asked, "How much do you want to start?" I told him I should make as much as a Veterans Administration training officer. He asked how much that was, and I told him. He nodded, took a drag on his cigarette and a sip of his drink and said, "Okay. Start as soon as you resign from your State job." I found out later that I could have probably gotten twice as much salary without much discussion.

He told me that he would complete the purchase of the business school, and that I would manage it for a time, but that he had an idea that he would do much more than just operate the place as a business school. He then said, "I'll see you in January. I'm going home now." I had a job. I had no real idea what I would be doing and did not really care very much about that as long as I drew a paycheck.

In January of 1949, I took over the operation of the Berne Davis Business College. It sounded impressive. Actually, it was located in a large old home on South High Street, where the rooms were used as classrooms. The faculty consisted of four or five instructors, none of whom was hired on a full-time basis. Most of the students were veterans, but there were several young men and women just out of high school. The total enrollment of full and part-time students could not have exceeded seventy-five, if that. The building, the equipment, the faculty, and the students were all third-rate. I thought that I had gotten myself into a hell of a mess. I was discouraged from the beginning, but was told just to sit in my office, leave the place alone and not worry about it; when the semester ended in June, something would be done.

We lost money every month. I was bored and used every excuse imaginable to get away from the place. The only advantage to the situation from my point of view was that I was able to really study law. I had few interruptions. The disadvantage was that there was night school on Tuesday and Thursday evening's which meant that I was gone from home five nights a week.

I saw the Old Man only two or three times between January and June. When I needed money to pay bills and salaries, I called his son and promptly received whatever sum I needed. I was told that the Old Man had set a meeting for a Saturday afternoon in March at his son's house, and that I was to be there.

It was a big meeting. All of the people in authority in the trade schools were there. So was a man from Cleveland – one of the top people in the Cleveland Public school vocational education hierarchy. So was a court reporter. When we were all seated, the boss said that he had employed the Cleveland "hot shot" to prepare a new curriculum that he wanted us all to hear about, and comment on, after studying the transcript we had received from the court reporter. The meeting was so secret that one would have thought strategy was being plotted for the overthrow of the United States government.

Basically, what was outlined was a nine-month business education program for graduates of the auto mechanics school. It was designed to prepare the graduates for the operation of their own businesses. The idea was good and so was the proposed curriculum. The remarks that day were all favorable. When I read the transcript, I was impressed and could understand why the business school had been purchased. Not one of the persons present at the meeting had any derogatory comment to make that day, or later, so far as I know. I assumed that we would implement the program that June and continued to swivel at my desk at the business school. I did not know how the regular business school students would be taken care of, but I felt that it would be entirely possible to make the regular business school stronger with the influx of the necessary faculty and equipment to provide training for the auto mechanics. Nothing happened. The boss kept dodging me. Finally, about the first of June, I received instructions by telephone to close the school at the end of the semester, two weeks later. I was also told that the auto mechanics school would be moved to a new building July first and that I would move with it. I again had no idea what I would be doing, but at least I still had a job.

I hated to tell the students and instructors at the business school that the school would be closed, but I did. Actually, I thought that all of them would probably be better off someplace else. The business training for auto mechanics was never implemented, and I sold the equipment at the business school at sacrificial prices. The Old Man lost a considerable amount of money on the purchase and operation of the business school, and the vocational education expert had to be expensive. I never found out why the business training program was scrapped. It was a strange, frustrating period.

The new auto mechanics building was truly impressive as the school was setup – new equipment, every phase of training departmentalized. Expert instructors were decked out in white service manager's coats. The Ohio Department of Education was enthusiastic; so was the Veterans Administration, and so was I.

It turned out that my new duties were many. I became the office manager, school registrar, disciplinarian, go-between with the local V.A. office, and anything else the Old Man decided on.

The school registrar's job was interesting. I had to interview, approve, and sign up all of the applicants for admission to the school. They came from all over Ohio. Huge advertisements were placed in newspapers in every county in Ohio. The theme was always "Earn while you learn" in large letters. What was meant, of course, was that the Veterans Administration provided tuition, tools, manuals, and any other items that might be required for training, in addition to paying the veteran subsistence allowance while in school. The school also employed two or three salesmen who beat the bushes and hills for prospects.

Prospective students came into my office in droves for two or three days before the commencement of classes each six weeks. It was up to me to accept or reject them. Few were ever turned away. The school was in business to make money, and I had a great desire to keep my job.

I did use an application form which each prospect was required to fill out. Among other things, I was able to determine whether or not the man could read and write. I also used an extremely simple test. I still remember one of the questions and one answer I received. The question was "What force causes an object to drop?" Of course, the proper answer is "gravity," regardless of how it might have been spelled. The surprise answer that I received was "a loose bolt." I thought it was a good reasoning and checked the answer as being correct. Actually, if the applicant could read and write, and answered the test questions even partially correctly and, most importantly, had his certificate of eligibility from the Veterans Administration, he was admitted.

All of the trade schools existed only because of the G.I. Bill. Most of them were less particular than we were with reference to admission and standards. Thanks to our chief instructor, no student who could not do the work remained in school very long.

There was never a question as to the number of hours a student spent in class. Tuition charges were based on hours of instruction. A total of twenty-five clock hours a week was required of each veteran wishing to receive full subsistence allowance. A time clock was installed at the entrance to the classroom area, and each student punched in and punched out under the watchful eye of the chief instructor or his designate.

The chief instructor was outstanding and a real little Napoleon when it was necessary. He was only about five feet, six inches tall, and slightly built but, when necessary, absolutely fearless, and completely in charge. His own instructors were hand-picked, well-qualified men for the training they were required to give. All of them followed the manuals of instruction, and really put out as far as teaching was concerned; they were afraid not to do so. When the chief instructor was required to dismiss a student, he always explained the exact reason for the dismissal, and then looked the student in the eye and said, "It's been nice to have known you."

The office was not anything like the instruction area insofar as efficiency was concerned. There were three girls in the office, including the Old Man's daughter, who was very nice, very pretty, very intelligent, with absolutely no desire to do any work. Occasionally, she brought her baby with her to the office – a practice which did not add much to an efficient operation.

There was a tall, pretty redhead with a body that was outstanding. Naturally, she always wore tight-fitting sweaters. She was dumber than hell. The only way she could count was on her fingers, and when she had to count to twenty, took off her shoes. She filed. She did know the alphabet. She filed her lunch everyday under "L," and once, when I was looking for a certain set of papers, I got my hand in a melted chocolate bar, which she had filed under "H" for Hershey. She was always late for work, but when she was going to be really late, she always called me to ask whether she could come in C.O.D. This meant that she got a taxi cab and I paid the fare out of petty cash. On payday, I deducted her charges from her paycheck.

The third member of the group was a tall dark-haired gal in her thirties, married with a child or two. She had a lot of ability, but she spent most of each day on the telephone talking to her various boyfriends.

I could not fire any of them. The Old Man had to support his daughter anyway. His son ran around with the redhead, and the Old Man went to bed periodically with the tall dark-haired girl.

One Friday I discovered that several hundred dollars in cash was missing from the office. I called the Old Man before calling the police, because everyone in the office, including his son and daughter, could have had access to the money. He told me to report the theft to the police, but to keep quiet about the whole thing. Saturday morning when I was the only person working, a police detective came in. I gave him the pertinent details, including names and addresses of all of our office personnel. The following Saturday morning, he called me to ask whether anyone else was around. When I answered in the negative, he said that he would come out immediately. When he arrived and was seated, he told me that he knew and could prove who had stolen the money, but he said that he did not think we would want to prosecute. It was the tall dark-haired gal. He asked me whether I knew that she worked out of the Neil House on weekends, and occasionally through the week, as a prostitute.

I waited until Monday and then met with the Old Man and his son in the bar located adjacent to the school. I told them what I had been told. The son grinned and the Old Man ordered another drink, which he sipped while he thought. He finally turned to me and instructed me to go over and fire her, and also give her a month's pay. He said that I should hire another girl as quickly as possible.

The next day I went downtown to lunch with some of my cohorts and told them that I needed to hire a very efficient secretary-bookkeeper. I added that I preferred someone homely. One of my friends said he knew just the girl, someone who worked in an insurance office next to his office. I went back with him after lunch, and he took me in and introduced me to the woman. She was uglier than hell! I hired her because I was sure neither the boss nor the son would get involved with her.

I was right! Neither of the men went near her and she was efficient. Beyond those two virtues, I made a large mistake in hiring her. She was never *late* for work; she just didn't show up at all about once a week, usually on Mondays. I found out that she was the penitentiary warden's girlfriend and drinking companion. He sometimes got away from the stockade, and they really celebrated. She was so homely that I put her out of sight in a little cubbyhole office. I did not go near it except, when necessary, because the smell, a combination of dirt and alcohol, was horrible. One afternoon I got a telephone call from the bar owner next to the school, demanding that I come over immediately and "drag my God-damned secretary out of the bar." I did not look to see which one was gone. Although I had not missed her, I knew. When I walked into the bar, there she was, on the floor, swearing more admirable than any G.I. I had met while in the service. She had gotten completely bombed and had fallen off a bar stool. I fired her as soon as

I got her into the office. Subsequently, I hired a nice older lady and had no more secretarial problems.

Sometime in 1950, the Old Man called to say he wanted to talk to me in the bar. The Veteran's Administration was refusing to pay our school any money at all. He pleaded ignorance as to the reason, but told me that, until the matter was resolved, I was to cut expenses as much as possible in the office. He also told me that very likely our telephones were bugged, and that I was to discuss no school business on the telephone. This situation continued for two or three months, while the Old Man kept advancing money for the payroll and the daily operation of the school. Payday was Friday morning. I always drove to the bank and cashed my check before I distributed checks to the rest of the employees. None ever bounced, but I was always worried.

I had no real idea why we were having problems with the V.A. Our student records were absolutely accurate. So was our tuition billing to the Veterans Administration. I talked with the few training officers remaining in the local office, and none of them knew what the situation was.

The chief instructor and I frequently lunched together. Naturally, we discussed the possible reasons for the Veterans Administration's actions. Each entering student received a complete set of auto mechanic's tools and receipted for them. The chief instructor thought that the V.A. either had evidence, or at least, well-grounded suspicion that there was fraud in the handling of those tools. For one thing, many students who left the school without completing the course did not take the tools with them, and he thought perhaps the tools were being reissued and charged for a second time. None of the tool business was handled by school personnel. The Old Man came from Detroit, and one of his Detroit cohorts handled all tool sales to the school. It was also suggested that the tools purchased were excessively expensive, and that at least some of this excess went directly into the Old Man's pocket.

We never really did find out what was wrong. The Old Man hired a very well-known Cleveland attorney who filed suit in Federal District Court in Cincinnati asking that the court order the V.A. to pay all sums withheld. The matter came on for hearing before an arbitrary federal district judge who listened to our attorney, tuned out the V.A.'s lawyers, and ordered all sums withheld to be paid at once. I was relieved.

At the beginning of the year 1951, I quit my job in order to prepare for the February Ohio State Bar examination. It was not possible to work and review all that was necessary in order to pass the examination, and I did want to become a lawyer and be admitted to practice in Ohio. It had been a strange two years. I had met many different types of people — poor whites, poor blacks, dumb whites, and dumb blacks, the Old Man and his entourage, thieves, really tough, hard people, and some fine, ambitious ones. In retrospect, I sort of enjoyed it all, and I know that my overall knowledge of people grew immeasurably.

I did not think much about it at the time, but I had had four or five different jobs in a period of four or five years; yet I was not a ne'er-do-well. No one fired me and I made a lot of friends. It was truly a time of transition for the entire country, and certainly for me. I think the experience made me a far better lawyer later on than I would have been had I remained in the sheltered environment of teaching during my law school years.

I received my law degree from Franklin University the spring of 1950, even though I had not completed all of the courses required. I did not really finish school until December of that year. Attrition had taken its toll insofar as numbers were concerned. Many began law school at about the same time that I did, but we had a comparatively small group who completed the work. As I said earlier, the courses were not easy, but the routine required of all of us was most demanding. We all worked at some sort of job during the day and studied or went to class at night. We saw little of our families; social life was almost non-existent. A couple of my classmates had nervous breakdowns, three were divorced, and many of us had digestive problems from the food we ate, and the hours when we ate. It was not easy!

In the fall of 1950, those of us who were going to take the February bar examination commenced a bar review course. It might not have been necessary to take such a course if one were a genius, but none of us felt that we could pass the bar exam without the course. We were right. We needed it. Everyone who was in the central Ohio area took

A. B. Gertner's Bar Review. From sometime in October until January, we met for four hours on Thursday evenings, four hours on Saturday afternoons and seven hours each Sunday. Abe Gertner taught the course most effectively.

Abe was a short, slightly-built Jew. In many ways he was brilliant. He gave us mimeograph copies of cases from previous bar examinations, which we studied. When we were in class, he kept our attention by asking endless questions requiring short, quick answers. There were perhaps two hundred in the course and Abe had all of our names on cards, which he constantly shuffled. A student might be called upon two or three times in one session, perhaps not at all. He always had our attention. The way Abe taught the course was not dull, dry repetition. It was humorous and fun. I remember even now some of the questions he occasionally threw in. "What is the difference between a fifty-dollar divorce and a seventy-five-dollar divorce?" The answer was twenty-five dollars. Then he said several times, "When someone calls you to ask whether or not the police can put you in jail for doing so and so, always ask them where they're calling from."

During the intensive six-weeks' course just prior to the bar examination, we were in class five nights a week plus Saturdays and Sundays. I studied every day. Because I had quit my job, we had no money. I had to pass that examination the very first time.

The examination was a three-day affair. All of the questions were essay type. Thank God, I could express my thoughts on paper. Each night, I was completely exhausted mentally and, to some extent, physically. One of my fellow sufferers called me every night to go over that day's questions. He had been a very bright student, but I really hated his calls. It seemed to me after listening to his answers, that I might not have known anything, and that all of the time I had spent on the study of law had been wasted. We would not know whether we had passed the examination for a month. It was a hard, nervous time for all of us.

During the years that I worked for the trade school, our lives were not uneventful. Television came to Columbus sometime during the year 1949. All of it was black and white. Color did not come in for several years afterwards. Most of the television sets had twelve-inch, sometimes round, screens. We did not buy a set in the beginning, for they were relatively expensive and very much a novelty. We decided to purchase a set for Christmas and, after much shopping, bought a Dumont with a nineteen-inch circular screen. Compared to what we had seen, the picture seemed huge. There were not continuous programs. Very often all that appeared on a channel was the test pattern. There was always the news. There were televised sporting events, which I watch avidly when I could. There were game shows, programs for children, a few soap operas, quite a few movies. Ed Sullivan had a Sunday night variety hour that drew faithful large audience for years, and years, and years. Jack Benny, Bob Hope and George Burns were seen occasionally then. However, the big star and number one attraction during those early years was Milton Berle. All of the television programs were live and, or course, mistakes were made.

The Korean War began. Some of my friends who had retained a reserve status in the military were called into service once again. No one quite knew why so much American money and so many American troops were committed to what was supposed to have been a United Nations peace endeavor. It was true then that the United States was by far the most powerful military force on earth. The other militarily-important nations, including Russia, were still recovering from the devastation and death of World War II. Of course, then we were the only country which had the atomic bomb. Amazingly, enough, in view of what occurred later, there were few draft evaders, no huge demonstrations in the streets, no major protest to this war. We were still a united country. The people seemed to accept the roll of being the policeman of the world.

For good or ill, depending on the point of view, our Congress, and a reluctant President Truman, insisted on the division of Palestine and the establishment of the nation of Israel. Through Truman, Secretary of State George Marshall's plan for the rehabilitation of Western Europe, including West Germany, was implemented. There is, in my mind, no questions that our open pocketbook at that time saved Western Europe from chaos, complete collapse of their governments, and a Communist takeover.

What we did in those few Truman years still affects us and the rest of the world today. It is interesting to speculate as to what might have happened had we gone into our shell and built an "impregnable fortress America."

Evelyn and I were not too concerned about world affairs during this period. We were – mostly Evelyn – raising our young daughter, enjoying, and furnishing our new home, getting me through law school and the bar examination, and eating. We saw few, if any, movies because I had no time, and we had few babysitters. Occasionally on a Saturday night we got together socially with friends. Many times, there was no real food served. The host usually furnished just beer and pretzels. Occasionally the wives would have a potluck meal, and everyone brought whatever they could afford to drink. We were not the only ones who had little money in those years. Actually, we were better off financially than were many of our friends.

We bought a new automobile in 1950. When I worked for the State of Ohio, I drove our Dodge a lot of miles. The checks I got for mileage came in handy at the time, but I actually needed another car in 1950. I not only got the new car, but I also learned about bank plan financing. I purchased a green, two-door Buick Special, with what was called a torpedo body style, slanted from the front roof line through the trunk. It did not have much equipment on it – and no radio. Buicks, even the cheapest Special, cost more than I could really afford, but I suppose that I bought it as a status symbol, though I had little status.

In the fall of 1949, Jim and Virginia Henry moved into their new brick home next door, with doctor's office attached. As I have said, we had agreed that it would be nice to be next-door neighbors. We were happy when their house was finished and they moved in. Despite all sorts of arguments between Jim and me over the years, we have remained friends; our wives have seldom, if ever, had a dispute of any sort. Our children grew up together and are all close. Whenever either family had problems, and everyone does, help and sympathy and understanding were always forthcoming.

Jim, however, is an unusual individual. He is a truly fine, very dedicated doctor. He has a brilliant mind, bordering that of a genius. He can be very generous and helpful and understanding. I am certain, though, that he frequently thinks that he is God. He can be conceited and overbearing; he can be compassionate and understanding. He is part saint and part son of a bitch. His moods are absolutely unpredictable. We have had a long and stormy friendship over all the years. One of his problems with me is that he expects perfection, and I do not attain it. Actually, I don't ever come close.

Evelyn became pregnant again, despite the fact that she had been told by Jim and other doctors that she could not have any more children. We had built our home accordingly. One Saturday afternoon, Jim was paying us a short visit and, while drinking a beer, looked at me and said, "I examined Evelyn this week. Congratulations, you're going to have twins." I told him that he was full of shit. "Okay, you son of a bitch," he said. "This is the last time I'm going to tell you. You are going to have twins." I thought he was kidding and so did Evelyn.

One afternoon in April when I had a dental appointment and was in the dentist's chair, I received a frantic telephone call from Evelyn telling me that I had to come home at once to take her to the hospital. I broke all speed records driving home. Evelyn had had a doctor's appointment that afternoon, and during the examination Jim discovered that she was ready to deliver. She was about two months early. We hurried to the hospital and got her checked into the maternity floor. The nurses promptly started to induce labor, and we were on our way. Like any other prospective father, I stayed as close to the delivery room door as possible, paced the floor, and chain-smoked cigarettes.

It was very serious business to me, and I was nervous as hell. Suddenly, I heard cheering, yelling and laughter coming through the delivery room door. I could not understand what that was all about. The door burst open and out came a nurse carrying a newborn baby. She had a big grin on her face, showed me a baby boy and said, "The next one will be out in just a minute." Out came another nurse carrying another fresh new boy. She was laughing. Both nurses had been students of mine when I taught school. A yell came from the delivery room. Jim Henry was saying, "Come on in, you bastard. I told you you'd have twins. This is the best practical joke I ever played on you. I'll leave you alone from now on." He didn't.

I went home, because Evelyn was still out as a result of the anesthetic. The Henrys were over immediately, laughing and joking.

Eveyln's parents had been visiting us that day. I think the news shocked them. I had to explain to our daughter, Marcia, that she now had two brothers. At age about three and half, she was not very impressed. She remained quite unimpressed for a number of years.

I went back to the hospital that evening. Evelyn was partially awake but still not completely recovered. I told her two or three times that we had twin boys. The news finally registered fully, and she opened her eyes with an expression of surprise and horror and said, "God, that's an awful lot of kids." It really was a lot of kids. We called them Tom and Dick and prayed that Harry would never arrive.

Marcia and the boys in 1951.

They were premature babies and both of them were in the incubator. Grove City was still a small town, and the news spread quickly. I think everyone in the area was chortling me.

Our rather placid lives were changed completely and forever more. Our lovely, roomy house was suddenly too small. With my schedule, Evelyn had complete responsibility for their care, feeding and welfare. She had a small daughter, twin sons, a house, no transportation, no help, and a husband who was either working, in school or studying. Naturally, she became extremely nervous to

Summer 1951 Marcia (4) Boys 1

the point of a complete breakdown. One Saturday afternoon, when Evelyn wanted to go shopping to get out of the house and away from it all for a few hours, I volunteered to care for the children. After all, they slept most of the time, I thought. The truth was that, on that day, no one slept. Both twins had diarrhea, and I spent most of my time changing diapers. Feeding the two their bottles was also a good trick. By the time Evelyn got home, I was exhausted.

I had no really good offers to practice law with anyone. I had talked with one of the Ohio Supreme Court judges who was a political friend of the politician who was my boss when I first went to work with the Veterans Administration. The judge offered to talk to his son, a partner in a very large, very good firm in Cincinnati, about helping me go with them. That scared me. I did not feel that a graduate of a night law school could possibly compete with the young graduates of the prestigious Eastern law schools. Besides, I did not really want to move. I was offered jobs with several of the big law firms in Columbus at a dollar an hour. I thought that was an insult. I might have become an understudy for the lobbyist for the Ohio Farm Bureau. The job paid about two hundred dollars a month. I could have sold life insurance and specialized in estate planning, but, at that time, I did not realize what the potential really was in that area.

I had known that I could practice with Tom White and Bud Rankin. Tom's father died sometime after he talked me into going to law school, and after Tom had been in practice for a short time. Bud grew up immediately across the alley from Tom. Although he was somewhat younger, Bud was always around when we were children in elementary and junior high school. Bud had retained his reserve commission after World War II and was called back into service very soon after my potential admission to practice before the Ohio bar. I knew that I would have an office.

During the waiting period between the time of the State Bar examination and the day of reckoning as to whether or not I had passed, I went to the law office almost daily. I knew nothing about the practice aspects of practicing law. At Franklin, we had had no legal clinic courses, no trial practice, nothing about office practice. Law school, then, was a study of case law with a minimum of experience in legal research. I knew nothing of legal forms. I had never taken a tax course. At that time I believe that most law schools prepared law students in the same manner. We were ill-prepared for what we were expected to do in order to properly serve a client.

The office itself had been established originally in 1913. Many of the lawyers who had occupied the suite over the years had distinguished careers in both law and politics. One had served as mayor of Columbus, another was then serving as a Common Pleas Court judge, several had been members of the legislature, and George Marshall, who was then a member of the group, was at that time a state Senator and later a judge. Tom's father had served as the attorney for the Anti-Saloon League, had appeared before the United States Supreme Court many times, had been an unsuccessful candidate for governor of Ohio on the Prohibition ticket and, in his declining years, served as a federal referee in bankruptcy and as chairman of what was then called the Ohio State Industrial Commission.

The office was located on the eighth floor at 44 East Broad Street. There was a huge lobby, six offices, one of which was immense; it had, at some previous time, served as a library. Two secretaries occupied desks in the lobby. At the time, I was very impressed with everything and considered myself most fortunate to become a member of the cast.

Actually, the building was old. The suite had not been painted in years. The carpet could have been the original from 1913. It was old and worn and dirty. The secretaries' desks were far from modern and there were several straight-back, worn-out wooden chairs and a couple of old-fashioned coat trees in the lobby. The individual offices looked little better. Nothing was new in any of the offices. None of the chairs were comfortable, including the desk chairs used by the lawyers.

I met everyone in the office. The secretary who worked for Bud, Tom, and George Marshall was young and had gone to work in the office directly from high school. She was bright and had absorbed much during her three years. She taught me a great deal about forms and office procedure. The secretary who worked for the other three lawyers was an older, high-powered, brilliant woman. She was always discontented with her job, because she felt that she was capable of doing better things. She proved it later as she accepted a responsible position as purchasing agent for two different colleges. George Marshal was older than we were by several years. He was a perfect gentleman, a prominent member of his church, did not drink, swear, or chase women. In his youth, he became an Eagle scout and that influence carried over into his adulthood.

Morris Lopper was a short, fat, hard-working, hard-drinking Jewish attorney. He had no home life, and was at his desk at five-thirty or six o'clock in the morning. Aside from frequent trips to a nearby saloon for a quick double shot of straight whiskey with a beer chaser, Morris had no social life at all. He represented several extremely wealthy clients and was recognized as an authority on real estate title, and real estate generally. Keith Martin was his partner. Among other clients, they represented a very busy savings and loan association. Keith, a tall, thin, quiet pipe-smoker, spent day after day examining abstracts of title, writing title reports, and closing real estate loans. It was drudgery. Herman Weisberg was their young lawyer. He was probably brilliant, but he lived in constant fear of Morris, and spent his days running errands and drafting legal documents.

Bud Rankin had always been too heavy. In his adult years he started a reducing diet at least once a week. Most of his diets ended when he impulsively brought in a sack of doughnuts and ate them all or drank a couple of chocolate milk shakes. He was a member of a prominent, wealthy, old Columbus family. When he was in college, he was a real big-man-on-campus type. Bud was always a little pompous and uncommonly funny. He never intentionally offended anyone but managed to upset a lot of people without realizing it. He would go to extreme lengths to be helpful to anyone, and always charged into everything rather like the proverbial bull in a China shop. He was, and is, very intelligent, and always completely disorganized. He took himself and everything else very seriously. Actually, most of the time I laughed at him, but there were frequent occasions when he exasperated me to the point where I had the urge to kill him.

Tom and I, friends from elementary school days and fraternity brothers, had always been close. Always a big, fat, good-natured kid, he was popular and very outgoing in college. The war changed him. He became quiet, somewhat introverted, slow to make a decision, somewhat tedious, methodical in his approach to a legal problem. Actually, he was a good lawyer and usually right when he finally unwound after taking the time to think the problem through. He would never have been successful as a trial lawyer.

Tom – out of necessity – had a job as an assistant clerk in the Ohio House of Representatives and, consequently, was out of the law office most of the time when the legislature was in session. Therefore, during my three or four weeks in limbo while awaiting the results of the bar examination, Bud Rankin was trying to educate me in the practical aspects of practicing law. The first thing he did was take me to the courthouse. I knew, of course, where it was located, but I had no idea as to what the various offices were doing. I knew that there were common pleas court judges, but I did not know the location of the court rooms; and the judges themselves, with one or two exceptions, were only _____ names to me. I quickly became acquainted with most courthouse employees and learned who to see in each county office to get advice and help. It was just smart to be friendly and to learn the ropes. Tom and Bud were not in court often, but their reputation with the judges were good, and their good names were transferred to me. We went to Municipal Court. I did not even know where it was located. I met the most important man in the Municipal Court hierarchy – the chief bailiff. He was the only person in that confused mess, including the judges, who knew how to do everything in this minor, kangaroo court. We went to the Federal Building and Bankruptcy Court. When we were there, the bankruptcy referee and assorted creditors were conducting a lengthy examination of an old, dignified attorney who was president of a bankrupt brewery. As he patiently, answered their questions as to why the brewery failed, I embarrassed Bud by saying in a loud whisper that the reason the brewery failed was that they made lousy beer. My comment drew a subdued laugh from the spectators who must have drunk some of the beer themselves.

Bud also explained to me about the office form file. There were forms for every conceivable document that might ever have to be prepared. Some of them were obsolete and probably had been in the office since its 1913 opening.

Bud also worked with me in the courthouse records office to introduce me to the continuation of abstracts of title. I had not learned in law school what an abstract of title was. Simply put, an abstract is the history of the title to a particular parcel of real estate as shown by the records located in a county courthouse. To search courthouse records is sheer drudgery. One is not required to be a lawyer or even to have any legal knowledge to perform the task. Abstracts are almost a thing of the past now, and title insurance is used most of the time, but title searches and a determination by a lawyer as to whether the title is good and marketable is required. I became quite skillful at this boring task, and got to be on a first-name basis with most of the courthouse office holders and employees. I learned a great deal about real estate title law as a result of performing the unpleasant task of record-searching for almost twenty years. Most lawyers refused to touch this sort of slave labor. In many ways, they were right, but, if you did enough of it, you ate.

During my training period, I got acquainted with the lawyer who occupied the suite at the opposite end of the hall. That office was a zoo. In a couple of instances two, and sometime three, lawyers shared the same office. When one of them had a client, the others took a walk. One of the men was in his late eighties and was horribly bent over and crippled. When he walked, he leaned on a cane for support. He had been quite famous, an excellent lawyer and was noted for being meaner than hell; old age did not improve his disposition much. Another was a tall skinny kid who later became successful and a senior partner in a large firm. Two others, young hustlers, became wealthy personal injury specialists. Another had been the prosecuting attorney in a small Ohio county, and probably should have remained there. Still another had held various high-important appointive political jobs. His party was out of office, and so was he. He had little law practice and seemed generally to be down on his luck. Three attorneys occupied large, well-furnished offices, each successful in somewhat unusual ways. One was a short, bald ex-drunk active in Alcoholics Anonymous. He represented a large assortment of lushes and said truthfully that he "specialized" in uncontested divorces and guilty pleas for drunk drivers. The second man, a large, tall, bald fellow was from a family in the funeral business. He wrote an unbelievable number of wills and handled a constant stream of estates. Every lawyer in that suite was colorful; but by far the most colorful and the greatest character was a short, fat, well-tailored, perfectly-groomed Jewish attorney, Milton L. Farber. At that time, he was an extremely well-known, headline-grabbing, trial lawyer. He was cultured, brilliant, a liberal's liberal, a best-selling author, and funnier than hell. We became friends immediately.

The day came when the grades on the Ohio State Bar examination were to be released. I did not wait for the next day's mail. I was in the office of the clerk of the Ohio Supreme Court early that morning. I had passed with flying colors! Actually, I received the highest grade of any of the members of my class at Franklin and was very high in the state. Two of my classmates failed the examination – one because he could not spell the word "judgment." Both passed the test the second time they took it and became successful attorneys. Naturally, I was thrilled and much relieved. I do not know what would have occurred had I failed. We were out of money, and I was out of a job. The chance I took really did not worry me until it was all over. What I did not realize at that moment was that passing the bar examination and making money did not exactly follow.

In any event, the successful applicants were duly sworn in as member of the Ohio Bar on March 29, 1951. My wife, daughter, and mother were there for the ceremony. It was a proud, happy day for all of us.

April 1951 — October 1958

Very shortly after I began the general practice of law, Bud left for active duty in the Army, and I inherited his office. The furniture in the office was old and somewhat shabby. It probably had been used when it was purchased. The chairs were wooden, as was the desk swivel chair. The small room had western exposure and on summer afternoons, was so hot it was almost unbearable. There was no fan and, naturally, no air conditioning. There were no drapes, but here were venetian blinds, which did not help the heat any, but did reduce some of the glare.

I usually had something to keep me busy from the beginning. At about the exact moment that I was being sworn in as an attorney, Milt filed a mandamus action against the State Director of Education and named me as co-counsel. Bud left me a stack of collection files. He had been doing collection work for the Columbus Credit Bureau. Some of my friends came to me to have wills drawn. I began to pick up a few divorce cases. None of the business was very lucrative, and I was not skilled at anything; consequently, it took me days to accomplish what should have taken an hour or two.

I found out quickly that Tom's father had outlived his law practice, and that the small amount of business that Tom and Bud had accumulated was minor in nature and not very productive financially. After paying the rent, our share of the secretary's salary, and the continuous expense of maintaining a huge law library, which we did not need, we were lucky to be able to draw one hundred fifty dollars a month. Our secretary was paid two hundred. I did not expect to become wealthy overnight, but neither did I expect to hit the poverty level.

Although there was little money, the experience I gained those first few years was almost worth the starvation. In the summer of 1951, about three months after my admission to practice law, I was the only lawyer in my part of the office, and Morris Lopper and I held the fort alone for three weeks. Bud had long since left for the Army. Tom was on Army Reserve duty. George was on vacation, and Morris chose that time to let his two associates take their holidays. I had to take all telephone calls, see all of the clients, and try to solve all of the problems for George and Tom's clients. I shudder now when I remember some of the advice I gave and the actions I took. Morris answered some of my questions, but Milt Farber really helped me very much. God, he was a good lawyer.

During this period, a friend from my days with the Ohio School of Trades came to see me with a major problem. He was one of three stockholders in a corporation called the Advance Scale and Manufacturing Company. Rudy, my client, was a great con artist, but dumber than hell. He had become involved in a promotional capacity with a real crook in the manufacturing of scales and had borrowed more money than any bank president should have loaned him to put into this business. He had also persuaded a "friend" to invest a considerable sum of money. The "friend" filed suit to dissolve the corporation and appoint a Receiver. In those years, when the common pleas court was in recess in the summer term,

Article from 4/6/1951

the judges took two-week periods of serving as the duty judge. This involved signing routine entries, handling emergency matters and hearing such cases as were required to be heard almost immediately. The corporate dissolution request was one of those cases required to be heard quickly. Judge Harter was the duty judge, so I decided that the smartest thing I could do would be to talk to him. Judge Harter was a peculiar sort, very much a holier-than-thou type. He categorized attorneys as either being completely moral, steadfast, upright, honest, worthy members of the Bar, or as being disreputable and unworthy. In fact, few were either all good or all bad. However, once he formed an opinion of an attorney's character, his mind never changed. Regardless, he was always unfailingly polite, boring, and addressing everyone as "sir." When I walked into his chambers, he had no idea who I was. I introduced myself and told him that I was newly-admitted to practice and had no idea how to proceed. He went out of his way to explain the entire procedure in great detail and told me exactly what to do. He asked who the attorney was who had brought action. When I told him, he shook his head in disgust and said, "Sir, I am certain that you will have no problem at all with this matter in my court."

On the day of the hearing, Milt Farber announced that he was going along just to observe. I sat at the counsel table; Milt sat in a chair some distance behind me. The opposing attorney was black and looked and talked exactly like Algonquin J. Calhoun of Amos and Andy fame. He was funny, but this was just a pose. He was one of the few lawyers I ever met who was completely untrustworthy. As he talked, Milt whispered to me, "Stand up and object." Later he whispered, "Move to strike that part of his statement," etc. I did not know what I was doing, but I followed directions, and Harter sustained me. When we finished, Milt was laughing and told me that had I moved to send the lawyer to the electric chair, Harter would have sustained that too. Harter ordered that Barber be appointed Receiver for the corporation and appointed me as the attorney. We liquidated the company, saved my client from possible criminal charges, succeeded in getting the other attorney's client indicted for embezzlement, and collected substantial fees for those days.

I could not begin to recite the matters I handled in any sort of chronological order. I had collection matters and minor lawsuits in the Columbus Municipal Court. My name was placed on the list to receive assigned criminal cases as defense counsel. I wrote wills, prepared deeds, did real estate title work and generally did a little bit of everything that a young, beginning attorney gets involved in. Some of those matters stand out in my mind, more than anything that happened later on when my practice became more lucrative and much more sedate, and much duller most of the time.

As did most young lawyers, I handled a countless number of divorce cases. Some of them were unusual. One of the first involved a couple who had been married and divorced four different times, three times to one another. I started to explain to them that I could not, ethically, represent both of them. They interrupted me and told me not to worry about that. That they knew a lot about divorces and would tell me exactly what to do. They were right. They knew much more about divorce than I did. When it was over, they each got married. I often wondered how many divorces each had, and whether they ever entered wedded bliss with each other again.

I do not know how I ever got her as a client, but a long-distance telephone operator came to me for a divorce. She was really something to see and the word "sexy" is not even a close description. From the top of her head to her toes, she exuded sex. She had a great body and every part moved when she walked. Naturally, she chewed gum. When a divorce was uncontested, it was necessary that the party seeking the divorce furnish two-character witnesses and one witness who could substantiate at least a portion of the testimony. It was a very perfunctory proceeding. My gal's witness came to my office to be briefed on their roles about half an hour before we were due in court. They wriggled down the main drag (High Street) and every male eye popped along the way. We traipsed through the courthouse with sensational results, including a few whistles. When we got in front of Judge Clifford to present the testimony, he did a double-take and smiled happily, proving that he was not yet too old to look. When we had finished and the decree of divorce was granted, my client looked at me and said,

"Now I ain't married anymore?" I told her that she was not. She said, "Look out, men!"

However, most of my female divorce clients were not quite so sensational. Most of them were homely, whiny, scrawny types. They came to the office crying when they told the stories of their husbands' transgressions. Sometimes while listening to them, I could understand why their husbands did whatever they were accused of.

A very shy, retiring, mousey little woman came to me wanting to divorce her husband of some twenty-odd years because he was a bartender and was never home. She was a church-going, God-fearing lady who disapproved of her husband's profession. They had one son who was much like his mother, and completely tied to her apron strings. I filed for divorce for her, and the husband contested. On the day of the trial, I met the husband—a big burly, hail-fellow-well-met, obviously a perfect bartender. I wondered why he did not want a divorce and was informed by his attorney that the husband wanted to continue to provide for his wife, because he did not feel that she was capable of taking care of herself and their son.

I put my client on the witness stand and, after she was duly sworn, asked her to state her name and address. She gave her name and then urinated on the witness stand and fainted. The judge recessed and continued the case. A public health nurse came rushing in and revived her. Her husband was in tears and promptly withdrew his answer. A week or two later she was granted an uncontested divorce. I did not see the lady or her son for several years afterward. When I did, she was much stronger and more self-reliant than she had been, and her son had changed completely for the better. Apparently, her husband had dominated both of them to their detriment.

There was, and to a lesser extent still is, slum housing adjacent to Grove City. Many of these dwellings were little more than shacks, having dirt floors, no plumbing of any kind and, in more than one instance, no outdoor privy. There were no lawns, only weeds; parts of old cars and other junk were everywhere. The places were filthy, smelly, rat-infested, health hazards. The occupants were equally crummy. An older—and smarter—lawyer referred to me a contested divorce involving two of the few married residents of the area. I should never have become involved and would not have except for the fact that somehow enough money had been secured to pay my fee.

My client and her husband had children, both legitimate and otherwise. Her "boyfriend" and his wife had children under the same circumstances. Probably so did my clients' husband's girlfriend and her husband. For all I know, their own children may have had children if they were old enough to breed. If a divorcing couple had children, a court investigator always interviewed the parents, checked the home and its surroundings, talked to the neighbors, and then made a report to the court as to the relative fitness of the divorcing parties to have custody of the minor children.

The day of the trial of what was to have been a contested divorce arrived. The other side did not appear, but his attorney stated that he was withdrawing the answer, thus enabling me to have my client secure an uncontested divorce. Everything seemed to be worked out favorable and easily. The bailiff called the case, and my client and witnesses stood up as I motioned them to follow me to the bench. Suddenly, Judge Rose, the Court of Domestic Relations judge, looked up at me and said, "Mr. Clark, ask your client to wait, and then come to the bench please." I did as instruct, and he leaned over and said, "I'm not going to grant a divorce in this case." I was shocked. No one ever lost an uncontested divorce. "Well, why in the hell not?" I asked. "I have just read the caseworker's report on the custody investigation," he replied, "and everybody is screwing everybody else in the whole damned area." "But, judge," I protested, "how will your not granting a divorce stop that?" "It won't, but it'll sure as hell slow 'em down!" the judge replied. At this point, I thought I had better make some show for my client so, in a loud voice I said, "Does this court mean to say that, without hearing any evidence in this matter, it will not grant a divorce?" The judge looked at me and smiled and said, "By all means, no. You may, of course, put on all of the evidence you wish, but after I hear it, I will not grant a divorce." There was nothing else that I could do. My client did not understand what happened, except I told her that, as a result of the investigation, she was still married. Naturally, every lawyer I knew had some sort of nasty comment to make to me. At any rate, I became well-known to most of the attorneys in town.

A Grove City gal whom I had known for years had been married and had two children. Her husband died. He had worked as a railroader, and she received a pension from the Railroad Retirement Board. Sometime later, she met and married a soldier who was stationed at Lockbourne Air base. She lost her pension as a result of the marriage. After a few months, her new husband was arrested and convicted of bigamy. He had married several different women and failed to divorce any of them.

She applied for the restoration of her pension and was advised that it could be restored only if she secured an annulment of the second marriage. The Ohio Supreme Court had ruled shortly prior to this time that an annulment could not be granted in Ohio. I went to see Judge Rose and explained the situation to him. He said, "I'll sign anything you wish so long as it says 'divorce.' But because the Supreme Court said that Ohio does not recognize annulment, I'm not going to grant an annulment." I thought about it, and decided to talk with Judge Reynolds, the senior common pleas judge, a wonderful judge and most understanding. He always said that in his decisions he hoped he had "wrought substantial justice." I explained in detail what had happened, told him about the Supreme Court's decision, and what Judge Rose had said. "Rose is wrong," he said. "The Supreme Court is wrong. File your petition, bring her in. I'll grant the annulment." I sent a certified copy of the decree to the Railroad Retirement Board, and her pension was restored. About six months later – out of caution – I got her a divorce.

Two young couples in Grove City, close friends, got together very often for social activities with their children, and as a foursome. There was too much togetherness. One husband and the opposite wife became involved in a very illicit relationship. I represented the two wronged parties and discovered outstanding examples of non-marital sex. My wronged husband came home unexpectedly one day and caught his wife and the other husband having intercourse in the family bathtub. (I tried to understand just how they worked that out mechanically.) I then learned that my "wronged wife" was having sexual relations with several different men in the community.

It was altogether a real mess. Divorces were granted, finally, to my two clients. Strangely enough, the two wives both got custody of their respective children.

In the early 1960s, I finally quit taking divorces. None of them were really money makers, and they all involved more time and trauma and nuisance than anything else. Divorce clients called me day and night, Saturdays, Sundays, holidays—anytime. There was always a new transgression on the part of their spouses, which I could not solve, and did not want to hear about. I almost always got mad at my client at some stage. In every other type of litigation, reason usually prevails. In divorce cases, the parties were never reasonable. They hated each other. The incident which finally induced me to refuse any further domestic matters involved a husband and a crazy wife. I represented the husband, thank God! One Saturday at about noon, my golf partner, a local doctor, had pulled into my drive to take me to the golf course. As I was ready to walk out the door, the telephone rang, and I foolishly answered it. It was my client's crazy wife. "I want you to know that I am just getting ready to kill myself," she announced. I was madder than hell at myself for being dumb enough to answer the telephone, and at her for calling me. My reply to her was, "I think that would be a God-damned good idea. Why don't you go ahead, and do it before you change your mind?" I then hung up and steamed out the door to my friend's car. He looked at me and asked what was wrong. I told him the entire story, and it frightened him. He insisted that I see her physician immediately and report the situation. I had no choice. He was driving. I burst into her doctor's office and told him the story. "Oh, Christ, she does this all the time," he sputtered. "She knows just how many sleeping pills to take. I'll get a call in about fifteen minutes from the emergency room. They'll pump her stomach and send her home. She just wants to get attention."

For quite a few years after I started to practice, the common pleas court judges alternated court rooms each term of court, so that a judge tried criminal cases for one court term only about every two years. The courthouse was old, and the criminal court room could house more spectators than could the others. Each term of court, for those of us who were willing to accept assigned indigent criminal cases, were required to have the judge place our names on the list for assignment.

Most young lawyers got on the lists for two reasons – the possible chance to actually try a criminal case to a jury and the fifty dollars the county paid for each case assigned.

Most of these assigned cases were not very glamorous. Upon notification of my assignment, I went to the county jail. These clients were <u>always</u> in jail. They not only could not afford to pay an attorney, but they could also not raise enough money to have a bondsman get them out of jail pending trial. The jail itself was old and dingy. It smelled scrubbed, but the odors of countless unwashed bodies, rancid grease, and onions cooked years ago combined to offend the nostrils. Attorneys conferred with their clients in a large area which was opened by a guard, who clanged shut the barred area full of curious prisoners staring out at the lawyer. He would yell out the name of the prisoner to be seen, let him out of the bullpen and into the area where we lawyers waited. There the prisoners (clients) and lawyers sat on hard wood seats, side by side in a corner of the huge room, hidden from the view of the other prisoners by a screen. The guard stood in the center of the room with his hand on his gun holster. Just sitting in that jail under those conditions was worth more than fifty dollars. Usually, when I started talking to my client, he admitted his guilt of committing whatever crime he was accused of. All he wanted was to work out a deal. Plea bargaining was in vogue then too. One client wanted to go back to prison as a parole violator, rather than on a new conviction, because he could get his old job back if he was merely a parole violator. Another, a loser three previous times, was indicted for burglary; he told me that he was not guilty, had alibi witnesses, and wanted a trial.

I had just secured the indictment of yet another of my assigned clients and was reading it and starting to ask questions when he jumped over me and ran into the middle of the room, screaming and crying. The guard and a couple of deputies seized him quickly, thank God.

I arranged with the prosecuting attorney to send the parole violator back to prison as a parole violator, after discussing the matter with the criminal court judge, who was agreeable. I had told my client that all he had to do was stay quiet and smile, he would be back on his old job soon. We went into the court room, and everything was working out perfectly until the judge asked the prisoner whether he wished to make a statement before sentence was pronounced. Instead of saying, "No, your honor," my client launched into a scathing attack on the judicial system, lousy cops, court judges, etc. when he stopped, the judge thanked him for his remarks, and then sentenced him to consecutive sentences on each charge against him in his indictment. If he is alive, he is probably still in the penitentiary, and I do not imagine that he ever saw his old job again.

None of my "not guilty" client's alibis checked out, but he still denied guilt and wanted a jury trial. I went to the prosecutor's office to advise them to set the case for trial. The prosecutor looked at the file, laughed and showed me the police report. It appears that on the night of the burglary it had snowed heavily, and that there were footprints leading from the burglarized residence to the house where my client was living, and the footprints matched my client's shoes exactly. The prosecutor would have him indicted and sent to prison for life as a habitual criminal. When I relayed this information to my client, he decided that he was guilty after all.

I had only one criminal trial on an assigned criminal case. This was a rather young black man who had been charged with armed robbery. He was very pleasant and cooperative. He told me that he had not committed the crime, and I believed him. He seemed quite sincere. The only thing that made me a little doubtful was that he had been in some sort of confinement every Christmas of his life from the time he was ten years old.

Henry Holden, by far the best trial lawyer in the prosecutor's office, and later a very good judge, prosecuted the case. Judge Gesseman, who had been my instructor when I took a course in contracts in law school, was the trial judge. My friend, Milt Farber, without any notice to me, came to the trial and sat behind me. After examination of prospective jurors, a jury of twelve was finally seated, and the trial began.

The problem with trying to convict my client was that the identifying witnesses, according to their testimony, saw him at night, running under a streetlight. It was almost like a free course in trial procedure for me. Judge Gesseman called frequent recesses and he and Milt talked to me, told me what I was doing wrong, and advised me how to proceed. Milt occasionally whispered questions or advice to me. While I could not use the language, my questions implied that "they all look alike" especially at night underneath a streetlight.

The jury was properly instructed and sent to the jury room late in the afternoon. They stayed out. The court recessed for dinner, and we returned. They stayed out. Finally, they sent word that they did not think they could reach a verdict. Judge Gesseman told them to continue their deliberations. Finally, at about midnight, they came in and declared my client guilty. I almost had a hung jury. The deciding factor was my client's criminal record. It is possible that he did not commit <u>that</u> particular crime, but, based on past performance, he sure as hell could have.

A Grove City businessman, whom I had known and liked for years, was charged with felonious assault. Among his many other activities, he owned and operated school buses. He was accused of molesting an eleven-year-old girl, the last passenger to be delivered on his busy route. He was not accused of rape, but rather of fondling her. He and his wife came to me and asked that I represent him, which I agreed to do. I never doubted his innocence; neither did his wife or family. His reputation in the community was good. Naturally, in a small town the word got around quickly as to the charges, and there were those who wanted to hang him without benefit of trial. The extremely sanctimonious insisted that my client quit driving a school bus immediately. He did quit voluntarily. Some even tried to force him to sell all his other buses, which would have been ridiculous.

I investigated the case as best I could, but there are never witnesses to this type of crime. It really became a matter of my client's word and reputation versus that of a child. I had my client take a lie-detector test, which indicated that he was innocent. I also had him examined two or three times by a clinical psychologist conversant with the type of activity involved. His report indicated that my client was psychologically incapable of committing such a crime.

I had found out that the child was pretty and appealing and would probably be a convincing witness in front of a jury. Judge Reynolds, criminal court judge that term of court, was a fine judge and I felt that he would give my client a fair hearing. After discussing the case with several other lawyers, and my client, I waived the right to a jury trial and tied the case to the court.

The girl was the only witness for the prosecution. She was a beautiful child. I listened to her testimony, and felt that she either was telling the truth, or should have been named the child actress of the year. I did not cross-examine her at all. Several character witnesses testified that my client was a hard-working good citizen, respected in the community. In those years, I could not use the results of the lie-detector test, but the psychologist was able to testify as to his conclusions concerning my client's mental stability and did so effectively. Finally, I put my client on the stand, and he denied guilt. His eyes shifted around the court room as he testified. Naturally, he was extremely nervous. His voice was strong enough, but he was not a very good witness. When the case was concluded, Judge Reynolds, without hesitation, found my client guilty, and continued his bond pending a probation report. I went to the bench to question the judge's reasoning. He told me that while my client was testifying, he kept trying to get the client to look him in the eye. He said, "Clark, he wouldn't look me in the eye." I found out, later, that he never looked anyone in the eye.

I was, of course, disappointed with the decision, but not totally surprised. The surprise was only that one of the major factors in the judge's conclusion was my client's lack of eye contact. I was confident, however, that the client would be given probation. He had no criminal record of any kind. He was a hard-working, solid family man and husband. He had always been a credit to the community. My psychologist's report was in the probation investigator's file, as was the result of the lie detector test.

On Friday morning I received a call from Judge Reynold's bailiff advising me that the judge wanted my client in court at one-thirty that afternoon for sentencing. I was worried then. I drove to Grove City, found my client at work, as usual, and delivered the message. I told him that he had better pack a bag and take it with him. Court opened at one-thirty, and my client's case was called. The judge asked whether he had anything to say before sentence was pronounced. He did not say anything. The judge then sentenced the client to serve a term in the

Ohio State Penitentiary, and the deputy sheriff led him out of the court room. I was indignant. I rushed up to the bench and asked why the client was not given probation. Reynolds looked at me, almost in tears, and said "Clark, I had to do it. I had no choice. I had to do it." He had been in Grove City the previous night at a party celebrating the opening of Beulah Park and was accosted by several of our "upright citizens" and a newspaper reporter, demanding that my client be incarcerated. Reynolds yielded to public pressure. I know that justice was not served by the penitentiary sentence. I never took another criminal case.

In those early years, I took almost any kind of legal business that came my way. I was frequently in the old-fashioned justice of the peace courts. The "J.P.s" were almost always non-lawyers. They had offices in their homes, and usually heard cases at night. Most of the disputes were between neighbors, and involved such important matters as straying and mischievous children or animals, disturbing the peace, disputes over small sums of money, and other similar items, important to the people involved, but not earth-shaking to society in general. Fees involved were even more minor than the resolution of the problems.

The Columbus Municipal Court was about one small cut above the J.P. courts. Minor criminal offenses were disposed of there, as were preliminary hearings on potentially serious criminal offenses. Traffic cases were heard, and evictions. Most cases in that court, however involved accounts allegedly not paid, judgments on cognovit notes involving sums insufficient to be handled in the common pleas court, disputes over money owed for whatever reason in amounts within the jurisdiction of this court. Lawyers served as judges, which really was an improvement over the justice of the peace system in effect in the townships. I had not been in practice very long before the justices of the peace were eliminated in Ohio, and cases which had been handled by them came under the jurisdiction of the municipal courts.

Some of the municipal court judges were good lawyers and good judges. Most of them were younger and hoped to move up to the more-exalted and higher-paying common pleas court. Three or four were older and just marking time until retirement. Some of the judges, both old and young, had ability; many more were limited, and some were terrible. Ability was not always the criterion for the election of judges. Actually, some of the non-lawyer J.P.s were much better than some of the judges.

At any rate, I tried numerous cases in municipal court. Almost all of them were tried to the judge for the reason that the cases were usually so unimportant that the loser could not afford to pay the costs of the jurors. In retrospect, those cases were great experience for any young lawyer. I had studied rules of evidence in law school, but the application of the rules was learned only by actual trial. I had to know how to ask questions of witnesses properly; what questions should be asked in order to develop a case; how to conduct a cross examination, and, most importantly, what questions not to ask. I discovered early that I should never ask a witness any question the answer to which I did not know, particularly on cross-examination of the witnesses on the other side. Unanticipated answers could, and sometimes did, completely ruin what appeared to be a winnable case.

I was involved in an important case in common pleas court wherein there were three or four different defendants. The case alleged that a business was sold to an unsuspecting couple who bought it based upon representations by the owners of the business as to the amount of business done, and the profits made. My client, a real estate broker, was not directly involved in any of these representations, but some of his salesmen were, in that they repeated to the purchasing plaintiffs what the sellers had told them about the business, without making an effort to determine whether there was truth in the statements made. This was an equity matter since it involved fraud and misrepresentation and was handled by the judge serving in equity court that term. Sure enough, Judge Reynolds was the equity judge. He did not hear *every* case I ever tried. It just seemed that way.

At any rate, my friend Milt was trying the case for the plaintiffs, and he put on his first witness, the defrauded husband, who had total memory lapse. He knew his name and address, and that he and his wife had purchased the business. He did not remember anything else that was pertinent to the case. Because he was extremely nervous, he drew a complete blank. Finally, Milt, exasperated, completed his questioning and it was our time for cross-examination. We lawyers looked at each other and all of us told the judge that we did not wish to cross-examine the witness – all but one, unfortunately. The plaintiffs at that point had not made any case at all. I do not know why this one idiot decided to cross-examine unless he was completely stupid or thought he should do something to earn his fee. In any event, he began to cross-examine the witness, and the more questions he asked, the more the witness remembered, going from drawing a total blank to total recall. The more questions the lawyer asked, the more the plaintiff remembered and the surer he became of his answers. The lawyer repeated, and repeated, and repeated, and then repeated several times more, the same questions. He went over the entire thing, time after time after time. Judge Reynolds, in an effort to shut the lawyer up, started answering the questions himself. The lawyer did not quit. The judge, then commenced singing the answers in rhythm to the beat of his gavel on the bench. God it was horrible! We all had an urge to choke the lawyer. Needless to say, our case was lost. We might have saved everyone time and money by quitting then.

Bill Stubbs, who worked for the Old Man at the same time I did, had practiced law before World War II. After his discharge from service, he went to work for the Veterans Administration as a contract officer in the headquarters office for Ohio. I do not know how he became acquainted with the Old Man, but he did. Stubbs did not negotiate contracts directly with schools, but supervised those who did. He knew Veterans Administration regulations and procedures extremely well; he had written most of those pertaining to school contracts. He also knew the people in the V.A. and was on good terms with them. Such a man could, of course, be of great value to anyone in the school business. The Old Man offered Stubbs a large salary and bonus to go to work for him. Stubbs accepted and worked successfully until the G.I. Bill had run its course and the schools either closed or operated on a limited basis. When Stubbs left, he had quite an amount of unpaid bonus due him. He asked that I sue the Old Man and the schools for breach of contract.

I knew the Old Man's lawyer—a tough, hard-nosed, damned competent trial lawyer. I thought that Stubbs needed to be represented similarly, so we talked to "W.B.," an equally tough, equally hard-nosed trial attorney. W.B. probably knew more law and more about appellate procedure than any other lawyer in Columbus. Because of his mean, abrasive personality, he frequently lost cases in front of juries, but seldom lost any that he appealed. Both sides thought this case too complicated for a jury to understand, and it was agreed that it be tried to the court. The trial judge was Bill Bryant, a political appointee, not a great judge, but one who did try hard. An added bonus was that the Old Man's lawyer and W.B. actively disliked one another. It was organized chaos. From the beginning of the opening statements the two yelled at each other. There were constant objections. W.B. called the other lawyer a liar, a thief, a crook, and a tool of crooks. The other lawyer laughed at him and yelled back remarks equally unflattering. The climax came when the two stood in front of the judge's bench toe to toe, and nose to nose, punching each other in the chest with their forefingers. The Old Man's lawyer said, "I'm not going to let this old son-of-a-bitch intimidate me." W.B. came back with, "In all of my years in practice, I have never heard anyone so reprehensible. This man is guilty of contempt of court and should be jailed." A stronger judge would not have permitted the conduct of either lawyer to reach that climax. Both should have been jailed just to cool them off.

We lost the case, as I was afraid we might, because the judge held that Stubbs' agreement was against public policy.

With only a little over a year in practice, I was called by one of the local Grove City area farmers, who told me that he and a lot of other farmers where having a problem with Columbus and Southern Ohio Electric Company, which was going to go through their land, erecting towers and stringing high-tension power lines. I told him to get as many together as he could and that we would have a meeting at my house to discuss the matter. Seventeen farmers and some wives showed up on the appointed night, and we met in our living room. Evelyn and the children had to evacuate the area, as frequently happened. I did not know anything about whether the electric company *could* go through the property as planned, but I found out before our meeting that it had the right of eminent domain. They could appropriate the property, but they had to pay "just" compensation to the farmers. We discussed everything imaginable that night that had anything to do with the problem. They agreed to hire me on the basis that I was to receive ten percent of whatever we could secure from the electric company. All seventeen landowners agreed to stick together, and did, to my amazement.

I learned quickly that the electric company was tough, close-fisted, and hard to negotiate with. Their settlement offers seemed ridiculous to me and to the farmers. I walked through every farm to see where the power lines would run and where the towers would be located. I got wet, muddy, and-- one day—smelly when I accidentally stepped in some fresh cow manure. The farmers loved it. I discovered that a friend's father, a retired employee of the electric company, had worked for the company all of his adult life obtaining right of way. I talked with him, drove him around the farms, went over the drawings with him as to location. He gave me really good advice as to the value of the land appropriated on each farm, and on how to handle the company.

I talked with each farmer, using the figures given to me—about five times higher than what had been offered. Finally, I got an agreed figure from each farmer as to what he would settle for. I had a conference with the company and presented our demands. They appeared to be horrified. I got mad and reminded them that they could try seventeen lawsuits if they preferred and left the meeting. I knew that they were in a hurry to get started on construction and could not proceed until they either obtained easements from the farmers, or tried the appropriate cases. They called me early the next morning and agreed to settle my figures. This was the first real triumph I had and the first big fee I received.

Not much business came to me as a result of my association with Tom and Bud; they did not have enough to keep themselves busy. It was up to me to procure business on my own. I never thought of little Grove City and its environs as being a source of business but thank God it was. The people came to me because they knew me and also because I made myself available to prospective clients at night and on Saturday. The phone at home rang night and day. I talked to clients on the telephone while eating dinner. I talked to them before breakfast. I talked to them anytime. At first, I loved it, but that novelty wore off quickly. I still took the telephone calls, but much less eagerly. My availability was not fair to Evelyn, the children or myself. When we built our house, we had a large living room and dining room area at the rear, and a large study facing the front. I had not really thought much about the room becoming an office, but an office it became. We certainly had not planned that our living room would become a waiting room, but that happened too. Sometimes the clients and my kids watched television together. Sometimes the overflow was large enough that the poor children were forced upstairs, where for a time there was no television.

Because I was young, broke, and stupid, I talked to everyone who wanted to see me, and handled almost everything imaginable, some of which I knew absolutely nothing about. I wrote a lot of wills almost from the beginning of my practice, which paid dividends in later years in the form of estates, and a very lucrative probate practice. Actually, I was being hired to probate estates very soon after I became a lawyer. From January of 1952 on, I prepared income tax returns for clients. I knew not a damned thing about tax at first, but the great bulk of the returns I prepared were pretty simple in the beginning and I did learn. I hated to do tax returns, but it was fortunate that I did them. The people who came to me for tax work became clients of mine for everything, and never considered seeing anyone else.

Law school did not prepare me for much of what I was forced to handle, but I did learn that one of the cardinal principles in will draftsmanship was, and still is, "keep it simple." A very active, important businessman in the Grove City area and elsewhere came to me to have his will prepared. I was honored and felt certain that if I did a satisfactory job for him, it would lead to future business. I bent over backwards to suit his every wish. When the will was drafted and submitted to him, he read it and signed it at once, stating that it was exactly what he had in mind. A year or two later he died, and the family came to me to handle the estate for them. In the interim between the will and the death, I had handled a few estates, and was getting a great deal of experience with real estate title. I read the will that I had been so pleased to prepare and was horrified. It would have been impossible to deliver good title to his real estate for years, if ever. The transfer of his personal property was cloudy too. I solved the problem by confessing my stupidity to the probate judge, who told me to prepare and file an action to interpret the will for the decedent, and also to prepare the necessary entry, straightening out everything that was wrong. I did as the judge suggested and he approved it all. The family was never informed by me or by the judge that I had really blown it when I drafted the will. I learned a lesson that I never forgot in later years and was never embarrassed by a similar problem.

Largely through the connections I had made with real estate brokers, salesmen, and investors as well as some of the farmers who owned land near Grove City, I handled several zoning and annexation matters. These involved getting property brought into the corporate limits in order that sewer and water might be available for developers. Our little town was commencing to grow as the demand for suburban property increased. I also was involved in innumerable requests for changes in zoning in the county, in Grove City, and in Columbus. Annexations were seldom controversial. They involved a hearing before the county commissioners in an effort to secure their approval and then a hearing before the council of the municipality to which annexation was proposed. People hate change. Sometimes there was no opposition to a proposed annexation, but there was also opposition to any proposed change of zoning. Neither the county commissioners nor city council ever decided a zoning case on its merits. If there were a lot of people in attendance at the hearing opposed to the change, it was voted down. Very often, the chairman of the board of county commissioners asked for a show of hands of those in favor and those opposed. I felt pretty stupid a lot of times because the only ones favoring the change were myself and my client. Everyone else was opposed.

Needless to say, politics, friendships, and good old-fashioned money entered into the thinking of those great decision makers. I suppose the same thing happens with state and national legislators, but I know what happens on the local level. I was about to lose a large annexation to the City of Columbus for the very good reason that it would create "islands" which were not a part of the proposal, and it would take time for city service to be extended to the new area. I had lunch with a couple of the commissioners and was doing nothing constructive to change their minds. One of the commissioners asked who some of the big landowners were whose land would be affected. I mentioned several names from memory and, when I named a certain man, one of the commissioners asked, "Dick, does he want to be annexed?" I said that he did. When I got back to my office, I called the landowner in question and had him talk with the commissioner. The annexation was approved.

I had a zoning matter once that also involved the county commissioners. There was much opposition to the proposed change, and after the hearing and the usual show of hands, the zoning request was disapproved. It could not be brought up again for six months. My client was the type who would not take no for an answer. Six months later the matter was presented again, and there was no one who opposed the change. I never did know who my client paid off, or how much, but I did find out that no notices were ever sent to the property owners in the area about the hearing date. Of course, this was entirely illegal, but it surely worked.

Handling an annexation to Grove City which was approved by the county commissioners, I appeared before the Grove City Council not anticipating trouble. I should never have felt that way. The plans for Interstate Route 71 called for the route to pass immediately east of the existing border of Grove City. The land to be annexed was on the other side of the proposed highway. Grove City did not want to bear the financial burden of maintaining the freeway, a situation which would have occurred had they approved the annexation. I asked whether they would approve the annexation if I could get the road moved further east. They chuckled and said sure. No one thought that I could get the road moved, and neither did I. I went to the governor's office and explained to a friend of mine that the location of this new road would stymie the growth of Grove City. This got me an appointment with the Director of Highways, State of Ohio. I took a letter from the mayor and a resolution from council with me. The highway director got out the map, looked at it and asked where I wanted the new interstate to be moved. I was not prepared for that question, but I picked out a location several miles to the east. The highway director marked where I pointed, and said, "Okay. If it is feasible from an engineering point of view, we'll do it." They did. I got a road moved and an annexation approved!

During those early years in the practice, I was involved in a number of important matters. I was hired by Minnesota Mining and Manufacturing Company (3M) to secretly purchase several tracts of land at the edge of Grove City. After this was finally accomplished, I got the property annexed to Grove City, and then rezoned for the construction of a really large industrial plant. They never built the plant, and still own the property.

When one of our local electrical contractors died, his son, in his mid-twenties, took over as president and general manager. He had some vision and plenty of guts, and took on all sorts of big industrial jobs, at first successfully. The company was making money and growing rapidly. Suddenly all of the quick success was brought to a halt. A very large job was greatly underbid, and the company could not perform. A bonding company was stuck badly. This resulted in default on other jobs and bankruptcy was the only answer. It was the largest bankruptcy in our entire Southern District of Ohio Federal District Court that year. Every Thursday morning for weeks, we were scheduled before the Referee in Bankruptcy for further examination of the judgment debtor. The creditors, mostly various bonding companies, thought that assets were concealed, or that my client had stolen large sums from the company. They could not believe the truth – that these jobs should never have been bid on, or bonded, in the first place. It was a case of a small company gambling too much to get too big too fast.

In early 1955, I broke up the partnership with Bud and Tom. I had felt for some time that I was carrying too much of the load insofar as bringing in income was concerned. When Bud had returned from Korea, we had remodeled the offices, which was traumatic in itself. We picked up an additional rental burden when George Marshall became judge. Theoretically, we should have had additional business from George's clients, but that was slow to materialize. I was tired of not being able to take home a decent share of what I brought in in income. I was tired of waiting for a lot of business to come in. I was also about half mad at Bud most of the time. He was, and is, one of the nicest, most helpful guys I ever knew, but in an office on a daily basis, I thought that he was a pain in the neck. One day it all came to a head when Bud told a secretary to quit doing some of my work in order to get his out. I raised hell, and said many bad things, most of them profane. Poor Tom was working at the State Legislature that day and could not get me quieted down. Either later that day, or the next, we sat down and discussed it all quietly, and I told them both that I really did want out of the partnership. Although I later had various office associations, I did not enter into another partnership for twenty years.

I got lucky and persuaded our secretary to come to work for me. Actually, she had the choice and opted to go with me for whatever reason. Good secretaries are hard to come by, and she was great. I got lucky again, and was able to rent a small office next door to the suite where I had been located. I bought some furniture, not much because it did not take much to furnish the office. It was really tiny, but I was proud of it, and happy. I was strictly on my own for the first time in my working life.

Left To Right: Richard (3.5y.o.), Marcia Jo (6), Thomas (3.5y.o.). Evelyn made the coats of the twins.

Many things happened in the 1950s. Our three children grew and grew and Marcia, then the boys, went to school. Evelyn began to have a little more freedom. I worked it out so that she could have our car every other week by alternating driving with our neighbor. In 1954, Evelyn got a car of her own, a new Ford station wagon, light blue with a white top. She was pleased and so was I. Kids are not fun to raise when you cannot get out of the house.

We began to take family vacations in 1953. Our first vacation should have warned us never to take anymore. We decided to meet friends at Lake St. Helen in northern Michigan. They had been there previously and extolled its virtues. We were "lucky" enough to get a cabin adjacent to theirs, and altogether there were four couples and their children in the group. It sounded as if it would be great, but it was anything else but. On the way north, we stayed all night in Ann Arbor. When we went to dinner, the boys announced that they had to go to the toilet. It was a pay toilet, so one of them crawled underneath the door and got stuck. What a lot of noise and embarrassment! When we got to our destination the next afternoon, we discovered that our cottage had no modern facilities at all. The others did naturally. The weather was cold. It rained. The main occupation was fishing, and I did not fish. It was all capped one night when I woke up and had to go. It was raining and windy outside, and cold and damp inside. I knew that I was not going to the next cabin to use the bathroom. I went out to the edge of the porch, and unfortunately urinated into the face of the wind. The results were disastrous, and my language was sensational.

I do not know why we persisted in our attempts to vacation with small children, but we did. We went to Rye Beach on Lake Erie three years in a row—each year in a different, and improved, cottage, and each year with friends who split the cost of cottage rental with us. They too had small children. It is all confusing when I think about it now, but at the time we thought that we were having fun, and I guess we were. Younger people raise children, fortunately, the old people either can't stand them at all or spoil them.

One summer we spent a week at Lake St. George in upper New York. I do not remember where the idea for that trip originated, but we took our new, yellow Buick convertible, and headed northeast. The trip took an interminable long time. The children were all in the back seat, and they spent most of their travel time fighting with one another. At night, we stayed in one motel room – yes, all five of us. Lake George and the surrounding area was beautiful, but the lake itself was ice cold. As far as I was concerned, it was to be admired, but not entered. We ate in more Howard Johnson restaurants than I thought existed. The kids love them, and the fried clams were edible. We drove through part of New Hampshire and Vermont after we left Lake George and got as far north as the Maine border. Then we headed home through parts of Massachusetts and Connecticut, and somehow arrived in New York

City late afternoon. I drove across the George Washington Bridge and down the New Jersey Turnpike in the five o'clock traffic and was petrified. I kept going faster and faster because I felt certain that the traffic would run over us if I dared slow down. Getting off the damn thing was difficult. I missed at least two exits because I could not get near the exit lane.

The next day we had our first experience with the Pennsylvania Turnpike. After the New Jersey turnpike, it was a pleasant drive, and then we came to tunnels. No one had told me about them. I could not see well, the exhaust fumes were impossible with the top down on the convertible. The next day we got home, and I carried the luggage upstairs and dropped it. When the entire trip was ended, I was trembling and could not stop. I needed a vacation to recover from the vacation. But it all accomplished its purpose. I went back to work cheerfully.

Friends of ours had gone to a place in Michigan a couple of years in a row called "North Lakes Resort," and said that it would really be a great place for kids. All meals were served in the main lodge, and when Evelyn asked how to dress for dinner, one of the gals advised her to wear a clean pair of shorts.

We made our first trip to North Lakes in 1957. Because of the roads, it took about twelve hours to get there. Again, all five of us stayed in a single motel room. That first year, the twins got into a fight at three o'clock in the morning. I wanted to strangle both of them but resisted the impulse. We had found our vacation spot at last. With and without children, we continued to go there for about nine years.

The place was located on the shores of Lake Bellaire near the village of Bellaire, in northern Michigan. The cottages were not fancy, to say the least, but the maid mopped them out every morning. I think that we made our own beds. There were no refrigerators in the cottages, but there was a cooler which was filled with fresh block of ice daily. The plumbing was old-fashioned, but adequate. Three meals were served daily. We generally ate breakfast as a family, and the breakfasts were good. Lunch did not amount to much and very often those of us who played golf in the morning, ate lunch at the golf course. Dinner was always filling, but the food was hardly gourmet.

There were, however, camp counselors for the children—really glorified babysitters. However, the counselors took over after breakfast and continued until about four in the afternoon. It was heaven for parents, and the kids loved it too. The lake was shallow and warm, and there were row boats in quantity. The kids rowed and tried to fish, but I do not think there were any fish in that lake. The adults were all friendly and relaxed. More than half were doctors, and if rest and relaxation were what they needed, they had found an ideal spot.

Evelyn and I, and quite a few others, played nine holes of golf each morning, swam, took sunbaths, and napped each afternoon. From four to five, the children and adults cleaned up, and the cocktail hour started at five. When the dinner bell rang promptly at five-thirty, kids took off on the run for the lodge dining room. The adults had more drinks and got to the dining room just before its seven o'clock closing time.

Those were wonderful years, enhanced by the owners, Chet and Agnes, with whom we became friendly. Chet was always neat in appearance, had a very dry, crackling wit, and was really a true "egghead." He was bald and his head was somewhat egg-shaped. In the winter, he taught in the local high school. Agnes supervised the kitchen and, upon occasion, took to serious drinking. Naturally, she joined our cocktail parties. In fact, on rainy days, she occasionally showed up in mid-afternoon at our cottage, where Chet usually could find her. They were charming people and added much to the establishment by their presence alone.

Dr. George Smith, his pregnant wife, Peg, and their four children were there that first year. We did not see very much of Peg that summer, but we got well-acquainted with accident-prone George. He attempted to water ski though he could not get up, but he was persistent and pulled his rib cage apart enough to keep him from much more exercise. He got stung by either a bee or a hornet; whatever it was, it was a man-hater because a lump appeared on his leg about the size of a small orange. As he was parking his automobile to go home, I went over to watch the action and say goodbye. While we were chatting, the trunk lid fell and hit him on the head. We got a get-well card and everyone who remained the following week signed it. We found out later that when he got home, he was hospitalized for a few days while he healed. Over the years, the Smiths have become among our closest friends. We planned vacations at North Lakes so that we could be there together. Our kids became friends and looked forward to seeing each other. One year, one of their two boys managed to get a fishhook in son Dick's ear, while the boys were out in the row boats attempting to catch non-existent fish. They rowed to shore quickly and we saw what was wrong. George looked at me and solemnly said, "Jesus Christ, Dick. We'd better get this kid to a doctor." George was a specialist in obstetrics and gynecology but didn't know much about fish-hook removal.

At the 1952 Republican National Convention, Dwight D. Eisenhower defeated Senator Robert Taft for the presidential nomination, and easily defeated Adlai Stevenson, the Democratic nominee. In 1956, Ike again defeated Stevenson. It was, looking back now, a wonderfully peaceful, orderly eight years. Eisenhower ended the Korean War but on an unsatisfactory note. We did not win Korea, but neither did we lose. Our troops came home, and the casualties were ended. No nation dared defy us and start trouble, because of Ike's reputation as a resolute general. For a time, we had the atom bomb, and the Russians had not entirely perfected theirs.

At home, we were prosperous people. Employment was high, and both interest and inflation were very low. We were a proud people. We were still patriotic, law-abiding and generally happy. We were all horrified, yet curious, when Senator Estes Kefauver and his committee publicly investigated organized crime, and we saw the evil faces and heard the tough, menacing voices of mobsters on our own television screens. We saw and heard Senator Joseph McCarthy, and his committee "investigate" communism. For a time, he was fascinating, then disgusting, then nauseating. He ruined many fine reputations over nothing except bare insinuations of communist sympathy. He finally met his "comeuppance" when he attempted to investigate the Army, and the Army retained an exceptional, courageous lawyer, who showed McCarthy to the country as he really was. When his fellow senators voted to censor him, I shed no tears.

President Eisenhower seemed above all of this, although now I wonder why he did not state that McCarthy was a villain. Ike's chief of staff, Sherman Adams, accepted a rug as a gift and Ike fired him! My God, I wish every President since had followed this precedent.

During the 1952 campaign, Richard Nixon, Ike's vice-presidential candidate, was accused of accepting some illegal contributions. Ike made Nixon go before the nation on television to "bare his soul" to the American people. Nixon made his famous "Checkers" speech, in which wife Pat and little dog Checkers appeared. Whether Nixon was honest or dishonest in those years, we will probably never know, but he convinced the American people of his honesty, and remained on the ticket.

In September of that year, Nixon made the major address at the Republican State Convention in Columbus and attended a reception afterwards in the Ionian Room at the Deshler Hotel, for some of the more influential Republicans. I did not have a ticket for this event, but my friend, "Ears" McCracken, with whom I worked at the Veterans Administration, grabbed a couple from some source and took me. I shook hands with Nixon. (He had sweaty palms and seemed somewhat ill at ease.)

In 1953, I decided to run for the local school board. Heretofore, I had heeded advice not to enter politics, but I guess I did not think that being on the local school board of education was political, and it really should not have been. I was elected overwhelmingly, as were two of my friends. We had the best situations. We simply wanted to do whatever we could to improve the school system. I had taught school and had a master's degree in education. I was a practicing attorney and felt that I could help considerably. One of the other two new members had been a college instructor at Cornell, and the other was a physician. We all three had children in school and more to follow, so our interest was truly genuine.

We were sworn in as members in January of 1954. The only persons in attendance at most board meetings were the Board members, the superintendent, and the clerk of the board, who was also the school secretary.

We performed such housekeeping acts as the approval of the payment of bills, and other similar items the superintendent brought before us. This suited me fine. I wanted to get acquainted with the schools' operation and I did not want to make any waves my first year in office.

Actually, nothing unusual occurred until early fall of 1954. We had been somewhat busy planning a new elementary building, which later became known as the J.C. Sommer School. We interviewed potential architects who had experience in planning and supervising the construction of school buildings.

Early in 1954-1955 school year, I was asked to attend a special meeting of the Board. We were told by the superintendent that the band director had been not only insubordinate, but actually was defiant in refusing to obey an order from the principal. The principal reported the matter to the superintendent, who talked to the band director, and got the same results. The superintendent wanted to suspend the band director indefinitely, and ultimately to dismiss him. The band director was highly competent, but like most perfectionists among musicians, thought that music was the ultimate, and that nothing else mattered so long as he accomplished his goals for his band and music students. On the recommendation of the superintendent of schools, the board voted three to two to suspend the bandmaster, and then, after a hearing, if he requested one, to dismiss him.

I was one of the majority who voted for suspension and dismissal. We felt that he was no different from any other employee, and that he should carry out the orders of his superiors. The two who formed the minority thought that he was such a good band director he should be retained. I also think that they had a better idea of his popularity with the general public. They loved that band and had an active band booster's association.

When the word got out that we were taking steps to fire the band director, all hell broke loose. I was besieged with telephone calls, some threatening and some profane; some from people who had always been friendly to me, some from my clients who informed me that they were now *former* clients. We received two petitions, each signed by about eight hundred people. One petition supported our action one hundred percent. The other was decidedly uncomplimentary and very much opposed to our action. The entire community was split. There are still people living in Grove City who have not spoken to me since that time—more than thirty years ago.

Prior to this time, no one attended school board meetings unless he wanted something specific. No one showed interest in the monthly business meetings. After the suspension, it was necessary to hold a series of special meetings, and the citizenry overflowed our biggest classroom and milled around in the halls. All of a sudden, everything that we did was of interest. Our board president was too patient and listened to everyone. The band director hired the most prominent lawyer in Columbus to represent him, and many members of the Grove City Band Association contributed to his defense fund. The board was too conservative to employ outside counsel. We used an assistant Franklin County prosecuting attorney who was no match for the great trial lawyer. Attempts were made to work out a compromise of some sort without success. Naturally, the Columbus newspapers got into the act, and everything that was done became front-page news. It was so bad that I spent more time talking to newspaper reporters, other board members, and local citizens than I did practicing law. In fact, while all of this was going on, I felt that I would have been personally better off never to have started law school, because the board was looking to me for advice and guidance.

Finally, a hearing date was set for an afternoon because we felt that there would be fewer people present. God, the people poured in, and we had to move into the combination auditorium-gymnasium to accommodate the spectators. It filled rapidly. The whole affair was much like a three-ring circus. In retrospect, I think we handled the entire matter poorly. The statute provided for a public hearing and a right to appeal from any adverse decision. We could have listened to the superintendent, principal, and band director tell their stories without benefit of statement or examination of witnesses by legal counsel. We did not need to provide seating for everyone in the area. We acted on the advice of our lawyer and held the most formal hearing imaginable. Witnesses were sworn, formal examination and cross examination was undertaken. It was a full-scale trial, and the board asked me to serve as acting chairman, and to rule on the evidence. The whole fiasco lasted two afternoons and two evenings. Both days when we recessed for dinner I went home, across the street, and mixed myself a couple of martinis to ease the pain. The trial lawyer chopped up our witnesses and had them so confused that they reversed themselves completely, and the poor assistant prosecutor did not have enough ability to rehabilitate them. At the conclusion of the hearing, we felt that we had to lift the suspension, or it would be reversed on appeal. I hated the whole proceedings and cursed my ignorance and our entire board's being so honest and conscientious.

The school district changed and merged with two or three others to form a large school system. Only one of us would agree to serve on the new consolidated board. We had had all we wanted of public service. Our annual salary was twenty-four dollars. The band director continued to be insubordinate and was dismissed again. He was not given the type of hearing he received from us and remained dismissed. He appealed and lost. That ended his problem but did not end the bitterness.

I was active in all sorts of local activities during the 1950s. I supposed that some of it was done for purely business reasons, but most of it was because I loved Grove City, and genuinely wanted to help the town and my own family.

I was appointed chairman of the Grove City Park Board. The town had a park with baseball and softball diamonds but a very limited amount of playground equipment for children. We ran what were called "homecomings" (really street fairs) and built several good asphalt tennis courts and bought the necessary playground equipment. Counting the nightly "take" with the carnival people was always interesting. I thanked God for my years of working at the racetrack. Those carnival operators were real thieves.

About a half dozen of us got together and decided that the town should have a swimming pool. We needed one for years, but now we actually got it built. It took a lot of planning. We talked with swimming-pool operators, builders of pools, and people from other towns who had somehow gotten pools constructed. Gradually, our own plans took shape. The legal work was all on my shoulders. I set up a non-profit corporation, was able to dodge the problem of blacks by limiting membership to Grove City residents. I got my non-profit corporation approved by the Internal Revenue Services as non-taxable, and approval for the sale of bonds from the Ohio Division of Securities. We sold bonds and raised the money we needed. The pool was ready for construction.

When a lawyer, who had been recalled to service because of Korea, came back, I told him and the others that all of the work was done, but that if anything else came up he should do it to help out the community. He agreed. The next thing I heard, he was being paid on an annual retainer basis, plus representing the board of the swimming pool. When the facility was dedicated, my name was not even on the commemorative plaque. Anyway, it had been a nice pool over the years.

Because of my wife, I became active in the Methodist Church. It was a small church with no money and few problems. I was asked to serve on the church board. This pleased Evelyn, and I did not think I could get into trouble by participating. The chairman moved away and, of course, resigned. I became chairman pending the next election. At this point, the board members, encouraged by the preacher, decided to build a new church.

Everyone should get involved in building at least one church. Some of our Christians in spirit were quite un-Christian in actuality. In fact, some folks were downright nasty. The congregation had to vote in open meeting. The methodist Bishop presided. I'm glad that I didn't have to handle that meeting. After discussion of the matter at great length, and after revealing numerous evidence of very squeaky pocketbooks, the congregation voted by a small margin to build. The church hierarchy hired professional fundraisers and then sent in a new minister—one who was more or less forced on us. He came for the sole purpose of making certain that the church got built, regardless of personal feelings, ethics, or the imparting of religious doctrine to the church membership.

I refused to serve a full term as chairman of the church board, but I agreed to serve in any way that I could otherwise. I might as well have continued as board chairman. I was involved in acquiring the land from one of the toughest, tightest old Dutch farmers in the area. He was Lutheran and, I think, believed that all Methodists should be consigned to the fires of damnation. I sold the old church building to the local Masonic lodge, and eventually sold the parsonage. I incorporated the church in order to make these transactions easier, and to borrow money without having to file and go completely through a lawsuit. All of this was, naturally, done for nothing, but I think someone did thank me.

I understand that some of the church members did not want to help pay for a new church. I did not expect to be paid for my legal services. I even understood the ingratitude of many of my brethren. What I did not understand, however, was the attitude of the minister which the church imposed on us. I do not remember, now, what he was saying to me in one of the many business meetings we had at my office at home one evening. However, the words finally sank in. He was outlining some chicanery which was absolutely fraudulent. I put down my pen and said, "Jesus Christ, Jim. I cannot permit you to do this. We're a church." He looked at me with a smirk on his face and replied, "Dick, this preaching is for Sundays, but the other six days of the week is just cold business." I know most ministers are not like that, but I have never since felt right about Methodist Church ministers or the Methodist hierarchy which ran all of the churches, state and national. I have been deeply suspicious of most churches and most religions ever since.

In the spring of 1954, Evelyn and I joined the London Country Club, as did our next-door neighbors, the Henrys, and another couple we knew well then. I really do not know exactly why we joined, except that we saw a lot of Bill and Lee Brokaw who were from London originally and had been members of the club for a year or two. I also think that perhaps the membership fees were so cheap it seemed a shame not to join. As I recall, annual dues in 1954 amounted to sixty dollars. The following year they were raised to seventy-five dollars, and everyone complained. We have been members at London ever since. Many of our friends are from there, and much of our social life has centered around its activities.

The City of London, Ohio, is a small county seat town located about twenty-five miles west of Columbus. It is a prosperous community surrounded by rich farmland. London Country Club had, and still has, quite a few very well-to-do members. Quite a few of those members are farmers, and it is not uncommon to see several half-ton pick-up trucks parked beside Cadillacs, Chryslers, and Buicks. Club members are not all wealthy, however. It is a true cross-section of the community—barbers, plumbers, electricians, and mechanics mixed in with doctors, lawyers, dentists, bankers, and businessmen. It does not matter to any of those people how rich or important one is, or thinks he is; every member is judged by how he or she behaves and fits in with the others.

The golf course was and is today only a nine-hole course. For a long time, it contained small, relatively flat greens which were not trapped. The fairways were not watered. A friend who belonged to one of Columbus' finest country clubs played the course several times as my guest and complained that the course was a cow pasture. Of course, part of his problem was that he did not score well when he played our course, although he was really a good player. Several years later, the course was revamped. Some fine elevated greens were constructed, sand traps seem abundant, and the course itself is much better cared for.

The club house was small, poorly furnished, and minimal in every sense of the word. The men's locker room was an atrocity—poorly lighted, with lockers so small they required one to wad up his clothes and stuff them in. There were only a couple of showers, both temperamental. The tin on the shower floor stuck up in spots, and it was not unusual for someone to cut a foot. Thank God, I was never in the ladies' locker room. I heard that it was worse. About 1960, the old clubhouse was enlarged. It was never really fancy, but, compared to those early years, it became a palace.

Despite the meager facilities, it was truly a great spot. The kitchen staff was black and so were the waitresses for a lot of years. The food was wonderful. The London Country Club never installed a pay bar where alcoholic beverages were sold by the drink. Beer was sold, but those people did not want to spend the money to get as drunk as they frequently did by ordering drinks by the glass. Almost every member kept a fifth or two in his locker, and so did some of the lady members. It was a generally accepted fact that the Ohio State liquor store in London sold more booze per capita than any liquor store in the state.

The parties were always great. Back in the earlier years, many of the members were really characters. Just listening to them lie to each other while sipping a drink or three was real entertainment. I relaxed at London. I did not feel that I had to impress anyone at London. I was certainly not going to pick up any legal business there, and I know that I became accepted by the members because I made no attempt to push myself, and we did enter in.

To write about the happenings at the club during the years we have been members, the people and their antics, the many golf stories, the golf course's beauty with its graceful old willow trees, gigantic oaks, and the maples, could well be the source of a book which I hope gets written one day by someone – hopefully me.

I truly believe at this time in my life, that the 1950s were the happiest, most interesting, and perhaps most productive of my adult years. I seem to remember them most fondly.

I purchased a 1953 Buick Super two-door hard-top painted Chinese red, with a black top and black cloth interior. Some of the money for that car came from the easements sold to Columbus and Southern. It was truly a monster of a car. It was huge, heavy, extremely hard to maneuver because it was automatic, but it was a modern version of Buick's dynaflow. I was proud of it in spite of its imperfections. It was sure as hell the biggest, reddish car around.

In 1955, Eveyln and the children were going to visit her parents in Florida, driving her 1954 station wagon. She felt sorry for me, because they were to be gone over Father's Day. The car that Buick was advertising that year in all the magazines was a yellow convertible with a black top and red plastic interior. She ordered it for me through a salesman she knew—a member of the London Country Club. (She did not pay for the car, she just ordered it.) Naturally, I was proud of it. It did not have power steering either, nor power brakes. The automatic transmission was better, however. I do not remember whether power steering and power brakes were available in 1955. I assume that they were not, because had they been, I would have ordered them.

I was so pleased with the convertible idea that I drove it with the top down constantly that first summer. Only rain caused me to change. It was quite an experience to climb into the plastic seat while wearing a pair of golf shorts after the car had been setting in the hot sun with the top down for about six hours!

One Friday evening in February of 1957, I mixed a pitcher of martinis and started drinking them prior to dinner. (I know it was a Friday evening because I did not drink through the week, only weekends in the evening.) I glanced at the used car ads, which was an unusual thing for me to do unless I planned on trading cars, which I had no intention of doing at that time. I noticed an ad for the sale of the Buick dealers' wife 1957 Buick Century convertible. I knew I had to buy it. After finishing my martinis, and dinner, I took son Richard with me and announced that we were going to Saeger Buick "just to look." I took Dick along because he loved new automobiles. As I feared, the ad was a come-on. I forget, now, what the problem was with the used car, but they did just happen to have two new ones. One was red and white with a white top, power steering and power brakes, power electric windows and power seats. I made them an offer I thought they would accept, and they did not—that night. On Saturday morning, damned if they didn't call me and accept the offer.

That was the fastest car I ever owned. The speedometer would register one hundred twenty-five miles per hour, while the car was still accelerating. I do not know how fast it would run. I do know that it had brakes inadequate for that car. That "bargain" had one other problem—it was a lemon. The radiator went bad. The cloth top became frayed and shredded through no fault of mine. Finally, it was leaking transmission fluid in ever increasing amounts. I decided to trade it quickly and started an afternoon of shopping at an Oldsmobile dealer. The Buick looked beautiful, everything was going my way, until the appraiser came back quickly, handed me the keys, and said he was not interested. When I asked what was wrong, he told me it would not run in reverse. I bought transmission fluid on the spot and drove to Saegers as quickly as possible and traded right then for Buicks' largest four-door hardtop. The lemon now was Saeger's car. They may have gotten to me in the beginning, but I got even.

I cannot discuss motion pictures of the era. We did not see them.

With three kids and little money, especially for babysitters at fifty cents an hour, we could not afford movies. Most of our entertainment was from the programs shown on the television screen. Everything was still in black and white. The stars were Milton Berle, Sid Cesear, Dean Martin, and all sorts of sporting events. We played some bridge and attended an occasional party. Many of the parties were bring-your-own-bottle, poker and Tripoli complete with sloppy joes. Children? We took them.

I am still amazed at how much we did on a small income. I know that everything is relative and that one hundred dollars then is the equivalent to three to three and half times that amount today. Margy, my very young, hard-working, bright secretary, kept belting out deeds, notes, mortgages, land contracts and title opinions. We acquired our real estate license, and it more than paid the overhead. In addition, I was taught a lot about real estate by Pete Gire. I learned how to evaluate property. I learned how to borrow money for investment purposes, and I was led by Gire and his salesmen into some good money-making deals. Evelyn and I began buying, at discount prices, property that was already sold on land contract. We often were able to borrow one hundred percent at low interest because of the discount. We used the interest difference as part of our income and spent it accordingly. When the land contracts were paid off, and most were relatively soon, we took our profit.

Jim Henry and I loaned money to a man who was a builder, developer, and Baptist preacher. He was in such bad shape that we had to take title to the entire subdivision he was developing. We paid off the liens and mortgages, advanced money as needed to build streets and water and sewer lines, and got paid, gradually, as lots were sold. To complicate the problem, the builder died. We finally got our money back and took our profit, which was usurious, in lots which we ultimately sold. We made money, but I know now that we were lucky to escape intact.

We had been told that Evelyn could have no more children after Marcia and a miscarriage. Accordingly, our house was designed for a family of three until we had twin boys. Over the one-car garage was an unfinished storage area which our contractor quickly made into a nursery. The only problem was that the boys got bigger, and older, and the only entrance to their room was through our daughter's bedroom. Something had to be done. We either had to buy, build, or remodel. Our "wonderful" house was no longer adequate. We looked at houses in Upper Arlington, a wealthy suburb of Columbus, but concluded that we did not want to live there. We looked at acreage around Grove City on which to build. There seemed to be something wrong with each location. Finally, we found a beautiful spot on a hill overlooking one of the holes at Oakhurst Country Club. Because a lawyer friend of mine owned it all, I knew I could buy it for very little money. He had told me to look at it, and said it would not cost me much. I had done him some favors.

As Evelyn and I sat admiring the view, I said, "If we're going to build, this is it." We then started talking sense. We would have to have a well and a septic tank. A driveway curving up the hill would require a snowplow in the wintertime. The yard would be large, and uphill. It would be beautiful, but hard to maintain. Evelyn would be forced to haul our children to all their varied activities. We decided to stay in our own home and remodel it.

Remodeled House

Thank God, we employed an architect. He tied everything together so well that the house did not have a remodeled look. We built a large two-car plus garage; enlarged the living room-dining area by removing a small screened in porch at the rear; opened up the back of our living room by installing a heavy sliding-glass door that opened onto a huge cement terrace. The former garage became a small office and waiting room. What had served as the office became our downstairs bedroom. The half-bath, and a portion of the original office, became the downstairs bath. It all blended together and, when it was finally properly decorated to Evelyn's satisfaction, it became a comfortable home once again, and still is.

1958–1964

Walt Barrett, Ed Fitzgerald, and John Phillips had their offices together at 33 North High Street. I never really knew the reason, but the Ohio National Bank, which owned the building, asked them to move. They, in turn, asked me to join them and take over a big suite.

I thought that I needed an office association with other lawyers. My little two-room office was small and, while I could, and did, talk to Milt Farber, Tom and Bud, and occasionally Morris Lopper or Keith Martin about legal problems, it was not the same. I needed someone to talk to in my own office. I was lonesome practicing by myself. I definitely did not want a partnership, but they were not partners. Walt had a good-sized law library, which was also a plus. I felt certain that we could get along well in an office. In any event, after talking to my secretary about it, I told them I would go with them.

We started to look for office space and finally selected a suite in the Buckeye Federal Building at 42 E. Gay Street.

Compared to 44 E. Broad Street, this building was a palace. There was a two-level parking garage underneath the building, which was convenient, but the building had been constructed about 1942 when automobiles were much smaller than the huge monsters that we drove around in the late 1950s.

The suite we selected had a long, huge lobby, which accommodated both clients and secretaries more than adequately. The lawyers' offices were all large and extremely quiet. We also had a large library, which we had painted a bright yellow and dubbed "the canary room." When the offices were all decorated and carpeted, it was an impressive layout.

On the evening of the last day of October 1958, Margy and I moved in. We were required to move at night by both buildings' management because we would not tie up the elevators during working hours. Fortunately, we did not have a lot to move, and we were straightened up and ready for business the next morning. I do not believe that I hit anything in the basement garage that first morning, which was an event worth noting. In my first month, I made enough of an impression that, by almost popular demand, my parking space was moved into the first level, and Cleve, the black major domo of the garage, advised me that I was just to pull into the basement, and he would be happy to park the car for me. That arrangement, with few exceptions, continued for all the years that I had offices in the building.

It was a fun office. There was entertainment of some sort almost every day. Ed Fitzgerald did little or no work. He really did not have to work. His father died, Ed was the only child, and inherited a fortune. Later on, his Aunt Molly died, and inherited quite a bit more. Generally, he arrived at about ten-thirty in the morning, jollied the three secretaries for a few minutes, went into his office, and called his stockbroker. He then, as a rule, dialed the three-working lawyers on the intercom for the purpose of arranging lunch. Upon his return from lunch, he lay down to read the *Wall Street Journal* and usually took a nap until about three o'clock, at which time he went home. Ed's first wife had died after suffering a long time from cancer. After a suitable period, Ed remarried, this time a wealthy widow from Indianapolis. On their wedding anniversary, she bought Ed a Rolls Royce. After that, we went to lunch in style. I felt like the King of Siam when I rode to lunch in the back seat of the Rolls. The only trouble was that, while Ed took us to lunch in his car and planned where we were to go, he did not buy our lunch.

Walt had a practice that was all his own. Some of his clients were very good citizens, some were a little on the seamy side. The good thing about Walt's clients was that they all paid him and some of his fees were outstandingly imaginative. He did a lot of collection work. When he had to repossess something, he seemed to make it his. He brought in a set of bongo drums, and stored them in the library. They remained there until the office broke up some years later. He did a great job when he defended a Chillcothe resident for murder. The man only could raise fifteen hundred dollars in cash, but he owned a pick-up truck, which Walt took as part of his fee. I do not remember whether this was the same case in which he acquired the cement mixer, but I do remember that he got a cement mixer from some source and gave it to his wife as a Christmas present.

John Phillips had something new happen to him every day. John was the most colorful lawyer I ever knew, even including Milt Farber. Almost all of his clients were characters. Some were completely nuts; others were just peculiar. John had the smallest, least impressive of the four offices. It bordered on being shabby; so was much of his clothing. His pants bagged at the knees, his suit coats did not fit, and both were usually wrinkled. John did not worry about it. He got excellent jury verdicts when he tried cases. He said the jurors felt sorry for him, and that he did not intend to change the "studied seedy look" that he affected.

Ed's office, as might be expected, was beautiful. He had a professional decorator who spared no expense, and it certainly showed the rest of us up. Walt's office was also impressive. He had purchased a huge desk and a chair of equivalent size. After all, Walt needed everything big-sized to fit his bulk.

I did not spend the money for furniture that Ed and Walt did. I bought new draperies, and a green, plastic covered couch. A client who was a cabinet-maker made me a credenza in lieu of paying his bill. My office still looked nice.

There was no separate air conditioning in the building at the time; consequently, Walt, Ed and I bought window units. John refused, saying that air conditioning was unhealthy. We made him keep his office door closed in order to keep the lobby and library reasonably cool. John practically stripped when he was in his office because of the heat. When a client came to see him, he, of course, was dressed completely, including his necktie and jacket. One day, however, his secretary buzzed him on the intercom and announced that two clients were waiting to see him with reference to a large estate which he was handling. He quickly dressed as usual, and went into the lobby to greet them, bowing and scraping as he went. His secretary immediately arose from her desk and shoved John back into his office. She told the clients that she had to see him for a moment before the conference. She shut his office door, pointed at his feet, and said, "Find your shoes and put them on!"

Of course, John kept his large window opened wide, with the result that when his door was open, a blast of air either came into his office or left it. One day he had a cognovit note lying on his desk and, as he was engaged in talking to another attorney on the telephone about collecting on the note, his secretary opened the door and the note blew out the window and on down Gay Street. John hung up the telephone, caught the elevator, and went running down Gay Street. He rescued his note just as it was about to go down a sewer. We all put the lack of air conditioning down as part of his eccentricity. I now think that he was too damned tight to spend the money.

Many people knew that Ed Fitzgerald was rich. I doubt that any of them knew much about his legal ability. He attracted wealthy clients, talked to them long enough to find out the problem, and then called in either John or me—usually John. He did insist on a full share of the fees. Rich he was, but a charitable institution he was not. When George Wolfe joined us a couple of years later, he started referring everything to George Wolfe. The only actual work that Ed did was insurance subrogation claims. This was not a lucrative business, but the only other job, to my knowledge, that Ed ever had was as an insurance claims agent, and that he understood.

It made a great deal for John. He shared a secretary with Ed, thus actually having a full-time secretary for half the wages. About all Ed did was have the secretary type an occasional letter, and John kept her busy almost full time. Their secretary was young and pretty and occupied the front desk, where she served as a kind of receptionist. She worked there for about three years.

Margy's desk faced the front of the room just outside my office. Because we still did a lot of real estate, the poor girl was almost always busy, and did not get much time to engage in horsing around that went on. Walt's secretaries did not last long, but he sure had some dandies. Thank God, they sat at the rear, opposite the entrance to Walt's office. The first one that I remember his having was ugly as hell—a Lebanese Catholic with no sense of humor. However, she was probably the most efficient gal he had. I don't think that she appreciated all of the conversation and conduct in that office, because she did not stay too long. She became a teacher in a Catholic school at less money than she made in the office. He had one so-called secretary that he actually was trying to teach how to type. I could see why he hired her. She had a tremendous set of breasts. But John said that when she sat at the machine, they activated the space bar, and perhaps that's why she couldn't type. Another one that I remember was a really good-looking young redhead. I found out that an older man kept her in a swank apartment and bought her expensive clothing when she was in high school. My favorite, though, was actually pretty efficient. Once she didn't show up for work for three or four days and did not call the office. Walt was concerned, but one morning the mystery was solved. A detective showed up and told us that she was the night manager of a downtown club, and that she was running a stable of whores out of a back room. The thing the police seemed to object to was that she was taping everything and blackmailing the customers. He had other secretaries, probably, but they must not have been quite so outstanding.

Margy quit at the end of 1960 because she got married, and then, of course, became pregnant. They did not have "the pill" in those years, but she probably wanted to have a child. I did not cry—I don't think—but I was damned unhappy. She was truly a fine secretary, and she had worked for me almost seven years. I knew that replacing her would not be easy.

The original source for secretaries for me was one of the most commercial education teachers at West High School in Columbus. We had taught together in Grove City when I first started teaching. When Ruth got pregnant and quit working for Tom, and Bud and me, I talked with this gal, and she sent Marilyn. Marilyn was young and had not much experience, but she was well-trained, loyal, and just beginning to be a good secretary. She got married, her husband went into the Army and was shipped to El Paso, so Marilyn quit. We called the commercial education teacher again, and she sent me a very pretty little girl with very little experience. Margy worked with her for a month training her and, while Margy was there, the work was pretty good. When Margy finally left, the work was terrible, and I knew the poor girl would never make a legal secretary. She was dumber than hell. I called Ruth Grannon and went to see her the first Friday after the new girl had taken over by herself. As usual, Ruth was a little hard up and told me that she would gladly start working the following Monday morning and would continue into the future. She came to work on schedule and her training consisted of my pointing out the location of the desk and chair. I gave the little girl two weeks' pay in lieu of notice. Everything would have been fine, except that Ruth managed to get pregnant.

I remembered that Marilyn, now back from El Paso and employed, had a sister, Susie. Although already working for one of the radio and television stations, Marilyn felt Susie would quit and come to work for me if I could stand her. I had lunch with her and, while she seemed a little wacky, I enjoyed her, and I knew that she was bright. She came to work a couple of weeks later, and it was an experience. She was smart and could do almost anything involving secretarial skills. The only trouble was that she really did not want to work. She frustrated me. Sometimes I would give her work to do that I needed in a hurry, but realized I could not hear the typewriter purring as it should be. One day when this occurred, I went out to find out what she was doing. She was filing her fingernails. I said, "Susie, I told you I'm in a hurry for that work." She looked at me with wide eyes and said, "Don't worry. I'm thinking about it." Another time I yelled at her about something that she was supposed to do but did not. She said, "Mr. Clark, when you yell at me like that, it makes the hair on the back of my arms stand right straight up." Once I noticed that she seemed to be mending the inside of my jacket. Later, I took it to the dry cleaners, and when I picked it up, the owner laughed and asked, "Where did you get that label? It's one of the funniest things I ever saw." I pleaded ignorance, then looked at the tag on the inside. It read, "This garment was made from 100% pure horse shit." It turned out that Fitzgerald had provided her with the label, and Susie needed no further direction as to what to do with it.

Susie was really just a wholesome, nice-looking girl. She was far from beautiful, but she did not seem to have much trouble getting dates. I had not counted on her being elected queen of Policemen's Ball. Every cop in town seemed to congregate in the office. Photographers took pictures of her from every possible location in the office. They stood on other secretaries' desks, on chairs, etc. Her picture was in every newspaper in the area. God, I was glad when that was all over.

In less than two years, Susie was married and was about to move to St. Louis.

I asked her if she had any friends who would be interested in her job, and she kept describing someone who, according to Susie, was blonde, beautiful, and built. I guess even her curves had curves. I said, "But, Susie, can she do the work?" Susie replied, "No, but I just think you need to have a little fun." For some reason, Susie refused to help me out. So, I had to turn to the employment agencies. The girls the agencies sent over were, by and large, terrible. They could not type or take dictation. They did not seem to have much of anything going for themselves. Susie watched them come and go and kept reminding me of the blonde. Finally, an agency sent in a black girl. At that time, there was much more prejudice than there is now, so I told the girl that I had just hired someone that morning and had not yet had time to notify the agencies. When the girl had departed, Susie came in immediately and said, "I'll get you a secretary, and she can do the work!" She did. She talked Donna into quitting school at Ohio State and coming to work for me.

Donna was a very attractive, dark-haired girl, the exact opposite of Susie. She didn't talk, worked hard, but would not have won the prize as Miss Congeniality. She was good, though, and stayed with me for almost seven years. By the time she left, she had gotten married, saved money, decided that it was time to get pregnant, gave a month's notice, and quit. As precise as she was, she probably had the date of birth of her child all worked out in advance.

John and Ed had three secretaries while we were together. Carol was young and pretty, Mary was young, pretty, and skinny; I do not remember much about the third girl. The only funny story about them was that John had an old guy, a real estate broker and a good client, who evidently fancied Mary. Accordingly, whenever he entered the office, he put five dollars on her desk and tried to pinch her. This upset her, of course, but I always wondered what there was to pinch.

Several outstanding events took place in that office. Once we decided to have a party lunch in the library (now George Wolfe's office) men only—no wives or secretaries. We invited "Taps" Schorr as a guest. Each of us was assigned by Fitzgerald to bring something. Taps was to furnish the martinis, so he brought a gallon of them. George did not drink, so there was plenty to go around—and it did. By this time, we had switched our luncheon spot to Benny Klein's, a local bar. So, a couple of us bought kosher corned beef sandwiches on rye and stole enough kosher dills to supplement the sandwiches. Somebody had brought brownies, someone else all kinds of snacks. All in all, it turned out to be a great party and very little in the way of work took place that afternoon.

I had a good client in my practically soundproof office one afternoon and, when the conference was over, opened the door to find John playing the bongo drums, Fitzgerald standing on the front desk taking pictures, and everyone else parading up and down the lobby. Fortunately, it turned out that my client had a sense of humor. He joined the parade.

As I mentioned earlier, George Wolfe moved into the library. He had been an assistant prosecuting attorney in charge of delinquent personal property taxes, and the Franklin County Grand Jury, and the "the flower fund" in the prosecutor's office. The prosecutor, Sam Devine, was a fraternity brother of both George and me. When Sam was elected to Congress in 1958, George went with him as administrative aide. George hated Washington. I took the family to Washington for a visit in the summer of 1960, and met George there. He asked whether there was any possibility of his coming into our office to commence the practice of law, sometime after the November election. I told him that I would check and let him know. I also told him that getting started is tough and warned him that it could be a long time before he made any money. At any rate, he came to Columbus, and we let him use the library and Susie's office skills. A client of mine wanted a lawyer in his real estate office. So, I sent George down a day or so a week. He got Margy to type for him at home, so he made out pretty well on a very low overhead. Most importantly, Sam set up a Columbus office, and paid George well to run it a half day each day. He could afford to eat.

I think that it was in 1962 or very early 1963 that Ed Fitzgerald "retired," and he and his second wife moved to Florida. This did make a difference to us all. We were used to Ed. We missed his luncheon arrangements, and we really missed the stability of having him around.

John, of course, missed him financially. He had to pick up the full tab for a secretary, and all of us had to pay more rent.

John solved the problem quickly. One of his friends was a real estate broker who said that he needed an office downtown, mostly for mail delivery, and to have a secretary take his telephone calls. John moved into Ed's office, which was much larger. The broker had an office full of beautiful new furniture delivered. John hired a new secretary, Frances, and he and the broker paid her salary. The entire arrangement was strange. The broker was well-known and highly successful in development, putting together huge deals constructing and operating apartment complexes, etc. He was hardly ever in the office, except to go over his mail. He was the only real estate broker I ever heard of who had an unlisted telephone. I asked him about that, and he said that he did not want to be bothered. He said that when he saw a deal that he wanted, he went after it, and did not want to be involved otherwise.

It worked out fine for all of us, the broker paid his share of the rent, and it was wonderful for John, because he got half his secretary's salary paid, and I do not think the secretary ever so much as typed one letter for the broker.

Finally, George moved out and set up an office with Taps Schorr, and Phil Herzing moved into the library. The entire office had always had colorful people, and Phil certainly fit in. He was a rich man's son, but at that time was out of favor with his father. He wore Brooks Brothers suits, which were threadbare, and Brooks Brother shirts with frayed button-down collars. At that time, Phil was not very successful in the practice of law. However, the one area where Phil shone was with the ladies, he loved them all. His hair was turning gray, he was reasonably tall, handsome, and distinguished looking. In short, he was attractive to women. Phil had attended Yale as an undergraduate, and he told us that in those years, senior professors taught freshman courses. He said that the first day of college, first class, was Elementary Psychology. The professor entered the classroom, went to the podium, and said, "Gentlemen, we will begin this course by discussing sexual intercourse, and I wish to make my point of view quite clear. Some of it is good, some is better, but it is never bad." Phil told us that he listened to the professor very intently that day and had followed the old professor's precepts ever since. He always had a story to tell about his exploits, and from what I saw, I believed him. One story that he told us centered around an apartment which he occupied during the time when he was between marriages. He said that one evening he answered the door to find a large irate man, who asked "Are you Phil Herzing?" Phil admitted that he was, and the man burst into his apartment, saying in a loud voice, "You son of a bitch, I'm going to kill you. You have been screwing my wife." Phil raised both hands, palms out, and said, "Wait a minute, sir. Let's talk this over. Which one are you?"

For me, during those years, the practice of law prospered steadily. I still did a great amount of real estate work. Much of it was dull, hard work, but it did help pay the overhead. Some of this work got complicated. I was becoming known for some expertise in that field. I cleaned up some titles that were most difficult. I put together several large real estate transactions involving large sums of money and some rather difficult agreements.

I organized quite a few corporations, partnerships, and other business entities and, generally, represented small businesses to a much greater extent than I had earlier. I continued to handle an ever-increasing number of estates, adoptions, and guardianships. I tried several real estate matters to the court, and even had the temerity to try two or three cases to a jury.

I continued to handle divorce cases and hated almost all of them. In all other adversary proceedings, it is usually possible to effect a reasonable solution. People involved in divorce were never reasonable. They hate each other. Most of them cannot afford to be divorced if they have dependent children. They owe money for automobiles, furniture, appliances, clothing, a house, and are on the ragged edge of bankruptcy to start with. Two households are financially impossible for the average couple to maintain. Divorce clients should all be charged for each telephone call. The attorney fees would become astronomical, especially when the attorney represents the wife. If one had the patience and the time, it would be easy to spend about twenty hours a day just listening to the spouse's past and present transgressions.

Somehow, as my practice became more lucrative, it became a lot less colorful. I became more selective in my choice of clients. Of course, they had to be able to pay me, which is a thing I learned with experience. Any lawyer can have more legal business than he can possibly handle, if he does not worry about money. I also began to demand some measure of respectability on the part of the prospective client. I quit taking just any warm body. That body had to be relatively clean in any respect. I refused cases where I felt that the prospective client was shady. I also learned a lot about the chances for success in litigation, and advised prospective clients when I felt that there was little or no likelihood of winning. I do not mean to imply that I was saintly in my practice, but it did seem only right to try to prevent futile litigation, from the client's point of view, from mine, and from the court's.

I remember that I purchased three very different automobiles in those years. When I traded the convertible that would not reverse, I bought a white 1959 Buick Super, four-door hardtop. It had huge tailfins, with the result that a stiff wind would cause the car to move around. The back end actually seemed to elevate when the wind was just right. I then traded for a 1962 Ford Thunderbird convertible that was really quite a car. It was all black with a red vinyl interior and had one feature that was outstanding. To put the top down, it was unlatched at the top of the windshield, a button was pushed, and the top went straight up in the air, the trunk lid flew open facing the car's interior, and the top then folded gently into the trunk, and the trunk lid went back down and locked, by screwing itself into position. To close the top, the reverse was true. It was all automatic. To my knowledge, they were made for only three years, and not many were sold. It was a great car, but not very practical, especially for a family. Fortunately, we had purchased a Chevrolet station wagon in 1960, and used it for all family trips.

In 1964, I really went overboard and bought a Chrysler Imperial four-door hardtop. It was all white with beautiful black leather interior. The car was huge and hard to maneuver. It was very comfortable to ride in, and really did seat six people comfortably. The car had every gadget that had been invented to that time. This was the first car I owned which was air conditioned, and it had a rather difficult to operate cruise control. By the mid-1950's power brakes, power steering and power windows were common.

We seldom went to the motion picture theaters. Much of our entertainment took place at home. We had a large stereo and played it frequently. We bought a color television, and the entire family watched T.V. Sunday night was family night. We usually were all at home, had popcorn, a fire in the fireplace, and watched the Sunday evening programs. The highlight for all of us seemed to be "Bonanza."

Evelyn and I partied a lot on the weekends, traveling in three or four different groups. Actually, as we all became more affluent, the parties became more lavish. No longer did everyone bring their own bottle, and a potluck dish. There were a lot of cocktail parties and dinner parties. Each hostess tried to outdo the other. We men seemed to measure the success of the party by how drunk everyone got.

We started going out to dinner in the better restaurants frequently. During the mid-fifties in the fall, much social activity centered around the Ohio State football schedule. We took in all of the home games, and every other year, joined the invasion of Ann Arbor, Michigan, to attend the Ohio State-Michigan game. We went to Michigan on Friday and returned on Sunday. There was a large group of our friends who all made reservations together at one of the Detroit hotels. We designated a different couple each time to have a suite, and we partied there. Gradually, through friends from North Lakes Resort, we got acquainted with a group of Michigan people who entertained us when we went up there, and we entertained them when the game was played in Columbus. Those were great parties and great times. A group of us went to Chicago twice to party and attend the Ohio State-Northwestern game. The second time we did this was a disaster. We went on Thanksgiving for a Saturday ballgame. By game time, we were all exhausted. Sometimes one can have too much of a good thing.

During golf season, we spent a great amount of time at London Country Club. I routinely played golf Thursday afternoons, Saturdays, and Sundays. Evelyn played on Ladies Day, in all of the club events, and very often on Saturday or Sunday. Many times, on Sunday afternoon, we played together and with our boys as they became interested. The boys took golf lessons and played with some of the other members' children. Marcia, our daughter, was left out. She had no interest in learning the game. The boys made some of their spending money by caddying for me on Saturdays and in the tournaments. Once a year we had what was called a "Calcutta." Team captains, the best golfers in the club, were appointed by the chairman of the tournament committee. They, in turn, selected their teams from those who had signed up to play in the event. The game itself was "best ball with handicap." Each club member had a handicap based on his ability to play. This meant that every player received a certain number of strokes which would arbitrarily, and hole by hole, be subtracted from his actual score. Best ball simply meant that the lowest score on the team on each hole was counted as the team score. On the stag night before the date of the "Calcutta," an auctioneer auctioned off the teams to the highest bidder. The teams themselves could buy their own team in competitive bidding with others. It was an exciting evening and quite a lot of money was gambled. If the winning team and the second and third finishers were the owners of their teams, they made a killing—several hundred dollars each. The whole thing always intrigued me and, although I was a poor golfer, with my high handicap I was always an asset. I always played better in the games than I ever did any other time and made money several times.

The Michigan people came to Columbus for the 1964 Ohio State-Michigan game on the Friday afternoon before the game. There were dinners and cocktail parties and much drinking. Evelyn finally dragged me out of the hotel where they were staying late Saturday night. As always, it was a hilarious time. The next morning Jim came from next door. Evelyn said, "Dick, Jim and I want to talk to you." They both looked quite serious; I knew something was terribly wrong. Jim said, "Clicky (my London Country Club nickname), it's Calcutta time. Get up for it. Evelyn came to the office this week and said that when she was routinely checking her breasts, she found a small lump on her left one, and asked that I check it. It is there and it may be malignant. She is going to the hospital tomorrow. Dick Zollinger will be the surgeon." "I didn't want to tell you until now, and spoil the weekend," Evelyn said. I was stunned. How brave she was to go through the weekend, and really enter in! How young she was. I felt as though I had been kicked in the pit of my stomach. I really do not know where the twins were when we talked. Marcia, of course, was away at college.

Jim went home and we talked further. Evelyn had even arranged for a cook for our evening meals and another gal to clean and straighten up the house. She had thought of everything for our comfort as she always did.

I took her to the hospital the next afternoon and checked her in. She was operated on a day or so later. The lump was malignant, and a radical mastectomy was performed. When I was told what had occurred, I cried. I cried for myself, I cried for our children, and mostly, I cried for Evelyn.

I went home to face the children. Marcia had come for vacation from school that day. In the middle of trying to explain, I broke down, and we all cried. When we stopped, we were much closer, and much braver. I went back to the hospital that evening and saw Evelyn. She was still groggy, and in a state of shock. The next day was Thanksgiving and, after seeing Evelyn, I took the children to Thanksgiving dinner. It was not a joyful occasion.

Evelyn was hospitalized for about ten days and, under the watchful eye of one of the special nurses, exercised her left arm until it exhausted her. She started her X-ray treatments. Finally, I got to bring her home. She was weak from the treatments and was required to rest most of the time. She was happy to be home, and God knows her family was too. I prayed for her recovery every night for five years. Thank God, she was one of the lucky ones!

Our children were growing up all too soon. Through Marcia's high school years, our house across from the high school, became an annex for her friends. I got used to girls in the kitchen during breakfast. I sometimes had the urge to kill but suppressed it. They were always there before every home athletic event and sometimes after. Evelyn loved it. The best part as far as I was concerned was that we had a pretty automatic check on our daughter's activities. She graduated in the spring of 1964 and entered Denison University that fall. The boys took over for her in high school, but we did not have boys in the house at breakfast.

I decided to again involve myself in local, Grove City, politics. A friend and client of mine was by far the most successful, and one of the most respected persons in the entire community. At retirement age, he had already relinquished control of the day-to-day operation of his business. He was still president of the local bank but had a vice-president who actually ran it. Grove City had just adopted a new charter which called for a strong mayor, supported by an administrator of his own choosing. Almost everyone on the charter commission had my friend in mind as the ideal person to serve as the first mayor under the new charter. He agreed to run and was opposed by a man who had been serving on the city council, but who had very little to offer in comparison. I had nothing to do with the campaign other than to make a small contribution. My friend should have won easily. He won by one vote. I decided that the campaign had been poorly run, so I became a ward committeeman on the Franklin County Republican Central Committee and, in short order, took control of local Republican politics. Four years later when my friend ran for re-election, his opponent was the same man he had defeated by one vote. I ran the campaign, and we won by a huge majority. During all the time that I ran things, we kept control of council. It really was a matter of organization. I got the people—and the candidates—working block by block, door-to-door. Being on the Central Committee was a sort of added bonus. Although I had a very small voice in what happened in county politics and City of Columbus politics, I did know what was going on. The county chairman was a typical political boss. He ran the organization completely. No one defied him, and very few ever questioned him. He passed out rewards to his friends and vanquished his enemies. He made deals with the Democratic chairman, with the result that certain offices were perpetually Republican, and other Democratic. The Central Committee had a few meetings. Bill Schneider, the chairman, headed everything himself; the Central Committee was a rubber stamp of his decisions. One reason, of course, that he was never seriously questioned was that he was almost always right. When the committee did meet, it was always at the Hotel Fort Hayes—a dinner meeting with unlimited quantities of any kind of drink known to man, steaks, or standing rib. Everything was absolutely first class. When dinner was over, Bill went to the podium, explained the purpose of the meeting and briskly got the meeting's business underway. Usually, it was a meeting called for selection of candidates to run for nomination. Selection was equivalent to nomination, and, for a majority of offices, nomination meant election. Occasionally, Bill ran a candidate for the purpose of getting him defeated in order to remove him from the political scene. Fortunately, when he made a deal with the Democratic chairman, he called someone into his office and asked that they run as a sacrificial candidate. He made it a point to reward him later, either by an appointment to a really good political job, or by running him as a serious candidate and winning. I know that all of this sort of thing still goes on, but few have ever been as adept as was Bill Schneider. Further, there was never a hint of scandal during his reign. Bribery was unheard of.

    Jim Henry and I built a six-family apartment building on the near west side of Columbus in a rather bad area called "The Bottoms." In order to get the lot and requisite space needed, we had to buy an old run-down brick house which was rented sort of room by room. Jim was a very busy doctor. I was busy, too, but it was sort of up to me to collect the rents each week. Christ, what a mess. I understand that many have become wealthy by being slum landlords. I think they earn every cent. We got the damned house sold and finally got the apartments built and rented. The reason we built where we did was because of its proximity to Mt. Carmel Hospital. Jim thought that we could keep the place rented to hospital personnel. Initially, we did have two or three doctors and some other hospital employees, but as they moved out, they were not replaced by others. Instead, most of the people who wanted to rent them were undesirables. My mother was handling the apartments for us because she owned some and had experience, whereas neither Jim nor I had time to fool with them. Even so, I had to evict a couple of the tenants for non-payment of rent, and one because the other tenants complained that the lady operated a "house of ill repute"—delicately speaking. The apartments were on a corner, and one night a drunk failed to make a turn and managed to land in the living room of one of the lower apartments. Fortunately, we had plenty of insurance coverage. Ultimately, several years later, we sold these apartments and made some money. It was good preparation for the construction I got involved in later on.

The second Eisenhower term gradually drew to a close. It was a time of peace and harmony not seen since. I did not think much of Eisenhower as a President while he was in office. Looking back now to that time, I feel that he really did an excellent job. We were prosperous, at peace both at home among ourselves and abroad. We trusted him.

In 1960, Richard Nixon, who had been Ike's Vice-President for eight years, ran as the Republican candidate for President against John F. Kennedy. Originally, it seemed that Nixon would be elected easily. Kennedy was a Senator from Massachusetts who really had not distinguished himself in the Senate. The Kennedy money was, of course, behind him and money is always an asset in any political campaign. Even in October, Nixon was expected to win rather easily. However, the Republican strategy makers made a horrible mistake. They agreed to a televised debate between the two candidates. Kennedy probably did not have nearly the knowledge of the government and its problems that Nixon had. However, the Kennedy make up people did a magnificent job for the cameras. Nixon looked pale and pasty-faced, Kennedy young and vibrant. Kennedy was glib, but articulate. His magnetic, attractive personality came across much better than did Nixon's. No question that Kennedy won the debate. He also won exposure that he could not have acquired in any other manner. What had looked like an easy Republican victory suddenly became less sure. Election day came, and I recall that when I went to bed about three o'clock the next morning, nothing was settled. When I got up, it was still in doubt, and appeared to be so close that it all depended on whether Illinois went Republican or Democrat. Finally, all of the Chicago votes were counted, and Mayor Richard Daley, and his Cook County organization had carried Illinois. It was thought at the time that the election was completely fraudulent in Cook County, but for some reason, Nixon himself refused either to demand a properly supervised recount of those ballots, or to insist on a serious Congressional investigation. Eisenhower was no great admirer of Nixon, but he was furious at the apparently blatant dishonesty. Kennedy was the new President of the United States. From the day of his inaugural address until the day of his death and beyond, Kennedy entranced the American people as no President had since F.D.R. in his prime. In the eyes of the media, he could do no wrong. His wife was idolized too. Everything the Kennedys did was glamourized. Their reign was likened to Camelot.

The most important happening during the Kennedy years was, of course, the Cuban Missile Crisis. Nikita Khrushchev and Kennedy had met and, apparently the Russians badly misjudged the Kennedy character. They evaluated him as being rather weak and wishy-washy. He was neither, and if he lacked anything in toughness and determination, his brother, Bobby, his Attorney General and confidential advisor, more than supplied any additional will required. The Kennedys had great social grace, but underneath the veneer they were as tough as their father, Joe, who did not build his huge fortune by being a nice guy. In any event, the Russians backed down, and a nuclear war that seemed all too near was avoided.

Beyond that, Kennedy accomplished very little. Perhaps he was in office such a short time that he could not have gotten his programs moving. It seemed from his words that he was extremely liberal. In fact, his record was somewhat conservative. The last time the budget was in balance was during Kennedy's presidency and it had not been balanced for years prior to that. He was a great civil rights advocate but did nothing serious in the way of prepared legislation. He did send federal troops, investigators, and attorneys into Mississippi reluctantly and only because he was forced to do so by the actions of southern rednecks.

On the Friday before the 1963 Ohio State-Michigan football game, we were on our semi-annual trek to Detroit and Ann Arbor with our friends, Brooks and Helen Julian. Quite a few of our friends were going and we all had reservations at the same hotel as usual. George Smith had chartered a bus for Saturday to take us to the game at Ann Arbor and had ordered box lunches. It promised to be a gala weekend. We stopped for lunch in Bowling Green, Ohio. When we had finished and, on our way out, we heard that the President had been shot and had been taken to a Dallas hospital. Details were sketchy. We got into the car and turned on the car radio. All of the joy had been taken out of our trip. We drove on to Detroit, listening grimly to the reports. President Kennedy was dead—killed by an assassin's bullet. We checked into our hotel as did our friends. We had a party room where we assembled, but we were not in a party mood. Detroit was virtually closed down. Few businesses and fewer restaurants remained open. We were fortunate to make reservations, in a good restaurant nearby, and later learned the next day's football game was called off.

The Smiths came to our hotel early Saturday morning. We cancelled the bus, and the box lunches. Most of our group checked out and went home, but three couples of us stayed and spent Saturday in Detroit. We drove home Sunday listening to the news of Jack Ruby's murdering Lee Harvey Oswald. It was a sad, sad, unforgettable time.

Monday the entire nation was shut down, and we watched the Kennedy funeral proceedings on television with a sort of horrified fascination.

From my perspective, the country seemed to change from that time on. No longer were we a united people. Radicalism flourished. It began to be popular to question the government leadership. Patriotism became unpopular. Eisenhower had gotten us involved in Vietnam to a limited extent. Kennedy increased our involvement without protest.

Lyndon B. Johnson was, of course, sworn in as President of the

United States immediately upon notification of Kennedy's death. Johnson had always wanted to be President. He coveted the job. I am sure that he had nothing to do with Kennedy's assassination but, on the other hand, I doubt that he was as sad as he should have been over the event. He was a consummate politician—he became majority leader of the Senate after first going to Washington as a congressional aide when F.D.R. was elected. Subsequently, he became a congressman, later a senator. He understood power and its uses. He understood legislative process as few Presidents ever had. When it came to getting legislation passed, he was without peer. Roosevelt had always been his idol, and he was a New Dealer all the way. Johnson caused more social legislation to be passed than Roosevelt ever did. He did not just give the advancement of civil rights "lip service" as Kennedy seemed to have done. He succeeded in securing the passage of virtually all of the civil rights legislation that was ever really significant.

In summer of 1969, Barry Goldwater was nominated as the Republican candidate for President after a truly bitter fight which split the party. Goldwater was extremely conservative. He was dead honest, saying exactly what he thought, regardless of whom it might offend. He even angered me with some of his statements, and I was sorely tempted not to vote Republican. Goldwater said that he would, if elected, use whatever means might be required to defeat the Viet Cong, and win in Vietnam, whereupon Johnson promptly branded Goldwater as a warmonger and himself as the peace candidate. Of course, Johnson was elected so overwhelmingly that there was talk about the destruction and probably demise of the Republicans as a national party.

In the early fall of 1964, it looked as though our office was starting to disintegrate. Our broker decided that he did not need either the office or secretarial service. I could understand that. I never understood why he ever had the office in the first place, or thought he needed it. It also appeared that Phil Herzing had a political job lined up and would be leaving soon. John Phillips and I decided that it was too much trouble to keep looking for desirable people to move in to help meet the overhead. We also decided for various reasons that we would try to find office space in the same building for ourselves only and eliminate our association with Walt. We talked to the building manager, who told us to look at some space on the eighth floor, which we found was already occupied by some other lawyers. The manager said if we liked the space, whatever changes we required would be made. We said we really hated to take space already occupied by other lawyers, but the manager assured us that he was going to evict them anyway as they were way behind in their rent. He then added, "and besides one of them is running a whorehouse out of the office at night."

January 1965 — October 1971

John and I took over the new office space sometime in November but, according to our wives, the space needed decorating badly, so we stayed in the big suite until sometime in December. Walt rented space in another (new) building. We hired a decorator who just might have been a little "light on his feet." I always suspected male decorators whether I should have or not. John had his choice of offices. I had an ulterior motive in telling him that he could have first choice. One office was in a corner of the building, with a door which opened into the hall. I knew he would choose it; it gave him a way to sneak out without anyone knowing it. I did not want it because the door took up wall space that I needed for my sofa.

The decorating in John's office was limited to carpet, draperies, and painted walls. John refused to have anything to do with decorating the combination lobby and secretaries' office. Accordingly, it had bright gold and blue striped carpet, and a mural of Chinese bamboo shoots on the wall that faced the entrance door. It was about as unusual as any lobby I ever saw. When Susie, my former secretary, came and paid us a visit, she looked around and said, "Sush, where are the hair dryers?" I had a mural with a Chinese motif as well. It was called "The Chinese Bird Market." How or why I ever agreed to all of this, I'll never know.

The offices were adequate. We had a small, narrow space that we used as a combination file room and library. We even had to purchase a few books. All that I owned in the way of law books were the Ohio Revised Code, some form books, and a probate manual. John never had owned anything. The books in the library in the big suite belonged to Walt.

The new office was not particularly a fun place in which to practice, as contrasted to the good times we had when we were all together in the big suite. My secretary was always extremely quiet, hardly ever smiled, and tended to business. John's secretary was a widow, trying to raise her children on very little money, and was serious and perhaps a little bitter. On top of that, John managed to agitate her, and some of her frustration occurred when he vanished from his office out the side door without bothering to tell her. He frequently did this to avoid a telephone call, and occasionally to avoid seeing a client waiting for him in the lobby. I never heard her explain that one, but it is little wonder that she got upset.

It was a serious, almost grim office. About the only humor that was supplied came from John or one of his clients.

One day I received an unwelcome telephone call from an auditor from Internal Revenue. He said that he was assigned to audit my income tax return for the previous year, and wondered when it would be convenient to meet with me. I did not tell him that, as far as I was concerned, it would never be convenient. We set an appointment, and he arrived at the scheduled hour. First, he went over all of my deductions, and I satisfied him by producing the requisite checks and receipts. He then wanted to see our records on our other income from land contracts, and mortgages, and our capital gains. He meticulously did all of the arithmetic on each item. He had no fault to find with any of it but did make a finding as to my methods of depreciating my car. By this time, I had a luncheon appointment and told him so. He had not even started on my office records – my major source of income. I told him that after lunch he could work with my secretary since she handled the record-keeping on all office income and expenses. I took him out to her desk and introduced them. She looked up and glared at him. He turned to me and said, "You know, I don't really think it's necessary to audit your office records." We shook hands and he left permanently. I was glad that day my gal was a little different. With some of my secretaries he would have moved in.

My law practice flourished. I represented two or three out-of-state corporations on land acquisitions and zoning matters. Some of their products did not work as advertised. In other cases, their customers failed to pay as they should. I represented a small country bank for a couple of years until the president objected to my fees. I charged them an hourly rate, and he raised hell because I charged them for telephone calls. He must have thought that telephone calls did not take time. I handled several appropriations cases, and made money because I took them on a percentage basis. On one of those cases, Judge Harter helped me when I filed a pleading late; he ordered the Deputy Clerk of the Courts to back-date the filing.

I got involved with a couple of real estate operators who purchased locations at almost every exit ramp from the interstate that was constructed throughout Franklin County. All three of the county commissioners were friends of mine politically; so was the secretary of the zoning board. It all helped. Some re-zonings were a little controversial. Usually, the only people at a zoning hearing who favored the rezoning were the person who would gain as a result of the change, and the attorney representing the petitioner. Everyone who lived in the area was usually present and raising hell against any change. Since the county commissioners are elected, they do not go against the wishes of the majority very often at zoning hearings.

I had one case that had been turned down by the Franklin County Planning Commission, and by the Franklin County Zoning Board. It then went to the county commissioners for final decision. The night of the hearing, the hearing room was packed. There was standing room only. The entire Pleasant Township Civic Association was present and upset. I thought to myself that I had no chance to win in the face of all of that opposition.

Several people spoke against the change after I had made my presentation. I had told the truth. There was to be a service station, and possibly later on a motel and restaurant. The zoning requested would also have permitted a bar or any type of drinking establishment. The chairman of the Township Association got up and said in a nasty, insinuating tone, "How do we know that a filling station and possibly a motel and restaurant will be located on that ground?" The commissioners had heard enough. The chairman of the Board of County Commissioners said, "We know because that's what Dick Clark says is going to be there. All who are in favor of the rezoning say 'aye." It was rezoned unanimously. Needless to say, I did charge a very substantial fee for that one. Incidentally, twenty years later, there is still only a service station on the space.

To get the office space we occupied, John and I were required to sign a five-year lease. We hesitated to do this, but, as it turned out, it was the best thing that could have happened to us. Tom and Bud had acquired a sizeable group of lawyers, and a busy title insurance office. They wanted to lease the entire eighth floor, and particularly our space since it was at the front where the elevators opened. We talked to the management, and to Tom and Bud, and finally agreed to move into other space at the end of the hall on the same floor. In return for our cooperation, the building manager employed an architect to design a truly modern office suite for us. It was virtually the same as it would have been to move into a new office building. We had all sorts of built-ins, sliding doors, bookshelves, concealed radiators, etc. They really gave us deluxe accommodations. My office was papered with grass cloth. I was damned glad to get rid of the Chinese Bird Market and the Bamboo Shoots that I gone along with previously. John's secretary was happier because he could no longer use an outside door to escape. There was none.

All of this occurred in 1968, so we really had only about three years in the first of our two offices.

When I taught high school, Percy Rider was the principal as well as chemistry teacher. There were no disciplinary problems to speak of because the students had great respect, coupled with quite a little fear. Percy had been a first sergeant in a cavalry outfit in World War I, which was the high spot of his life. He had a World War II style moustache and always wore tan, square-toed army shoes, and a sheepskin coat during the winter. His wife, Mina, taught elementary grades in a small country school system. They had no children. Percy owned and operated a good-sized farm in Madison County during all the years that I knew him, and neither he nor Mina ever missed a day's teaching because of snow drifts or road closings. He always had a couple of riding horses, and when not being active otherwise, rode over his land and all the territory surrounding. No fence seemed too difficult for him to jump.

After retirement, Percy and Mina traveled literally all over the world. Percy even drove the Alcan Highway years ago.

Mina was severely injured in an automobile accident, and Percy crawled out of the wreckage, shook-up, but otherwise fine. He really was a tough old bird. I settled Mina's case against the driver of the other vehicle for the limits of his insurance policy. I only regret that he did not have more insurance. He had nothing else. Mina never fully recovered, physically, from the accident.

Two or three years later, I learned that they both were in a nursing home in Grove City. I was surprised that Percy ever left the farm, but he did shortly after Mina.

They were not in the same room for some reason, perhaps because Mina was the first to enter the home. I learned that neither of them was doing very well; accordingly, I went to visit Percy. I was amazed. He was emaciated and simply stared at me. He knew nothing and no one. I did not visit Mina. I could not face two in one day.

A few days later, I was told that Mina had passed away and that, within a matter of a few hours, Percy died. He must have intuitively known of her death and willed his own. I knew of only one other instance of a similar nature. A baker and his wife got into a hell of a fight, which went on all night. She had to take him to work very early the next morning. A semi-truck, fully loaded, was approaching on the other side of the road. She deliberately pulled across the road in front of the semi, and both she and her husband were killed instantly.

At any rate, I had written wills for both Percy and Mina several years earlier where in each had left everything to each other, and in the event of simultaneous deaths or deaths within thirty days of one another, to diverse relatives. They had named a farmer friend of theirs as their executor, and apparently had told him to employ me as attorney for the estate. The estates were complicated because of the times of their deaths, and their various relatives. Each of them had acquired a fair amount of money in addition to the farm and equipment. I was surprised, because they had done this on teachers' salaries, which were never high.

The executor and I went through the residence methodically. That was how we found most of their bank books. We found miscellaneous papers and documents which absolutely were without value to anyone. This sort of thing happens time after time. Many safety deposit boxes that have been maintained for years contain nothing except old receipts, outdated insurance policies, and the like.

We did find a sugar sack filled with coins from every foreign country that they had ever visited. Neither of us had any idea as to their value. I volunteered to take them to a coin dealer and get them appraised. The bag was heavy, and I carried it for several blocks to the dealer. For a fee, he went through them coin by coin and valued each individually. It turned out that the vast majority were not worth their face value, and the appraisal cost more than the coins were worth.

There were some items of furniture and household goods that we felt were probably antiques. Everything was old, whether antique or not. Much of Percy's farm equipment was antiquated and of little value. The executor suggested that the best way to dispose of all of their tangible personal property was by selling everything at auction.

We hired the best-known auctioneers in central Ohio. They went over the entire house, outbuildings, and the farm itself looking for saleable items, and came up with things that we thought were valueless. They advertised heavily and stressed that they were auctioning Percy and Mina's Rider's property. Without permission, they even included Percy's automobile which, while it was not an antique, was not a thing of beauty either. The Grange, a farmer's organization, asked to serve food. Percy and Mina were well-known. In their years of teaching, they influenced a lot of lives, and they were also active in numerous farm organizations.

The auction was held on a cold, clear, sunshine-filled Saturday in early winter. We had expected a crowd. We got a flood of people. The Grange had not anticipated the numbers either and ran out of food shortly after noon. They did, however, continue to sell hot coffee out of their huge tent until late afternoon when the auction was over.

I do not remember what the final sale amounted to, but it was far beyond our appraisal and expectations. The auctioneers even sold an old rusty bucket that they had picked up someone place on the farm. The bucket had a hole in one side; yet it sold for three dollars. The auctioneers took the large bag of coins, and carefully put them into several small sacks. They auctioned these off one at a time, telling different tales about the Rider's trips. The bidding got higher and higher, and each sack brought more than all of the coins were worth.

After my experience with that auction, I have never hesitated since to sell personal property in that manner.

Years earlier, several children of a deceased farmer came to the office I had in the front room at home. There was no will; hence no one had been appointed to serve as the executor of the estate. I got them all seated, after bringing in some dining-room chairs. My question was, "Which one of you will serve as administrator?" I thought that would be pretty easy to answer, but it was not. A story verbal battle began, all of them shouting and accusing one another of all sorts of horrible things. I stood up and told them I would leave and return in half an hour, and that if they had not settled everything by then, they would have to go someplace else. When I came back, everything had quieted down and they had agreed on an administrator, and from then on everyone cooperated.

I handled an estate for a family who were clients of long standing, as had been their deceased father. He was a real character. In his lifetime, he had given each of his children a farm plus God only knows what else but had never filed a gift-tax return. One of his sons brought him in to see me two or three different times for the purpose of having me explain to him the necessity of gift tax returns. He was deaf and wore a hearing aid. When I started to talk and he found out what I was talking about, he would turn off the hearing aid. The result was that when he died, he had only about ten thousand dollars left. Things got complicated, and each of his children had to come up with a substantial amount of money in order to satisfy Internal Revenue, the State of Ohio, and my attorney fees. Fortunately, three of the children had money. I do not know how the other one came up with it. The father had never bothered to make a will either; consequently, all three sons were equally eligible to serve as administrator of this estate, since they all lived in the same county as the old man. The daughter could not serve, because she was a resident of New York City. I explained this to all of them and asked which of them wanted to be administrator. They all did. Two of the three were very bright. I had them draw straws; naturally the dumb one got the short straw.

Sometime later I got a telephone call from an attorney in Manhattan who was drafting a will for the daughter. He said she had requested that I serve as her executor, even though I was a non-resident of New York State. I had known her for years and had represented her entire family, virtually from the time I became a lawyer. I told him that I would do so. Because she was about my age, I did not really expect to ever have to serve. She died, suddenly, within a year.

I knew that she owned a farm in Ohio, as well as a considerable amount of stock in the local bank. I had to make a trip to New York to meet with her attorney, whom I had hired as my attorney, and to get access to her safety deposit box in order to properly inventory her estate. The attorney was in Manhattan, and her safety deposit box was in a branch bank in Queens. One of her brothers knew that she used Bache and Co. in Rockefeller Plaza as her broker. The attorney and I discussed the procedures and both he and his secretary agreed that I could take the subway to Queens and still return in time to deposit with the brokerage house any stock I found, and then meet him for lunch at his club. I decided to take a taxi instead.

I was amazed at the amount and variety of stock in that box as well as bank books, certificates of deposit and some very helpful notes to me. I had kept the taxi waiting, took the stock to Rockefeller Plaza, established an account as executor, got receipts for all of it, and went to the club, which occupied an entire floor of the Hotel Pennsylvania.

As I entered the hotel, I followed instructions and told the elevator starter that I wanted to go to "Squadron A-1," whatever that was. A large number of elevators stretched across the entire wall. The starter looked at me, smiled, and said, "A-1 is A-1, Sir. I'll take you there." With that, he opened the door to the first elevator inside the building entrance and took me directly to the floor. It opened into the club itself. When I stepped inside, a fine-looking black man in a uniform greeted me, asked for my belongings—-hat, coat, and brief case—inquired as to whom I was to meet, advised me as to the location of the lawyer, indicated that my host had not arrived, and asked what he might serve me. While I sat sipping my first martini, my host arrived, and ordered his martini. We chatted, ordered another drink, and went into the dining room. The food, drink, service, and furnishings were all excellent. The prices for lunch were so reasonable for New York that I was amazed.

I commented to that effect, and he said that I might be interested in the story of Squadron A-1. During the Civil War, a group of what I am certain were young New York socialites organized a calvary squadron which became known as Squadron A-1. After the war, they did not disband, but ultimately purchased land in New Jersey, just across the river from the city, to drill on, exercise their horses and the like. When one person dropped out, some person considered acceptable to the group was invited to join the squadron. Later, they fought as a unit in the Spanish-American War and in World War I. They entered service together as a unit in World War II, but then they were disbanded because the Army no longer had need for a volunteer cavalry unit. After the war, the squadron members decided against continuing to drill and ride and therefore had no further need for the land which, by this time, had become very valuable. The squadron sold it, set up the club, and maintained it with the income from the proceeds of the sale. He looked at me, smiled, and said, "Wouldn't it be interesting to be the last man left alive from the squadron?"

From Squadron A-1, my attorney insisted that I walk with him to the Princeton Club to see, as he put it, what I had missed. He had offered to sponsor me there during my stay in New York and had told me that the accommodations were far nicer and less expensive than anything available in downtown Manhattan. I had declined because I did not want to become too obligated to a lawyer I had never seen and did not know much about—one who was representing me and the estate for which I was responsible. The rooms were large and beautifully furnished. We then went into the bar adjacent to the dining room for an after-lunch farewell drink. On the way out, we looked into the dining room, which was filled with dowagers in big hats who were sedately drinking and having either a late lunch or an early tea.

During the general time frame of my trip to New York, I was interested in novels by John O'Hara. A year or so after the trip, I picked up O'Hara's <u>Butterfield Eight</u>, which I had not read earlier for some reason. At one point in the book, O'Hara listed the criteria for a real bluestocking member of New York's high society. My host met all the qualifications, to my amazement, including graduating from Princeton and membership in Squadron A-1. I must confess that I became more impressed than I was when I was there, both with my host and Squadron A-1.

During the 1960s, I began to make money from the practice of law. Each year seemed better than the previous one. I felt comfortable and even moderately successful. As a matter of fact, I really thought that things would only get better in the future. Then came the year of my awakening. I really do not remember what year it was, but it was in the late 60s. There was no explanation for it that I know of. No one was mad at me, and I was busy, but nothing of any consequence came in to me. The largest fee that I received all year was for fifteen hundred dollars. I had to really hustle to keep my financial head above water. Strangely enough, and thankfully, the following year was very good and continued to be for several years. I had heard that almost every attorney had occasional bad years and that their income can fluctuate greatly from year to year. I can swear to it!

I had not normal vision from birth. I had no vision in my right eye, and my left eye could not be corrected to so-called normal. I wore glasses from the time I was three years old. Since my eyesight had always been bad, I had compensated and adjusted to the point that I functioned normally. My parents had not made an issue of my visual problems when I was growing up, fortunately, and, therefore, I never thought of myself as being handicapped. However, some time in 1968, I began to notice a change in my so-called "good eye." I was not making as quick an adjustment when I went out into the sunlight from inside, and vice versa. Sunlight bothered me when I was driving and walking the downtown streets. I was not able to recognize people on the streets as well as I had, nor was I as comfortable driving an automobile as I had been. I knew that the time would come, sooner or later, when I no longer would be able to practice law in a normal manner in downtown Columbus. I did not discuss my feelings with anyone—not even Evelyn—but I tried to decide on my future course of action. When I saw my ophthalmologist for my annual checkup, I described the situation to him. He told me that I was in the beginning stages of the development of a cataract on my good eye and advised me that I would have gradually-increasing difficulty and should consider making some sort of change in my routine.

I decided that I should set up shop in Grove City. I talked with Evelyn, and she agreed. I was certain to lose some of my law practice, but over a period of time I would have had no choice. A friend of mine, a former student, had a law office in Grove City. Gene Gunderman was several years younger than I, but I liked him and trusted him, so I talked to him about the two of us getting together for the purpose of building an office building in Grove City to house our law offices. He readily agreed, and after a considerable amount of looking, we found an ideal location (3083 Columbus Street) for our purposes.

At this point, after we had acquired the land, I told John of my plans and invited him to join us. He did not want to leave downtown Columbus, and he had no desire to come to Grove City full time. I also told my secretary, Donna, that I would eventually move my office. She was not enthusiastic, but she was never very enthusiastic about anything. Sometime later, Donna gave me notice that she was going to quit work in a month and said that she wanted to stay at home and have a family.

I had never wanted a Grove City girl in my law office for the reason that a lawyer-client relationship must always be, and remain, confidential. Grove City was a small town even though growing rapidly, and I was afraid that a local girl might say something she shouldn't. But I decided that this time I virtually *had* to hire a Grove City girl if I intended to have my office there. I knew several local girls and older women who were secretaries, but the first one I thought of contacting was Marianne Smith. I had known her when she was a little girl coming into the drug store to get an ice cream cone. When I returned from the Army, she was a senior in high school and a student of mine. She even typed some letters for me then, which I dictated to her. Subsequently, I had represented her and her husband, and her grandfather. She was an executrix of her aunt's estate, and I had served as her attorney. She was a secretary at the high school, and I doubted that she would want to change jobs and come into Columbus to work. If she was interested in working for me in Grove City, she would be excellent. I called and she agreed to come to work. She must have enjoyed it, because she remained in the office for more than fifteen and a half years. She has been a real asset, always.

After considerable trauma, which included discussions with architects, builders, and lenders, we finally hired an architect to plan an office building. After we agreed on the plans, we asked for bids from competent builders, and they were all so high that we were shocked and did not think that we could build at all. Finally, through friends of the Gundermans, a builder agreed to revise the specifications and see what he could do that would satisfy us as far as price was concerned, and the architect as to the specification's revision. Everything came together and, after shopping for money, we built a small office building in Grove City. We moved in the first of October in 1971. John Phillips and I shook hands and both felt sad. We had practiced law together for thirteen years without having any problems of any kind with the relationship. As John put it, "Other lawyers thought that it was the most unusual association that they knew of." It probably was. Our type of practice was different, and so were our clients. In fact, John seemed to attract characters, all of whom were involved in the most unusual situations that I ever heard of. I remember two of his favorite expressions. One was, as he shook his head, "Where do they come from?" The other, "Oh, Jeezus Christ, you ought to hear what happened to me this morning!" A book could be written about John, and really should.

One of his clients had enough mental problems to be declared mentally incompetent to handle his own affairs. I never knew whether John was his guardian, or the attorney for the guardianship but, anyway, one of the problems the nut had was that he felt the F.B.I. watched him constantly. When he was at home, he said he was watched through his television set; it stared at him constantly. When he left home, the F.B.I. tailed him. He came into John's office one afternoon completely terrorized and announced that "they" were in the hall just outside the office door. John said, "Now we have had enough of this. I'll take care of this once and for all." With that, he went out into the hall, carefully making sure that the entrance door to our office was left open, and yelled, "All right, you dirty sons-of-bitches, this has gone far enough. Get out of this building and quit bothering John Paul! And leave his television set alone, or I'll fix you!" He came back in after a minute or two, and said, "They're gone now, and you're safe from now on. They'll never bother you again." This satisfied his client and solved his F.B.I. problem.

John received a telephone call one afternoon from one of his clients who was in jail and wanted John to come over to get him out. His client said that he had no idea why he was in jail; that the police just arrested him. John went to the police department and discovered that his client was charged with indecent exposure. He talked with one of the arresting officers and was told that the client was running down one of the busiest streets in Columbus with no clothes on. John then saw his client and asked him why he had done this. After all, it was January and very cold. The client replied, "I was walking along talking to Jesus, and Jesus told me to disrobe at Broad and Third, and then to run out to Franklin Park and back. All that I was doing was jogging for Jesus."

One of John's friends was an assistant prosecuting attorney for Mahoning County in Youngstown, Ohio. Youngstown and its environs were a heavily-industrialized area, filled with various ethnic groups and crime of all kinds. It was a tough, wide-open county, and a mob center. Naturally, his friend and probably the police and other law enforcement personnel were mob controlled.

Mobsters owned bars, night clubs, and so-called "private" clubs, all of which were required to be licensed by the State of Ohio to sell liquor, obey the liquor laws, and abide by the regulations established by the Ohio Department of Liquor control. Those people laughed at laws and regulations and periodically were visited by investigators and inspectors who cited them to appear before a State Liquor Board for their transgressions. The Board could mete out various penalties according to the seriousness of the offense, including closing the establishments for various numbers of days, and even permanent loss of their liquor licenses.

The friend referred many of these people to John, who represented them surprisingly successfully before the board, which was in Columbus. These thugs came into the office frequently, frightening all of the secretaries because they looked, talked, and acted exactly like a movie gangster. They wore hats which they seemed never to remove; their coats bulged from carrying a gun in a shoulder holster. One of them must have been a real big shot because he was always accompanied by a bodyguard, who looked tougher than any of the others. He wore an overcoat even on warm days in the spring. I suspect that he carried a submachine gun underneath the coat. John called them "members of the Youngstown Rod and Gun Club." It was a very lucrative clientele, but John became frightened himself after one of his clients was found lying alongside the Ohio Turnpike, shot in the head; and another was blown up as he attempted to start his Cadillac in his garage one morning. Once he had a meeting in the Sheraton Hotel bar with the mob's top burglar, just out of jail on a two hundred fifty-thousand-dollar bond. The police had staked out a large grocery warehouse on a tip and caught him on top of the Big Bear Warehouse. The bond was very high for those days, but the mob had put up cash to bail him out. He wanted John to get the bond reduced to one hundred thousand dollars so that he could jump bond and disappear. The mob had given him permission to do this, he said, but would have killed him had he run for two hundred and fifty thousand dollars. He told John that he would give him "ten big ones" up front. The burglar's bodyguard suddenly became startled and drew a gun in the bar. So did the burglar. John was really afraid, and apologized profusely, as he told the burglar that he really did not think he could help him out.

The end of any association with that group came when John's friend was running for county prosecutor with the endorsement of the Democratic party, which was tantamount to election in Mahong County. One evening at his home he received a telephone call to the effect that if he did not withdraw as a candidate, he would be put into a sack of cement and thrown into the Mahong River. The next day he let word get out that he was considering dropping out as a candidate. That night he received another telephone call with the same threat if he *did* withdraw. He left town that night and disappeared for several weeks, returning only after the election, and after he was advised through his wife that he would be safe if he returned.

John had a client whom he called "the man with the twos," who showed up periodically for various reasons. The guy wore two neckties, two shirts, two coats, two pairs of pants, and two pairs of socks. I supposed he would have worn two pairs of shoes and two hats if he could have figured out a way to do so.

One of John's long-time clients owned a bar which must have been extremely popular. It had to be in order for the client to pay for all the damages resulting from his own transgressions, not to mention John's legal fees. The fellow appeared harmless enough when he came into the office, always well-dressed, soft-spoken, and intelligent.

The first episode that I remember occurred when one of his customers got into a loud, profane argument in the saloon. John's client came out from behind the bar, picked up a pool cue, hit the customer over the head and broke the stick. The part of the cue which remained in his hand had a sharp point, and John's client stabbed the fellow three or four times with it. Fortunately, the customer was wounded only slightly. The client was charged with aggravated assault and battery and a couple of other offenses. John got his client off, which amazed everyone, including the client.

Another miracle occurred when one of the bar customers started to leave without paying his bill. When the client yelled at him and told him to come back, the customer told him to go to hell, went out the door, climbed into his car and took off. John's client ran out the door, jumped into his Cadillac and started chasing the fellow down a busy, rather wide, one-way street. He put his window down and started shooting at the guy while speeding after him, driving with only his right hand. The police got into the chase and finally got John's client to stop two or three miles south of the bar. The client was charged with speeding, reckless operation of a motor vehicle, discharging firearms within the city, and shooting with intent to wound. John worked it out somehow so that his client pleaded guilty to discharging firearms, and all of the other charges were dropped.

Shortly afterward the client drove into a service station which displayed a sign that read, "If we fail to clean your windshield, your gasoline is free." The attendant failed to clean the windshield, or if he did try to clean it, John's client was not satisfied and refused to pay for the gasoline. The attendant ran to the front of the car and spread his legs and his arms in order to prevent the client's departure. The client started his engine and proceeded forward, the attendant draped over the hood, and drove out of the station and down the street. The attendant either fell off or jumped off the hood, escaping with only minor injury. I do not remember what the charges were, but John pulled off another miracle and his client got off completely.

A few years later, this malefactor ran for sheriff of Franklin County. Fortunately, he was badly beaten in the primary.

John composed a little ditty which he sang to a tune and rhythm all its own; "It's unbelievable. It's inconceivable. But yet, by God, it's true!" John's clients all seemed to be colorful characters and, of course, he was a bigger character and more colorful than any of them. There was a new John Phillips story every day that either had me laughing or shaking my head. In any event, those days were never dull.

Lyndon Johnson was inaugurated as President of the United States in his own right, after posing as the candidate of peace. Shortly after the inauguration, the Vietnam War escalated substantially, and with it came the disaffection of many of our young people. There were peace demonstrations, draft dodgers who went to Canada, and downright defiance of authority. The blacks, who had benefited from Johnson's "Great Society" programs and advocacy of civil rights legislation, rioted in the ghettos and burned-out huge portions of several large cities. Johnson could have run for a second full term as President in 1968, and he certainly would have been nominated had he stayed in the race, but he announced that he would not be a candidate after his defeat in the New Hampshire primary.

In the 1968 campaign, Hubert Humphrey, Johnson's vice-president, was defeated by Richard Nixon. Nixon inherited the Vietnam problem, but did little to resolve it; actually, in some ways he deepened the war further. There were further demonstrations, riots on the campuses of many colleges, rioting even in Washington, D.C. Nixon was completely frustrated by the lawlessness, the apparent lack of patriotism of too many of our young people, and the fact that he knew, as did many others that, unless we set out on a deliberate policy of laying waste to the entire country of Vietnam, we were in a no-win situation.

One Thursday afternoon early in September of 1965, I had played golf at London Country Club, as was my custom. My son, Tom, was with me that day. After golf, Tom and I drove home in the Chrysler Imperial. As I neared the corporate limits of Grove City, I took my foot off the accelerator, the car coasted down to the speed limit. The road was narrow. Almost immediately upon our entrance into the town, I noticed two young girls starting to walk across the road. They were looking in my direction, and I assumed that they saw the car. One girl stopped completely, but the other kept on. When I realized that she was going to walk directly into the automobile, I slammed on the brakes and turned the steering wheel sharply to the right in an effort to avoid her. The car went into a skid as she walked into the left front, and I struck her. I do not know why the little girl failed to stop. Because the automobile was white and she was looking into a setting sun, perhaps she did not, or could not, see us. I blew the horn when I realized that she was in my path, just as I hit the brakes. It was all too late. She died instantly.

I was in shock. I opened the car door and just sat with my feet and legs outside the car. I talked with the Chief of Police and answered his questions. Finally, a friend of mine drove me home in the car. Evelyn greeted me sympathetically, as did some of our friends. I tried to eat and could not. I did not want to see anyone or talk to anyone. I went to bed to avoid any contact. Jim Henry came over, walked into the bedroom, and asked me what the hell I was doing in bed. I asked him to go get some sort of shot to knock me out. He said, "I'm not going to give you a shot of anything, you son-of-a-bitch; get out of that bed right now and face it. Furthermore, no matter how hard it is for you, go to your office tomorrow and face reality." It was hard to do. I refused to drive Eveyln's car to work, and could not even look at my own car.

It was fortunate for the sake of my sanity that the little girl's parents and grandparents did not blame me. Apparently, no one did, including the police, but I blamed myself. I finally started driving again because I had to, but I was extremely nervous behind the wheel for a long time. I got rid of the Imperial as soon as I could; I hated to drive it at all. Gradually, I recovered from the trauma. However, I can never forget the incident. It bothers me to this day and always will.

Socially, during all of those years, we continued to attend parties, have dinner out, usually with friends, went to the dances and other social events at London Country Club, entertained at our home, and all of the rest of the futile things that everyone we knew did. When I write about all of this now, it sounds rather dull, but we did not think so at the time. We thought we were having fun. I joined what was called the "Y.B.M.C." or Young Business Men's Club, which was composed of business and professional people. It was supposed to be an honor to belong, and I guess it was because, periodically, people were not accepted who had applied for membership. The club's only purpose was to put on an all-male song-and-dance extravaganza once a year, at a suitable time in early March. In addition, there were about three other dinner dances a year, all of which were formal. Many of the members, many of whom were no longer young, used these parties as an excuse to get drunk in formal attire.

I also joined the University Club of Columbus which was, and is, a very good downtown club. I joined it ostensibly for business purposes, because everyone seemed to use one of the downtown clubs as a tax write-off. As it turned out, I really used the club a lot for business lunches, and several times worked out some lucrative deals there over drinks and lunch.

The main dining room was somewhat formal with a view overlooking the State House. There was a very gracious hostess who knew all of the members and their wives by name and seated each group as rapidly as possible. There were white tablecloths and napkins, nice silver and chinaware, attentive waitresses, and excellent food. Clients were impressed. My wife loved it. Women were not permitted in the dining room before one o'clock. I suppose some women felt that there was discrimination, but I never heard about any protests. There were no black members in those years, and so far, as I know, no black applicants for membership. Today, the club has both women and black members.

A place I frequented was the informal downstairs barroom. The bar itself was a "stand up" affair, no stools. There were tables and chairs, with the same lunch menu as one had in the main dining room. Needless to say, there were no white tablecloths, and the entire atmosphere was very friendly. The bartender, Ray, had been there for years—long enough to have become an institution. There were some members of the club whom Ray would not permit to so much as set foot inside the entrance. There had been protests to the board of directors without avail. Ray ruled with an iron hand. One waitress took care of all of the tables with efficiency and great good humor. She adopted most of us. In my case, she frequently limited me to two drinks, no sweet rolls, and no dessert. When I asked either her or Ray for another drink, I was always to say, "I will have a drink." I asked about that finally and was told that if I were arrested for drunken driving after having been in the bar, the testimony could truthfully be that they knew that I had *a* drink.

Suddenly, our children grew up. Marcia got married in early 1967, while still in college, and produced a daughter in August. It all worked out eventually. Despite everything, Marcia did graduate from Denison University in 1968, which took a lot of courage on her part. We have always loved our granddaughter, Courtney Jo.

Our boys graduated from high school in 1968. Although they were twins, they were unalike. They had different interests, different friends, and never seemed to agree on anything. Both boys did well in high school. They were not as good students as was their sister, but few were. Tom played on the high school basketball team, which in that time was an achievement, because Grove City had consistently fine teams. Dick was in all sorts of activities and became senior class president.

Dick went to Muskingum College for a year, but that school was too religious and too small for him. He said that the most exciting thing he did was to join the village fire department. He transferred to Bowling Green State University his sophomore year, and from then on had all the action he wanted. Tom went to Miami University at

Oxford, Ohio, and adjusted too well. Both boys benefited from going away to college, and from being separated from one another.

When the boys left for school, Evelyn and I were completely alone for the first time since Marcia was born in 1946. True, they all came home on occasional weekends and during summer vacation. Marcia was nearby, and we saw her and her husband and our granddaughter often but were basically without family. That fall we took the first vacation the two of us had without children since World War II. We drove to New Orleans and visited various other points of interest. Actually, we had a marvelous time, and pretty well became convinced that life without the responsibility of children was really a lot of fun. We took a Florida vacation that winter, went to Torch Lake to visit our friends, the Smiths, in the summer of 1969, and to San Francisco and Las Vegas that fall. We had made our adjustment.

October 1971 — September 1981

On the evening of the last day of September of 1971, I moved from the Buckeye Building into our new office building in Grove City. Leaving John and the familiarity of the Buckeye Building after almost thirteen years was not easy. Almost all of my memories of that period are still very happy ones. It was hard to believe then, and is even now, that thirteen years had gone by from the time when John and Walt and Ed and I had gotten together in the suite.

In any event, I was more or less ready to go to work the next morning in Grove City. In all honesty, I probably should have stayed in the Buckeye building another month for the reason that, although the building itself was complete, it was not really ready to properly function as a viable office. The carpet had not been installed and the cement floors were noisy and dusty. As yet, there were no draperies, which were necessary to cover the floor-to-ceiling windows screening the offices from the view of passersby. My office faced Columbus Street, the second busiest street in town, with a traffic light at our corner location. Automobiles would stop for the light, the drivers peering into my office and frequently blew their horns. I waved to them and cursed the lack of privacy. It seemed very much as though I was practicing law in the front yard. I doubt that my clients enjoyed being the subject of such interest. The practice of law and the confidentiality attendant with it, never was intended to be available to the curiosity of passing spectators. Gunderman and I had ordered new desks for our offices, and for our secretaries, new matching stainless steel files, lobby furniture and chairs, an impressive table for our combination conference room and library. All in all, it was complete chaos for a while, and not an orderly transition.

Gradually, everything fell into place. The carpet was installed, the draperies arrived, all files placed in the proper filing cabinets, the library books in place, wallcovering hung. Finally, we felt that we were really in good operating condition and ready at least to hold an open house for our clients, potential clients, friends, and the curious.

We sent invitations to all of our clients and friends, various dignitaries, and a few people we wished would become clients. The weather that day was lovely, for which we were grateful. It might not have been on the second Sunday in December in Ohio. The offices were beautiful. Our wives and secretaries served as hostesses, and my children helped with punch and cookies and other goodies. We hoped for a good turnout, but the crowd was even better than we had hoped for. The parking lot was overflowing all afternoon, and we were told that automobiles were parked two or three blocks away. It was wonderful, and all of us were very proud. When the afternoon was over, I went home, had a drink, and went to bed. I was too exhausted to eat.

Many things occurred in connection with the move to Grove City. Gunderman and I decided that we needed a young lawyer in the office, partly to occupy our third lawyer's office, and partly because there were many things that came to us that we no longer wished to handle. I no longer wanted the drudgery of searching real estate titles in the courthouse, and I had no intention of taking divorce cases again.

We felt that between us we could keep a beginning lawyer reasonably busy, and that the influx of people to the new building would help. We brought in Donald Drake. Don had not taken the Ohio State Bar Examination, so he clerked for us until he took the exam and passed it. Don was older than the average law school graduate, as both Gundy and I had been. He had graduated from college as an engineer, and spent several years in California before returning to Ohio State to attend law school. His wife worked as a secretary in order to put him through school, and was willing to continue to work while he got started. They had a child and were buying a home. We were pleased to get him to agree to come with us.

We had office space for rent and were anxious to get it rented to someone with a compatible business such as real estate, insurance, or accounting, because we felt that the offices would help each other. The space was designed so that it could accommodate two different tenants. Mel Girbert, a real estate broker and former builder, took one of the spaces in early 1972. We were pleased not only to get the space rented, but because Mel was really well-known and well-thought-of in the community. Late in 1972, we rented the other space to Mike Morely, a young insurance man, who opened a general insurance agency. We had our ideal mix of law, real estate, and insurance. It all prospered.

Even though I had lived in Grove City for years and knew the community and the people well, I had problems adjusting to a different working environment. I no longer had the daily drive to and from Columbus, which in a way was an improvement, but it was different. I did not walk to work very often, as I should have; the walk only took about five minutes. I drove, for the reason that I frequently did need a car in connection with work, and I did not want to go home for lunch any more than Evelyn wanted me to. I closed the little office at home, and we converted it into sort of den. This meant that for the first time since I commenced law school twenty-five years earlier, I had nothing except an occasional meeting to occupy me at least two nights a week. This was a mixed blessing, for the reason that I saw all of the clients in the new office during ordinary working hours. This meant that I had to change my working routine in many ways in order to get the day-to-day work accomplished. I worked most Saturday mornings, sometimes on Sunday and sometimes at night in order to keep up with the workload. I also sifted out a lot of minor problems and referred them to Don, which helped us both.

The office was much more informal than it was when I was downtown. Clients came in without appointments and expected to see me at once. If I did not have a client in the office, I saw them. Some came in wearing work clothes which were not always too clean. Sometimes they smelled of sweat from their labors, but some of the worst offenders were damned well-off financially. So, I didn't worry much about either what they looked like or smelled like.

Lunch was different too. The choice of restaurants in Grove City was limited. In the old downtown area, there were two or three places where the food was average, but much of it was counter service, and the idea was to eat quickly, pay the check, and get out. I was not geared to that routine. Lunch for me had been a leisurely affair where I socialized with my friends, picked up the news as to what was happening or was going to happen. Often, I had a drink at lunch. Grove City was not set up for that. A bar was a bar, and a restaurant was a restaurant. It was sad, but the best place to eat in the community was the local Holiday Inn. I did manage to have business in Columbus frequently, and when I was there, I almost always had lunch with some of my old friends. That did much for my morale.

The law practice itself did not change. I still did much in handling real estate deals, although I had Don Drake do the title searches. I was involved in some business deals which seemed to be complicated, and which offered enough of a challenge that my interest was aroused. Many of these did involve real property. I found that my probate practice increased substantially.

Perhaps some of this could be attributed to my move to Grove City, but most of it came about because my clients were getting older and were dying. I wrote more wills and got into estate planning to a greater extent because it was more convenient for people in the area to come to me than it had been. I also was getting involved in handling personal injury cases. I had never had very many of these, and hence did not feel that I could do a truly good job for the client without help. I used Bob Herron for all personal injury work that came to me.

Bob was, and is, a consummate personal injury trial lawyer, but a cantankerous, miserable, mean son-of-a-bitch. He is a good friend of mine, completely honest, a great drinking companion, but a bastard, nevertheless. It may be that he became bitter as a result of too much exposure to the tensions of trial work. Another lawyer friend of mine made the observation that all trial lawyers are nuts. He may have been at least partially right. John is, shall I say, eccentric, and Milt Farber was different too, although neither of them were mean. They both saw humor in almost every set of facts. Bob did not. Perhaps it was the hand that life dealt him.

Bob and his wife adopted two children, built a home in the country, and moved in. Possibly because of loneliness, his wife became alcoholic and finally died as a result, leaving Bob with the two young children to raise. It was not easy either for Bob or for the children. They had an artificial Christmas tree which the daughter always wanted to put up right after Thanksgiving. Bob, of course, explained to her that it was much too soon. One year she kept pleading and arguing. Bob became completely beside himself, got the tree out, carried it outside, started a fire and burned the tree. Of course, he later felt horrified and ashamed at what he had done, and bought a new, much larger tree the next morning.

We were in a judge's chamber prior to commencing a trial, and in response to a question, the judge stated that he would make a certain ruling. Bob became incensed, shouting that any judge who could possibly make such a ruling was a dumb bastard and did not deserve to remain on the bench. I insisted that Bob take himself to the men's restroom, and I soothed the waters until time to go into the courtroom.

Any lawyer who has ever been involved in a jury trial knows that it is not possible to predict what verdict will be returned by a jury. Bob and I tried an appropriation case wherein the City of Columbus took my clients' property for the construction of a superhighway. The building was old, but it was a landmark in the south end of Columbus because it had housed a tavern operated by my client and his wife, and by his father and grandfather before him. The city had offered him a ridiculously low figure; naturally, he refused to accept. The city deposited money with the court and took the property. I negotiated but could not get them to agree to pay more than fifty thousand dollars, which my client thought was an insult. So did I, because the appraiser we had hired thought that we should get up to twice that amount if we appealed and tried the case to a jury. The appraiser was excellent, and always did well in front of a jury. Unfortunately, the appraiser became seriously ill a few months before the trial, and it became necessary to hire another appraiser suggested by the first.

The trial date finally arrived, and the jury selected. The city's experts, naturally, testified that the property was worth an extremely low amount. Our appraiser insisted that the property was worth one hundred and twenty-five thousand dollars. Appraising real estate is not an exact science. My client and his wife said that if they were selling the property, they would not take less than one hundred fifty thousand. Both were effective witnesses.

After all of the testimony had been given, the attorney for the city asked for recess, which was granted. He came over to us and said that the City of Columbus would pay our client eighty-seven thousand five hundred dollars if we would dismiss the case. We told him that we would talk to our client, recommended that he take the settlement offer, and give them an answer the next morning. We tried very hard to get the client and his wife to agree to take the offer, telling them that they might receive much less from the jury. They both said that such a sum was an affront. We told them to sleep on it and give us their final word the next morning. We even suggested that we might get a little more out of the city, perhaps one hundred thousand. The next morning, our clients stated that they would not willingly settle for anything less than one hundred fifty thousand dollars.

We told the other attorney, who of course refused. We told the judge to bring back the jury. Closing arguments were made. The judge instructed the jury, and they departed for the jury room for their deliberations. While they were out, the attorneys, the judge, and his bailiff all put down on a slip of paper the figure they expected the jury to determine. The lowest figure was that of one of the city attorneys. He guessed seventy-five thousand. The highest was the judge who guessed one hundred twenty-five thousand. When the jury came in the foreman announced that the verdict was for sixty-two thousand dollars. Our client and his wife were, of course, heartbroken, and Herron and I were truly sorry for them. Everyone was surprised.

No one can predict how a client will react either. We had a personal injury case which we had evaluated at about twenty-five thousand dollars. Our client thought that it would be great if we could get that much. About a week prior to trial, the insurance company offered to settle for forty thousand dollars which, of course, we gleefully accepted. We got the client into my office and relayed the good news to him. He did not want to take the offer, because it was too much money, and he was truly worried about the insurance company. We finally got him to agree, reluctantly. If he hadn't, I think either Bob or I might have choked him to death.

Sometimes clients say something very unexpected. We had a case involving a woman who I had represented for years. She was a hardworking salty old gal much like her husband when he was alive. She had her Volkswagen Beetle stopped at a traffic light and was clobbered from the rear. She had a truly terrible whiplash injury and was really hurt. I knew her well enough to realize that she was not just putting on an act. The driver of the other car carried a minimum amount of liability insurance which, then, amounted to twenty thousand dollars. The client had heavy medical expenses, was not able to return to work for a long time, and still had pain constantly. We demanded that she be paid the full amount of the insurance policy. Because there have always been so many doubtful claims for injury resulting from whiplash, the insurance company almost laughed. We got ready for trial, and the attorneys for the insurance company took my client's deposition. They asked the usual questions. She told them about her pain and that she returned to work only because she had no money. In answer to a question, she said that she had been involved in a previous automobile accident which was entirely her fault. They asked if she ever had any other claims for accidents. She said that she had filed a claim for workman's compensation just recently. I did not know anything about this. She was asked what her injury was. She turned red and asked us whether she had to answer. We told her yes. She then said, in an embarrassed voice, 'I burnt my tit." The least anyone in the room did was grin ear to ear. She then said that she was carrying a cup of hot soup to a table during her lunch break, when the paper cup collapsed, burning her. When things quieted down, they did pay the policy limits. She would have killed them on a witness stand.

The most pitiful couple I ever knew were both injured in an automobile accident. I had known them for a long period of time, going back to my days of working for the State Welfare Department. Even then, he was a born loser, with a very minor job working in the print shop. When the Democrats came into power, he was fired. I was never sure whether it was politics or incompetence that brought this about. He called me and, after he whined for a while, asked whether I could get him a job. Eventually I was able to help him. I heard later that he had developed heart trouble and was not able to work at all. I heard nothing more about him for several years until he called me at home one evening. He asked whether his gas could be turned off just because he didn't pay his bill. I knew that life had not gotten any better for him. Several more years went by, and then he called and asked me to come to his residence to talk with both of them. He told me of their auto accident and said that they had no transportation although he was no longer able to drive.

I went to see them. They lived in a small house which they rented and had only the barest of furniture. His wife had heart trouble also. The accident did neither of them any favors. Both had been in the hospital as a result of the accident, but they had both been in and out of the hospital for a number of years anyways. I never knew how they lived. I do not know how they got food, or how they got medical attention. I think their son helped them as much as he could. I am certain that they both received assistance from welfare.

In any event, Bob and I both felt that they had good personal injury cases, and that we could get them enough money that life would become easier for them. The insurance company did not feel as we did about the value of their cases, because of the pre-existing disability. We prepared to go to trial, and our clients seemed eager to go to court, because they felt that the money awarded to them would be their salvation.

The trial date finally arrived. The lawyers met with the judge in his chambers, and settlement of the cases was discussed. After much wailing, the attorneys for the defendant who, of course, really represented his insurance company, offered ten thousand dollars as the settlement figure for both cases. We did not want to settle for this, but we were obligated to inform our clients of the offer. We advised that they not accept the offer. Even though it seemed to them to be a huge sum of money, they both agreed to refuse the offer.

We went into the courtroom. A jury was selected, and opening statements were made by both sides. Our first witness was my friend, the former employee in the print shop. He did a magnificent job of testifying. We knew that he had the sympathy of the jury and of everyone in the courtroom, except the hard-hearted lawyers for the defense. The court was recessed for lunch. The attorneys for the defendant asked that we allow their expert medical witness to testify out of order, promptly at the reconvening of court for the afternoon session. Bob did not want to agree, but I nudged him and said that we would permit it. I knew the doctor very well and was damned sure he would not show up after lunch or at any other time unless he was dragged into court kicking and screaming. It looked good to us, and we enjoyed our lunch. When we returned, the doctor was nowhere to be found, but my clients were. The wife was so frightened that she had become ill and was afraid that she would have another heart attack. She could not go on the witness stand. They asked that we settle the case and let them go home. I could have cried in frustration. We got the other lawyers to agree to settle all claims for twelve thousand five hundred dollars. Bob and I had thought that if the wife testified as effectively as the husband had done, the jury might well have awarded them fifty thousand, particularly with no medical testimony available to the defendant. Damn it, I'm still frustrated. Those poor people were losers to the end.

I really did not get involved in a great deal of trial work during all of the years that I practiced. That was not through choice. For reasons unknown to me, trial work did not come my way. Fortunately, I began handling estates and other probate matters from the beginning. As I got more established, I got more and more estates. They were not all large, but enough were that I was comfortable with them when they were large enough to require the preparation of federal estate tax returns, and to be audited. Most of those came to me after I got to Grove City.

Sometimes the most exciting thing about an estate is the day the attorney fees are paid. Almost always the attorney is very well paid for his services. Occasionally, however, he more than earns the fee.

Carl was a hard-working farmer who just barely made ends meet on his small place. He was of German descent, as was his wife, and as were most of the old farmers in the Grove City area. They were among the group I had represented in the right-of-way battle against Columbus and Southern Ohio Electric years earlier, giving them more money than they had ever seen. Later, they got more cash for an exit ramp that took some of the frontage, and even more when a road was widened. When Carl died, under the terms of his will, his one-half interest in the farm was inherited by his widow. She, of course, was already the owner of the other one-half interest. They had three children, all of whom had become at least somewhat successful; one son had become truly rich, and he was named executor under the terms of the will. I had never represented him, but he came to me because I had been his parents' lawyer. I had, of course, known him for years. He was a helluva character.

Because of the location of the farm, adjacent to an exit ramp from the outer belt, and on a very busy four lane highway, I knew that the land was very valuable. I also knew that I wanted the most accurate appraisal of the land, because of the tax consequences. I talked with the probate judge who appointed one of the most successful real estate operators in the Columbus and Franklin County area. The appraiser did a very painstaking job and really analyzed the property. He finally gave me an appraisal of five hundred thousand dollars for the entire tract. I do not remember how many acres were included, but there were less than one hundred acres, and considerably less than that of usable ground.

Not too long after the appraisal was made, the executor and I were having a three-martini lunch in the bar at the University Club. He asked me what I thought the attorney fees would amount to, and I told him that it was hard to tell at that point. I said that I knew it sounded stupid, but that they could range anywhere between fourteen thousand and seventy-five thousand dollars, depending on what had to be done, since I knew that the farm would have to be sold. He said that he had been thinking about the fee, and that he felt that fifty thousand would be fair to everyone, but that I had to prepare a trust for his mother since she could not even comprehend the kind of money she would have. We agreed on that amount, and I earned every cent of it.

Both the executor and I had contacts, and between us we got the word around that the property was for sale. We thought that we could sell it without employing a real estate broker. We had several "lookers," and a few "nibblers," but no real action for several months. Finally, a very large developer offered eight hundred thousand dollars for the property. However, they required a six-months option for engineering studies, and zoning. We huddled, and finally told them that we would agree, provided that they paid eighty thousand dollars for the option, which would be applied to the purchase price at closing, but would be kept by us if the option failed for any reason other than a failure to be able to obtain proper zoning. Believe me, the agreement was not a simple one. Their attorneys and I prepared drafts back and forth, and finally agreed. When the final agreement was signed, we received the option money which, of course, we put out at interest. The zoning was approved as I was certain it would be. The engineering study had been completed, and it seemed that we would close the sale on schedule. However, the developer was purchased by a major steel company anxious to diversify, and we were notified unofficially by the president of the company we had been doing business with that the steel company did not like our deal. He told me that he thought they were wrong and added that he would deliver his formal letter to me personally and would bring with him all of the engineering data which he wanted to give to us. He said that this had cost about seventy-five thousand dollars. He followed his verbal promise, and handed me a huge amount of engineering data, drawings, etc. We now had an even more valuable tract to sell, plus our eighty thousand dollars.

The executor received a telephone call from a real estate broker-turned-developer. I had known him for several years and thought that he was always on the ragged edge of going clear broke. I never knew where he ever got money enough together to do anything, and he had blown two or three deals that I knew about. He wanted to meet the executor and discuss purchasing our tract. I told the executor what I knew, and warned him not to agree to any option, and not to agree to the estate accepting anything except cash at closing. I said that I thought it was a waste of time, but I told him to meet the guy and listen to the proposition, but to sign nothing unless I saw the proposal first. We agreed that a million dollars cash at closing would be our goal.

The meeting took place and, while it was in progress, the executor called me and said that they (more than one man was involved) had started out offering to pay a million dollars for the ground. I asked whether they knew about the engineering and zoning, and he said that he did not think they did. I told him to go back into the meeting and tell them about it and say that we would accept a million one hundred thousand dollars. They agreed. A contract was prepared and signed by everyone within twenty-four hours. Within a month, the closing took place at which we received two cashier's checks totaling, as my executor said, "a mill and one."

We could not close the estate and distribute the money. For many tax reasons, it was necessary that an amended federal estate tax return be prepared and filed reflecting the true value of Carl's half-interest in the farm. In the meantime, we had all of the money which needed to be placed at interest. I shopped the banks and placed it for ninety days at eight and one-half percent interest.

When the ninety-day rate was due, I received the bank's check for the full amount plus interest. We still could not close the estate because the Internal Revenue Service had not released the estate from tax liability. I again shopped the banks and was able to place all of the money at eleven percent for six months. This amount of interest seemed unheard of at the time but, fortunately for us, interest rates were up. Finally, we were able to close the estate. The tax returns had been approved, and the estate released from further tax liability. Checks were written to everyone who had anything coming, including myself, and everyone was happy.

On the larger estates I felt that I always earned my attorney fees and usually the heirs agreed. The problems were usually with the Internal Revenue Service. Each large estate paid a considerable amount of federal estate tax, but the I.R.S. audited the returns as a routine matter. Most of the agents were nice, but they were all anxious to make a finding that further tax was due. This was the only way they could justify their existence. It seemed to me that I was constantly engaged in a battle of wits with them. One or two agents were completely unreasonable, and I got so that I was as unreasonable and hard to deal with as they were. I learned my lessons early and, as a result, frequently was able to save the estate money in estate taxes. It was never a matter of cheating. I knew better than that, and I educated my clients accordingly, so that everything in the way of taxable property was reported as it should have been.

Occasionally, I was surprised to learn that the auditor had found something that I knew nothing about, but in each instance the news was welcomed, because additional property of value went into the estate. Needless to say, my clients were surprised and happy to find it. The place where I differed with an auditor occasionally was over the appraised value of real estate, some tangible personal property, small businesses, and small closely-held family corporations. I learned early that it was always desirable to use the most competent appraisers that I could find, and then to stand fast despite the agent's claims, and rely on the reputation of the appraiser I had selected.

Not every estate was grim, routine, and boring. Some were really fun, sometimes because of the challenges and sometime because of some of the people involved. A husband had died leaving everything he owned to his widow. The estate was surprisingly large. In addition to a thriving business and some real estate, there were two safety deposit boxes filled with securities, savings and checking accounts in diverse banks and savings-and-loans, as well as certificates of deposit. His widow and executrix were not very interested in letting me know the extent of the property, partly because she wanted to hide it, partly from forgetfulness, and partly out of perversity. The estate was started, the inventory and appraisement filed, and then she came in with a shopping bag full of items of intangible personal property that I had no record of. I asked where these were found and she replied, "Oh, they were in the oven." It turned out that the lady had never cooked one meal in twenty-five years, and the oven of her kitchen stove was a storage area for valuable papers. I finally finished the estate, but I had a feeling that, somehow, there were assets which did not surface. Two or three years later she died, and her son was designated as the executor of her estate. I felt sorry for him. She specifically stated in her will that he was not to be paid anything for his service. Never did an executor deserve to be well-paid more than he. We made as complete a search as we could of her home in an effort to make sure that we found everything. We filed tax returns and paid taxes, we went through an audit, closed her estate, and made distribution. He then called and told me that he had discovered another twenty-thousand-dollar certificate of deposit at the local savings-and-loan, in both the husband's and wife's names. We reopened both estates, paid additional taxes, distributed the remainder of the money, and closed the estates. Two or three months later, we repeated the process for a lesser amount. About a year later, he came in and handed me a savings account book in a small savings-and-loan in downtown Columbus, discovered quite by accident, in the amount of ten thousand dollars plus interest. We did not open any estates. I will not divulge how we got the money out of the savings-and-loan, but I will say that it was done. A crime was committed, but had she been around, one or both of us would have throttled her.

I received a telephone call one afternoon from a man who identified himself as Dr. VanDeWater. His wife had died, and he had given a lawyer in Columbus five hundred dollars to start her estate, but the attorney had done nothing for three months except pocket the money. He said that he had seen the probate judge, and that the judge had called the lawyer and had the money brought to the court. The judge gave the money back to the doctor and had advised him to see me, since the doctor lived only a short distance outside Grove City.

Now I had heard about this doctor, unfavorably, over a number of years. He was a well-known physician with a large practice in the south end of Columbus at one time. His father before him was a doctor at the same location. He and his wife—I am not certain which number she was—were getting a divorce. At one stage of the divorce proceedings, he was served with a court order by a deputy sheriff while at his office desk. As the deputy approached the desk, Vandy opened a drawer, pulled out a revolver and attempted to shoot the deputy. The deputy disarmed him, handcuffed him, and took him to the county jail, where he remained for some time. This made headlines in the Columbus newspapers. Later on, he rented a farmhouse and some acreage from a client of mine. He and another wife owned riding horses and wanted a place in the country to keep them. My client went to the farm one Saturday and was greeted at the gate by the doctor with a double-barreled shotgun pointed at the car windshield. I had to evict the doctor, his wife, and the horses from the property. All in all, I had the feeling that this guy was nuts and potentially dangerous. I told the doctor that I would call him back, that I was not sure I had the time to properly represent him. I then called the judge, who was a friend of mine, and tried to get out of handling any of it but was told that I had to take the matter off the court's hands, and to keep the doctor and his stepchildren away from the court.

I met the doctor and three very greedy stepchildren. The doctor was vague and the stepchildren demanding. What had happened was that he had married this woman a couple of years previously and had been generous with her. He had bought her some good jewelry, put bank accounts in joint names, and had purchased and furnished a comfortable, newish home in a nice area on the outskirts of Grove City. He had the property placed in both names. She brought nothing to the marriage of a material nature except herself and her three children. He owned two or three other pieces of real estate and had deeded her a half-interest in them as well. He never had much luck with women. This one died without a will, owning half of his property. Under our laws, her children inherited two-thirds of her newly-acquired wealth, and the doctor one-third.

The entire matter was more trouble than it was worth. The doctor accused the stepchildren of stealing from him, which they probably were. They accused him of trying to keep them from getting their fair share of their dear departed mother's "hard-earned" estate. I think that he would have done exactly that had he known how to get away with it.

I developed a fondness for Vandy. He was on both drugs and alcohol and was in outer space much of the time. He turned in his license to practice medicine and, when the residence was sold, moved into an apartment on the far east side of Columbus. He wanted to get the estate closed in order that he might move to the northern part of Ohio and live with his mother. All property was sold, and the net proceeds deposited in an estate checking account. I kept the checkbook and all records in my office, except for the building which had housed the doctor's office and an apartment. We could not sell that, try as hard as we could. The doctor needed money; her sons were screaming for money. I ran them out of the office. I finally got authority from the court to make a partial distribution of the assets to relieve the immediate pressure but did not get rid of the problem entirely. The building was a real "white elephant."

I would have much preferred not to have ever heard of that estate, but Vandy was unusual enough that sometimes it seemed to be almost worthwhile. After he had moved, he called one day to ask a question which I could not answer without referring to the file. I said, "Doctor, I'll have to look that up and call you back. What's your phone number?" He hesitated and then said, "Oh, I really don't know. You see, I never call myself." He called my home one weekend and told my wife that he had a solution for disposing of the real estate which had not been sold. She, of course, told him to call the office. He called on Monday and, when I asked how we could dispose of the property, he said, "Let's torch the place. There's plenty of insurance. Do you know a good torch man?" Then there was the time that he told me of not being able to sleep one night shortly after his move into the apartment. He turned on the television and sat watching the Notre Dame-Navy game. He suddenly realized that it was summer and not fall, and that it was also the middle of the night. He said that he was terrified, because he thought that all of the people who said that he was crazy were right. Then he realized that he had cable in his new apartment and decided not to call the wagon. Perhaps he should have.

Ultimately, the real estate was sold. The doctor and the greedy stepchildren all came to the closing with their hands outstretched to receive their checks. I said goodbye to the doctor that day and he left for the northern part of the state to live with his mother. I later read that he had shot and killed himself there.

Son Tom went to law school in 1972 and became an attorney in 1974. His last year in law school he worked in my office as a law clerk. He wanted to practice law with me, and I wanted him to do so. We converted a large storage area into an additional office, and he commenced practice at the end of 1975. We entered into a partnership the first of the year in 1976. Although I had reservations about a business relationship with a member of the family because I did not want any ill-will created, it all worked out. I was always pleased, and I think that Tom was also. I was able to switch many things to Tom, and my clients accepted it, which they would not do when I attempted to refer them to Don Drake. Tom attracted business of his own, and did very well for a young, eager lawyer. A year or two later, Don left us, at least partially, because he realized that Gunderman was nowhere near retirement and that Tom was obviously going to take over for me eventually. We had an extra office and needed a lawyer. Jack Briggs and Gunderman had gone to law school together and were friendly, and I knew Jack was a good lawyer. His only problem was himself. He was, and is, an alcoholic. He talked to Gene and asked to come into the office. We discovered that he had not been drinking for about two years and decided to take a chance with him. He has not always kept this record going. We threatened to throw him out periodically. Somehow, he remains.

My eyesight steadily deteriorated. I gradually quit driving except for negotiating the two blocks between home and the office, which I did only in order to have an automobile available. Marianne, my secretary, and Tom when he came into the office, drove me where I needed to go and did routine errands for me. I hated it, but I was virtually office-bound and could no longer take off on my own to visit with my cronies in Columbus, and to lunch at the University Club.

In 1971, I began to experience severe pain in my right eye that at times became so severe as to be almost unbearable. I had never had vision in that eye, but my ophthalmologist could not determine the source of the pain. He finally told me to get into his office while the pain was occurring. I made it one day, thanks to Evelyn, and he discovered that a cataract which had always been present had somehow broken loose and periodically was causing pressure. I went to the hospital directly from the doctor's office. He followed and was able to reduce the pressure through the use of medication. He told me later that had the pressure not yielded to medication, he would have been forced to remove the eye. In any event, he did remove the cataract. The pain disappeared, and I do not believe it caused any problem to the other eye.

A cataract formed on my so-called "good eye," gradually becoming worse, and worse, and worse. I could see as well as I ever had to read and to watch television but, other than that, it seemed that I was looking through a window which became dirtier and dirtier. Every time that I saw the ophthalmologist, I raised hell. I wanted him to remove the cataract. He was as determined not to operate. His reason was that if the operation went wrong for any reason, I could be completely blind.

September 28, 1978, I watched the Monday night football game on T.V. and then went to bed. In the middle of the night, I awoke with a horrible pain in my left eye. I arose, took some aspirin, and found an ice bag which I put on the eye to relieve the pain. I noticed that the lights appeared dim, but I did not have sense enough to realize that I was losing my vision. I went to bed and to sleep. Later I awakened again for my nightly trip to the bathroom. I flipped the bathroom switch, but there was no light. I called Evelyn. I asked her whether or not the bathroom light was on, and she told me that it was. I knew then that I was completely blind. Neither of us knew what to do. We decided to wait until about seven o'clock that morning and then to call Jim. I even went back to sleep for a time. I do not know whether Evelyn slept or not.

Jim told us to go to the emergency room at Mount Carmel Hospital immediately. We dressed. Evelyn had to lead me to the garage and help me into the car. I saw nothing. No movement, no light, no shadows appeared. I felt no emotion. I was numb and more or less in shock. I do know that when one is completely blind, everything is black.

We made it to the hospital and, after answering the usual questions concerning our ability to pay, I made it into the emergency room with Evelyn's help, I disrobed, and was given the usual hospital gown. Then I was placed on the hardest table ever made. I am certain that cement would have been softer. I explained to a doctor the nature of my problem, but this did not prevent the routine chest X-ray, E.K.G. and blood profile. I was finally advised that Dr. Moses, my ophthalmologist, was on his way. I tried to be comfortable on the table, but that was not possible. Dr. Moses and his son, who was just commencing the practice of ophthalmology, arrived. They both labored steadily to bring down the pressure on my eye by the use of drops. Finally, the pain eased, and I gradually got so that I could see a little. Dr. Moses got me admitted to the hospital.

I remained there from Tuesday morning until Sunday. I do not yet know the reason for my lengthy stay. I do know that, despite my protests, I had another chest X-ray, E.K.G. and blood profile. Even then, hospital costs were unnecessarily high because of such foolishness. The doctors saw me each day, and used further drops to reduce the pressure as much as possible. Young Moses explained that I had an acute glaucoma attack caused by the large, fat cataract. I still wonder whether or not my problem would have been as serious as it is had Doctor Moses, Sr. operated when I virtually begged him to do so. I understand why he was reluctant to operate. He was afraid that I would not get a good result and would be blind as a result of the operation. I thought about all of this while hospitalized. I was not even angry. I seemed to be incapable of any emotion. I could not cry. I didn't swear. I wish that I had been able to break the numbness. I was simply resigned to my fate.

Evelyn was extremely faithful about seeing me and staying with me each afternoon. I did not want her to come to the hospital at night. It was, and is, a dangerous area. She read the newspaper to me, told me all of the news each day, and was cheerful and happy, and kind. I never had appreciated her as much as I did during that time, and since.

The doctors released me on the following Sunday. I had to return to the hospital on the following Thursday to have the cataract removed Friday morning. In the meantime, I was able to return to the office and work. I needed to do this. A very large estate needed much attention, and there were other matters that I needed to dispose of before surgery, and what I knew would be a lengthy period of time away from the office. I could not see enough to read. Marianne was my eyes. Son Tom was my legs. With their help, and out of sheer desperation, and with some will power, I got matters well straightened out in three days and was able to return to the hospital relieved at the situation in the office. At home during that period, Evelyn looked after me, and babied me a little.

Cataract surgery was not as simple in 1978 as it is eight years later. I was under some sort of anesthetic. I knew that they were operating on me, but I could not move. I heard conversation, but it was far away. After surgery, I spent time in the recovery room. My eye was bandaged and, of course, I could see nothing. The only time the bandage was removed until the following Monday evening was for examination by one of the two doctors. This continued until Monday evening when young Moses came in with a pair of cataract glasses. I was able to see with the glasses, but everything was distorted. Doors looked very tall and narrow, people either huge or tall and thin. Gradually, I saw almost normally. About two days later, I was allowed to go home. God, it was great to be at home again, free of that damned hospital. I did not realize how much I disliked being there until after I was discharged and safely at home. I had been in the hospital on two other occasions, but I had not minded it either time.

I had to remain reasonably quiet until sometime in November. I took small walks with Evelyn. We got out occasionally for a ride, but Evelyn had to be exceedingly careful about sudden stops, in order not to jolt the damaged eye. It was a very close time with Evelyn. However, both while I was hospitalized and at home recovering, I did not want to see my friends. I know that I was making a difficult adjustment to a strange world for me, and I really did not enjoy seeing or visiting anyone. Part of the problem was that the cataract glasses I wore were not prescription lenses for my eyes and, even though I gradually got used to them, certain objects were still distorted. For example, the light from automobile headlights and streetlights looked triangular in shape even though I knew that they were round. The shot glass that I always used when mixing my evening martinis appeared to be huge. The result was that I missed the glass, and Evelyn had to make my drinks for me. I could not read but, strangely enough, I could watch television which looked as it always had. Actually, I was able to enjoy the baseball playoffs and the World Series. Those events and the weekend televised football games relieved my boredom and sense of frustration. I had to cheat twice and go to the office — once was for the purpose of beginning an estate for a valued client who would not let Tom commence the work. I went over, met with the client, asked the necessary questions while Tom took notes. He then began the estate anyway. The other was to meet with two important clients who wanted me to listen to a proposal for an agreement to purchase the corporate stock of whichever of the two died first. Such an agreement was to be funded by life insurance. I recommended that this be done, and eventually I prepared the "buy-sell" agreement required. I was glad to have the excuses to go over to the office. It relieved the boredom of just sitting at home doing nothing.

Finally, young Dr. Moses did the refraction and wrote the prescription for my lenses. He told me that, when I got the new glasses, I could go back to work, and that I was then released to live as normal a life as possible. I was thoroughly enchanted to be able to return to the office, and to become useful again. I had never realized previously how important work can be to one's ego. I was even exceptionally nice to clients for quite a length of time after my return.

Things were different from what they had been. I had felt for some time prior to my final eye blow-up that the volume of business which came to me had decreased. Some of this was through choice on my part. I did refer many items of business to Don Drake, and later to son Tom, that I simply no longer wanted to handle. The result was that I lost business and our office lost work that I would have loved to have taken care of. Then, too, it had become essential that Marianne and Tom drive me to wherever I needed to go in performing my duties outside the office. Many noticed this, and felt that my eyesight was failing, which of course, was true. When I had the eye operation, the news spread rapidly throughout the community. After all, Grove City was still a small town, even though it had become a part of suburban Columbus. I lost more business when this occurred. Fortunately, I was really doing well financially because of the estates that kept on coming in without much interruption. I could still see well enough to take care of them, and Marianne and Tom both helped me tremendously. I was at the point where I could not have continued without their assisting me almost every day.

I had other business as well. I was lucky enough to get an occasional personal injury case, and I had acquired a really fantastic real estate client. Tom benefited more from him than did I because of the amount of real estate title searches involved. The client bought farms at bargain-basement prices. He paid little cash for them, and usually persuaded the seller to carry notes and mortgages. He also borrowed heavily from Federal Land Bank and the Production Credit Association. Much of the land which he bought had subdivision potential, and he usually was able to sell some lots quickly enough to keep well ahead of his debt obligations. Some of his purchases were complicated enough that my services were required. It was usually a real challenge to my ability when I worked out some of these deals. He was a lawyer himself, a C.P.A., a real estate broker, and he was fun. I needed him in order to be able to feel that, in spite of my physical problems, I still had some ability.

Unfortunately, my eyesight worsened, and it became more and more difficult for me to function as a lawyer should. I not only could not travel, but I was also having increasing difficulty in reading. Neither Tom nor Marianne complained, but I felt a sense of guilt and felt as though I was imposing on them.

In January of 1981, after much thought and conversation with Evelyn, she and I went to the Social Security office. I do not remember how many times I went there, or how many interviews I had, but I had decided to retire on September 1, 1981.

This decision was the hardest one that I ever made. I was not mentally prepared for retirement. It seemed that this would mean the end of life for me. I did not want to tell anyone that I was retiring, but I was forced to confide in son Tom and Gunderman, both of whom were entitled to receive six-months' notice under the terms of our respective partnership agreements. I had lunch with Tom and, when I told him that I was quitting, I choked up so much that I could not speak for a few moments. After that experience I gave Gundy written notice so that I did not have another emotional problem.

I knew that I had to tell Marianne. However, her husband had just died unexpectedly, and I did not want her to have any further trauma at that time. Because Evelyn and I were leaving for Florida, I decided to wait until my return in order to break the news to her. Tom and I did take Marianne to lunch to celebrate her completion of eleven years of working for me. Anyone who stood me for that length of time deserved lunch at least. Marianne had not returned to work at the time. She was taking care of thank-you notes and the many other matters which had to be handled subsequent to the funeral, but she did come over for her luncheon. When she went to the powder room, Tom insisted that I tell her of my retirement upon our return to the office. He said that he was afraid that she would hear about it from someone else. So, I took her into my office and told her. She cried, and I was emotional again. It was a sad ending to what had been an occasion to celebrate.

After our vacation, I returned to the office and to work. There were numerous clients who had to be told that I would not be able to complete work on their problems. I believe that they were all genuinely sorry that I was quitting. I felt happy, yet sad too. One always is happy to know that he is appreciated. I had never thought much about it before, but I began to realize that I did mean a lot to many people, and that in a small way I had become somewhat of an institution in the community after more than thirty years. I was sad too that it all had to end. It was a bittersweet time really.

I got through it all. I made the arrangements to sell my law books and furniture, and to sell my half of the office building to Tom. Each such endeavor hurt. On August 1, the last of my furniture was removed. I stood in the empty office alone for a few moments and tried to control my emotions. Finally, I walked out and closed the door. It was the end of what had been my life, and the beginning of something unknown, which I feared.

The period was certainly not without significance. Richard Nixon was President in October of 1971. The Vietnam War was still continuing while Nixon sought means to end it. The spirit of détente continued with Russia. Nixon was consummate leader insofar as our foreign policy was concerned. Early in 1972, he went to China and established what has become a more or less friendly relationship with the Chinese. Nixon's re-election seemed to all of us to be a foregone conclusion. In June of 1972, the Watergate break-in occurred — Democratic National Headquarters was burglarized. It seemed to be such a foolish thing to do. I had little doubt that Nixon had approved of it, or at least knew about it in advance. I was surprised as were many others when Nixon and his top aides, including John Mitchell, denied any knowledge of it. I thought then, and I still do today, that it would have made little difference if the Republicans had come forward at once and claimed full responsibility. That sort of political "dirty tricks" had gone on in Washington for years. Besides, I could not understand what was so important in Democratic Headquarters as to warrant a burglary. Nixon defeated Senator George McGovern by the predicted landslide and was sworn in for his second term in January of 1973.

Watergate did not disappear as it certainly would have done had Nixon admitted in the beginning what actually took place. Nixon kept on insisting that he was innocent of any wrongdoing and was not a crook. The more he and his cronies protested their innocence, the tougher the investigation became. It developed that for reasons unknown, Nixon had taped every conversation in which he ever participated while in the Oval Office at the White House. Poor, dumb, Spiro Agnew, our Vice-President, was forced to resign and was subsequently convicted of tax evasion, and other little matters such as having been on the take while governor of Maryland, and in some of his previous offices. Had it not been for Watergate, there probably would have been no action taken against Agnew.

As the entire mess continued to occupy the full attention of the media, more and more charges were made, and it became necessary for more and more denials to be issued. It also became apparent that Nixon could no longer function effectively as President of the United States. Congress was so preoccupied with the impeachment proceedings against Nixon that the entire government was at a virtual standstill. I do not know whether there was ever any possibility of any sort of sneak attack on us by the Russians, but then—if ever—would have been ideal from an enemy standpoint. In any event, General Alexander Haig functioned as White House Chief of Staff and, for a time, virtually ran the country. Nelson A. Rockefeller, who succeeded Agnew as Vice-President, resigned, and Gerald Ford, Speaker of the House of Representatives, was next in line to become President. During Nixon's last few days in office, there were many rumors that he had become mentally unstable. Those rumors might very well have been true, and if they were, it certainly was understandable.

In any event, Nixon resigned as President, and Ford took over.

Ford was exactly what was needed at the time. He was perfectly honest, a friend of Republicans and Democrats alike, and trusted by the entire country. The long, sad ordeal was ended at last. Ford immediately pardoned Nixon for any and all crimes with which he might have been charged. This action was criticized, probably more by the bloodthirsty press than by the politicians. In my judgment, with the perspective of time on my side, it was the wisest move that could have been made. Watergate was finally over, and an era of good feeling could and did prevail. Ford was rather dull and plodding. He was a politician and not a statesman, but the dark clouds that seemed to stay over the White House began to dissipate. If he did nothing other than restore the confidence of the people in our government, his place in history should be assured.

In 1975, a former governor of Georgia, Jimmy Carter, began to make himself known among Democrats. He made speeches throughout the United States, wherever asked. He shook hands, smiled continuously, and was not taken at all seriously by any of the country's leaders within the hierarchy of the Democratic party. They all felt that when the time came, Senator Hubert Humphrey would be the candidate once again, or Ted Kennedy, or Senator Scoop Jackson, or perhaps one of the other heavyweights in the Democratic party. By the time the leaders got around to really thinking about the Democratic presidential candidate, they discovered to their horror that Carter had the nomination virtually sewn up. Carter was truly a political phenomenon. He was not the type who would ever please the average politician. He was a born-again Christian, a real rock-solid Southern Baptist. He did not use alcohol or tobacco in any form. His record as governor of Georgia was mediocre at best, and he had managed to split the old-line Georgia Democrats. He was a real "do-gooder" and a civil rights activist from a small town called "The Plains" just large enough to be called a town. He had graduated from Annapolis and had served in the Navy. In the opinion of many, he was the least-qualified candidate for President since Calvin Coolidge.

Gerald Ford was the Republican candidate as expected. However, there were some problems before, during and after the Republican convention. Ronald Reagan was the darling of the conservative members of the Republican party of which there were many. He wanted the presidency and refused to wait his turn gracefully. Perhaps it was his feeling that the age factor would enter in were he to be a candidate at a later time. In any event, he did not lose the nomination gracefully, and he did nothing to aid Ford during the campaign. Nonetheless, it seemed to me that Ford would defeat Carter in November. Whether Reagan's active support would have turned the tide in Ford's favor, no one knows. The election was close enough that in all probability Reagan's help would have carried the day. In any event, Carter was elected President of the United States.

Ten years later, I still feel that the Carter election did nothing to enhance our country in any manner. A fuel crisis in 1973 while Nixon was still President occurred because the Arabs banded together in a cartel for the purpose of increasing the price of oil, by greatly decreasing its production. Nixon did not solve the problem of a fuel shortage, neither did Ford. The Carter administration announced that it would solve the problem. Our domestic oil companies made matters worse, particularly in the area of the production and distribution of natural gas. Our houses and offices were cold. President Carter, in his wisdom, decreed that a temperature of 68° was very adequate in the daytime, and that 60° was high enough at night. There was much disobedience and some pneumonia as a result, but the problems were not solved. Inflation ran wild, and interest rates rose to historic highs. The economy was truly out of control.

In 1979, the Iranians captured fifty-five Americans in our embassy and in Tehran. Supposedly it was a student uprising and a protest against our assistance in keeping the Shah on the throne in Iran against the will of the people. Carter had withdrawn our support, and the radical, fundamentalist Moslems took control. I do not know how we could have gotten the hostages released unharmed by any act of superior force which we might have exercised. The hostage problem was the major crisis of its time. It caused the oil problem, inflation, and high interest to recede into the back pages of the newspapers, and the end of the nightly newscasts. Almost in desperation, Carter ordered a military attempt to get to the hostages and free them. The plan failed because our military equipment was in horrible condition, our personnel improperly prepared. It was a disgrace.

The 1980 presidential campaign was at hand much quicker than seemed possible sometimes. Carter, of course, being the incumbent President, was nominated with little trouble, although Ted Kennedy was certainly the Democrats' sentimental choice, and did create some bitterness. Many Democrats felt that Carter had little chance to win the election regardless of whomever the Republicans nominated. The Republicans conducted a very spirited, hard-fought primary. Reagan was the front-runner, but George Bush made a good showing. Howard Baker, the Senate minority leader, did poorly as did Bob Dole and John Connally.

By the time the Republican convention was held, it seemed certain that Reagan would be nominated, and so he was. Reagan approached Gerald Ford as his possible vise-presidential running mate. Although it is doubtful that Ford had any intention of running, it made for a fun evening watching and listening to the maneuvering. Finally, Bush was called in and agreed to be the candidate for vice-president. God knows what promises he made, but he has been Reagan's errand boy ever since.

Perhaps because of Reagan's inherently conservative views, perhaps because of some of the lunatic fringe who surrounded and supported him, but more likely because Carter did have an appeal to the so-called common man, the polls showed the election to be close. A debate wherein Carter was clearly the loser may have been the deciding factor, perhaps it was the hostage crisis. Whatever the reasons, Reagan won a surprisingly close victory, and Carter might have won under only slightly different circumstances.

Many significant happenings occurred in our own family.

In addition to the office building, Evelyn and I built two twin singles, side by side, on Gladman Avenue in Grove City. We paid seven thousand five hundred dollars for the land and borrowed one hundred percent of the construction money. I simply used a little leverage by placing a blanket mortgage on the twin single we had built previously and the two we had contracted to build. Subsequently, we sold the earliest of the three twins at a profit and applied the proceeds to the loan. I do not know at this point why we sold the first structure. We did not need the money at the time, and the profit we made on the sale was not great. I know that I did not anticipate the tremendous inflation that took place in real estate as well as everything else, but who did?

Son Richard married Maureen Terry in June of 1972. He had graduated from college in March of that year and had a brand-new job as a drug salesman in Lansing, Michigan. We loved Maureen but thought that they were at the time dumber than hell to get married. They had no money and it scared us, even though Evelyn and I did get married on my overseas furlough. Maureen got a job immediately teaching school in the Lansing area and, between them, they got along fine financially.

They had a very nice wedding and reception. I realize that Maureen's mother gets upset to this very day about an incident which took place during the wedding ceremony. When the two knelt at the altar, the bottoms of Dick's shoes were exposed. The word HELP was spelled out on his soles. One of his college friends, an usher, thought of performing this small act of kindness for his friend. He was ably assisted by the best man, his brother Tom.

In August of that same summer, Tom married Karen Kirby, whom we had come to know during their college days at Miami. We learned to love her in the summer of 1972 when she stayed with us while she worked at her first full-time job with what is now Bank One. We thought that they were stupid too. Tom and Karen had just graduated from Miami in June, and Tom planned to attend law school that fall. We were willing to pay for his tuition and books but had no intention of supporting either him or them. They lived on her salary, and struggled, but they made it somehow.

Dick and Maureen did not stay in Lansing too long. In the summer of 1973, they informed us that they were moving to Florida in the Fort Lauderdale area. Neither of them had jobs. Maureen got a teaching job shortly after they arrived, and Dick became an Orkin man, complete with uniform, and truck, I suppose. Fortunately, Dick got a sales job with a surgical supply company, and the two purchased a house in Pompano. I thought that they were settled, but in another year, Dick, who could not read a note of music or carry a tune, went to work as a salesman for his father-in-law in the piano and organ business. At least they returned to Columbus. In March of 1978, while we were in Florida, they had their first child, Elizabeth Terry Clark. I called her Betsy just to tease her, until one day she cried, and so I have called her Libby ever since. Her brother Kevin was born in February of 1980. Like his father, he has been a con artist from the time he could talk.

Marcia, Mike, and Courtney moved to Winston-Salem, North Carolina, in 1973, and then to Baltimore. As a consequence, we did not see them as often as we would have liked, although we did keep in touch with them by mail and telephone.

After much soul-searching and a great deal of looking on both coasts of Florida, we purchased a condominium on Honeymoon Island at Dunedin, Florida, in January of 1974. At the time, we both thought of it as being a vacation home. It did mean that we spent much vacation time there, but we were not completely inhibited about traveling. After the boys were married, we had no reason for staying at home. As a matter of fact, in addition to two or three visits a year to our condo on Honeymoon Island, we took four very nice trips. In July of 1973, we went to Europe with Carey and Adele Pace who had "stood up" with us when we were married. The four of us have been close friends ever since.

We were not on a tour, but the Paces had been to Europe two or three times, previously, and really did know how to travel. Adele had taken a course that winter in conversational French and did well enough to get us around France. We had a travel agent plan our entire trip and arrange all of our air and hotel accommodations.

It was, to us, a marvelous trip. We were in Paris for a week, including Bastille Day. We rented a car and drove through France's champagne country. We visited Luxembourg, then drove through Alsace Lorraine, and some mountainous country into Switzerland, where we stayed in Lucerne and Zurich. From there we were in Germany briefly and had just a taste of the Black Forest. We crossed back into France at Strasbourg, where we turned in our rented car, and boarded a Dutch ship for a trip down the Rhine to Rotterdam, and then to Amsterdam. We took the train to Brussels and had our first experience with a high-speed European train. From Brussels we drove to Brugge, then back to Brussels and home. We were gone about five weeks.

I would not attempt to write a travelogue of everything that we saw and of all that occurred. It was wonderful insofar as I was concerned to visit all of the historical sites that we crowded in, although I could have done with fewer cathedrals. I loved seeing the castles along the Rhine on our one-day tour which effectively covered the entire duchy of Luxembourg. I enjoyed the sounds, the differences in languages, the excellent wine, the fine beer, and the Dutch gin. I must confess, uncultured slob that I am, I loved the food every place we ate. I supposed that Evelyn would say that I literally ate and drank my way through Europe.

Since we were not on an organized tour, we had more than the ordinary amount of unusual experiences happen to us.

We landed in Paris at Orly Airport and cleared customs. I do not know how it happened, but I became separated from the other three and got lost without having left the terminal. I didn't panic, however, because I knew the name of our hotel, and decided that I could find a taxicab and get there. I went out a door to see whether I could find them, and there they were. Evelyn was in more of a dither than I was over my mysterious disappearance.

We checked into our hotel, changed clothes and Evelyn and I decided to go to a nearby bank and get some French money in exchange for traveler's checks. We returned to the hotel and took naps in order to catch up with the jet lag. When we awakened, Evelyn discovered, to her horror, that she no longer had her passport. We both had visions of all sorts of dire consequences. She finally remembered that she had had to show the passport at the bank. We rushed to the bank, but it had closed for the day. The next morning, we were at the bank bright and early. The clerk remembered her, and smilingly handed back her passport.

Pace told of a small, out-of-the-way restaurant that they had visited on their previous trip to Paris. It was on the Left Bank of the Sienne and was called "Café de Roger." Pace said, and Adele agreed, that the place was simply a neighborhood restaurant, frequented by college professors from the Sorbonne. We got a taxi, but the taxi driver had difficulty finding the location. Finally, we got to the area. The driver pointed to an alley where the café was located, but he refused to drive any further. We paid him and walked into the alley to the restaurant. Fortunately, it was still daylight. On entering, we discovered that there were no individual tables. Everyone sat at long tables with other patrons. I do not think that there was a college professor in the entire area, and there certainly were none in that restaurant. I am certain that all of the patrons were native Parisians except for the four of us. A reasonably well-dressed man came in and sat with us, and in very good English told us of other restaurants in the area that he thought we might enjoy. After he left, the waitress started playing games with the male patrons. She had some way of taking off our neckties without actually untying them. The price for return of the tie was a kiss. Apparently, she had missed one of the virile Frenchmen, because all of a sudden, he was standing on the top of his table, taking off his pants and underwear. Completely exposed, he calmly threw the undershorts toward the waitress. Pandemonium set in. The restaurant was closed immediately, and we were urged to leave through the kitchen. As we filed out, Roger, the owner and chef, and a former member of the French Resistance in World War II, took a look at Evelyn and gave her a little pat on her rear.

As we arrived in the darkened alley, our dinner companion stepped forward with another man who did not look too friendly, and said to us, "This man is hungry, give him all your change." We did so promptly. No further words were exchanged, and we vacated the alley and the area as rapidly as we could. We did not see a taxi anyplace, kept on walking, and walking, and walking and finally reached our hotel.

The next evening, we went from the ridiculous to the sublime. Our concierge made reservations for us at Tour D'Argent, one of the very finest restaurants in the world. We decided that this was one night to splurge. We sat downstairs on small sofas and sipped drinks prior to being escorted upstairs to our table. There was no doubt as to what our main course would be. It had to be duck. Duck was the only entrée featured. However, there are various ways of cooking duck, and I believe that they served all of them. We ordered a good bottle of wine, ate exotic desserts, watched members of the Vietnamese peace delegation live it up, and generally had a wonderful evening. Evelyn even bought a ceramic duck to take home. We then got the bill, which was, of course, astronomical for the year 1973. I handed them my American Express card, and discovered to my horror that they would not accept it. We had left our traveler's checks in the hotel. Pace had paid his bill in cash and loaned us enough to pay ours, barely able to get out of the restaurant.

I also discovered that white shoes were not the proper thing to wear in Europe as a dress shoe. Unfortunately, I had not brought another pair of dress shoes with me. I do not think that we saw any other man in white shoes on the entire trip. In Strasbourg, a couple of idiots pointed at my feet, jabbered at one another, and laughed. I did become a little self-conscious and wanted to hide my feet.

We went to the Moulin Rouge the night before Bastille Day. It was a memorable evening. The floor show was outstanding, and the food was quite good. However, we were not prepared for what faced us when we exited from the night club into the street. The French were in the streets and had already begun their celebration of Bastille Day, shooting skyrockets back and forth across the street, throwing large firecrackers and what we used to call "cherry bombs" at each other. They were cheering, screaming, shooting, and drunk. If we were not caught up in the middle of a riot, I hope never to be near one. Automobile traffic was non-existent and, of course, no taxicabs were to be seen. We ran for two or three blocks in order to get away from the mobs, and finally saw a taxi which, unfortunately, had already picked up a passenger. We waved frantically. The driver stopped and the passenger, a wonderful English lady, let us in. After she was delivered to her destination, we were taken to our hotel. We had detoured around other mob scenes on the way and were truly thankful to get to our rooms. When we left Paris, we picked up our rental car. We were well-provided with all sorts of maps and were directed to what we would call a freeway to take us out of Paris and to St. Cloud. We were lost within three blocks. Apparently, we must have gone through a traffic light or committed some sort of traffic violation, because a huge French gendarme appeared at the side of our car and stopped us. He looked impressive in his helmet, blue uniform, boots, and white gloves. Adele was able to make him understand our problem and destination. He motioned for us to follow him, and he led us to the entrance to the St. Cloud expressway. When he got to the entrance, he pointed with a grand gesture and his white-gloved index finger. It was great! However, as soon as we exited at St. Cloud, we were lost again.

We were lost every time we came to a town larger than a village. We were lost in every country in which we drove. It made the trip more interesting.

In Luxembourg City, we found our hotel easily, but no place to park. We unloaded the luggage, got checked into the hotel and were advised to park in the public parking lot across the street. We could see it from the hotel entrance. Pace and I headed toward the lot, and our wives went on up to our rooms. We could not get there. We had to make a turn, since the street was one-way. The next thing we knew we had driven across a bridge, and then all over the city. Finally, we got lucky and got on the right street to get into the parking lot. We had no Luxembourg money, and the attendant would not let us park until we got some in order to pay in advance. Finally, he kept me hostage while Carey went to the hotel to get the ransom money. I could see our wives leaning out the windows of our top-floor rooms, laughing, waving, and motioning for me to come on. It was just as well that no one within hearing distance understood American profanity.

On our last night in Europe, we stayed in Brussels. Our travel agent had, of course, made the reservations and had included the usual chit which was payment for the room. This one was different, however, because it had more than the name of the hotel and the date of our stay. It said, "good for one lovely twin-bedded room." I really thought that the travel agent had made a special effort to provide truly deluxe accommodations on our last night, although lodging arrangements had been excellent throughout the trip.

After driving around Brussels for quite a time trying to locate our hotel, we found it. From the exterior it did not resemble any of our other hotels; the place looked shabby and old. We were greeted by a woman who might have owned the place. The decrepit elevator was so small that only the old lady as operator, the luggage, and one person could ride at the same time. The rooms were horrible, old, dark and dingy, and undoubtedly dirty. Evelyn did not want to stay there. Fortunately, we had not registered, and still retained our passports.

We all went downstairs to the lobby because the car was to be picked up at the hotel. Evelyn and Adele went to look at a Ramada Inn which we had noticed about a block down the street. Pace and I waited in the lobby. The chair in which I sat had broken a spring which kept jabbing my rear. We began to notice some action. Girls and men came in, rode the elevator to an upper floor, stayed a time, and then returned. I turned to Pace and said, "This joint reminds me of a French whorehouse in the Napoleon era."

Evelyn and Adele came back with the news that we had a room at the Ramada Inn and a bellboy was on his way with a cart. The Paces stayed, but we got out. I guess that the old lady was mad and threatened to call the police, but of course she did not know where we were.

The Ramada Inn was new. The room was great, and the place had a genuine American bar, complete with Jack Daniel's.

The next morning, we got a taxi, picked the Paces up at the curb in front of the flea bag and got to the airport. We cleared security and were in line to board Sabina for our trip home when we were asked to step out of line. I thought the police had found us and that the old woman would get her revenge. Instead, we were asked to ride first-class since they were overbooked in tourist. We got the Paces on with us, and first-class on Sabina was truly first-class, and especially because we did not pay for it. What a way to end a trip!

Early in 1974, we were having dinner with a group of our friends. I must have been drinking, because when Brooks and Helen Julian asked whether any of us wanted to meet them in Hawaii that fall after they attended a bankers' convention, I immediately said that we would be glad to. My God, we had just purchased our Florida condominium, and had to furnish it! I wonder where I thought the money would come from! Come to think about it, I wonder where it did come from.

At any rate, we booked a trip to Hawaii in October of 1974. We stopped off in Los Angeles for two or three days and visited Evelyn's brother, sister-in-law, and their family. What an experience that was! It was not just disorganized, it was chaos. They gave us their bedroom and bath. Thank God, there was a separate shower in addition to the bathtub where there was a huge bucket of paint located in the middle of it. We used the shower. I think that her brother was supposed to have painted the bathroom before we arrived but did not get around to doing it. All was confusion. The daughter's husband, ex-husband, or boyfriend—I'm not sure I ever knew which—had been given his walking papers by the daughter but kept showing up in an effort to get her back. He kept threatening to slit his wrists. I finally said that I did not care whether or not he sliced himself, but I did want him to hold off until after we left. I did not want to miss the airplane to Hawaii. The son needed a clean shirt in order to go out on a date, but there were none ironed, so he was told to go purchase a new one. I drank a lot.

We flew to Hawaii on a 747. This was an event for us since we had not even seen one before. We were both very impressed with the plane's hugeness. It was a pleasure to be able to walk up and down the aisles, to go to the bar, and have a drink, to be able to stretch out in the seat a little, and to have reasonable comfortable seating.

The Julians met us at the airport in Honolulu and transported us to our hotel in the auto which we had agreed to rent together. Since Brooks had been staying at the Kahala Hilton while attending the convention, we were agreed to live in the lap of luxury for a few days. It was a truly fine hotel, and damned expensive.

While we were in Honolulu, the Julians took us on a series of conducted tours. They had been to the Islands several times previously and loved it all. They were great tour guides and, as always, fun to be with. From Honolulu we flew to Maui and stayed in a hotel on the beach. We took one trip while there, without the Julians, to gaze into the crater of a volcano which was no longer active. It was quite high up a mountain. I was impressed as was Evelyn. I cannot pronounce the name much less spell it. We were there very early in the morning, the only people there for a short time. Then came the inevitable busload of Japanese complete with their cameras. There were Japanese everywhere we went while in the Islands, and they did take pictures constantly.

The Julians had been to the Island of Hawaii previously, and did not want to see it again, but felt that we should spend some time there. We flew over, landed in Kona, rented a car, and toured the immediate area, saw the black beaches, and then drove to Hilo. Naturally, we had a flat tire, but a wonderful young Hawaiian driving in the opposite direction saw our situation, turned around, changed the tire, and refused any money for so doing.

We stayed that night in Hilo, drove out to the Mauna Loa volcano the next day and walked around enough to be impressed with its potential when it emptied. We visited a macadamia nut farm, saw the trees growing, then boarded a plane for Honolulu where the Julians again met us at the airport and transported us to our hotel on Waikiki Beach.

The hotel was fine, but not quite the same category as the Kahala-Hilton had been. We spent a day looking over the tourists and the crowded streets near the beach, and then sunning ourselves and swimming.

We flew out the next day for San Francisco, the Julians taking a different flight because they were going directly home. Evelyn and I enjoyed Hawaii. We were glad that we went there, but neither of us had the same feeling about the Islands that many people, including our friends the Julians, seem to have. The Islands are not calling us back and I am glad because I know that the hordes of tourists are much greater, and that prices—which were high even then—are now confiscatory.

We had taken a vacation in San Francisco in the fall of 1969 and fell in love with it as does everyone else. It is a beautiful city, and a charming cosmopolitan area to visit. I presume that it would be a great place in which to live, but we were amazed at the great increase in traffic. Peak morning and evening hours certainly create one huge traffic jam.

We stayed at the Clift House. It was old, but its large rooms were well-furnished. We were impressed with the service and the consideration that the employees gave to the guests. As we arrived, the huge, impressive black doorman asked our names and never failed to greet us by name when we entered or left the hotel. By the time we got to the desk clerk to register, he greeted us by name. When we got to our room, I picked up the telephone receiver to ask for ice and glasses, and the operator said, "Yes, Mr. Clark, what may we do for you?"

Certainly, San Francisco is my favorite city in the United States, and ranks first behind Paris and Vienna among cities we have visited in Europe. Admittedly, we have not visited all of the great cities in Europe, and none in the rest of the world.

The Central Ohio District Golf Association had a golfing trip to Munich and Vienna the following September. It was for only ten days and included a stay in Munich during the Oktoberfest with good accommodations. We had no intention of playing golf, but we did think the trip inexpensive, so we talked the Gunderman's into going with us. It got really inexpensive, because I purchased a ticket on the winning Calcutta team at London Country Club and got a thousand dollars just a week or two before we were to depart.

The Oktoberfest was worth seeing and hearing. While German bands played almost continually in all of the huge tents, the Germans drank beer, ate, sang, and almost marched when martial music was played. I understood, after that experience, how Adolph Hitler was able to organize the Nazi party after World War I.

We loved Vienna. It seemed such a lovely, gentle city after Munich. Instead of martial music and beer, we listened to Strauss waltzes in Stadtpark as we sipped our wine or ate huge ice cream sundaes smothered with whipped cream. We ate the tortes and other pastries offered everywhere and discovered why there are few skinny Viennese.

We took no more trips for several years. Neither my eyes nor my pocketbook were in good enough order for travel. Besides, we did feel that we should spend our vacation time in our condo in Florida. We started going there two or three times a year for two to three weeks. November and March were musts, and we were there in June on three or four occasions. We rented the place in January and February for three or four years, and then decided not to rent it anymore.

In late summer of 1980, we were having a picnic in the grove at London Country Club, as was, and to an extent still is, a great Friday night pastime. Howard and Betty Sturgeon were there, of course. They own a little house overlooking the golf course, and they live there during the summer months, and in Florida the rest of the year. They talked about a trip that they were planning for the following spring. They love to travel and have been many places throughout the world.

The trip was to board the Queen Elizabeth II at Port Everglades at Fort Lauderdale, cruise up the east coast to New York City, dock there on Easter Sunday, and then sail to Southampton, England. There they would disembark and spend a week in London before flying home. It sounded great to Evelyn, and since neither of us had ever been on a ship, or to London, I thought that I might be able to make it, with Evelyn's help.

The Sturgeons encouraged us to join their group, and we signed up with the travel agency in Sarasota, Florida, to make the tour the following spring. It sounded good, even to me, although knowing that I would not be able to fully enjoy the sightseeing as I had on our previous travels.

Our friends, the Paces, had retired and were living in Fort Myers. They love anything having to do with travel, and when we told them about our plans, they offered to drive us to Port Everglades in order that they might see the ship and wish us Bon Voyage.

The "QE2" is huge. The biggest passenger ship ever built, it was quite comfortable to be on, for which I was duly thankful. I had no trouble walking around and, for all I knew, could have been in a huge floating hotel, except for the fact that it was not possible to get off at will.

We pulled into dock at New York City on Easter Sunday, early in the morning. We passed the Statue of Liberty, and I was thrilled to be able to really see it from our porthole. The sun seemed to be perfect for me, and I loved the sight. Our daughter, Marcia, and granddaughter, Courtney, had driven up from Baltimore to see us and the ship. Easter Day in New York was another thrill. I could not see nearly as well as I wanted, but the sounds of the people, their accents and, in many instances foreign languages were wonderful to hear. The smells of food being sold on every street corner was intriguing. After lunch at The Plaza, which was damned expensive, we walked from Central Park for blocks and enjoyed Fifth Avenue on Easter. We boarded ship later that afternoon and began our sail to Southampton. It took five days and, despite the nice stateroom, the wide variety of good food, and all of the shipboard activities, I was ready to get off after a day or two. Somehow, being miles away from the sight of land or of anything except water did not appeal to me.

The ship was scheduled to dock at Southampton at about five o'clock in the afternoon on Friday. Before lunch that day we began to receive instructions via the public address system to the effect that we were to have our bags packed and placed outside our stateroom door right after lunch, and that we were to vacate our stateroom early afternoon in order that the rooms might be cleaned, etc.

Suddenly, a very authoritative, very British voice came through. "This is the captain speaking. I have just been in touch with Southampton by radio and have been advised that there is an industrial disturbance among the dock workers, and that each of the passengers will therefore be required to remove his or her luggage from the ship. There will be further instructions." The damned dock workers were on strike! The ship's crew would be unable to handle the luggage because of the unions. It was a mess.

Periodically, we received instructions, most of which were confusing, but given to us by a female with yet another authoritative British voice. It was at that time that I began to develop an active dislike for the British.

All of the passengers were upset. There were some very elderly passengers, and some disabled passengers, who could not possibly carry their own luggage from that ship. The voice asked that younger people able to assist report to a designated area for instructions. Finally, we were told that our heavy luggage would be removed from the ship in the ordinary manner—by conveyor—but that we then would have to assume full responsibility for its transportation. We were told to vacate the staterooms and go to one of several designated areas to disembark. There was, once again, total confusion. We stood around and listened to several sets of conflicting instructions. Most everyone aboard was angry. Actually, we were all madder than hell. I imagine that everyone wanted a drink, but all of the bars were closed. Finally, I sat down on stairs which I suppose went someplace, and waited until things sorted themselves out, and Evelyn persuaded me that we actually were going to get off the damned boat.

I did carry off a bag which contained my remaining three or four bottles of Jack Daniel's, Evelyn's cosmetic case, and whatever else she thought was of too much value to risk. We were two or three hours late getting onto the dock, and then had the problem of finding our luggage, locating our bus, etc. It was dark. We were hungry, tired, thirsty, and still mad.

I do not know how long it took us to get from Southampton to London, but supposedly the staff at our hotel was prepared to serve us a late supper upon our arrival. We were so late that the dining rooms were all dark. We found that the bar was open, and I managed to consume three or four drinks in a short time. We discovered that a very old, very proper-looking waiter was going from table to table, slowly and methodically taking orders for what looked like tiny tea sandwiches. After receiving the order, he then disappeared, made the plate of sandwiches, and returned. We decided that we were not hungry enough to wait all night for that to transpire, so we found our room, took in our luggage, which, partly because of Evelyn's earlier efforts, was intact, and went to bed. My dislike for the British was increasing rapidly.

I could not detail everything that we saw and did in London during that week. To me, it was not a great experience. I know that we attended the theater twice and saw the Saturday matinee performance of "My Fair Lady," which was well done, and an evening performance of "Bringing up Rita." I slept through much of the final act, partly because the play was lousy, and partly because the actors spoke a language I could not understand. It was their version of English. Evelyn was angry and embarrassed and took me back to the hotel quickly. This suited me fine. We went into the bar, and gradually the after-theater-goers in our party straggled in. They all left early too, and agreed with me that it was not a great performance.

We rode the underground, a remarkable quick way to get around the huge city. We rode also on two double decker buses. They started up too quickly for me, but the underground cars did not wait for the passengers to be seated either. I was a little terrified in my attempts at riding on the public transportation system. I did like their taxis though, and I loved the cockney cab drivers.

The pubs were all great. We ate lunch in them as often as we could. The food was good, and I enjoyed all of the waitresses. They were pleasant and very efficient, and called patrons "love," "lovie," and "dearie." I had only one good dinner during the week we spent in London. That was at the Brown Hotel. I know that London had good restaurants, but they were not included in the price of our tour. I had understood that the English had never been noted for having great cuisine, and I believe that.

We were housed in the Russell Hotel, which really had nothing to recommend it except that it was clean. The Russell was old, and certainly not located conveniently to anything, except for the British Museum, which we should have gone through, but did not.

I resented the superior, almost insulting, attitude of the waiters in the restaurants, the hotel personnel from the clerks to the concierge, including the bartenders. Some tour guides were overly-impressed with their own vast knowledge. I saw better personally on a Sunday morning public transportation bus tour and learned more from listening to the driver than I did at any other time during the week.

I had one near catastrophe. Sturgeon had advised me to calculate how many bottles of booze I would consume on the trip, then take it with me, because of the high costs at the bars on shipboard, and in London. I thought that seven liters of Jack Daniel's should last for two weeks. I miscalculated by a day and ran out at noon the day before our departure. We found a liquor store a block or two from the hotel. Sturgeon was right! The cost of American whiskey was shocking. The cost of anything in the store was outlandish, but I finally settled for a pint of scotch with a brand name I never heard of before or since. It was about ten dollars and was the least expensive item we saw that looked drinkable.

For a day or two before we were scheduled to fly back to the United States, we kept hearing reports of another "industrial disturbance." This time it was the air controllers. They did not close down all of Britain's airports at the same time, but did it selectively for specified periods of time, I presume to aggravate the public even more than might have been the case had they closed all of the airports at one time and kept them closed. The result was that airports were jammed throughout Europe, and airplanes were backed up waiting to depart for some portion of the British Isles. It was not known when, or whenever, London's Heathrow would be closed or for what length of time. The morning, we were required to vacate our hotel, we were informed that Heathrow would be struck, but no one knew at what hour or for how long. Nevertheless, we were loaded on buses, bag and baggage and transported to the airport ---there to await our fate.

When we arrived, we joined hordes of confused, angry people who were noisily raising hell in all sorts of languages. The strike was on! Some found seats. The lines were long to get into the restrooms. I finally elbowed my way to a bar where the bartender, knowing that I was American, suggested that I have a martini, insisting that he knew how to make them. I should have known better. It was terrible. Evelyn and I finally got to a table where we planned to eat lunch. We were joined by a delightful young Irish banker, who observed that I was finishing a martini, and promptly got me another, unfortunately. Evelyn was able to get us something to eat. The food was horrible.

After a few hours, we learned that planes were again in the air. Soon thereafter we were told to go to our gate, and to prepare for boarding. After we walked for quite a distance, we arrived at our gate, where we either stood or sat on the floor for another hour. Finally, we were allowed to board. After boarding the British Airways *747*, we sat. It was hot in that cabin. We sat and sat; it became hotter. After a considerable time, the engines were started and we taxied out to a runway, prepared to take off. We sat. Other planes were flying, but we were not. The air traffic controllers must have disliked our pilot, crew, and all of the passengers. We finally took off about six hours late. The airline gave us free drinks. I thought that was damned big of them. I bought a couple more drinks, talked to the people I was sitting with, ate whatever food was served, and took a nap. I was not able to sit with Evelyn or any of our group. We dozed and talked. The plane was packed. It was hardly possible to walk around, and I could not see well enough to do this anyway. It was a long, boring, tiring trip. The plane was near Miami, finally, and all of the passengers were stirring. Evelyn discovered that she had lost her gold earrings. They were never found.

The plane finally landed sometime after midnight. I carried our luggage through customs and then up steep steps. There were no skycaps. We discovered that all connecting flights had long since departed, and the airline had to put us up overnight at a motel at the airport. The room we were given had not been occupied for some time, but it was adequate. Evelyn found ice and I had a large shot of my London scotch. We went to bed after having been up for twenty-eight hours.

After about four hours' sleep, we were awakened and transported back to the airport where we were served a free breakfast. Eventually, we got to our plane for Fort Myers and the Paces. The plane held about twenty passengers and a stewardess. It was an old-fashioned prop affair, but we really did not worry about it. It landed and the trip was over. All we had to do was visit the Paces, which was no hardship for us. We were just too tired to drive back to Dunedin that day.

I had never harbored any ill feeling for the English prior to our trip. I have since. In every other country we had visited on previous trips, I had enjoyed the people. My ancestors all came from England among the early settlers in America. I knew, after that experience, why they had left.

Several unpleasant things occurred during that decade in addition to the big "eye blowup" in September 1978.

My mother died in November of 1971. She never got to see the new office building, and I know that she would have loved it, and would have reported to all of her friends with pride. She had been afflicted with arthritis for several years and was in constant pain. The disease had settled in her hip and she was able, only with great difficulty, to use a cane for support. She was too proud to use a walker.

She had been quite independent into her mid-seventies and maintained her apartment and usual lifestyle. Indeed, she worked for the State of Ohio until she was well past seventy. She had lied about her age so much that I doubt whether she was certain as to how old she really was.

She finally told me that she thought she had better move to Grove City in order to be near me and my family. She had suddenly become insecure. She built a house and moved into it, which was indeed a mistake. Her friends were gone. I saw her fairly often, but this was not a substitute for the life she had been used to. She still drove her car. I could not tell her she could no longer drive. She would have paid no attention to me. She drove into Columbus to play cards with her friends, and I shuddered every time that I knew about it. Jim Henry was her doctor, and he told me what I already knew, but did not really want to admit. She was becoming senile, and sooner or later I would have to take over her affairs. I tried to talk to her about her checkbook, and she got really mad. Finally, she let me see it one day, and it was a real mess. She had always been a very good businesswoman, and my worst fears were confirmed. She knew that I would take action soon unless things were changed rapidly.

The next thing I knew, she was visiting retirement homes. I did not want to appear too eager, because she was contrary enough to drop the idea if she thought that I wanted her to move into one of them. Finally, she asked that I go with her for the purpose of looking at one that was just being completed. She liked it, so naturally did I. She moved in as soon as she could after having disposed of all of her furniture, crystal, dishes, and silver. What she did not get sold, we brought home. I got her house sold quickly.

She loved the retirement center, and miraculously got completely back to normal mentally. She had people around again. She could talk with them. She developed entirely new interests. Unfortunately, her health became worse. She was hospitalized twice. Her hip bothered her more and more. Finally, she announced that she was going to have a hip replacement, which was then a relatively new procedure. She did undergo the surgery and was able to walk much better. She was almost pain-free, and quite encouraged.

A month or so after the operation I received a telephone call to the effect that she was hospitalized again with what was thought to be a stroke. She was at least partially paralyzed and came and went mentally. She died in the hospital. Her doctor thought that probably a blood clot had broken loose as a result of the surgery and got to her brain. We did not permit an autopsy. What good would that have done?

I had developed an occasional, very severe pain in my right eye which was truly disabling while it lasted. The ophthalmologist could see nothing, and finally told me to come into his office when the pain occurred.

It developed one afternoon, so I called Evelyn and had her drive me in. As soon as the doctor looked at the eye, he insisted that I go directly to the hospital. What happened was that the cataract on that eye, which so far as I know had always been there, had been knocked loose and was floating in the eye. When it came to rest, it caused severe pressure and acute glaucoma.

The ophthalmologist came to the hospital, and over an hour or two later was able to reduce the pressure on the eye sufficiently to alleviate the pain. He then scheduled me for cataract surgery on his normal operating day, which was Friday. I do not know whether it was Monday or Tuesday afternoon when I went in, but I really had nothing to do until the Friday surgery. The cataract was removed, the eye bandaged, and I was returned to the hospital room and sentenced to complete inactivity in bed. I even slept on a very small, extremely hard pillow. It all seemed futile to me, because I knew that there was no vision in the eye anyway.

After a week, I wanted to go home. The various residents, after dutifully checking my eye each day, finally told me that even Doctor Moses, conservative as he was, could not possibly keep me hospitalized any longer. He came in very late on Friday afternoon and told me that I would be required to remain over the weekend. I protested loudly and profanely. He asked why I wanted out so badly. I told him that I wanted to go home, watch the Kentucky Derby on television, eat some snacks, and drink several martinis. He said that I could do all of those things in my hospital room, but that if I were released from the hospital, I would have to release myself.

Fortunately, Evelyn was there during all this conversation, and she did calm me down. She brought in a pitcher of martinis and the snacks the next afternoon, and we celebrated the Kentucky Derby in the hospital.

Evelyn had a hysterectomy, which was painful for her, and frustrated her greatly because she could not get right up and start working hard immediately. I do know that when she was ill and hospitalized, I felt tremendous sympathy and love for her.

I had a hernia operation. I had swung strong at a golf ball and had immediate severe pain. A blood clot soon developed which made Jim Henry nervous enough that he called the surgeon and scheduled me to be operated on.

Evelyn and I knew the surgeon all too well. He had operated on her both times. We had spent a weekend with the surgeon, his wife, and the Henrys, and had seen them socially on occasions.

By the time of the hernia operation, Dick was considered to be the most outstanding surgeon on the staff at the hospital. He did not examine me prior to the day of the surgery. He had a female resident do that. He told me later he thought that I would enjoy her more. I agreed. Just as they were ready to wheel me to surgery, he came charging into my room, complete with surgical gown, etc., looking, or attempting to look, as much like a nurse as possible. He said, sweetly, "Lift up your nighty, honey," patted the hernia, and then said, "I just wanted to make sure what I was operating on. It'd be hell if I cut in the wrong place."

I developed pneumonia as a result of the anesthetic. My lungs were not great anyway because of having smoked cigarettes continually from age sixteen. I did not know that I had pneumonia until I was to be released. No one bothered to tell me.

I don't know exactly how it happened, but I had a room that seemed to be the attic of the hospital; it was not on the regular surgical floor in any event and was not air-conditioned. It had western exposure. One hot September afternoon while Evelyn was with me, our new Methodist minister paid me a visit. I had not met him, nor had Evelyn. We both greeted him warmly, and I was attempting to be extremely nice because Evelyn really is a good Methodist, and I did not want to embarrass her by being anything else but very nice.

Unfortunately, my friendly surgeon chose this time to make rounds. There he was, dressed in a powder-blue, expensive-looking suit, looking very handsome and distinguished with his white hair. He had a full retinue of medical interns, residents, and nurses following, and hanging on his every word. He said, "Evelyn, how you doin'?" Ignoring the minister, he looked at me and said, "Go take a shower, you son-of-a-bitch. You stink. And while you're at it, rip that God-damned tape and bandage off, and I'll be back." Without thinking, I said, "Rip it off yourself, you bastard. It'll hurt." He left, I took a shower, the preacher stayed. I think the minister was intrigued. Back came the surgeon and his entourage. The female resident removed the tape and bandage. After Dick checked the wound and told me that I could go home the next day, the resident said, "What about the pneumonia?" "Jesus Christ," he cried. "Let me go look at his chart." He came back and said, "All you've got is a little temperature. You'll be all right. Go home in the morning." He left, the minister left, and I laughed. Evelyn didn't know quite what to do. In a few minutes the resident returned and said that the doctor had discharged me, and that I could go home at once.

Now that I have written about the entire decade, and have time to reflect, I realize it was a truly eventful period for me and for my family. I wonder what should be classified as the most eventful period on my life. Probably the 1940s from my own perspective, but also from that of the world. To me, every period in which I have lived was an interesting time. I might not have enjoyed it all, but it was never dull.

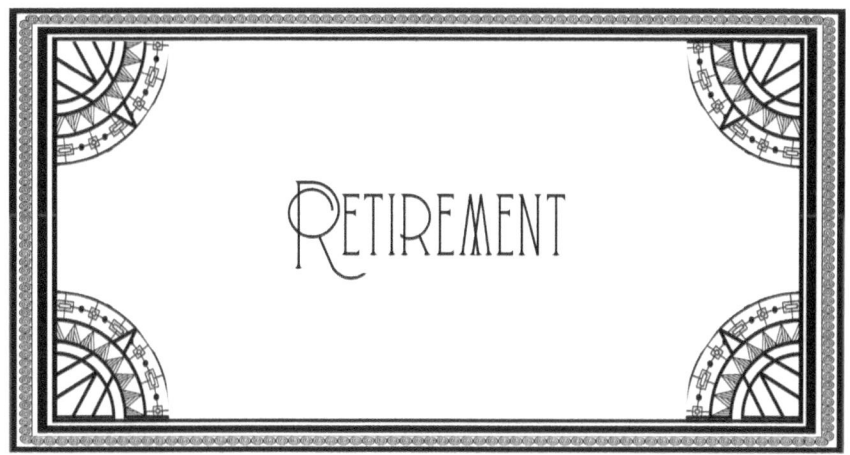

RETIREMENT

As I indicated earlier, when I came to the conclusion that I had to retire, I was completely devasted. When the day finally arrived, I was tearful. I had a couple boxes full of personal items that I took home with me. I thought that they were important to me at the time, but I do not now know where they are. Some of my office furniture was transferred to son Tom's office, and the rest sold to a dealer in used office furniture. Finally, my office was completely empty. I stood inside it for a few minutes until I could regain my composure and then walked out and closed the door on my working life.

There were two or three retirement parties, including a large party that Evelyn insisted that we have. We held it at the Grove City Country Club and did not label it as a "retirement party," although it really was. We had cocktails, dinner, and dance music. It was a good party. One of my friends even supplied a strip-tease dancer. I wished that my eyesight was better. I never really knew which of my friends was so thoughtful, although I had some suspicions.

The parties were over with soon enough, and I had an adjustment to make. So did Evelyn. She had to adjust to me being at home and underfoot. She had the problem of my being around for lunch. We were both uncertain as to how we would get along financially in retirement. Our lives were changed completely.

In my case, one of the hardest of the many adjustments was to get used to the fact that I really was not in life's mainstream any longer. I had to face the realization that I was not important if I ever had been. I had to learn that I had nothing useful to occupy my time.

I walked to the office frequently. I even talked with some of my former clients and helped the transition for Tom. Everyone was wonderful to me. I was still welcome in the office, but it was not my office any longer.

Evelyn and I had decided that we would spend the fall and winter in our condominium in Florida. When I bought the place, the thought of it serving as anything other than a vacation home never entered my mind. In 1981, prior to our last trip to Europe, we stayed in the apartment for six weeks. We had become somewhat acquainted with a few people in our building and had joined Dunedin Country Club. It was not as though we were entering a new phase of life with which we were totally unfamiliar.

Royal Stewart Arms

We had stumbled into Royal Stewart Arms (the name given the complex) in 1972. We stayed two or three nights at Innisbrook, a well-known golf convention and vacation resort. We did not want to play golf on that day, so we took a ride and explored the area. We saw signs directing us to visit Royal Stewart Arms, and we followed the arrows to the location on Honeymoon Island where the complex was under construction. To reach the island required crossing the Dunedin Causeway, which is about two miles in length. It offers a spectacular view of the water as it is crossed, and gradually buildings loom into view. At that time, the two smallest buildings, Aberdeen and Berwick

—every name was very Scottish—had been built and fully occupied for some time. Clydebank and Dunoon, larger three-story buildings, were completed and occupied as well. The first of three eight-story high rises, Elgin, was nearing completion. We had seen the models and were taken by one of the salespeople to one of the upper floors of the Elgin building to see what the units would be like. The view was spectacular! We had St. Joseph's Sound directly in front of us, and Caladesi Island and Hurricane Pass just across a small expanse of land and water. It was a beautiful, clear day and we could see the high-rise buildings on Clearwater Beach, eight miles away. The water sparkled in the sunlight, the sand was white and clean, and there were a few small boats in the sound. Evelyn was enraptured and wanted to buy one right then. I was thrilled with the idea myself, but I had not planned to even look at condominiums just then, and absolutely no intention of purchasing one.

Not quite two years later, we had decided to purchase a vacation condo, and we knew by then that we wanted to have a place on the west coast of Florida. It was much cheaper there and, at that time, not nearly so crowded.

We had flown to Florida to spend Christmas of 1973 with Evelyn's parents who lived at Delray Beach, and also to see son Dick and his wife who, by then, were living at Pompano Beach. I had been told that there were some new condominiums located on a golf course in the Clearwater area. They sounded good to us, so we flew to Tampa, rented a car, and stayed in a motel on Clearwater Beach. We spent two days looking at condominiums in the Clearwater, Dunedin, and St. Petersburg area. Nothing suited us. We kept remembering Royal Stewart Arms, but there was nothing for sale there at all.

We were packed and just ready to leave for the airport to fly home, when the real estate broker who had worked so hard for us, called to tell us that two re-sales had just gone on the market in the Elgin Building at Royal Stewart Arms. We told him to take his wife along and go look at them, and that we would call them when we got to our home later that afternoon.

We talked to them late that Sunday. From the description, we selected one of them and told the broker to send up a contract for our signature. Naturally, by Monday morning Evelyn had changed her mind and wanted the other one. I called again, the contract was written accordingly, and early in 1974, we became the proud owners of a condominium (7 Elgin Building, #409) we had never seen. My wife has reminded me often that had we purchased one in 1972, as she had wanted, it would have cost us five thousand dollars less.

At any rate, we had decided that as part of our newly-retired lifestyle, we would spend about six months in Florida during late fall, winter, and spring until early May, and six months at our home in Grove City. I could not have handled staying around home knowing that my office and my clients were two short blocks away. I doubt that son Tom could have handled it either.

There are ninety-three living units in our building: more than four hundred in the entire complex. Our little enclave is known as a community for adult living. What it really is, is a settlement of little old ladies, many of them widowed and living off their deceased husband's money, pension, and insurance. Most of them are not sweet, although a few are wonderful. Little old men are referred to unaffectionately as "old farts," who may be married or single. Some older married couples live in peace and harmony, while some do not. Some of the folks there are quite well off financially, some moderately so, and some who have a hard time making ends meet.

Each condominium association has rules. My God are there rules! One rule sometimes seems to contradict another. A person may purchase a condominium unit owning a house pet. The pet may move in and live with its owner, but when it dies it may not be replaced with another. Consequently, the place is almost entirely devoid of dogs and cats now that it is fourteen years old.

Children under the age of sixteen may not remain on the premises for longer than two weeks at a time. An attempt was made to fix the minimum age for permanent occupancy at forty, but this failed, not because it is probably an illegal restriction, but because it was felt that one of the "old farts" might want to marry a sweet young thing, and none wanted to interfere with the romance. I really do not know all of the rules even after much time spent there. In that way, I can either apologize for one of my transgressions when one occurs and is called to my attention, or I could tell the person bringing my violation to the fore to go straight to hell.

I was at the swimming pool one afternoon when the owner of a unit in another building was showing his brother our recreational facilities. Posted, prominently displayed, were the rules for the use of the swimming pool. The brother stopped, sipped his drink, looked at the other and said, "There are sixteen rules here. You have innumerable condominium rules. There are only ten commandments."

Very few people in the entire complex are still gainfully employed. Taking care of our small apartment units comprises about half a day a week. None of us really has anything to do. The problem is how to occupy our time.

Some walk a mile or more a day, and then disappear until the next day. Some ride their bicycles around the roads in our complex, out the road on the State Park property to the beach, up the causeway to the small shopping center and back. Many bicycles, chained and locked, have rusted. So have their riders.

We have a fishing pier in connection with our recreation area. There are quite a few people, most of them men, who go to the pier frequently. They fish—at least they get a line in the water—and then they talk to one another. On a daily basis, few fish of any significance are caught, but amazingly enough, occasionally good-sized fish will be reeled in in abundance. In the winter, when the "renters" are occupying quite a few units in each building, the pier is crowded almost daily.

The recreation hall has a daily quota of pool players. There are several poker games each week, and blessed is the man who is invited to participate in more than one game a week. On second thought, maybe he is not so blessed; he probably just plays bad poker and contributes heavily.

The ladies have bridge on weekday afternoons, and I think that there is occasional mixed bridge, exercise classes and bingo.

Then there is the swimming pool. The same people are there daily, mostly women. Some of them even swim a little, but it is mainly a place to get together to gossip. The amazing thing is that an outsider—which I definitely am at the pool—can stay away for months, and on the next visit can eavesdrop, and the conversation is the same. They talk mostly about the restaurants each visited either for lunch and dinner, and compare notes on cost, quantity, and quality. It does not seem that any of them ever agree. They discuss the soap operas on television. They raise hell about the operation of each building as well as the entire complex. They all want to fire the management, and they actively dislike their duly-elected officers.

These people are so entrenched that they all sit together in the same location each day. In the unlikely event that a stranger has had the temerity or misfortune to occupy a spot in their area, harsh words may be spoken, and at the least there are glares at the poor creature.

There are shuffleboard courts. While shuffleboard is favored by most Florida retirees, the courts at Royal Stewart Arms are seldom occupied.

The tennis courts are occupied constantly. One group plays every morning at eight. I have wondered what would happen if they all arrived one morning and found the courts already occupied.

There are a godly number of golfers who play on various days of the week at different hours. Several play at Dunedin Country Club, leaving about seven-thirty in the morning at least three days a week. Tuesday and Thursday mornings are ladies' days at Dunedin, and several women charge out early on these days.

There are some who head for the shopping malls almost daily. There are some who simply go out for lunch each day, and many make it a big deal to have dinner out two or three times a week. It is entertainment.

There are cocktail parties about every night and some, unfortunately for their health, are too popular and get invited to too many of them.

I suspect that almost all of the residents have at least one or two drinks every day. I am afraid that each building has a few alcoholics. It is surprising that there are not more because of the genuine lack of purpose in most of our lives.

There are residents who are seldom seen by anyone. I supposed that those unfortunates must have friends and relatives someplace. Most of all those physically able attend church frequently. I know that at their ages, and mine, they all want to get right with God. I should attend, and I even think about going sometimes when Evelyn leaves. She goes to church infrequently, but I know would attend regularly if I would go with her. I may start going one day, but slothful habits are hard to break.

The universal pastime is to complain about the transgressions of the officers of the various condominium associations, and the so-called "Master Board." The owners elect them, and then bitch. Serving as a board member is a truly thankless task. Naturally, it is difficult to find people, qualified or not, who will agree to serve. There are exceptions, but most board members will serve only one term. There are some, however, who continue year after year, until they have finally lost most of their friends, and notice that many people do not speak to them anymore except at board meetings, when they listen to all of the hell-raisers on whatever the current gripe may be.

Many of our friends from Ohio live in the area. The Julians visited us and liked the place so much that they purchased a unit in the next building. The Wolfe's live in Dunedin year around, as do the Moore's in St. Petersburg—an hour's drive away. The Frys' have a place about twenty minutes from us, and our next-door neighbors, the Henrys, bought a condominium no more than fifteen minutes from us. Even our friends, the Smiths, who now live on Torch Lake, Michigan, since George retired as a doctor in Detroit, have been renting a place in our building for three years during the season, and rented in our area two other years.,

It is very reassuring to have all of these people around. It also gives us a considerable social life without benefit of any friends that we have made in Florida.

During the last five years, we have become acquainted with most of the unit owners and many of the tenants in our building, and more than a few from the other buildings in our complex. We have made some good friends there, and we see them socially as well. The result of all this is that we are as busy socially as we want to be. Thank God we are not among those who seem to be invited to cocktail parties every night. We do enough of it as it is.

Our Florida routine is somewhat varied. We do walk a little more than a mile most mornings, Evelyn plays golf occasionally, and bridge about once a month. We go out to lunch two or three times a week, usually to Dunedin Country Club, but not always. We have drinks out often either with friends at one of the many fine, really good restaurants, we go to cocktail parties, and are invited to dinner at various friends' residences. Naturally, we entertain too.

Evelyn is now on our Board of Directors, is the treasurer, and loves it. I don't think she knows as much as she should about financial statements which she receives and which is provided by management, but she does.

I spend time writing my memoirs, which has entertained me immensely; whether anyone else will be entertained remains to be seen.

I have become involved with an organization called "Channel Markers," which provides assistance of all kinds to the visually impaired. I have taken courses there each winter for the last four years, the last two winters participating in a creative writing class. The instructor is completely blind as are most of the students. Volunteers read what we produce, and the class and teacher comment after listening to the reader. The instructor has a fine mind and is amazingly cogent in his comments. I entertained them last winter with character sketches, which they enjoyed to the extent that the instructor asked me that I continue to write one each week during the semester.

Anyways, that is our life in Florida. We are both reasonably busy, not bored very often, and going along with retirement and the aging process pretty well so far. Of course, I wish I could see; there really can be a lot to do in retirement.

The other six months of each year, we have spent at home. We love it at home but are not really as active as we seem to be in Florida.

I am no help at all to Evelyn, and the result is that she must take care of the yard and the house herself. Yes, she has some help, particularly with the yard, but she has to pull weeds and take care of her flowers and her vegetable garden. Our Florida condo is too small to live in for six months at a time. Our home is large and requires that Evelyn work harder than she needs to. We should sell the place and move into some place requiring no more effort than our condominium apartment; another condo or a retirement home seem to be our choices.

We are both reluctant to make a move at this time, but we both know that it is inevitable.

We have been members of London Country Club commencing with the year 1954. Evelyn and I both have played a lot of golf there, even though the course is twenty-two miles from our home. Evelyn still plays as often as she can but is somewhat handicapped by the fact that I can no longer play.

Over the years, we have made friends at the club, with the result that much of our social life centers around it, and London people. We are entertained by them frequently and, of course, reciprocate. We go to dances and parties at the club. The most fun to us are the Friday night picnics "in the grove." These are very impromptu affairs, and many of the same people participate week after week. There is really a beautiful grove of trees at the top of a hill overlooking the golf course. Over the years, the club has supplied picnic table and grills. Everyone brings whatever they wish to grill, some sort of dish which becomes a part of a pot luck, and a considerable quantity of alcoholic beverages, which they consume.

Of course, we see our children and their families fairly often. We see our friends in Grove City and Columbus, but generally speaking, there is more of a vacation-like feeling to Florida.

I did go to the office almost daily for a couple of years. I did my writing over there, and I felt almost as though I was still working. Actually, I did help out with advice, which the lawyers frequently solicited as they always had. Gradually, I went over less and less. Everyone was working hard, and I did not want to bother them. Besides, my old office had been rented to a title insurance company which had the right to use the library for their real estate closings. The result was that I frequently had no place to sit.

I feel that I have lost more and more of what little vision I had left. It is more difficult for me to read and write. Walking to the office is a chore, and I am much more hesitant to cross the street which is necessary to get to the office.

One of our friends in Florida had a sign on her door which says, "Old age is not for sissies." That's true. Several of our friends have had serious illnesses and operations. London Country Club has become a virtual geriatric society. Certainly, that is true in Florida. The emergency squad seems to be called to our complex at least once each week. Several of our friends have died. It happens more frequently each year.

In my own case, 1986 has not been such a great year insofar as my health is concerned. There is still some question in my mind as to whether I would ever have developed cancer of the colon. All of the doctors who checked me both in Ohio and Florida assured me that I would probably soon and recommended an operation. I had it, and the staples in the incision did not hold. In addition, I could not urinate. The result was that I had two operations on the same day—surgical repair and prostate! Indeed, I had three operations in ten days, and developed congestive heart failure. I spent a total of twenty-five days in the hospital, and I am still recovering nine and a half weeks after the last operation. I am nearly recovered and can only thank God for permitting me to make it through. I also thank God for Medicare and other supplemental health insurance. I am more and more certain that some form of national health insurance is necessary for everyone's protection from financial disaster. I am also convinced that curbs should be made and enforced on doctor and hospital charges.

The 1980s have been the Reagan years. Ronald Reagan defeated Jimmy Carter in the 1980 election largely because Carter and his administration were unable to release the hostages held prisoner in Iran. We were shown as impatient, a "paper tiger," and inept. Carter and Reagan debated, which was a mistake. Carter was colorless, Reagan an actor. The American people seemed to place too much emphasis on their debating skills.

Reagan has become the most popular President in our history. He makes a great appearance; he is highly articulate. Even most of the media seem to support him, or at least do not try to tear him apart as they have every President since John Kennedy. I never was a fan of Reagan even though I have been a Republican all of my adult life. In 1976, had Reagan supported President Ford as he should have, Ford would have defeated Carter. In the 1980 presidential primaries, Reagan promised to substantially increase defense spending, sharply reduce taxes, and also balance the budget. George Bush, then a candidate for President, called Reagan's proposals, "voodoo economics," which, of course, it was and is. Unfortunately, Reagan set out on his program, with the result that we now have such a huge budget deficit that we are virtually bankrupt, and economically have become no more than a second-rate nation.

Walter Mondale was Reagan's opponent in 1984. The American people gave Reagan the greatest vote in our history. But we really had no choice. Mondale would have been a disaster.

Some good things have occurred as a result of the Reagan presidency. Lyndon Johnson's Great Society is rapidly being dismantled as it should be. I do not believe that we can support financially the huge number of programs instituted during the Johnson years. The problem is that we have increased defense spending beyond all reason. I was in the service, stationed at Wright Field. I saw the waste there. I know that the more the military is given, the more it wastes and the more it wants.

The 1980s brought substantial reductions in the size of our automobiles in an effort to make them more gasoline efficient. This process was commenced in the 1970s, and it is amazing how well they have been accepted. It is also amazing to me that the United States' auto industry is in the process of becoming second-rate. The Japanese and the Europeans apparently produce better cars than we do at more than competitive prices.

Steel, textile, and shoe industries are in trouble. Asiatic countries are producing shoes and textiles of good quality much cheaper than we can. Europeans are producing steel under heavy government subsidy and sell it cheaper than we do. The result of all of this is that much of our manufacturing has been lost, perhaps forever.

Drugs of all types seem to possess much of our youth, and many others into their thirties and forties. This was unheard of until the early 1960s.

Our entire culture seems to have been in transition for more than twenty years. Our music is much different, much of our literature, drama and art seems far out to me. I suppose that what we did and wrote and sang baffled the elderly when we were becoming adults. The world does change. I think, though, that it has changed more rapidly in the last twenty-odd years. I sometimes think much of the change began with the assassination of President Kennedy. Kennedy was not too many years past his youth, and the young identified with him. Then, in a matter of minutes he was gone.

Even our taste in food and our eating habits are different. We have come into an era of "fast food." We line up to eat junk. McDonald's is a household word with our grandchildren. Hamburgers and French fries are staple daily food for millions of children and young adults.

In our case, the retirement years have produced two more grandchildren. Tom and Karen have a son Tommy, and a daughter, Katie. That gives us a total of five and I know that we have two generations to follow us. I trust that our grandchildren will continue the production line.

In retrospect, I have lived through a remarkable period. I was born at the end of the first World War, lived my earliest days of consciousness in a very small, old-fashioned town with all of its inconveniences and all of its values. When I moved to the big city, the country was at the height of the so-called Jazz Age. There really were rumble seats, roadsters, the Charleston, and slickers. There was prohibition. There was great prosperity and a stock market boom. We were as a nation, convinced that we were the greatest country in history.

I also lived through the 1929 stock market crash and the Great Depression. I saw what it did to the lives of all of us. I had known that my family was not well-to-do, but I realized that we were poor in 1934. When my father found himself without a job in Marion, Ohio, there was no unemployment compensation, and no welfare then.

I lived through World War II. I even served in the Army for nearly three years. Friends of mine were killed, others wounded either physically or psychologically. We experienced rationing and wage and price controls. The atomic bomb ended the war but began the nuclear age with its constant threat of destruction of the world or a large part of it.

The immediate postwar period was wonderful. We were at peace. Prosperity returned. My friends came home from all over the world, and I was again a civilian.

Historically speaking, we were involved in the Korean War. However, I was not affected by it at all. The Eisenhower years brought a peace and prosperity which continued until the assassination of President Kennedy in 1963.

There was our involvement in the Vietnam War. This caused our young people virtually to revolt. I was concerned also because of my own boys who got, thank God, high enough draft numbers that I knew they were safe. There was rioting on our country's campuses, buildings were burned, classes disrupted, and colleges closed. I never understood this. I was a product of a time when no one questioned the how and why of our entry into a war. When drafted I felt, as did we all, that I had to serve.

The civil rights movement pushed forward rapidly in the 1960s and continues to progress today, although at a much slower pace. The blacks, however, were not satisfied with progress in the late 1960s, and rioted in many cities across the country. I never understood why they burned down their own areas.

I followed President Nixon and the entire Watergate fiasco with great interest. Had he not resigned, Nixon would most certainly have been impeached and removed from office. I never understood why Nixon did not have all tapes destroyed after it became known that there were tapes. Stupidity was the problem, I think. Nevertheless, I still feel that in many respects Nixon was a good President, if not a great one.

We lived through Carter and the hostage crisis. I do not believe that he will be remembered as anything other than mediocre.

I have lived from the beginning of radio, silent films, talking pictures, color movies, television both black and white, and color video cassettes. I saw rather primitive automobiles in the early 1920s and have lived through their progression to the sophisticated turbo engines of today, from autos with side curtains to those air-conditioned models we all seem to drive today.

I cannot think of all of the changes and improvements that have come along as a result of our inventiveness. We are now well into the age of the computer, and this has passed me by completely. I do not understand computers. Neither do I comprehend how we were able to place men in space and send them to the moon.

I know that my life and Evelyn's and our friends are more nearly over than midpoint. I have few regrets. I am glad for our marriage and our children and grandchildren. I am glad that we have had and still have so many good friends. I am glad that I practiced law, but I enjoyed everything else I did as well. It did not always appear that way when it was happening, but, aside from my blindness and the infirmities of age which are now beginning, I have enjoyed my life. I have had a good one.

Afterword
By Courtney Jo Barr

This book is a snapshot of my grandfathers' life from 1918 to 1987. Born blind in one eye, and nearly blind in the other while writing his autobiography, my grandfather captures events, and cost of items as a young man growing up in Grove City, a once small suburb of Columbus, with astute mental clarity. Educated in history, economics, then law, high school teacher turned attorney, he loved Ohio, the Buckeyes, golf, drinks, politics, friends, family and 3174 Park Street. It has been a tremendous joy to uncover my grandfather's writings and discover that even as a history buff, he questioned political decisions being made in his time. I believe ancestral autobiographies, capture a perspective in time that can help us piece together past truths, as if we are a time traveler back to their era.

In regard to the age-old question of Nature vs Nurture, my grandfather writes (page 50), "Zoology was of more interest to me because it was elementary genetics. I learned that heredity does, in fact, play an important role in the lives of us all. I learned that intelligence — or lack of it — is inherited. My father said it very well: 'You can't plant peas and get sweet potatoes.'" On that same page, adds, "We read George Bernard Shaw's and Eugene O'Neill's plays, poetry by Ogden Nash and other modern (for then) poets and playwrights. We did not read prose to the best of my recollection. It amazed me so much at the meaning, the themes of some of these authors. I did not understand the symbolism of many of them because I did not sense its existence until the instructor pointed it out to us. I wonder whether all of the rather hidden meanings were really there, or whether they existed only for the instructor and the intellectual few. I always thought plays were written to entertain." I wonder, can this same symbolism be said of autobiographies as well? Can only intelligent people see symbolism in writings? Do only intelligent people seek knowledge? It seems to me, the internal application of knowledge leads to wisdom, and wisdom allows for truths to be revealed. He mused (page 62), "I had many courses in history. Some were dull, some extremely interesting. I know that at the time I knew a lot—facts, dates, the interrelation between historical periods, and the repetitive aspects of history from earliest times. All that I retain now is an appreciation for the broad sweep of history and the predictability of what is occurring today. As Henry Adams wrote quite a few years ago in The Education of Henry Adams, 'Look at the past, compare it in the present, triangulate and see the future.'" In order to augment our knowledge and understanding of our society in 2024, may we seize upon Henry Adams directions and combine it with our modern-day awakened intellect, along with the wisdom and symbolisms in this book.

A new history class could be taught from my grandfathers' writings by using examples he has given and comparing them to what truths we know today. An infamous Q epistle "future proves past," comes to mind. Although there are many within these pages, following are a poignant few that spurred critical thinking within me that the matrix and connectiveness of this world is real. For example (page 185), he writes, "It is because of the systems we set up, and people like myself who fit into the systems." Systems, in my opinion that have been purposefully corrupted and yet to be fixed, such as presidential election shenanigans we witnessed with Trump vs Biden, Bush vs Gore, he references in his period Dewey vs Truman (page 193), and Nixon vs Kennedy (page 271). Today it is common knowledge that Mayor Daley and Cook, 'Crook' County was indeed a hotbed of corruption. Election manipulations/selections made in the middle of the night have been happening for a long time. Chicago has long been known as the headquarters of organized crime. Have these organized crime syndicates truly gone away, or did they just become more adapt at deception and camouflage on a grander scale? Grandpa discusses other units of the mob that were active in Columbus and throughout Ohio, just one state out of our union. Are corrupt leaders still running our government and the bureaucracy? Did they create secret societies for concealment purposes, to groom corrupt future leaders?

Beyond election fraud, my grandfather busts the system of education (page 75) that children were passed no matter if they could read or write. He ponders (page 79) neither money, nor bussing children, solves the issues, and provides insight and solutions on how to fix the defunct educational structure, which applies today. If the ruling class truly wanted an intelligent populace, our illiteracy issues would be easily fixed, but then again, an intelligent and healthy populace is hard to govern and control. There is not much profit in a smart citizenry. He writes (page 168), "I thought then, and I think now, that teachers' salaries were, and are, totally inadequate for the amount of education, training and dedication required of anyone in the teaching profession who really prepares himself properly to do a decent job of educating young people. When I started, many people went into the educational field only because there were few jobs available in anything else. Some became teachers because they were truly dedicated and, in the alternative, others because they felt totally inadequate to handle any other employment. Today, I am very concerned that only the less fit is finding their way into teaching. The result of all of this is that the young student is not receiving a first-class education. Standards for teacher certification must be raised, and teaching salaries must be substantially increased, regardless of where the money comes from."

Throughout the book, my grandfather highlights bureaucratic waste, judicial and political corruption at the micro and the macro levels, and how it began. He draws attention to the degeneracy of the local church, and the hunting of communists and gays in the military in the 1940s. He questions Roosevelt knowing about Pearl Harbor before it happened. Stationed at Wright Patman Airforce base in Dayton, Ohio, my grandfather was assigned to investigate the mass disappearance of large equipment. He writes (page 155), "I was in unauthorized, top-secret areas that I knew nothing about." There was no explanation, or paper trail as to where the large equipment had gone so the disappearance was attributed to a sudden fire. Case closed. As part of my awakening, it dawned on me the possibility the equipment was taken and used for subterranean (underground tunnel) applications, unbeknownst to the general public, or those in service. He states (page 133) "…including several really hot shot test pilots who would — and could — fly anything upside down, sideways, straight up, and sometimes straight down. Conservatively, there was a crash a week at Wright Field. We were the experimental and procurement headquarters for the Air Corps." Today, it is speculated that this base was where the Roswell alien craft was taken along with its alien 'corpses'. My grandfather doesn't hold back regarding the media's influence on young minds, (page 98), "Patriotism seems now to be a dirty word. Either people today are much brighter and better educated than we were, or else the media have exercised tremendous influence over our thinking. Whether this is good for the country, I am not so sure." He references the brief Kennedy era (page 272), "In the eyes of the media, he could do no wrong. His wife was idolized too. Everything the Kennedys did was glamourized." Then adds (page 319), "As the entire mess (Watergate) continued to occupy the full attention of the media, more and more charges were made, and it became necessary for more and more denials to be issued." This shows that media creates the circus to draw the public's attention away from what's really going on — a look here not there scenario. In that same section, he ponders, "Besides, I could not understand what was so important in Democratic Headquarters as to warrant a burglary." There was obviously more at stake than photographed campaign documents and installed telephonic listening devices, yet the media could not or would not dig deeper. This says to me, the burglars wanted to get caught and that deep state shenanigans were occurring for a much larger and dastardly purpose. He writes regarding Reagan (page 352), "Even most of the media seem to support him (Reagan), or at least do not try to tear him apart as they have every President since John Kennedy." As of this publishing in 2024, the tearing apart of Presidents has continued as part and parcel for the legacy media. In my opinion, the media is disrespectful as a complete affront to our country whose 'talking heads' add zero value, making media the enemy of the people, along with the entire television (tel-lie-vision) industry. History books tell us one of man's largest accomplishments is 'landing' on the moon. My grandfather wrote in the second to last paragraph, "Neither do I comprehend how we were able to place men in space and send them to the moon." That's it. That's all the attention he gives the matter, which solidifies my thoughts that the entire moon landing was a Stanley Kubrick filmed fabrication.

Grandpa Richard inspiring a two-and-a-half year old future author, Courtney Jo Barr's, love of books and writing during Christmas of 1969.

My grandfather was a studious, critically thinking, humble, trustworthy and unpretentious man, who knew more than this book goes into. He lived in his truth. The truth is out there, and with today's global communication, more available than ever before, if one is willing to sift through the lies perpetrated upon humanity. An autobiography is novelty, and the universe loves novelty. Each of us has a personal story to share. My grandfather, like each of us, was uniquely created by the Almighty God for a purpose. God wants these stories purposefully told to educate and uplift humanity. I hope and pray I have honored God and my ancestors by publicly publishing my grandfathers' life story. May God bless us all and our unique contribution to the world.

To believe in the life of love, to serve in the light of truth, to walk in the way of honor.

SIGMA NU CREED

First Honors-First Semester, 1932
S.A.R. Contest
School: Indianola Junior High School
Pupil: Dick Clark (14 years old)
Topic: A More Perfect Union

When the Constitutional Convention met in 1787, the theme of its efforts was a more perfect union. Among the notable there were Washington, Hamilton, Franklin and Madison. It was indeed a great gathering.

Under the Articles of the Confederation we had no chief executive, no central government, the states were individual governments and they were very jealous of each other. We had a Congress which could make laws, yet without the states' consent, could not enforce them. Congress could levy taxes, yet could not collect them. It could declare war, yet unless the states desired, could not raise an army.

When the Constitution was written, it was done on the basis of putting the national government on a pedestal above the state governments. Before the national government was made supreme, we had no place in the world as a nation, and the European countries took great advantage of our weakness. We were heavily in debt to European countries and they were clamoring for payment. Notwithstanding these conditions, the makers of the Constitution did their work so wisely that only nineteen amendments have been added to it.

Today we are one of the foremost nations and instead of being in debt, we have been for a number of years, the chief creditor nation of the world. All this is due (1) partly to our wonderful form of government, the gift of our forefathers, (2) partly to the splendid leaders of our history and (3) to the good qualities of our American people as a whole.

Our present-day needs call for men as brilliant and purposeful as those who wrote our constitution. We need wise leaders to solve our problems of government, many of them as momentous as the problem of 1787, problems such as unemployment, our national deficit, the gangster problem, the liquor problem and control of various forms of radicalism. If we succeed in solving these problems, we shall be preserving and perfecting our union.

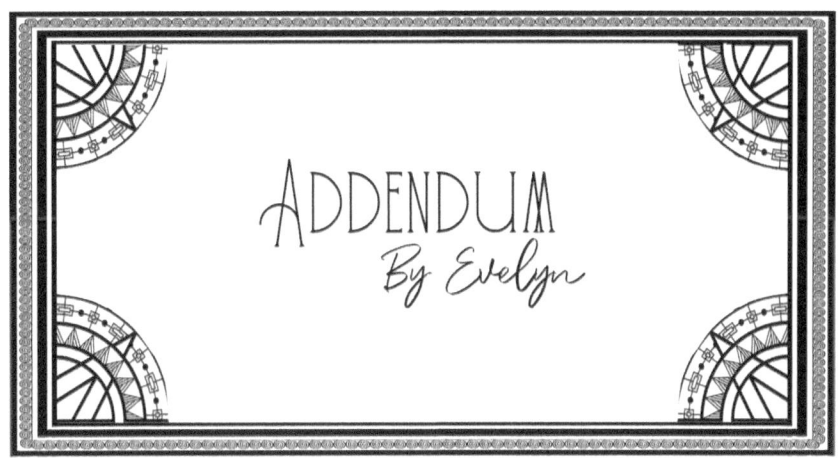

ADDENDUM
By Evelyn

Richard Guy Clark was a devoted husband and father. He was an outgoing, warm person, liked by all who knew him. The tragedy of his death was a severe shock to me and our children. His death was due to choking on meat in a restaurant (Beachcomber) in Clearwater Beach, Florida on January 11, 1987.

This picture was taken on Christmas Day of 1986, just a mere two weeks before Richard passed away.

Angel Flying on the Ground: Letters of a Gentleman's Pursuit
True Tales of a Buckeye Legal Eagle

To purchase copies, please visit
AngelFlyingontheGround.com

www.ingramcontent.com/pod-product-compliance
Lightning Source LLC
Chambersburg PA
CBHW030226100526
44585CB00012BA/231